CHEVROLET PICKUPS 1973-1998

How to Identify, Select and Restore Collector Light Trucks and El Caminos

John Gunnell

©2007 Krause Publications
Published by

700 East State Street • Iola, WI 54990-0001
715-445-2214 • 888-457-2873
www.krausebooks.com

Our toll-free number to place an order or obtain
a free catalog is (800) 258-0929.

All rights reserved. No portion of this publication may be reproduced or transmitted in any form or by any means, electronic or mechanical, including photocopy, recording, or any information storage and retrieval system, without permission in writing from the publisher, except by a reviewer who may quote brief passages in a critical article or review to be printed in a magazine or newspaper, or electronically transmitted on radio, television, or the Internet.

Library of Congress Control Number: 2007936902

ISBN-13: 978-0-89689-614-7
ISBN-10: 0-89689-614-5

Designed by Kara Grundman
Edited by Tom Collins

Printed in China

To my daughter Sue, who I miss immensely. She was the best daughter anyone ever had and always supported my passion for old cars and trucks.

ACKNOWLEDGMENTS

One cannot put together this type of book without direct or indirect help from many people and sources. Among those who have contributed to my efforts to research the history of Chevrolet trucks and gather photos of them are: Robert C. Ackerson, Bob Adler of Adler's Antique Autos, Kari St. Antoine of the Chevrolet Communications Staff, The Antique Truck Club of America, Dave Barthmuss of the Chevrolet Communications Staff, Susan Berkowitz of LMC Truck/Long Motor Corp., Terry V. Boyce, Mark Broderick of the Chevrolet Communications Staff, Chevrolet Motor Division, Tom Collins, George H. Dammann, Terry Davis, Mike Garwell, Steve Hanson, Dayna Hart of GMC Division, Robert Hensel of All Chevy Acres, Tom Hoxie of the Chevrolet Communications Staff, J. David Hudgens of the Chevrolet Communications Staff, Elliott Kahn, Roy Kaple, Ralph Kramer, Edward S. Lechtzin of the Chevrolet Public Relations Central Office, Michael Levine of *Pickup Trucks.com*, Jack L. Martin, Mary McElyea of the Chevrolet Communications Staff, Gregg D. Merksamer, Motorbooks International, *Old Cars Weekly, Old Cars Price Guide*, Vince Sauberlich, Frank Senkbeil, Bill Siuru, *The Standard Catalog of American Light-Duty Trucks*, Edward Stanulis of GM Corporate, Forest "Chip" Sweet, *Vintage Truck, Charles Webb* and Donald F. Wood.

The great majority of images appearing in this book are factory-issued images that were distributed in press kits at auto shows. They show the trucks in original condition. Any photos contributed by truck owners are individually credited. Photo collections used for books are never complete and anyone wishing to submit a photo of their Chevrolet truck for use in future editions of this book is encouraged to do so. The publisher's name and address are included on the publisher's information page. Any photos used in this manner will be fully credited if and when they appear.

The biggest acknowledgment in this book goes to the great pickups and other light trucks built by the Chevrolet Division of General Motors. Chances are pretty good that if you're reading *Chevrolet Pickups 1973-1998* you own one of these trucks, which are usually promoted as hardworking vehicles that are "built like a rock."

Chevrolet started building trucks in 1918. A Flareboard Express model — which is basically a big pickup truck — was in the lineup right from the beginning. However, the first "real" pickup model of the type we had today arrived in 1928. So that makes our year of publication, 2008, the 80th anniversary of the Chevrolet pickup as we know it.

Table of Contents

Acknowledgements	3
Introduction	5
Historical perspective	7
1973-1980 C/K Pickups	8
1981-1987 C/K Pickups	32
1988-1998 C/K Pickups	59
El Camino	109
LUV & S10	116
Other Chevy Trucks	130
Factory Factors (Options & Info)	143
Customizing & Restyling	181
Collecting & Restoring	196
Truck-O-Mobilia	208
1973-1998 Chevy Pickup and Blazer	215
Information Department	249
Chevy Trucks Prices	263

INTRODUCTION

WHAT A DIFFERENCE 20 YEARS MAKES

This book puts the spotlight on two series of Chevrolet full-size pickup trucks — the 1973-1987 models and the 1988-1998 models. In addition, it covers other Chevrolet trucks including El Caminos, LUVs and S-10s. Since early full-size Blazers were essentially short-wheelbase 4 x 4 pickups, we had to make room for them. By this point, it seemed silly not to at least mention other light-duty Chevrolet trucks that collectors are interested in. So we threw in the rare Vega Panel Express and the Suburban, which shares front sheet metal with the big pickups. Then it seemed foolish to leave out S-10 Blazers, Chevy vans, mini vans, Tahoes and MPVs. In fact, even the Tracker made the cut.

The bulk of our research (the book's three major chapters) traces the product history of Chevrolet C/K and R/V pickups. Practically everyone has heard the "C/K" designation for the big Chevy trucks. The "C" trucks are the conventional two-wheel-drive models. The designations C10 or C1500 are used on 1/2-ton-rated trucks, while a C2500 is a ¾-ton and a C3500 is a 1-ton. The "K" prefix designates four-wheel-drive versions of the same models.

The R/V designations arrived in 1988 and bear some explanation. Chevy started phasing in a redesigned pickup for model-year 1988. Some people assumed that new R/V tags went with the new trucks, but the opposite was true. The *new* trucks adopted the *old* C/K designations. However, certain models — such as Crew Cab pickups and Suburbans — continued to be built with the old–design sheet metal. These became R/V models, instead of C/K models.

The reason this book starts with 1973 models is that my previous book *Chevrolet Pickups 1946-1972: How to Identify, Select and Restore Chevrolet Collector Light Trucks, Panels and El Caminos* (Motorbooks International, First Printing 1988) featured the previous models. The book you have in your hand is the long-awaited sequel. If it sells anywhere near what the previous one sold, the publisher will have the automotive version of a "Harry Potter" novel.

We're convinced that the timing is perfect for a book about 1973-1998 Chevy pickups. Susan Berkowitz, of Long Motor Corporation (parent company of LMC Truck Parts) tells us that her firm is enjoying strong sales of parts for these "later-model" Chevy pickups, especially the 1988-1998 models. We are also beginning to see these trucks at shows, cruise nights and other hobby events.

John Gilbert, the editor of Primedia's *Classic & Custom Pickups* magazine, says that the 1988-1998 are Chevy's "first real *sport* trucks." We think the company made sporty trucks as far back as the '50s, but we appreciate John's viewpoint on the trend towards the newer models that he's seeing out in California. Like we say, the time is ripe for a book about 1973 and newer models.

This book was planned as a "clone" of the 1988 book. Why mess with success? However, we found that some updates had to be made to various sections. The passing of 20 years really does bring many changes. For instance, other than the low-production Vega version, no true "panel trucks" were built in the late-'70s, '80s or '90s. Also gone completely was the sedan delivery model.

The 1983 trucks were lighter than their early 1980s counterparts, but had the same cab size and bed size.

Chevrolet introduced an all-new range of full-size C/K pickups as 1988 models. The new trucks were 3.5-in. narrower, but the interior had more leg and shoulder room. The new models had larger doors that extended upward into the roof line.

We found that pickup truck designs lasted longer than they used to. In the earlier book there were five chapters for 1944-1946, 1947-1955, 1955-1959, 1960-1966 and 1967-1972 full-size pickups. The longest lasting of these early Chevy trucks was the Advance-Design, which survived nine years from 1947-early 1955. In contrast, this book has only three chapters on full-size trucks and the newest type covered remained on the market for 11 years.

The chapter on "Factory factors" gives a much more elaborate breakdown of Vehicle Identification Numbers (VINs) for Chevy trucks and the numbers also tell us more about the vehicle than they used to 20 years ago. In the same chapter, the list of engine options is much, much longer than it was for 1940s, 1950s and 1960s models. Even the paint color information is different today. There are more color choices and more use of metallic type paints.

In the chapter discussing the options for modifying a Chevy pickup, we found a lot of changes. What we used to call a "hot rodder" years ago is now a "tuner" and the person we used to call a "customizer" (or "kustomizer" if you lived in Southern California) has become a "restyler." Vehicle-modification techniques have changed, too. "Crate engines" aside, power plant swaps are required less than they used to be, since most Chevy pickups come from the factory with a V-8. However, a lot of high-tech "upgrades" can be made to that stock engine.

Changes have also occurred in the collecting- and-restoring market niche. The prices of older trucks continue to climb, the cost of a good restoration continues to zoom and the number of hobbyists with professional-quality shops at home has gone through the roof. Restoration parts for older models are coming on stream a lot quicker than they used to, thanks to booming interest and trade organizations like SEMA. We also have new tools, new equipment, new paints, new shops, new parts suppliers, new magazines and new clubs to help us find, fix and have fun with vintage Chevy pickup trucks.

As you can see, this book isn't strictly a history like some other books. Although it gives you the basic techs and specs for your pickup, it also provides you with information about collecting, restoring and modifying it. The size of the book doesn't lend itself to step-by-step restoration techniques or customizing tips, but it does layout the basics and direct you towards good sources of help. The list of parts and services in the "Information Department" should be invaluable for both rookie and veteran truck collectors. Need a part or a club address or a tool supplier? The info you need is probably listed.

One thing this book has that the 1988 book didn't is a price guide to the collector values of 1973-1988 trucks. Krause Publications is the world's leading provider of collector-vehicle pricing, so it was possible to add the Chevy truck prices database to all the other good stuff in this book.

Now for the disclaimer — like my earlier book, this one is dealing with many topics that haven't been researched or written up before. That leaves the door open for minor errors. For instance, much of the historical information in *Chevrolet Pickups 1973-1998* is based on printed sales literature and press releases that the manufacturer (Chevrolet) issued. Often, these are put out months in advance of actual vehicle production and there can be last-minute changes that cause variances from the printed information. We have strived to keep our typos and goofs to a minimum, but if you spot one, please let us know right away so that we can make a correction before the book is reprinted.

Thanks for listening…we hope you enjoy our book!

John Gunnell
KP Books
Iola, Wis.

HISTORICAL PERSPECTIVE

CHEVROLET PICKUP TRUCKS 1973-1998

Chevy has been building trucks for 90 years. The first was put together in 1918. Only 879 trucks were made that year. By the end of 1919, sales were up to 8,179. By 1929, the 500,000th Chevy truck was manufactured. By 1933, the company was America's largest truck maker and held a 50 percent share of the market.

The earliest Chevrolet trucks had four-cylinder engines. The venerable "Stovebolt" straight six was adopted in 1929. A V-8 first appeared in mid-1955, when Chevrolet's truck lineup was revolutionized with a new "Task-Force" design. It replaced the popular Advance-Design model, which had bowed in 1947 and survived until early 1955. The classic Advance-Design styling was the inspiration for today's SSR specialty model.

The half-car-half-truck El Camino arrived in 1959 to combat Ford's Ranchero. By 1964, the El Camino re-appeared on the Chevelle chassis and a compact Chevy Van replaced the radical rear-engined Corvan, which had been based on Chevy's first compact car platform. The 9 millionth Chevy truck of all time was built that year and the 10 millionth unit was put together during 1966.

By the early '70s, the popularity of Chevy trucks was booming bigger than ever and part of the reason was a growing product line. The Blazer 4 x 4 Utility Vehicle arrived in late '69 and the Vega Panel Express was a new-for-'71 model. Mini pickups sourced from Isuzu of Japan bowed under the LUV name in '72.

This book picks up the Chevrolet pickup truck story — (or should we say the Chevrolet pickup/truck story) — in 1973 when a rather glittery new full-size C/K model replaced the clean-lined '67-'72 trucks that became "Quick Classics." The new trucks seemed boxy and big and had interior designs that rivaled the Madras plaid sport coats of the era. When they were introduced, vintage truck lovers scoffed at the concept that they could ever replace the trucks that came before them. Today, they are the darlings of a new generation of collectors who grew up with them. This is the book that these enthusiasts have been waiting for.

1973-80 Chevrolet C/K Pickups

1973: AUTOMOTIVE LUXURY WITH TRUCK DURABILITY

Enthusiasts know that the 1967-1972 Chevy "Custom Sport Truck" design has been very popular with collectors for over 20 years. During that period, the 1973 and later pickups were largely overlooked in the collecting hobby. According to Susan Berkowitz of LMC truck in Lenexa, Kansas, that is changing today. Susan says the older trucks have become too costly for younger restorers to do, so the later models are "where it's really at right now."

Chevrolet's conventional light trucks for 1973 were totally restyled and marked a departure from earlier designs. The basic styling introduced that year could be called Gen X. It would stay about the same, other than detail changes, through 1980. In 1981, it was mostly updated to enhance the aerodynamics a bit. The "aero" edition lasted for seven more years. With a 15-year market run, you can tell these were great trucks. If they had not proved popular with buyers, they would have been gone after three years.

The immediate impression of the 1973 Chevy pickup was of a slightly bigger, slightly wider, slightly boxier truck that somehow looked "airier." While a truck is a truck, the new model looked new. The cab

This 1973 Chevrolet C10 Fleetside long box pickup has Silverado trim. Note how it is two-toned with the lighter color on the roof of the cab and down the center of each body side. These trucks had a massive, airy feeling. Old Cars Weekly Collection

wasn't drastically changed and the visual refreshment was mainly in the lower sheet metal. Soft-cornered rectangular wheel wells contributed a great deal to the new look and the body sides had more "tumble home" at the bottom.

In true mid-'70s fashion, the new trucks looked bright and luxurious. They offered fancier trim packages. Two-tone finish was common. Woodgrain accents were added to the up-market models inside and outside. Chevy followed the trend towards increased use of plastic and vinyl parts and the public tended to equate this with a cheapening of the product. However, these pickups had plenty of truck durability built into them and would prove themselves sturdy and tough over the long haul.

A sculptured cove or depression in the sheet metal ran along the belt line of these trucks. It gave the new models very clean and distinctive feature lines. Also contributing to the Chevrolet's good looks was a radiator grille with a simple "eggcrate" insert that brought back memories of the classic 1955 Chevrolet passenger-car grille. An in-the-windshield

Some lucky-feeling fishermen are getting ready to unload their ATV to take them and their rods a little further into the wilderness than their ½-ton Stepside pickup can carry them. Note the white sidewall tires. John Gunnell Collection

Chevy thought this picture of a high-steppin' '73 K20 Fleetside pickup made a good publicity photo. It carries the Cheyenne trim package and wears a "350" engine call-out on the left side of its grille. Old Cars Weekly Collection

radio antenna was one new item that didn't catch on; curved side window glass was one that did. The cab doors now opened into the roofline and roof drip rails were no longer used. At the rear, buyers found a new easy-to-open tailgate.

A widened interior featured a powered, flow-through ventilation system. A new dashboard design grouped all instruments and controls in a semi-circular cluster within easy reach and view of the driver. To start the truck, you now inserted the key into a switch on the steering column and it had an interlock designed to combat thieves. The steering wheel was reduced in diameter and a new energy-absorbing steering column was adopted.

All models had longer wheelbases. The C10 two-wheel-drive and K10 four-wheel-drive pickups with the smaller 6-1/2-ft. cargo box came on the standard 117-1/2-in. wheelbase, which was used only for these models and small chassis-only trucks. A six-passenger version of the 1/2-ton pickup was introduced. Another change involved relocating the fuel tank to a spot outside the cab on rear section of the right frame rail.

The C10/K10 pickups with the 8-ft. box featured a 131-1/2-in. wheelbase. This wheelbase was also used for many 1/2-ton chassis models and all basic C30 models. The C20/K20 trucks, except Carryall Suburbans, were also on a 131-1/2-in. wheelbase.

Longer wheelbases were provided for Chassis-and-Cab models and the new Crew-Cab trucks. Crew-Cab bodies that seated six could be had as an option on all 3/4- and 1-ton pickups. The Crew-Cab option cost about $1,000. The box used with factory-made Crew-Cab pickups was the 8-ft. Fleetside box.

There were numerous technical changes. A 454-cid V-8 was introduced as an option for standard trucks. Although the 454 used more gas than smaller engines, collectors who love their trucks "loaded" with options consider it a desirable option today. C10 models used rubber control arm bushings for a quieter and smoother ride. Leaf springs replaced the rear-coil springs used in 1972 on C10/C20 models. Four-wheel-drive models were fitted with longer front springs and a standard front stabilizer bar.

All of the pickups now used a Salisbury rear end. Only the C10 had this feature before. On C20 and C30 pickups an Eaton locking differential was optional. It locked in upon a 100 rpm difference in the rear axles and had a governor to keep it from locking-in at above 15 mph. Full-time four-wheel-drive was introduced. It was available only in combination with both a V-8 engine and Turbo-Hydra-Matic transmission.

All truck configurations offered in 1972, except the "Longhorn Pickup," continued to be available with the new 1973 styling. Stealing a model name from

This 1974 Chevrolet C10 Fleetside pickup seems to be kicking up a little dust for a company photographer. It carries the "long" 8-ft. cargo box and, according to the engine call-out badge, has a 350-cid V-8. John Gunnell Collection

In 1974, the Crew-Cab pickup was offered on both the ½- and ¾-ton chassis with a choice of two-wheel drive or four-wheel drive. Buyers could also pick from a Fleetside box or the Stepside one shown here. John Gunnell Collection

Another leisure-activity trend in '74 was the swing towards recreational vehicles. This C20 Fleetside "Camper Special" is fitted with the 8-ft. box and a big 454-cid V-8 so it can carry a Week-N-Der slide-in camper unit. John Gunnell Collection

The mid-'70s was an era when the four-wheel-drive movement was gathering steam. This 1974 Chevy K10 Fleetside long-box pickup truck has the upscale Silverado trim package. John Gunnell Collection

Cadillac, the C10 with 6-1/2-ft. bed was nicknamed the "Fleetwood." This truck is rarely called by that name today. Available trim levels included Custom, Custom Deluxe, Cheyenne, and Cheyenne Super.

1974: VIRTUALLY UNCHANGED

After the complete restyling of Chevy pickups in 1973, the 1974 trucks were virtually unchanged. Minor exterior differences included four new paint colors, improved "below-eye-line" outside rearview mirrors and optional new bright roof drip moldings.

Technical developments for model-year 1974 included use of a full-time four-wheel-drive unit on all V-8-engined 4 x 4 models. Also, brake systems were now computer-matched to the gross vehicle weight rating of each truck. The new braking system included a lining sensor on the front disc brakes. It sounded an audible signal when the pads needed replacement. In addition, all pickups had larger front disc and rear drum brakes, as well as a new hydraulic booster power assist called Hydro-boost.

Interior refinements included foam instrument panel padding with all trim levels. All models had an energy-absorbing steering column and, on all models with automatic transmission, an anti-theft ignition system was used.

The 1974 models made their debut on September 2, 1973. Calendar-year production was 838,959 units. This did not include Vega panel trucks, El Caminos or LUV mini pickups. Chevrolet held 29.44 percent of the U.S. truck market. On a calendar-year basis, this was Chevrolet's second best year in truck sales in history with sales of 885,362 units and production of 896,130. The model-year figures were, however, even more impressive with 975,257 sales and 925,696 trucks built to 1974 specifications. This production total includes trucks built in Canada for sale here, but does not include LUVs (which are included in the sales total). An all-time production record, for the Flint, Mich. factory (339,678 trucks) was also set. On a calendar-year basis, 85.5 percent of Chevrolet's truck output was V-8 powered, 15.1 percent had six-cylinder engines and a mere 0.4 percent were diesel engined.

BASIC CONTENTS OF 1973-1974 TRIM PACKAGES

Custom: The Custom was the basic pickup with plain black rubber window gaskets and white-painted bumpers. The grille shell had bright metal finish. The vent window pillars and frames were flat black. The standard hubcaps were painted. Rear moldings around the taillights and tailgate were not available on Customs.

Custom Deluxe: The one-step-up Custom Deluxe trim level Included a full-width bench seat with comfortably-padded seat cushions and back rest, vinyl seat upholstery and door panels, steel roof panel painted in the main exterior color, a black rubber floor mat extending to firewall, padded arm rests, padded sun shades, a courtesy lamp, a prismatic rearview mirror, a foam-padded instrument panel, bright upper and lower grille outline moldings, bright headlamp bezels, bright outside rearview mirrors, bright door handles, a white-painted front bumper, white hubcaps and wheels and bright Custom Deluxe nameplates.

Cheyenne: Included in the Cheyenne package was a bench seat with full-depth foam cushions and back rests, custom-grained vinyl upholstery (or nylon-and-vinyl upholstery), special door trim panels, a cab headliner, deep-twist nylon carpeting extending to the firewall, color-keyed garnish moldings, an ashtray-mounted cigar lighter, a Custom steering wheel, Cheyenne dashboard nameplates, door- or manually-operated courtesy lights, extra acoustical insulation and all Custom Deluxe exterior items, plus a cab-mounted cargo lamp, bright metal cab trim and moldings, bright upper body side and tailgate moldings and central taillight appliqués for Fleetside and Cheyenne nameplates.

Cheyenne Super: The top trim level added upper lower body side and wheelhouse moldings and a chrome-plated tailgate release. Cheyenne Super nameplates decorated the front fender sides and dashboard. A new offering was the "Big Dualie" type C30 pickup with dual rear wheels.

This 1975 Cheyenne K10 Fleetside pickup is finished in Skyline Blue with the upper cab finished in Frost White. This profile view of the truck shows how much ground clearance it offered. Gregg D. Merksamer Collection

1975: Market Turmoil . . . "Sticker Shock"

Styling changes for light-duty conventional trucks were headed by revamped grille with a larger grillwork, clear-lens parking lights and new front fender model identification combining model nameplates and series identification plaques. A restyled tailgate with a quick-release control was used.

Starting in 1975, all trucks with under-6,001-lb. GVWs (except LUVs) were equipped with catalytic converters, which significantly reduced hydrocarbon and carbon monoxide emissions to meet 1975 EPA standards. Chevrolet promoted trucks as having "newly-designed engines with increased efficiency." However, one enthusiast publication recommended that since the converter added to cost, it might be a

Chevy ads sold this 1975 Custom Deluxe C10 Fleetside Pickup on the basis of its low price. With a new High Energy Ignition (HEI) system, the '75 operated more economically on unleaded fuel than its '74 counterpart. Old Cars Weekly Collection

12 | Chevrolet Pickups 1973-1998

The oil-change recommendation for the 350-cid V-8 under the hood of this 1975 C20 Fleetside pickup with the Scottsdale trim package was changed from 6,000 to 7,500 miles that year.
Old Cars Weekly Collection

good idea to specify chassis equipment sufficiently heavy-duty to exceed a 6,000-lb. GVW so a converter wasn't required.

Introduced on all 1975 engines except the LUV's, was a high-energy ignition (HEI) system, that delivered a hotter and more consistent spark for better starting power. Also introduced was an outside air carburetion intake and an early fuel evaporation system that provided faster engine warm up after cold start. Chevrolet's stalwart 250-cid six-cylinder engine had a new, integrally-cast cylinder head with improved-flow intake manifold. All 1/2-ton models with this engine had a larger standard clutch. Extended maintenance schedules were adopted. The Big Dualie pickup, with dual rear wheels, was one of several equipment offerings.

The 1975 Chevrolet truck exterior colors were Skyline Blue, Hawaiian Blue, Catalina Blue, Grecian Bronze, Buckskin, Yuba Gold, Moss Gold, Willoway Green, Spring Green, Glenwood Green, Crimson Red, Rosedale Red, Saratoga Silver, Sante Fe Tan, and Frost White. Two-tone color options came in conventional, special and deluxe combinations, each requiring specific moldings packages.

The 1975 trucks were Introduced September 1, 1974. Calendar-year sales: were 771,518 trucks.

This 1975 Cheyenne K10 Stepside pickup was finished in Rosedale Red (a brownish color) and had a Frost White cab with double-wall construction. It rode a 117.5-inch wheelbase.
Old Cars Weekly Collection

Chevrolet Pickups 1973-1998

BASIC CONTENTS OF 1975-1980 TRIM PACKAGES

Custom Deluxe: Custom Deluxe became the base interior. It included a foam-padded bench seat with blue, green, red or saddle plaid upholstery, a body color steel roof panel, black rubber floor mat, padded arm rests, courtesy lamps, prismatic rear view mirror, foam padded dash, bright upper and lower grille outline moldings, bright headlamp bezels, silver plastic grille insert, bright outside rear view mirror, bright door handles, bright Custom Deluxe nameplates and white-painted bumper, hubcaps and wheels.

Scottsdale: The Scottsdale package ($137 to $199 extra in 1974) included full-depth foam padded seats, wood-grain door trim inserts, an ash tray cigarette lighter, door or manually-operated courtesy lamps, bright door sill plates, color-keyed rubber floor mats, a high-note horn, patterned nylon cloth upholstery with vinyl trim, and all Custom Deluxe exterior features, plus a chrome bumper, chrome hubcaps, chrome body side moldings on Fleetsides, bright windshield and window trim, bright-rimmed parking, side marker and taillights, and Scottsdale nameplates.

Cheyenne: Cheyenne trim ($258 to $315 extra in 1974) was the next notch on the totem pole. It added full-depth foam seat cushions, a choice of custom-grained vinyl or cloth-and-vinyl seats (bucket type optional), an ash tray-mounted cigarette lighter, wood-grain door panel inserts, door or manually-operated courtesy and dome lights, extra cab insulation, and all Scottsdale exterior items, plus bright metal cab back appliqués and moldings, bright upper body side and tailgate moldings, central appliqués for Fleetsides, and Cheyenne nameplates.

Silverado: At the top of the line, a Silverado option ($312 to $531) replaced the old Cheyenne Super package. It featured 7-in. thick seat foam, richer basketweave nylon cloth or buffalo hide vinyl, full gauges, wood-graining on the dash panel and door panel inserts, door storage pockets, carpeting, an insulated headliner, extra body insulation, and all Cheyenne exterior items, plus lower body side and tailgate moldings, wheel lip moldings, Scottsdale nameplates, and a tailgate appliqué on Fleetsides. All pickups could be equipped with an optional glide-out spare tire carrier.

This C10 Special Stepside with the sporty 6-1/2-ft. box has a special trim package with body striping, chromed front and rear bumpers, Rally wheels and white-lettered tires.
Old Cars Weekly Collection

This stop-action photo was taken during the filming of a television commercial in which a 1976 Chevy Fleetside pickup was driven over railroad ties at high speed to demonstrate how well its suspension rode. Old Cars Weekly Collection

This 1976 Custom Deluxe Fleetside pickup was equipped with special "Inflation-Fighter" content including a full-foam seat, a painted rear step bumper and a special heavy-duty 3-speed manual transmission. Old Cars Weekly Collection

In 1976, Chevy started using the term "Big 10" to promote the 1/2-ton pickup with the longer cargo box. This one is a Fleetside version with Cheyenne trim. Despite a full load it seems to be zooming along. Old Cars Weekly Collection

1976: New Bonus Cab One-Ton

Conventional trucks included the Chassis-and-Cab, Fleetside and Stepside Pickups. Also new was a Bonus-Cab pickup and the traditional Crew-Cab model, both on a stretched wheelbase. The Bonus-Cab had two doors, but the cab was extended for added passenger space. The Crew-Cab had four doors and a full rear seat. The one-ton C30 series offered the same models. The C10 and C20 trucks could be had with four-wheel-drive.

In 1976, the grille texture was changed slightly and the engine call-out badges were moved from in the grille. The 400-cid (actually 402-cid) big-block V-8 was replaced with a 400-cid small-block V-8.

Custom Deluxe was again the base interior and was about the same. The next step up was Scottsdale trim. Cheyenne trim included new ribbed pattern velour or buffalo-hide vinyl upholstery (vinyl bucket seats optional) and other items usually associated with the Cheyenne. At the top of the line again was the Silverado option.

Standard Colors

 Skyline Blue
 Hawaiian Blue
 Catalina Blue
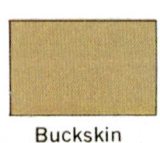 Grecian Bronze
 Buckskin
Yuba Gold
Moss Gold

 Willoway Green
 Spring Green
 Glenwood Green
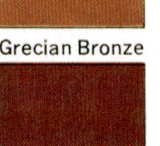 Crimson Red
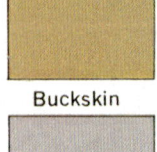 Rosedale Red
Saratoga Silver
Santa Fe Tan
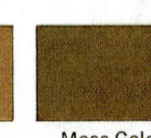 Frost White

Chevrolet Pickups 1973-1998

A road's-eye view of Chevy truck toughness.

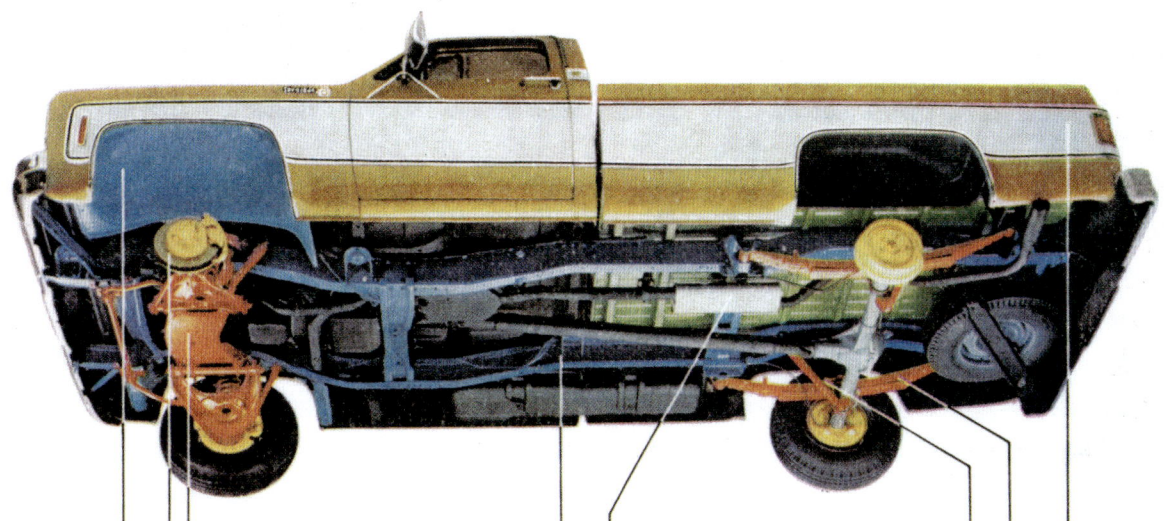

Massive Girder Beam independent front suspension uses steel control arms, friction-free coil springs. Wheels step over rough spots individually, helping smooth the ride.

Computer-matched brake systems have fade-resistant front disc brakes, fin-cooled rear drum brakes and power assist (most models) tailored to the truck's GVW rating.

Full front wheelhousings help protect fenders and engine compartment from road spray and rocks. All-steel, one-piece inner and outer fender panels form a double wall for structural rigidity.

Ladder-type steel frame uses deep-section channel side rails, riveted crossmembers for strength, rigidity and durability.

Aluminized muffler uses heavy-gauge metal for shell and baffles. Aluminum coating inside and out adds corrosion protection.

Counter-angled rear shock absorbers are slanted, one forward and one aft, to help keep rear wheels firmly in contact with the pavement during acceleration and deceleration with heavy loads.

Multi-leaf rear springs provide a good ride with light loads, progressively firmer support as cargo weight increases.

Double-wall construction adds strength and durability in many important areas. Fleetside body side panels, doors, upper cab panels, windshield pillars, roof, cowl and hood.

YOUR MONEY'S WORTH. MILE AFTER MILE AFTER MILE.

This ad purports to show the way that a road looked at a 1976 Chevrolet Fleetside pickup. That seemed to be a good way to promote eight of the truck's most outstanding features. Gregg D. Merksamer Collection

A 1976 Chevy K20 4 x 4 Fleetside pickup sloshes through some wet stuff in this factory publicity photo. Now, we don't recommend your doing this with your collector truck, as it might cause rust. *Old Cars Weekly Collection*

All Chevrolet pickups could be equipped with an optional glide-out spare tire carrier. Stepside pickups with the 6-1/2-foot box were not ignored, they were available with a new trim package including special striping, chromed bumpers, Rally wheels and white-lettered tires. The package was offered in four body colors: Blue, Orange, Red or Black. Exterior colors for other models were Skyline Blue, Hawaiian Blue, Catalina Blue, Grecian Bronze, Buckskin, Yuba Gold, Moss Gold, Willoway Green, Spring Green, Glenwood Green, Crimson Red, Rosedale Red, Saratoga Silver, Santa Fe Tan, and Frost White. Two-tone color options came in conventional, special, and deluxe combinations, each requiring specific moldings packages.

The 1976 Chevy trucks were introduced on October 2, 1975. Model-year sales (not production) of light-duty pickups totaled 682,039 units. J.T. Riley was sales manager for Chevrolet Motor Div.'s truck group. Chevrolet was America's leading truck-maker with its strong 35.02 percent market share for calendar-year 1976.

1977: Retirement Age

Chevrolet Motor Division turned 65 years old in 1977. It was old enough to retire, but had no intentions of doing so. Beginning in 1977, the C30 one-ton models joined the C10 and C20 trucks in offering four-wheel-drive. Called K30s, the trucks so-equipped carried a heavier-capacity 4,500-lb. front driving axle, instead of the 3,800-lb. axle used with 3/4-ton four-wheel-drive models. Other equipment on the K30s included a modified 7,500-lb. rear axle, power steering, and a standard four-speed manual transmission.

Also for model-year 1977, all Chevrolet conventional trucks had a new grille arrangement with four (rather than eight) vertical dividers and two (rather than three) horizontal bars. A secondary mesh was placed behind the major grille sections.

Single-unit combination tail, stop, back-up lights replaced the former separate units on Stepside pickup truck models. A new option for pickups in general was the Sport package. It included special hood and body side striping, and white-spoke or Rally wheels. The

On the left is the '77 Chevy Fleetside Sport in Mariner Blue with special hood and side striping and styled wheels. On the right is the same-year Chevy Stepside Sport with special striping, wheels and a roll bar. Gregg D. Merksamer Collection

This 1977 Chevrolet "Big 10" Scottsdale Fleetside pickup is finished in an attractive two-tone combination featuring Lite Blue and Mariner Blue. The optional spoke wheels give it a sporty look. Gregg D. Merksamer Collection

Chevrolet Pickups 1973-1998 | 19

This 1977 C10 Cheyenne Fleetside pickup is finished in Mariner Blue and Frost White. The white spoked wheels were a regular production option or RPO. Old Cars Weekly photo

This shows the 1977 Scottsdale bench seat interior with Buffalo-hide embossed vinyl seat trim. Scottsdale exteriors had a chromed front bumper, spear-type side moldings and other up-level decorations. Gregg D. Merksamer Collection

This shows the 1977 Custom Deluxe bench seat interior. It featured plaid-pattern embossed vinyl seat trim. It was available in a choice of four colors. A matching rear seat was standard in Crew Cabs. Gregg D. Merksamer Collection

The Cheyenne trim level for 1977 regular-cab models only included this ribbed-pattern velour cloth seat trim, plus door trim with simulated chestnut wood-grain panels and storage pockets, plus carpeting. Gregg D. Merksamer Collection

A Glide-out spare tire carrier provided convenient access to the spare tire under the pickup box. This was a big help when an overhanging camper unit (popular in the '70s) was carried in the cargo bed. Gregg D. Merksamer Collection

Silverado trim for 1977 included this ribbed-pattern velour cloth seat trim. Other features of this top-of-the-line package varied according to whether the truck was a regular cab, Crew Cab or Bonus Cab model. Gregg D. Merksamer Collection

Sport tape stripes followed the body feature lines and continued in tiara fashion across the roof. On Fleetside models, the "Chevy Sport" lettering appeared on the upper sides of the cargo box. Similar lettering went on the rear spare tire cover of Stepside trucks.

Appearance changes to the 1977 truck interiors consisted of new seat trim colors, fabrics and wood-grain trim. From top to bottom, pickups again came as Custom Deluxe, next-step-up Scottsdale, Cheyenne or top-of-the-line Silverado versions, all of which had similar content to before. Joining the optional equipment list was an Operating Convenience package with power windows and power door locks. These could also be ordered separately and represented a first in the truck industry.

Another new-for-1977 option was an Exterior Decor package. It included a spring-loaded hood emblem, two-tone paint and color-coordinated hood striping. Six new two-tone color schemes were offered in this package. They featured a secondary color on the hood, between body side moldings, and on the roof of cab models. Also offered were new wheel covers for 1/2-ton models and an inside hood release.

Under the hood of full-size Chevy trucks, the big 454-cid V-8 was still a fairly common sight. Starting this year it was fitted with double-honed piston walls and modified rings to improve its oil consumption habits. Also debuting was a new method of gasketing rocker covers and a redesigned distributor cap and rotor.

Exterior colors for 1977 were Mariner Blue, Cordova Brown, Saratoga Silver, Lite Blue, Cardinal Red, Buckskin Tan, Holy Green, Russet Metallic, Hawaiian Blue, Santa Fe Tan, Mahogany, Red Metallic, Colonial Yellow, Frost White and Seamist Green.

1978: Strong Market Again

All Chevrolet pickup trucks available during the 1977 model-year were retained for 1978 with no additions or deletions. Chevrolet introduced a new

The 1978 C20 Fleetside pickup truck with Cheyenne trim looked great in this in a two-tone combination of Mariner Blue and Lite Blue. Another thing we miss from this era is those shiny bright metal mirrors. Gregg D. Merksamer Collection

The 1978 Chevy pickups came in a choice of these 15 colors in either solid or available two-tone combinations. Gregg D. Merksamer Collection

Dual rear wheels provided "Big Dualie" with the capacity for hauling large loads or towing large fifth-wheel trailers. This is a K-30 1-ton 4 x 4 version finished in solid Colonial Yellow. Gregg D. Merksamer Collection

Loaded with cargo and ready for a long day's work is a 1978 K10 Fleetside with two-tone white-and-blue finish. Full-time four-wheel drive was included with K-Series pickups that had automatic transmission. Gregg D. Merksamer Collection

24 | **Chevrolet Pickups 1973–1998**

Here's the short-bed version of the '78 Fleetside pickup in a White and Mahogany color combination. Sport decals decorate the hood, body side and tailgate and the Rally wheels look sporty, too. Gregg D. Merksamer Collection

This 1978 Chevy Stepside with the 6-1/2-foot cargo box was affectionately called the "Shortie." It has the Sport package with bold multi-tone decal striping to set off its Black and Colonial Yellow paint. Gregg D. Merksamer Collection

GM-built 5.7-liter V-8 diesel engine for use in the 1/2-ton two-wheel-drive C10 pickup. Its design features included aluminum alloy pistons with three rings, a cast-iron regrindable crankshaft, three-inch diameter main bearings, rotary fuel-injection plug, electric glow plugs and a seven-quart oil pump.

Custom Deluxe was the basic trim level. The next-step-up was Scottsdale trim. Cheyenne trim added the regular extras. At the top of the line was the Silverado option. The C30 pickup with the dual-rear-wheels option was now called the "Big Dooley."

Exterior colors for 1978 were again Mariner Blue, Cordova Brown, Saratoga Silver, Lite Blue, Cardinal Red, Buckskin Tan, Holly Green, Russet Metallic, Hawaiian Blue, Santa Fe Tan, Mahogany, Red Metallic, Colonial Yellow, Frost White, and Seamist Green.

Chevrolet reported an all-time record of 1.34 million truck sales in 1978. The number of trucks registered by Chevrolet dealers, per sales outlet, was 215 units, up from 187 in 1977. Calendar-year registrations came to 1,275,787 trucks, while calendar-year sales stood at 1,233,932 units.

By '79, the tough-looking Stepside was becoming increasingly popular for off-road use. This K10 "Shortie" was perfect for carrying dirt bikes to the beach. GVWRs up to 6200 pounds were offered. *Gregg D. Merksamer Collection*

'79 Fleetsides were available with exciting factory-installed Sport packages that included special two-tone paint treatments, sport striping, body-colored bumpers, color-keyed carpets and Sport identification. *Gregg D. Merksamer Collection*

1979: A Bad Market & Gas Shortages

Light-duty trucks had a smoother, more aerodynamic hood lip. New integral headlights and parking lamps complemented the "aero" look. The grille had a new paint scheme. While it's true that the grille was of the same basic design as last year's, it was slightly narrower top-to-bottom. Also, the slotted area, directly below the grille, was now made of bright metal.

An optional sport grille had only two full-width horizontal members and a center bow tie against a blacked-out background. The base 250-cid six got a new staged two-barrel carburetor, and a dual

Cardinal Red and Frost White finish was the choice of the cowboy driving this 1979 Chevy C10 Fleetside pickup. It has the Deluxe two-tone style of paint with roof and body sides done in the contrasting hue. *Gregg D. Merksamer Collection*

250 Six

350 V8

Popular engine choices for 1979 included the 250-cid in-line six on the right and the 350-cid V-8 on the left.
Gregg D. Merksamer Collection

Factory full wheel covers and white sidewall tires give this 1979 Chevy C10 Fleetside pickup a glittery appearance. The top-of-the-line Silverado trim doesn't hurt its looks either.
Gregg D. Merksamer Collection

Colors.

Chevrolet again offered a choice of 15 colors in 1979 and some could be had in two-tone combinations. Gregg D. Merksamer Collection

Chevy's Trailering Special option included heavy-duty power steering, battery and generator. Certain V-8s and axle ratio combinations were required, as well as four-speed or automatic transmissions. Gregg D. Merksamer Collection

take-down exhaust system. There was also a new concealed fuel filler.

Custom Deluxe, Scottsdale, Cheyenne and Silverado trims were available. Exterior colors for 1979 were Frost White, Mystic Silver Metallic, Charcoal Metallic, Hawaiian Blue, Mariner Blue Metallic, Deep Blue, Shamrock Green Metallic, Holly Green, Colonial Yellow, Santa Fe Tan, Light Camel Metallic, Dark Carmine Red, Cardinal Red, Cordova Brown Metallic, Midnight Black.

The latest trucks were introduced in the fall of 1978. Calendar-year registrations came to 1,085,855 trucks and calendar-year sales included 644,775 pickups. That was a considerable softening of the market due to a gasoline shortage, which brought the entire car and truck industry temporarily to its knees.

TRUCK SERIES & MODEL	4.1 Liter 2-Bbl. L6 RPO LE3 (A)	4.8 Liter 1-Bbl. L6 RPO L25 (F)	5.0 Liter 2-Bbl. V8 RPO LG9 (E)	5.7 Liter V8 Diesel RPO LF9 (D)	5.7 Liter 4-Bbl. V8 RPO LS9 (E)	5.7 Liter 4-Bbl. V8 RPO LT9 (E)	5.7 Liter 4-Bbl. V8 RPO LF4 (A)	6.6 Liter 4-Bbl. V8 RPO LE4 (A)	7.4 Liter 4-Bbl. V8 RPO LE8 (A)
C10 & K10 PICKUP	Std.†		EC*(1)		EC*				
C10 BIG-10 PICKUP			Std.*		EC				
C10 DIESEL PICKUP				Std.					
C20 & K20 PICKUP	Std.(1)				EC(3)				
C20 & K20/C6P PICKUP		Std.					EC	EC(2)	EC(1)
C20-30 BONUS/CREW CAB		Std.					EC		EC
C30 & K30 PICKUP		Std.					EC	EC(2)	EC(1)
C10 & K10 BLAZER	Std.*		EC*(1)		EC				
C10 & K10 SUBURBAN					Std.				
C20 & K20 SUBURBAN					Std.(1)	Std.(2)		EC(2)	
C20/C6P SUBURBAN						Std.			EC
G10 SPORTVAN	Std.		EC*		EC				
G20 SPORTVAN	Std.				EC		EC		
G30 SPORTVAN						Std.		EC	

*Not available in California. †Not available on K10 in California. (1) C model only. (2) K model only. (3) Std. on K20. Std.—Standard. EC—Available at Extra Cost.

Nine engines were available in 1980 Chevy C/K pickups. This table shows the models and power options for each one.
Old Cars Weekly Collection

This is the 1980 Silverado trim interior package in Camel Tan. Old Cars Weekly Collection

Taking the dirt-bike-hauling test is a 1980 K10 Stepside "Shortie" pickup. It is painted in a Sport Two-Tone combination (contrasting color on bottom of body only) of Dark Camel and Santa Fe Tan. Old Cars Weekly Collection

Taking the haul-a-tree-trunk test is a 1980 C20 Fleetside Silverado pickup. It is painted in a Special Two-Tone combination (contrasting color on center body sides only) of Dark Camel and Santa Fe Tan Old Cars Weekly Collection

1980: Entering A New Decade

Chevrolet pickups had a new Argent Silver colored grille with 33 square openings. Silverados got new rectangular parking lamps. Inside, there were new gauges with international symbols. The seat back angle was changed for greater comfort.

There was a new thermostatic-controlled cooling fan. A single inlet dual exhaust system was new for the 292-cid six-cylinder engine.

The 1980 exterior colors were Frost White, Medium Blue, Light Blue Metallic, Nordic Blue Metallic, Emerald Green, Sante Fe Tan, Carmine Red, Cardinal Red, Midnight Black, and Burnt Orange Metallic. Also seen were new exterior graphics and eight new two-tones.

1981-87 Chevrolet C/K Pickups

1981: New Aerodynamics

Chevrolet's 1981 pickups had new aerodynamic grille and sheet metal treatments. The grille could be had with the square headlamps only in the top level or with a Halogen High-Beam option in which both grille levels held a square lamp unit at each end. Thanks to the use of new low-alloy steel body panels and lightweight window glass, various models were 87 to 300 pounds lighter than their 1980 counterparts. However, they still retained the same cab size and bed size as before. Electronic spark control was adopted.

A new one-piece instrument panel trim piece was used on the dash eliminating the vertical seam between the banks of gauges. Collectible trim options include the Chevy Sport, Cheyenne, Scottsdale, and Silverado packages. Custom and Custom Deluxe trims were more commonly seen.

Among light-duty power plants was a new high-compression 5.0-liter V-8 with ESC (not used in California) that was designed to give both economy and performance improvements. Also new for the season was a body with improved corrosion resistance, low-drag disc brakes, a new 6,000-pound semi-floating axle for specific models, a resume-type cruise control option, a quad-shock 4 x 4 front suspension, heavier-duty rear springs and a water-in-fuel warning lamp for diesel-powered trucks.

K20s and K10s adopted the new automatic locking hubs, and shot-peened rear springs. Standard on all models were high-efficiency radiators and a Delco Freedom II battery. Outside of California, a new 305-cid V-8 was standard equipment. Half-ton pickups had a quick-take-up master cylinder, plus lighter weight rear springs.

Calendar-year registrations of Chevrolet light-duty trucks came in at 650,460 vehicles. Calendar-year sales included only 403,487 big pickups, 15,473 compact S-10 pickups, 21,399 Blazers, 61,724 LUV pickups and 33,086 El Caminos for a total of just 654.990 trucks. Rising gas prices were blamed for the "bottoming out" of Chevrolet's light truck sales.

These para-sailing enthusiasts thought that the 1981 K10 Stepside Sport "Shortie" looked great in New Light Silver Metallic and Midnight Black, with optional white spoke wheels.
Gregg D. Merksamer Collection

BASIC CONTENTS OF 1981-1987 TRIM PACKAGES

Custom Deluxe: Custom Deluxe was the basic trim level. It included a foam-padded bench seat with plaid upholstery, a body color steel roof headliner panel, black rubber floor mat, padded arm rests, courtesy lamps, prismatic rearview mirror, foam padded dash, bright upper and lower grille outline moldings, bright headlamp bezels, silver plastic grille insert, bright outside rearview mirror, bright door handles, bright Custom Deluxe nameplates, and white-painted bumper, hubcaps and wheels.

Custom Sport: Custom Sport was the Sporty trim level. It included and bright Custom Sport nameplates.

Scottsdale: The next step up was Scottsdale trim with a full-depth foam padded seat, wood-grain door trim inserts, an ash tray cigarette lighter, door or manually-operated courtesy lamps, bright door sill plates, color-keyed rubber floor mats, a high-note horn, patterned nylon cloth upholstery with vinyl trim, and all Custom Deluxe exterior features, plus a chrome bumper, chrome hubcaps, chrome body side moldings on Fleetsides, bright windshield and window trim, bright-rimmed parking, side marker and taillights, and Scottsdale nameplates.

Cheyenne: Cheyenne trim included full-depth foam seat cushions, ribbed pattern velour or buffalo-hide vinyl upholstery (vinyl bucket seats optional), folding seat backs, ash tray-mounted cigarette lighter, chestnut wood-grain dash and door inserts, door-operated or manually-operated courtesy and dome lamps, and added cab insulation. The Cheyenne exterior featured all Custom Deluxe and Scottsdale features, plus bright metal cab appliqués and moldings, bright upper body side and tailgate moldings, tailgate center appliqués on Fleetsides, and Cheyenne nameplates.

Silverado: At the top of the line was the Silverado option featuring extra-thick seat padding, basketweave nylon cloth or buffalo hide vinyl trim, full gauges, wood-grain dash panel, door storage pockets, carpeting, an insulated headliner, extra body insulation, and all Custom Deluxe and Scottsdale exterior items, plus lower body side and tailgate moldings, wheel lip moldings, Silverado nameplates, and a tailgate appliqué on Fleetsides. Silverados had distinctive rectangular-shaped front parking lamps in their grilles.

A 1981 Chevy K10 Fleetside "Shortie" carrying peat moss, seed and other agricultural products. It has white spoke wheels and a slider-style rear cab window. Old Cars Weekly Collection

A 1981 C30 Crew Cab/Bonus Cab pickup in Colonial Yellow with a Frost White cab roof. Bonus Cab models lacked the rear seat of Crew Cabs, but had the same body. Gregg D. Merksamer Collection

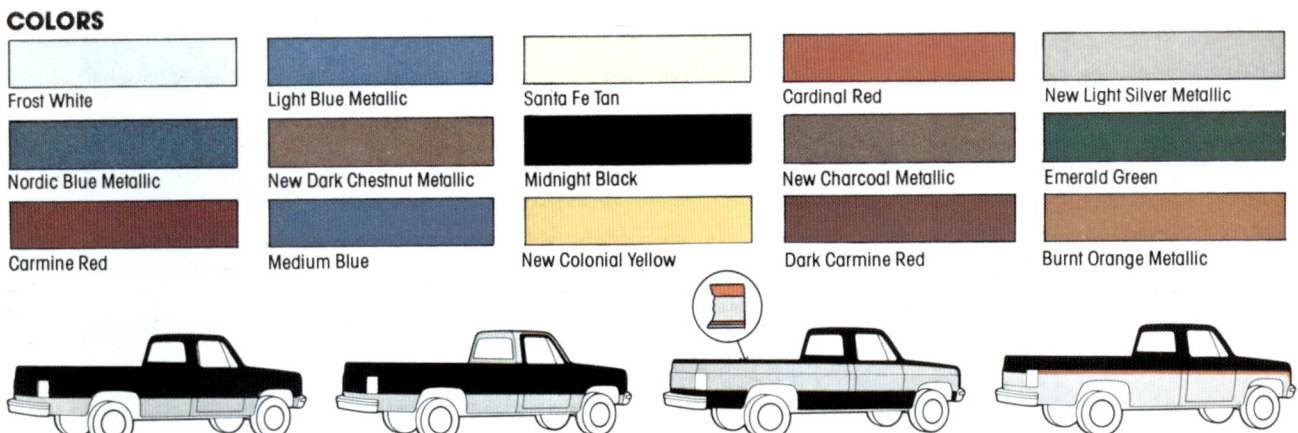

As had been the trend the past few years, Chevy offered 15 colors in 1981. Some could be teamed for two tones that came in the new Special, Deluxe, Interior Décor and Sport configurations shown. *Gregg D. Merksamer Collection*

The 1981 Silverado bench seat interior made for a roomy and well-appointed cabin. *Gregg D. Merksamer Collection*

New Silverado instrument panel

34 | Chevrolet Pickups 1973-1998

When a job at the Lakeside Rodeo required four-wheel drive, Chevy had the truck. This is a K10 Fleetside long box pickup with a dual-stacked headlamps grille in new Dark Chestnut Metallic and Colonial Yellow with white spoke wheels. Gregg D. Merksamer Collection

Shown here is the 1981 C10 diesel pickup with the 8-foot Fleetside box being loaded with bales of hay. The ice cube tray grille was new for 1981. This truck has the standard single-headlamps grille. Gregg D. Merksamer Collection

A convenient step between the door and extended rear fender was helpful when loading spools of cable in a Chevy Stepside pickup. This Santa Fe Tan long-box example has a silver-painted rear bumper. Gregg D. Merksamer Collection

The Carmine Red and Frost White truck is an '82 C10 Fleetside. The Light Blue Metallic job is a same-year C30 diesel with the Big Dooley option. The Silver Blue 4x4 is a K10 Stepside. The Colonial Yellow truck is a C30 chassis-and-cab fitted with a cabinet-type utility body. Gregg D. Merksamer Collection

Chevy dropped down to offering just these 10 colors for its 1982 pickup trucks. Gregg D. Merksamer Collection

1982: Chevy Tops Ford Again

Appearance features for 1982 Chevrolet pickups and their derivative models were virtually identical to the previous season, except a chrome grille became standard equipment. Improved rust protection was advertised. A new 6.2-liter Chevy-built diesel V-8 was available for larger trucks.

The base engine for half-ton C10 and K10 models and 3/4-ton C20 models was Chevrolet's trusty-and-true 250-cid in-line six-cylinder. A larger 292-cid in-line six was standard in 3/4-ton K10 trucks with four-wheel drive and in all one-ton C30 and K30 models.

This is 1982 Scottsdale vinyl trim in a rich Mahogany color. Note the textured vinyl floor covering and the four-wheel-drive lever mounted on the floor. *Gregg D. Merksamer Collection*

You could describe this gas-engined 1982 Chevy C10 Fleetside long-box pickup as a "dock worker" since it is carrying two oil drums on a dock. It's done in solid Light Blue Metallic. *Gregg D. Merksamer Collection*

Diesel power motivated this '82 C20 regular-cab Fleetside pickup with Scottsdale trim. Its cowboy-hatted owners picked a new Light Bronze Metallic and Almond paint scheme. It has the deluxe grille. Gregg D. Merksamer Collection

With the smaller the trucks, a three-speed manual transmission with a steering column-mounted gearshift three-speed was standard. However, the one-ton models came with a four-speed manual gearbox. Power brakes (except C10/C20), chrome bumpers and a bench seat were also regular equipment. Four-wheel-drive models came with standard power steering and K30 models featured a two-speed transfer case.

The Cheyenne trim level was eliminated. Custom Deluxe, Custom Sport, Scottsdale and Silverado packages were still available.

Calendar-year 1982 sales for Chevrolet light-duty trucks included 177,758 S10s, 8,161 S10 Blazers, 22,732 El Caminos, 24,103 Blazers and 393,277 pickups. Calendar-year production at U.S. factories totaled 658,066 units and included 209,517 compact pickups, 24,238 Blazers, 22,732 El Caminos and 268,080 full-size pickups. The final totals for calendar-year registrations were 758,107 for Chevy versus 733,120 for Ford. It was the first time since 1976 that Chevrolet had more registrations than Ford.

Aimed at the go-anywhere, do anything crowd that liked to go dirt biking in the desert, the 1982 Chevy K10 Stepside "Shortie" combined rugged looks with 4 x 4 versatility. Old Cars Weekly Collection

Hauling firewood is no problem for this Light Bronze Metallic and Frost White '83 C10 Fleetside with the 6.2-liter diesel V-8 under its hood. Note the chrome step bumper and non-sliding rear cab window. *Gregg D. Merksamer Collection*

1983: Scottsdale Package Revised

The big Chevy truck news in 1983 centered on sales and marketing, rather than product revisions. Overall, the American auto and truck industry realized a general recovery from the bleak period of the early 1980s. Chevrolet's overall market penetration in the light truck and van field rose by 1.58 percent to a 39.72 percent share of industry. Chevrolet dealers recorded 176 truck registrations per sales outlet in 1983, compared to 156 the previous season.

Chevrolet did slip behind Ford in calendar-year registrations for all types of truck however. For the calendar year, the company's van and light truck production in U.S. factories came to 848,580 units.

Chevrolet's Conventional-Cab C/K Pickups were unchanged in 1983, except for a revised grille treatment and new parking lamp placement. The grille featured a black-out look. The horizontal center-bar was finished in body color. The parking lights were moved from the bumper to the bottom of the grille.

Nicely dressed with chrome Rallys, raised-white-letter tires and a deluxe grille is this Colonial Yellow and Frost White '83 K10 Scottsdale Stepside. *Gregg D. Merksamer Collection*

Added corrosion protection was provided with the use of galvanized steel in the pickup box front panel and a Zincro-metal hood inner liner. Full-size 4x4s now used 15-inch diameter wheels and tires.

The Scottsdale trim package was upgraded slightly. Base Custom Deluxe and top-of-the-line Silverado trims were unchanged.

The 1983 Chevy trucks were introduced to the public on September 14, 1982. By the end of the calendar-year selling season, 904,672 new Chevy trucks would be registered. Calendar-year sales came in at 198,222 S-10 pickups, 106,214 S-10 Blazers, 24,010 El Caminos, 31,282 big Blazers and 412,533 full-size pickups. Calendar-year production: stood at 35,179 big Blazers, 28,322 El Caminos, 280,209 C/K pickups and 321,054 S-10s.

REVISED CONTENTS OF 1983 SCOTTSDALE TRIM PACKAGES

Scottsdale: The top trim level for 1983 was Scottsdale. It included a full-depth foam padded seat, wood-grain door trim inserts, an ash tray cigarette lighter, door or manually-operated courtesy lamps, bright door sill plates, color-keyed rubber floor mats, a high note horn, patterned nylon cloth upholstery with vinyl trim, and all Custom Deluxe exterior features, plus a chrome bumper, chrome hubcaps, chrome body side moldings on Fleetsides, bright windshield and window trim, bright-rimmed parking, side marker and taillights, and Scottsdale nameplates.

"Tough Chevy trucks are taking charge," promoted this Carmine Red and Frost White '83 C10 Silverado Fleetside long box. Gregg D. Merksamer Collection

COLORS

ALMOND | SILVER METALLIC | LIGHT BLUE METALLIC | MIDNIGHT BLUE | MIDNIGHT BLACK | MAHOGANY METALLIC | CARMINE RED | FROST WHITE | COLONIAL YELLOW | LIGHT BRONZE METALLIC

Back in 1983 all of the Chevy pickup colors had descriptive names like Midnight Black or Mahogany Metallic. These colors were not uniformly available on other models like Suburbans and Blazers. Gregg D. Merksamer Collection

An '83 C10 Scottsdale-level Fleetside pickup with full wheel covers and a deluxe quad headlight grille. Deluxe two-toning was based on Special two-toning with the second color on the roof and back of the cab. Old Cars Weekly Collection

1984: A Bold New Face

Chevrolet's full-size Pickup had a bold new grille featuring a bi-level design. There were three horizontal bars showing prominently in each section with seven less prominent vertical members behind them. Bright-plated grilles had a cross-hatch look, while the black-finished version appeared more horizontal. There were parking lamps behind the bars on the bottom and a yellow Chevrolet "bow tie" emblem on the body-color strip in the middle. Rectangular-shaped quad halogen headlamps were an option.

For better rust protection, two galvanized steel interior door panels were a new construction feature. Also new were semi-metallic front brake linings on C/K10 and C/K20 series trucks. New non-asbestos rear brake linings were used on most models. Plastic fuel tank stone shields were provided on all pickups and chassis-and-cab models. This was the first year for optional power windows and door locks on Bonus-Cab and Crew-Cab models, both of which came on a 164.5-in. wheelbase with Fleetside boxes.

A C10 Fleetside painted Apple Red and Silver Metallic in Chevy's Special Two-Tone manner. This option included body side and wheel opening moldings and other bright trim. Rally rims were extra. Gregg D. Merksamer Collection

The '84 spilt grille had eight vertical segments and six horizontal bars forming grids above and below a horizontal center piece bar with the Chevy bow tie logo. Gregg D. Merksamer Collection

Chevrolet trucks with deluxe two-tone paint had the cab and lower perimeter finished in the secondary color. Special two-toning meant only the lower perimeter was in the secondary color and there was bright trim on the body side and wheel openings. The Exterior Decor package included dual-tone body side finish and a rear tape stripe keyed to body colors, plus a hood ornament. The secondary color was used between the decal stripes and moldings.

Interior options for 1984 included standard Custom Deluxe trim, plus Scottsdale and Silverado options. There were 39 models in all. C10 and K10 pickups came in short box Stepside and long box Stepside and Fleetside models. C20 and K20 models came in Stepside or Fleetside form, only with the 8-ft. long box. The heavy-duty C20 added Chassis-and-Cab, Bonus-Cab and Crew-Cab models. Heavy-duty K10s came as Fleetsides and Stepsides with the long box. The C30 heavies offered three 4 x 2 and four 4 x 4 configurations in Chassis-and-Cab form for commercial and RV applications.

Sales during the 1984 calendar-year totaled 1,111,839 light trucks. Chevrolet promoted the U.S. Army's purchase of nearly 30,000 full-size Chevrolet 4 x 4 pickups 6.2-liter diesel V-8 engines. These trucks were said to be "regular production trucks like the ones you can get, except for a few specialized military adaptations like a special electrical system."

This well-preserved 1984 K10 Fleetside Silverado showed up in the swap meet at the Iola 2007 Old Car Show with a $12,500 asking price on the windshield sign. It was a highly-optioned truck.
John A. Gunnell Collection

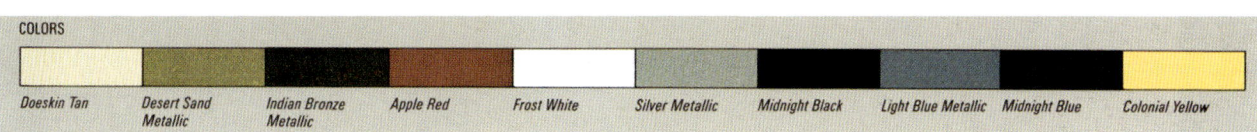

A few new colors like Desert Sand Metallic and Indian Bronze Metallic showed up in 1984, while others like Midnight Black were carried over. Gregg D. Merksamer Collection

Parking a nice '65 C20 in back of the Doeskin Tan and Apple Red '85 C10 Fleetside told buyers that "Chevrolet trucks last a long time." The '83 is a Silverado Custom with new Custom Two-Toning. John A. Gunnell Collection

The roomy and durable 1985 Chevy regular-cab Silverado bench seat interior. In this instance, it's trimmed with Chevy's Saddle Tan Custom cloth upholstery. John A. Gunnell Collection

Chevy catalog copywriters thought a picture including construction workers was the best way to reach buyers interested in this Light Blue Metallic 1985 C20 Stepside pickup. John A. Gunnell Collection

The 1985 Chevrolet Silverado pickup truck instrument panel was an impressive piece of industrial design. It included big, easy-to read gauges and well-thought-out controls. John A. Gunnell Collection

1985: 35 Years of Leadership

The 1985 Chevy sales catalog pointed out, "For three, and a half decades there have been more Chevy trucks in use than any other make." If that didn't make the new Chevys stand out, a redesigned front end did. The year's new grille had only a single horizontal bar intersected by seven vertical bars. There was a much wider, body-colored panel between the upper and lower grille sections. The headlight housings had more of a vertical look than last year's, although the rectangular lamps were again stacked

Chevrolet Pickups 1973-1998 | 47

Again in 1985, the Scottsdale Custom Cloth upholstery and interior trim was available in the Saddle Tan color. John A. Gunnell Collection

This crew of five husky lumberjacks could fit comfortably in this Doeskin Tan 1985 C20 Scottsdale Crew Cab pickup truck. Crew Cab models had two extra doors and one extra seat. John A. Gunnell Collection

| Frost White | Silver Metallic | Midnight Black | Light Blue Metallic | Midnight Blue | Colonial Yellow | Doeskin Tan | Desert Sand Metallic | Indian Bronze Metallic | Apple Red |

The 1985 Chevy full-size pickup paint options included these 10 colors in monotones. Or specific two-tone combinations
John A. Gunnell Collection

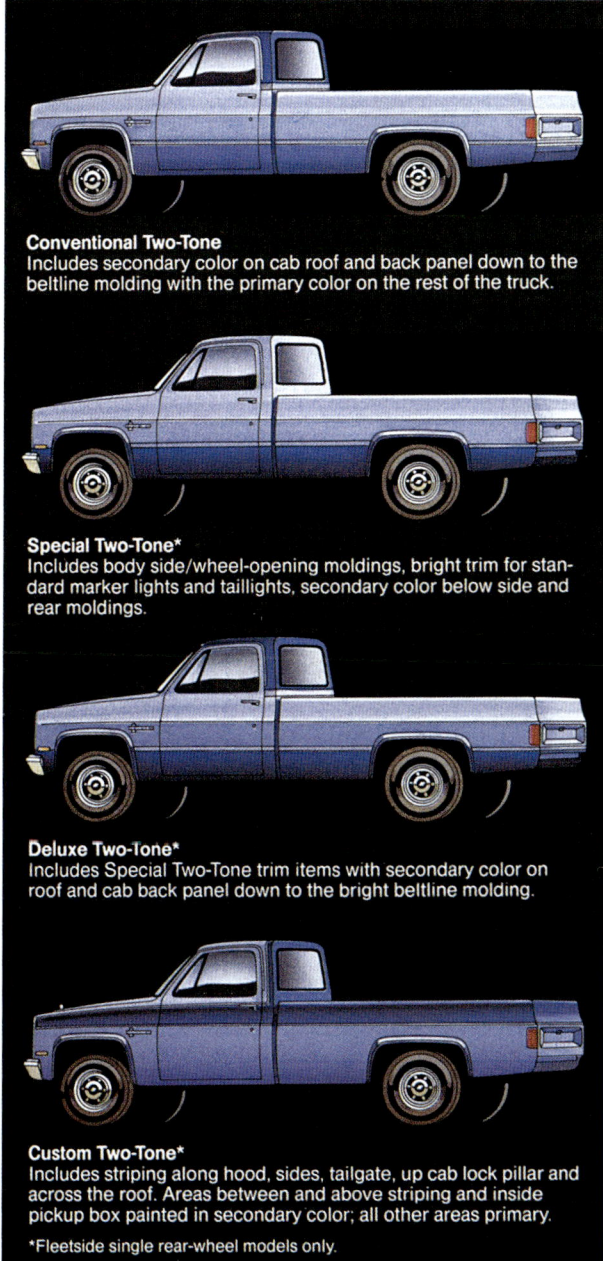

Conventional Two-Tone
Includes secondary color on cab roof and back panel down to the beltline molding with the primary color on the rest of the truck.

Special Two-Tone*
Includes body side/wheel-opening moldings, bright trim for standard marker lights and taillights, secondary color below side and rear moldings.

Deluxe Two-Tone*
Includes Special Two-Tone trim items with secondary color on roof and cab back panel down to the bright beltline molding.

Custom Two-Tone*
Includes striping along hood, sides, tailgate, up cab lock pillar and across the roof. Areas between and above striping and inside pickup box painted in secondary color; all other areas primary.

*Fleetside single rear-wheel models only.

The 1985 Chevy full-size pickup two-tone paint options included Conventional Two-Tone, Special Two-Tone, Deluxe Two-Tone and Custom Two-Tone. All but conventional came only on single-rear-wheel models. John A. Gunnell Collection

on top of each other. Amber-colored parking lamps at each side, on the bottom, were standard. When optional halogen high-beam headlights were ordered, the parking lamps were moved behind the lower grille.

A new custom two-tone body-color treatment was seen. It used the secondary color above the belt line on Fleetside cargo boxes, on the rear of the cab, on the doors and on the fender sides above the belt line. It was not used on the hood or window frames. This gave a sportier look (something like a tapering racing stripe) to the cab and fender sides.

Under the hood, as standard equipment, was GM's Vortec six. The trucks continued to come in a wide range of choices including 1/2-, 3/4- and one-ton series with long or short cargo boxes. Buyers got a choice of Fleetside or Stepside styling, Crew-Cab or Bonus-Cab configurations and 4 x 2 or 4 x 4 drive. A real "Country Cadillac" was the Crew-Cab Big Dooley with its flared rear fenders and dual rear wheels.

Custom Deluxe trim was standard. Scottsdale, and Silverado trims were again available. Scottsdales had color-keyed floor mats, plus added cowl and headliner insulation. Door-to-door carpeting, and velour or grained vinyl upholstery, were featured with Silverado interiors. Special two-tones, and Exterior Decor finish options were available. The latter included a hood ornament. Standard equipment now included fluidic-arm window washer/wipers.

Chevrolet introduced its 1985 models on September 21, 1984. Calendar-year production included 430,600 pickups and 1,325,491 trucks in total. Innovations: Every new 1985 light-duty Chevy truck delivered by a Chevrolet dealer in the United States came with a one-year, $10,000 seat belt insurance certificate from MIC General Insurance Corporation at no additional charge. Under the policy, $10,000 would be paid to the estate of any occupant suffering fatal injuries as a result of an accident involving that vehicle while wearing a GM seat belt.

Chevrolet Pickups 1973-1998

1986: Diamond Jubilee

Chevrolet kicked off a year-long celebration of its 75th anniversary as an automaker in 1986. By the end of this milestone year, the company would make 1,174,217 trucks of all types. Of these, 438,422 were full-size pickup trucks. New for the year was a high-tech instrument cluster for many models.

Continuing as standard equipment on full-size Chevy pickups was the Vortec Six. Electronic fuel-injection was added to the 2.8-liter V-6 for a nine percent boost in horsepower. With that and new swirl-port cylinder heads, it pumped out 155 hp and 230 lb.-ft. of torque. "It is the most powerful standard engine ever offered in a Chevrolet pickup," advised a Chevrolet press release.

The 5.0-liter and 5.7-liter gas V-8s, as well as the 6.2-liter diesel V-8, were used again. Diesel V-8 got a durable steel crankshaft, cast-aluminum pistons and glow-plug system for fast cold-engine starts. Diesel-powered trucks came with a 50,000-mile warranty and had up to 148 hp (on trucks with over 8,500 lb. GVW ratings.). An electric booster fan, mounted ahead of the radiator, was a new feature used with the optional 7.4-liter V-8.

The trucks continued to come in a wide range of choices. Custom Deluxe, Scottsdale and Silverado trims were again available.

Special Two-Tone paint decorates this 1986 C10 Fleetside Silverado. It is done in Light Blue Metallic and Frost White with Chevy's factory-style optional cast-aluminum wheels.
Old Cars Weekly Collection

This Nevada Gold Metallic K30 Fleetside Big Dooley Crew Cab Custom Deluxe pickup was also made to work hard. However, because of all the extras it includes, this would be a collector truck today. Old Cars Weekly Collection

Canyon Copper Metallic is the color that the factory applied to this 1986 Chevy C20 Stepside Custom Deluxe pickup. Old Cars Weekly Collection

Squirting Steel Gray Metallic paint on this K10 Stepside Custom Deluxe pickup does little to hurt its purposeful, utilitarian image. In later years, the plainer Chevy pickups would be called "Work Trucks." Old Cars Weekly Collection

Apple Red paint brightens the exterior of this 1986 Chevy C20 Fleetside Bonus Cab Custom Deluxe pickup. Bonus Cab models used the four-door body, but the extra interior space was used for storage, not seats. Old Cars Weekly Collection

Having been a volunteer firefighter for years, the author couldn't resist this photo of brave men and a "brave" V20 Fleetside Custom Deluxe 4 x 4 pickup battling a big forest fire. Naturally the truck is Apple Red. John A. Gunnell Collection

Chevrolet Pickups 1973-1998

Cast aluminum wheels

Styled wheels

Rally Wheels

Wheel covers

Buyers could dress their trucks up with many tire and wheel options in 1986, including the Cast-Aluminum, Styled and Rally wheels seen here. Wheel covers (lower right) were a lower-cost dress-up option. Old Cars Weekly Collection

In 1986, Chevy used 1956, 1966 and 1972 pickups parked behind a new C10 Fleetside Silverado to drive home the "longevity" theme. The new truck has the optional Exterior Custom Décor package. Old Cars Weekly Collection

In mid-'87 a new generation of C/K pickups bowed as '88 models, so the old-style '87 ½-tons were called R10 (4 x 2) and V10 (4 x 4) models. This is a V20 Fleetside Scottsdale with Special Two-Toning in Canyon Copper Metallic and Midnight Black. *John A. Gunnell Collection*

1987: Alphabet Soup

Chevy's full-size pickups (the type with stacked, square headlights that were called C/K models in 1986) became R/V models in 1987. This change was made because all-new full-size pickups based on the so-called GMT400 platform were being introduced in mid-1987 as the "1988" C/K models.

Although the GMT400 version were sometimes registered as 1987 trucks, the trucks were are covering in this chapter are the ones depicted in Chevrolet's 1987 Full Size Pickup sales catalog. These are the 1987 trucks that look like 1986 models, However, they had some improvements over the previous year's products.

Throttle body electronic fuel injection was fitted to both V-6 and V-8 engines in 1987. This system replaced the carburetor and allowed for higher compression ratios and greater horsepower. Both the 305-cid V-8 and the 350-cid V-8 were significantly more powerful for 1987. Computer controls were incorporated into the spark advance, fuel-to-air ratio, idle-speed and fuel cut-off functions to enhance both driveability and performance. Also for 1987, the engine-mounted mechanical fuel pump was replaced by an electric unit mounted in the fuel tank. This pump, along with a fuel pressure regulator, provided instant and constant fuel pressure for more precise

Here is the optional 1987 Scottsdale interior with Saddle Tan upholstery. Note the four-wheel-drive lever on the floor, indicating that this is a shot of the inside of a V10 regular-cab pickup truck. John A. Gunnell Collection

Here is the optional 1987 Silverado interior in Blue Custom Cloth. Note the Silverado nameplate on the glove box door and the carpeting covering the floor of the cab. Silverado was for luxury-truck buyers.
John A. Gunnell Collection

Chevrolet Pickups 1973-1998 | 55

1987 CHEVY PICKUP STANDARD EQUIPMENT

A front chromed bumpers.
Two right- and left-hand side doors.
Rear side doors on both sides of Bonus-Cab and Crew-Cab.
Removable tailgate with Chevrolet lettering.
Argent-painted molded plastic grille.
Single low-note electric horn.
Bright metal hubcaps with black trim.
Taillamps with integral back-up lamps.
Two rectangular headlamps.
Directional signals.
Parking lamps.
Front side markers.
Right- and left-hand chromed outside rearview mirrors.
Jack and wheel wrench.
White-painted wheels.
Two-speed electric windshield washers and wipers.
Right- and left-hand padded arm rests.
Instrument panel ash tray.
Rear door trim panel ash trays on Bonus-Cab and Crew-Cab.
Color-keyed molded plastic door trim panels.
Black rubber floor covering.
Outside air type heater and defogger.
Inside-operated hood release.
Speedometer with odometer.
Fuel gauge.
Switches and warning lights.
Insulation and sound-deadening materials.
Instrument cluster and cab interior lights.
10-inch prismatic rearview mirror.
Full-depth foam front bench seat with vinyl trim.
Full-width rear bench seat in Bonus-Cab and Crew-Cab.
Safety belts.
16-inch soft black plastic two-spoke steering wheel.
Energy-absorbing steering column.
Lockable instrument panel stowage box.
Dual padded sun shades.
Color-keyed molded plastic trim panels on side doors.
4.3-liter V-6 engine (in R10/R20/V10 models)
5.7-liter V-8 (in R20HD/R20 Bonus-Cab or Crew-Cab/R30/V20/V20HD/V30 Bonus-Cab and Crew-Cab models).
Three-speed manual (R10) or four-speed manual (all other models) transmission.
P195/75R-15 tires (LT215/85R-16C on base 4x4 models and LT235/85R-16 on larger 4x2 and 4x4 models).

This 1987 Chevy R10 Fleetside Silverado pickup from Arizona was another swap meet offering at Iola 2007. The 79,000-mile original had the 350 V-8 and overdrive automatic and a $9,500 asking price. John A. Gunnell Collection

fuel control during engine starting and driving.

The 262-cid Vortex V-6 was the standard base engine. For 1987 it was equipped with lower-friction roller-hydraulic valve lifters. These increased engine efficiency, while providing a three percent fuel economy increase. Chevrolet also installed new lower-weight Delco batteries with higher cold-cranking current for all gasoline engines. Cold cranking amperes were increased from 500 to 525 on the 4.3-liter V-6 and from 405 to 525 on 5.0-liter V-8s with automatic transmission and all 5.7-liter applications. They also climbed from 540 to 630 amperes on the 7.4-liter gasoline engine. The 6.2-liter diesel for 1987 continued to use two batteries, each with 540 cold cranking amperes. The RPO UA1 heavy-duty battery option for the 5.0- and 5.7-liter V-8 engines was revised to include an increased performance cranking motor for 1987.

Chevrolet Pickups 1973-1998 | 57

Vinyl trim, which was "in" during the '60s and early '70s, was "way out" by the late 1980s. However, Chevy's cheaper Custom Deluxe interior did offer pleated vinyl upholstery shown here in Saddle Tan.
John A. Gunnell Collection

Alternator changes for 1987 involved replacement of the standard 37-ampere output alternator with a 66-ampere alternator as standard equipment. The 66-ampere alternator had been an option in 1986.

Custom Deluxe trim was standard and included color-keyed all-vinyl upholstery (blue, burgundy, charcoal, mahogany or saddle tan), a black rubber floor mat, a padded instrument panel, and color-keyed molded door trim panels with arm rests. The mid-level Scottsdale package added a color-keyed rubber floor mat, a full headliner, added insulation, a choice of deluxe cloth or custom vinyl upholstery, and special Scottsdale identification. The top-level Silverado package added a color-keyed headliner, color-keyed carpeting, a custom steering wheel, full gauge instrumentation, and specific Silverado exterior trim.

Exterior and interior color selections were Frost White, Steel Gray Metallic, Midnight Black, Light Blue Metallic, Midnight Blue, Canyon Copper Metallic, Doeskin Tan, Nevada Gold Metallic, Indian Bronze Metallic, and Apple Red. Two-tone paint options included conventional with the cab roof and back panel in one color and the rest of the truck in another, special two-tone with a second color below the lower body side moldings, deluxe two-tone a combination of conventional and special, and the exterior decor package with the second color around the center of the body, between the upper and lower body side moldings.

Chevrolet general manager Robert D. Burger was way off in his prediction of 1.3 million truck sales. American truck-makers saw their sales volume reach a record 4.9 million units in 1987, but Chevy dealers retailed just 1,191,848 units, a six-percent drop from 1986. That put Chevy second in the truck-sales race, behind rival Ford. Of the total, 417,670 units were full-size pickups.

1988-98 Chevrolet C/K Pickups

1988: All-new Chevy Pickups

Chevrolet introduced an all-new range of full-size C/K pickups on April 23, 1987 as 1988 models. The new trucks were produced at three assembly plants—in Fort Wayne, Indiana, Pontiac, Michigan and Oshawa, Ontario, Canada. Adding sales appeal, as well as representing a new avenue of versatility, were the extended-cab models with optional six-passenger seating.

The wheelbases of the new models were 117.5 in. for standard models, 131.5 in. for long-wheelbase and extended-cab models and 155.5 in. for extended-wheelbase models with extended cabs. These dimensions were unchanged from the immediately preceding generation of full-size trucks, although the new models were longer than the older models.

The redesigned exterior was 3.5-in. narrower, but the interior had more leg and shoulder room, as well as more seat travel. The new models had larger doors that extended upward into the roof line and downward nearly to the bottom of the rocker. The new doors, along with a low step-up height and high headroom, made for ease of entry and exit.

Fleetside pickups had a cargo box that measured 49.15-in. between the wheel wells and 63.8-in. between the side panels. Numerous features, such as flush side glass, a modular-assembled bonded-flush windshield, single-piece door frames and robotic welding marked the latest C/K Chevrolet trucks as very advanced vehicles. Chevrolet went to great lengths to improve the fit and finish of its 1988 models. The use of hidden roof pillars and built-in drip rails eliminated matching problems on door cuts. The back of the cab and the front of the pickup box were both mounted on a single, one-piece fixture. This bracket eliminated mismatch of the two sections, especially when the box was loaded.

A new front end featured a single-piece grille that eliminated potential molding mismatch. There were single headlamps at each corner. The Silverado was equipped with dual halogen headlamps. Structural

The 1988 C2500 Fleetside Cheyenne in Flame Red. Looks very much like the author's trusty, plain-Jane '88 C1500 Cheyenne, but without the rust! John A. Gunnell Collection

INTRODUCING A LEANER, MEANER FULL-SIZE CHEVY.

The 1988 full-size Chevy

Introducing a whole new animal. A full-size pickup built new from the inside out. With the most standard power, most available V8 power and heaviest standard payload of any half-ton pickup.*

The 1988 Chevy. It's new from the inside out. And ready to work now.

*Excludes other GM products.

THE *Heartbeat* OF AMERICA
TODAY'S CHEVY TRUCKS

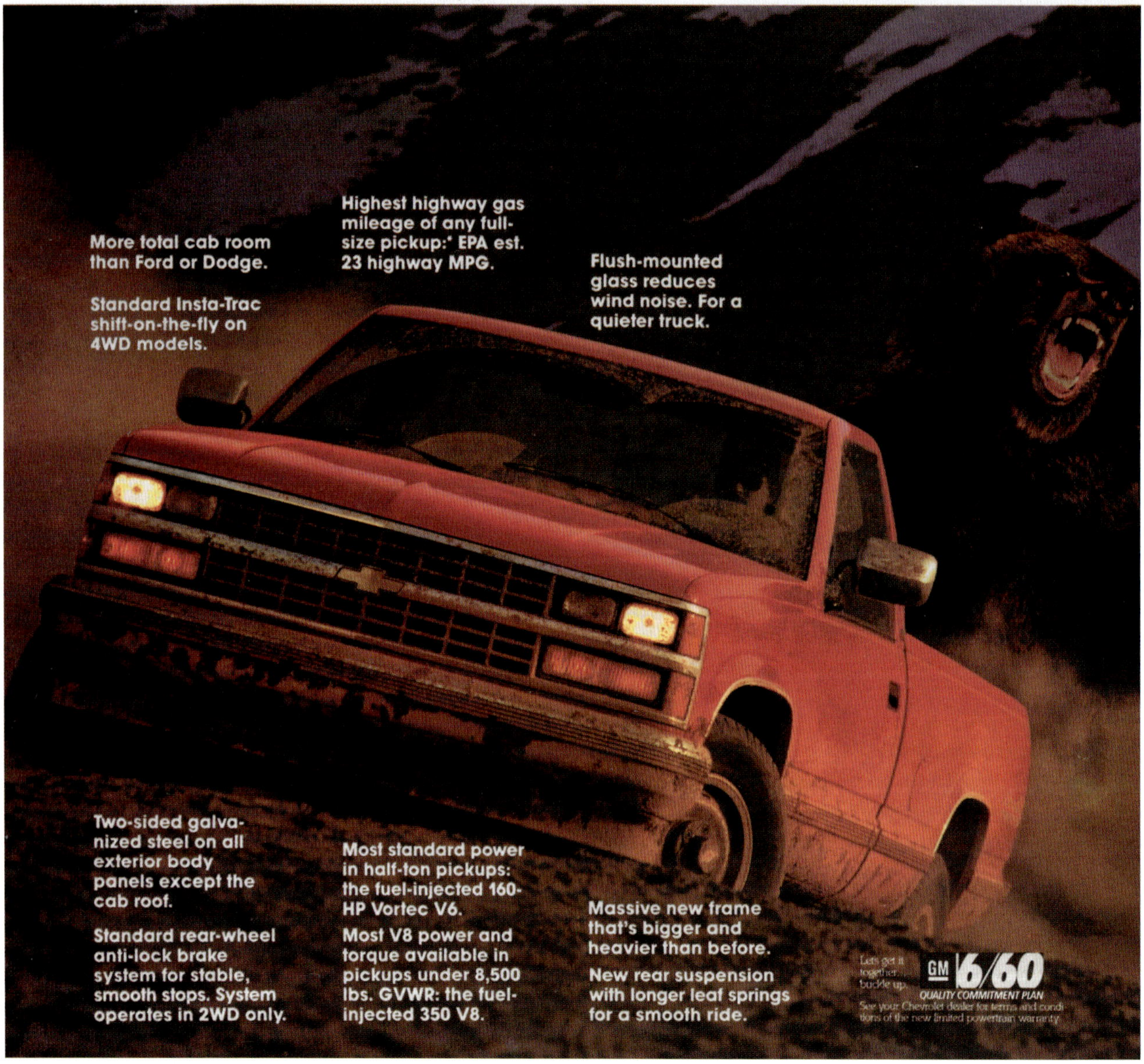

More total cab room than Ford or Dodge.

Standard Insta-Trac shift-on-the-fly on 4WD models.

Highest highway gas mileage of any full-size pickup:* EPA est. 23 highway MPG.

Flush-mounted glass reduces wind noise. For a quieter truck.

Two-sided galvanized steel on all exterior body panels except the cab roof.

Standard rear-wheel anti-lock brake system for stable, smooth stops. System operates in 2WD only.

Most standard power in half-ton pickups: the fuel-injected 160-HP Vortec V6.

Most V8 power and torque available in pickups under 8,500 lbs. GVWR: the fuel-injected 350 V8.

Massive new frame that's bigger and heavier than before.

New rear suspension with longer leaf springs for a smooth ride.

The ad outlined all of the new features — well, most of the important ones — of the all-new 1988 C/K pickups. It showed a rough-and-tumble K1500 regular cab Fleetside long-box pickup kicking up some mud. John A. Gunnell Collection

The standard 1988 Cheyenne interior featured a three-across all-vinyl bench seat with folding backrest that came in a choice of five colors, color-keyed molded door trim panels and electronic gauges and controls. John A. Gunnell Collection

rigidity was improved with double-panel construction for the roof, hood, fenders, doors and pickup box.

One of the most apparent features of the new generation Chevy truck was its greatly increased glass area that, at 4,256 square in., was one-third larger than the older model's. The use of a bonded, angled and curved backlight was credited with reducing glare. To improve visibility in poor weather, the wiper pattern was enlarged.

Improved anti-corrosion protection was a high priority for designers of the Chevrolet. The all-welded pickup box had a seamless floor without bolts for enhanced corrosion resistance. Two-sided galvanized steel was used for all major exterior panels, except the roof. All exterior sheet metal was primer dipped. Anti-stone protection was applied to the lower fenders, door and pickup box. Both the windshield and backlight were constructed without mitered corners.

The front bumper was devoid of attaching bolts. This had the dual result of improving appearance while also removing another source of potential corrosion. Prior to painting, all sheet metal panels were immersion-washed to remove contaminants for better paint adhesion. A uniprime ELPO dip treatment drew the protective primer into recessed areas. The color coat/clear coat paint provided a hard, high-luster finish.

The color selection for 1988 consisted of Brandywine Metallic, Sandstone Metallic, Pacific Blue Metallic, Adobe Gold Metallic, Sable Black Metallic, Quicksilver Metallic, Spice Brown Metallic, Summit White, Flame Red, and Iced Blue Metallic. Three optional exterior two-tone schemes were offered. Conventional two-toning placed the accent color below the lower styling line. Special two-toning included a multi-stripe decal at the upper styling line and the accent color below. Deluxe two-toning featured a multi-stripe decal at the upper styling line and the accent color between the decal and the lower feature line.

The new trucks adopted the old C/K10, C/K20 and C/K30 designations. Certain models, such as Crew Cab pickups, continued to be built with the old sheet metal. Instead of designating these C/K trucks, they were now R/V models. Stepside pickup trucks were not offered at first, but a new Sportside version arrived during the model year.

Chevrolet used three well-known names for the trim packages available for 1988. The base package was the Cheyenne, which was depicted as "a new value standard in full-size work trucks." The mid-range Scottsdale was described as "a big step up in a sensible blend of function and form." The Silverado, regarded as "the finest expression of the new '88

Black Metallic finish makes a K1500 Sportside "Shortie" pickup stand out. This one has the Deluxe grille. The Sportside was a modern interpretation of the Stepside body style. This one wears Rally rims. John A. Gunnell Collection

Chevy full-size Pickup," remained the top-of-the line trim package.

Two-wheel-drive Chevrolets featured an independent coil spring front suspension in all weight classes. The C1500/C2500 models used a semi-floating rear axle, while the C3500s had a full-floating rear axle. Four-wheel-drive trucks were fitted with a new independent front suspension with a hypoid driving axle and torsion bar springs. It used a new wire-form design for the upper control arms with lighter and stronger parts than the components previously used. The torsion bar springs and jounce bumpers were connected to the lower control arms. The torsion bars were computer selected to correspond with the truck's GVW rating and balance with the rear springs.

STANDARD FEATURES OF ALL 1988 MODELS

Standard interior features on all models were the following items:
Right- and left-hand arm rests.
Instrument panel-mounted ash tray.
Right side coat hook (also a left-hand hook in extended-cabs).
Painted areas in the same color as the exterior primary color.
Interior trim identical to seat trim.
Color-keyed molded plastic door trim panels.
Left-door jam switch-operated dome light.
Tinted glass (in all windows on extended-cab models).
Heater and defroster with side window defoggers.
Inside-operated hood lock release.
Speedometer, odometer and fuel gauges.
Warning lights for generator, oil pressure and engine coolant temperature.
Safety belts.
Service/parking brake.
Direction/hazard signals and high beams.
Insulation/sound-deadening material installed on the firewall.
Insulation/sound-deadening material under floor mats.
Insulation/sound-deadening material extended-cab-rear quarter and cab back.
Storage box on right side of instrument panel with beverage holder.
Instrument cluster and cab interior lights.
Shift point indicator light with manual transmissions and gasoline engines.
4x4 lighted display.
10-in. inside day/night rearview mirror.
Foam-padded and full-width bench seat with folding back rest and vinyl trim.
Safety belts for all seating positions.
15.25-in. soft black plastic four-spoke steering wheel.
Energy-absorbing steering column.
Left and right side padded vinyl sun shades.
Front chrome bumper.
Molded plastic Argent Silver-painted grille.
Single electric low-tone horn.
Black plastic hubcaps with 4x4 identification.
Back-up lights integral with tail lamps.
Two rectangular headlights.
Front and rear directional and parking lamps.
Front side marker lamps.
Removable tailgate with embossed Chevrolet lettering.
Mechanical jack and wheel wrench.
Silver-painted wheels,
Electric two-speed windshield wipers and washers.
All models were fitted with new anti-theft door locks with sliding levers integrated into the door trim panels.

The frame used on 4 x 4 trucks had an additional front cross member located under the transmission case. The 4 x 4 trucks also had a new "Shift-On-The-Fly Instra-Trac" transfer case system allowing for shifting from 4 x 2 to 4 x 4 high, and back, without stopping at any speed. The front axle disconnect system locked the front hubs automatically when the single lever operating the 4 x 4 system was pulled backward. This shifter was located in the center of the cab floor and was connected directly to the transfer case, rather than using cables. In the 4 x 2 mode, the front-axle disconnect allowed the front wheels to turn freely. In the 4 x 4 mode, the transfer case split the power and directed it equally to the front and rear wheels.

Rear axles used on 4 x 4 models were of the same type and capacity as the ones used on 4 x 2 trucks. The K1500 was available with an optional off-road chassis package consisting of a front differential carrier, engine and transfer case shields, front stabilizer bar, Delco/Bilstein high-pressure gas shock absorbers, and heavier front and rear jounce bumpers.

The standard V-6 engine for the K1500 and K2500 series had a new one-piece rubber oil pan gasket to help prevent oil leakage. As a midyear treat, Chevrolet introduced a new K1500 Sportside model on the 117.5-in. wheelbase chassis. It had a 6.5 foot long pickup box. The fiberglass rear fenders or side panels were flanked by functional steps to aid in loading and unloading. The Sportside was available

OPTIONAL TWO-TONES AND EXTERIOR COLORS.

CONVENTIONAL TWO-TONE places the accent color below the lower styling line.

SPECIAL TWO-TONE includes a multi-stripe decal at the upper styling line and the accent color below. (Not available on Sportside models.)

DELUXE TWO-TONE features a multi-stripe decal at the upper styling line and the accent color between the decal and lower feature line. (Not available on Sportside models.)

In '88, Chevy dropped to just three two-tone color options. Conventional had the accent color on bottom. Special had belt line stripes and an accent color below. Deluxe put the accent color between the base color.
John A. Gunnell Collection

Shown here is the optional Silverado interior for the new Chevy C/K extended-cab pickup. The rear seat was a separate option. John A. Gunnell Collection

with any trim level and with most appearance, convenience, and performance options offered for other 4 x 4 models. This new truck's body style designator was E62. Also introduced during the latter part of the 1988 model-year was a new instrument cluster featuring enhanced cluster graphics that increased clarity of instrument readings at all light levels.

At the start of 1988, Chevrolet had 4,910 dealers who sold Chevrolet trucks. They helped the company take a large chunk out of Ford's lead in light-duty truck sales in 1988, retailing 1,336,407 units compared to 1,173,675 in 1987. Ford's lead in the market segment shrank to 106,000 units. The thrust of Chevrolet's increase came from full-year availability of the restyled GMT400 C/K pickups.

Establishing and industry record of 71 trucks per year per employee, sales of just under 500,000 pickups were anticipated for 1988. Chevrolet also added Sportside and Extended-Cab Pickup models, plus a heavy-duty pickup with a 8,500-pounds-plus GVWR.

Calendar-year sales of new pickups included: 514,870 of the full-size C/K models, 248,768 S-10 and T-10 pickups, and 420 El Caminos (built from January 1988 to April 1988 only). The company's total truck sales were 1,354,491 units for the calendar year.

CONTENTS OF 1988 TRIM PACKAGES

Cheyenne: Included a Cheyenne designation on the rear cab side pillars and a choice of five interior colors: gray, blue, saddle, beige or garnet.

Scottsdale Package (Z62): *In addition to or replacing the Cheyenne content:* Dual electric high-note and low-note horns, Scottsdale nameplates on the rear cab side pillars, a chrome front bumper with black rub strip, a Chevrolet block lettering decal on the tailgate, a standard bench seat with cloth upholstery and folding back rest in the same color selection as Scottsdales offered, grained plastic interior door panels with soft-vinyl upper trim and integral arm rests, map pockets and Scottsdale identification on doors, color-keyed door-sill plates, color-keyed rubber floor mats (front compartment only on Bonus-Cab), a full-length mystic-colored insulated cloth headliner with matching retainer moldings, left and right-side coat hooks, and Scottsdale identification on door trim panels.

Silverado Package (YE9): *In addition to or replacing the Scottsdale content:* : Hood and cab-to-fender insulators, a deluxe front end appearance with Dark Argent Silver grille and quad rectangular halogen headlamps, a deluxe bright-accented front bumper rub strip, bright accent body side moldings, bright accent wheel-opening molding (single rear wheel Fleetside models only), deluxe tailgate trim with Chevrolet lettering over bright aluminum appliqué, Silverado identification on cab back pillars, custom vinyl seat trim in gray, blue, beige, garnet or saddle (custom cloth seat trim at no extra cost), soft-vinyl two-tone door trim panels with integral arm rests and door map pockets and door-closing assist straps and Silverado identification, color-keyed full-length carpeting, carpeted cowl/kick panels with insulators, carpeted cab back panels, a color-keyed headliner, cloth-covered sun shades with left-hand storage provisions and a strap, a right-hand vanity mirror, a custom four-spoke steering wheel, and a cigarette lighter in the ash tray.

CONTENTS OF 1989 TRIM PACKAGES

The base Cheyenne, mid-range Scottsdale and top-ranked Silverado trim levels were carried into 1989 with minor changes.

Cheyenne: Single electric low-note horn, power steering, rear brake drums with anti-lock brake system (operated in two-wheel-drive mode only), a front chromed bumper, a molded plastic grille painted Light Argent with Dark Argent air intake areas, single rectangular headlights, silver-painted wheels with black hub ornaments, all-season steel-belted radial tires (steel-belted radials on RPO RO5), a winch-type spare tire carrier mounted under frame (K1500 models only), right and left side fixed arm mirrors with adjustable heads and black finish, right- and left-hand padded arm rests integral with door panels (with grained molded plastic finish), three-passenger all-vinyl trim bench seat with folding back rest, right-hand coat hook, left-hand coat hook on Extended-Cab models, dark gray door sill plates, a dome light with switch in left-hand door jamb, embossed black rubber floor mats, tinted glass in all windows on Extended-Cab models, padded color-keyed left and right side sun shades, a four-spoke steering wheel, a 10-inch rear view mirror, a vinyl headliner in same color as retainer moldings (Extended-Cab models had cab upper, lower and side trim panels and a molded cloth color-keyed headliner with matching retainer moldings), insulation on dash panel, cowl top and sides and doors of regular-cab models, insulation on rear quarter and back panels and floor covering of Extended-Cab models, and extra insulation for models with diesel engines.

Scottsdale: The Scottsdale trim (RPO Z62) contained the following added equipment: A front chromed bumper with bumper rub stripes, black plastic body side moldings, black wheel opening lip moldings (except on K2500 C6P, dual rear wheel models, and Sportside trucks), color-keyed door panels with grained molded plastic finish and soft vinyl trim, map pockets and Scottsdale emblems, left- and right-hand coat hooks, color-keyed door sill plates, dome light with switches in left and right side door jambs, color-keyed embossed rubber floor mats, a full width storage tray behind seat on floor, and a color-keyed cloth headliner, Regular-Cab and Extended-Cab models had matching retainer moldings, color-keyed door pillar and roof side panels, and additional insulation on their headliner.

Silverado: The Silverado trim package (RPO YE9), had all this equipment, plus an additional electric high-note horn, Silverado exterior nameplates, dual rectangular halogen headlights, black plastic body side moldings with bright trim, hood and cab-to-

With all of the changes for model-year 1988, the next season brought modest changes, as reflected by this K1500 Fleetside regular-cab pickup being hard to distinguish from models of the previous year. John A. Gunnell Collection

fender insulators, door panels with two-toned soft vinyl over plastic trim, door panel map pockets, door closing assist straps, door panel Silverado emblems, color-keyed floor carpeting, padded, color-keyed left- and right-hand sun shades with cloth covering, a storage strap on the left side unit and a visor mirror on right side unit, gauges for voltmeter, engine coolant temperature and oil pressure (replacing warning lights), a cigarette lighter in ash tray, color-keyed carpeting on the cab back panel, and insulation on regular-cab back panels.

The content of the V3500 Crew-Cab and Bonus-Cab models differed slightly from the other 4 x 4 Chevrolets. The Cheyenne package for these big pickups had white painted wheels, bright metal hubcaps with black trim (on single-rear-wheel models), exterior below-eye-line mirrors, an AM radio, a two-spoke steering wheel and a heavy-duty heater and defogger.

With Scottsdale trim, these trucks included a full-width front bench seat in a choice of dual-woven cloth vinyl trim or all-vinyl pigskin trim, a door-operated dome lamp with bright trim, color-keyed rubber floor mats (for front compartment only in Bonus-Cab), full-length mystic-colored insulation for headliner (with matching retainer moldings) and insulation under the cowl panel or headliner, plus on the cab back panel.

The V3500 Silverado package had bright body side and rear moldings with black trim, plus bright wheel-opening trim on Fleetside single-rear-wheel models only, an underhood reel-type lamp, a bright tailgate appliqué, bright trim for the front marker lights and taillights, special color-keyed plastic door panels with cloth inserts and vinyl stowage pockets (plus carpeting and bright trim strips on lower portions), a right-hand visor mirror, a headlamp warning buzzer, a two-spoke steering wheel with bright trim on horn buttons, a mystic-colored full-length cloth headliner and extra-thick insulation on floor panels.

Extensive changes took place in the brake system used on the C/K series trucks. The parking brake cable was given increased protection from rocks and road debris by revised routing and the addition of a shield. To reduce brake noise a new molded, semi-metallic brake lining material was used. A new 28MT starter motor and revised engine dipstick lettering were used on 6.2-liter diesel engine-equipped models.

A new Borg-Warner Model 1370 transfer case with an electrically actuated synchronizer was offered for K3500 models with dual rear wheels. This allowed RPO RO5 dual rear wheels to be ordered on 1-ton R/V Pickups and Chassis-and-Cab models. This development also increased the available GVWR on the K3500 1-ton four-wheel-drive trucks to 10,000 lb.

Chevrolet calendar-year sales of new pickups totaled 521,358 C/K models and 228,691 S-10/T-10 models. Model-year new-truck sales included 551,223 C/K pickups and 241,866 S-10/T-10 Pickups.

At the Chicago Auto Show, a man on the '88 Chevy pickup design team showed us how lumber could be stacked in the box walls like this. This off-the-floor stacking allowed plywood boards to slide in below. John A. Gunnell Collection

The tailgate is removable.

Completely removing the tailgate from the all-new C/K pickup is a one-man operation, though not for 90-pound weaklings.
John A. Gunnell Collection

SABLE BLACK METALLIC

ICED BLUE METALLIC

PACIFIC BLUE METALLIC

SPICE BROWN METALLIC

SUMMIT WHITE

ADOBE GOLD METALLIC

SANDSTONE METALLIC

FLAME RED

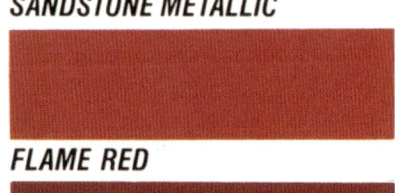

BRANDYWINE METALLIC

QUICKSILVER METALLIC

Chevy offered 10 colors for 1988 and still used descriptive names like Pacific Blue Metallic and Spice Brown Metallic that made it easy for buyers to picture various hues. Some could be teamed up in two-tones.
John A. Gunnell Collection

68 | Chevrolet Pickups 1973-1998

Two range-riding cowpokes discuss the merits of the '89 K2500 Fleetside Silverado extended-cab pickup. The 4 x 4 truck looks great with its Conventional Two-Tone paint treatment. John A. Gunnell Collection

1989: GM BEST SELLER

The "New Generation" full-size Chevy C/K trucks entered the 1989 model-year as the best-selling vehicles in General Motors' lineup. To meet consumer demand second shifts and overtime were added to production schedules. Also a good sign of the times for Chevy was the news from GM surveys that the C/K trucks had the highest customer satisfaction of any full-size pickup.

Numerous changes were found in the 1989 C/K models, in terms of their engineering as well as option availability and content. The regular-cab and Extended-Cab models had a new optional 4 x 4 sport graphic package. Chevrolet said it made "A bold statement for performance enthusiasts." Complementing the Sportside 4 x 4 was a new Fleetside Sport with a 6.5-foot pickup box that was available as an interim 1989 model. The 4 x 4 Sport models featured black-out wheel opening flares, bumpers, mirrors and a front air dam with tow hooks.

Eight exterior colors were carried over from 1988: Brandywine Metallic, Sandstone Metallic, Adobe Gold Metallic, Sable Black Metallic, Quicksilver Metallic, Summit White, and Flame Red. They were joined by three new colors: Smoke Blue Metallic, Caramel Brown Metallic, and Midnight Blue Metallic.

Initially, a new Dark Cognac replaced Saddle in the interior color offerings. In January 1989, Saddle rejoined Beige, Blue, Garnet and Gray as available interior colors. Beige and gray were not available for Extended-Cab models.

Three optional exterior two-tone schemes were again offered. The conventional two-tone (RPO ZY2) was available only on single rear wheel Fleetside models. The primary color was applied to the areas above the lower side body styling crease line (including the roof) with the secondary color below the crease line. Outlined block "Chevrolet" decal lettering was applied to the tailgate. A bright trim panel with lettering was applied when the Silverado option was ordered. The Special two-tone (RPO ZY3) also available only on single-rear-wheel Fleetside models. It included a multi-stripe decal applied over the paint break at the belt line. One color of paint was applied to the areas above the decal (including the roof) with the second color applied to the areas below. The Deluxe two-tone (RPO ZY4) also featured a multi-stripe decal at the upper styling line and the accent color between the decal and the lower feature line. Outlined block "Chevrolet" decal lettering was applied to the tailgate. A bright trim panel with lettering was applied when the Silverado option was ordered.

The big trucks retained the old look (and R/V designations) for several more years. This is an '89 R3500 Crew Cab in Smoke Blue and Gray Metallic. The colors offered on these trucks varied from C/K colors. *John A. Gunnell Collection*

Here's a bird's-eye view of the extended-cab pickup's roomy interior with optional front bucket seats and up-the-scale Silverado upholstery and trim. *John A. Gunnell Collection*

This is the 1989 Chevy C3500 chassis Ca6 in Summit White with special body equipment that was available from Chevrolet dealers.

1990: 454 SS — CHEVY'S "HOT ROD" PICKUP

Two new models, a new heavy-duty engine and more standard equipment than ever highlighted the 1990 Chevrolet full-size pickup lineup. Work Truck and 454SS were the names for two distinctly different new trucks. They were designed for different segments of the growing full-size pickup market.

The 454SS was a high-performance, limited-edition, up-level C1500 Regular-Cab 4x2 pickup. Its special option package contents were targeted to meet increasing demand for high-style personal-use pickup trucks. Equipped with a potent 7.4-liter EFI V-8 engine, three-speed automatic transmission,

This view does a good job of showing the 255.7-inch length of the 1990 V3500 Crew Cab pickup. This truck is Apple Red and came standard with Cheyenne interior trim. John A. Gunnell Collection

As we mentioned earlier, one of the plainest models Chevrolet had in its 1990 truck lineup was called the Work Truck. This is a W/T 1500 4 x 4 in White with black-finished grille, bumper, mirrors and hubcaps. John A. Gunnell Collection

Chevrolet Pickups 1973-1998 | 71

performance handling package, and 3.73:1 ratio rear axle as standard equipment, the 454SS delivered 230 hp at 3600 rpm. It carried a powerful torque rating of 385 lb.-ft. at 1600 rpm. Other power train standards included a heavy-duty radiator, engine oil and transmission oil coolers, and a locking rear differential.

The standard 454SS performance handling package (which was optional on other C1500 models) included 32 mm Bilstein gas-filled shock absorbers, a 32 mm front stabilizer bar, a .7:1 fast-ratio steering gear assembly, and heavy-duty jounce bumpers. The package also included five P275/60R15 steel-belted radial tires mated to five 15 x 7-inch styled chrome wheels.

The upscale content of the 454SS was as impressive as its performance and handling. The package also included high-back bucket seats with a console, a Sport appearance package, air conditioning, an AM/FM stereo with cassette and clock and graphic equalizer, a sliding rear window, a tilt steering wheel, power door locks and windows, electronic speed control and auxiliary lighting.

The 454SS was a slow-selling vehicle when it first came out and Chevrolet dealers gave buyers healthy discounts on purchases of trucks with this model-option. Also, an interesting pieces of Chevrolet truck sales literature was a full-line brochure that folded out and had a full-size picture of the 454SS on the obverse side.

The C/K1500 Work Truck "WT" represented a high-value, low-option regular-cab pickup aimed at truck buyers looking for a no-frills workhorse pickup. The WT was available exclusively in standard Cheyenne trim, but with a new grille added. It also included a body-color filler panel, charcoal-painted bumper,

The definitely-collectible high-performance 454 SS was released in 1990. This C1500 regular-cab Fleetside had the 454-cid V-8. It came only in Onyx Black with blackout trim, a 6-1/2-ft. box, fat tires and more. John A. Gunnell Collection

Chevrolet Pickups 1973-1998

The interior of the 454 SS pickup featured an exclusive Garnette Red plush cloth interior, luxury Silverado trimmings, special front high-back Sport Seats, a center console, a slider rear window, tilt steering and more. John A. Gunnell Collection

There were only seven factory colors for R/V pickup trucks in 1990. All of them were different than the colors used on the new-style C/K pickups. John A. Gunnell Collection

There were 10 factory colors for the new-style C/K pickup trucks in 1990. Some could be teamed up in specific two-tone combinations. These colors were not available for R/V models that used the "old" styling. John A. Gunnell Collection

and WT identification. Available in either 4 x 2 or 4 x 4 configurations, the WT carried a GVWR of 5,600 lbs. The maximum payload for the 4 x 2 and 4 x 4 versions was 1,711 lbs. and 1,331 lbs., respectively.

Chevrolet full-size pickup engine availability for 1990 included two V-6s, three gas V-8s and two diesel V-8s, depending on the model. A new heavy-duty version of the 4.3-liter EFI V-6 was available as the standard engine in C/K2500 models carrying the minimum GVWR of 8,600 lbs. and as a credit option on C/K3500s. The features that distinguished the heavy-duty 4.3-liter engine from its standard counterpart included a lower 8.6:1 compression ratio (versus 9.3:1) and a larger 3.0-inch low-restriction exhaust system for improved performance in heavy-duty applications. Horsepower and torque ratings for the heavy-duty V-6 were slightly lower at 155 hp at 4000 rpm and 230 lbs.-ft. of torque at 2400 rpm.

The standard 4.3-liter V-6 delivered five more horsepower and five more pounds-feet of torque at the same engine speeds. The 5.0-liter and 5.7-liter EFI V-8s were carried over from 1989. The 7.4-liter V-8 featured new electronic spark control to fight spark knocks.

The standard and heavy-duty 6.2-liter diesel V-8s were both back. They had revised power ratings because of a new rating system, though output was unchanged.

Full-size pickups continued to be offered in three trim levels called Cheyenne, Scottsdale, and Silverado. All three had expanded contents. Black Onyx, Catalina Blue Metallic, and Crimson Red Metallic were added pickup colors, while a new interior trim color was garnet. Chevrolet C/K pickups were produced at plants in Ft. Wayne, Indiana, Pontiac, Michigan and Oshawa, Ontario, Canada.

Full-size Chevy pickups were built in factories in Fort Wayne, Indiana, Oshawa, Ontario, Canada, Pontiac, Michigan and Janesville, Wisconsin. Calendar-year new-truck sales were: 464,730 C/K pickups. Model-year new-truck sales included 486,056 C/K pickups.

A 1990 Chevrolet pickup shattered a 37-year-old record at the Indianapolis Motor Speedway on October 26-27, 1989 by averaging 103.463 mph for 24 hours to win the Hulman Indy Challenge Trophy. The full-size Chevrolet C1500 Sport was assembled at a GM plant in Fort Wayne with sheet metal produced at the GM stamping facility in Indianapolis. It covered 993.234 laps or 2,483.085 miles around the 2.5-mile track, including pit stops for fuel, tires and driver changes.

The record, certified by the U.S. Auto Club (USAC), was announced when Chevrolet introduced the 1990 Indy 500 Official Pace Car, a Beretta convertible. The Hulman Indy Challenge Trophy — formerly called the Stevens Trophy — had belonged to a Chrysler, that averaged 89.93 mph in 1953. Driven by Indiana race drivers Steve Butler of Kokomo,

CONTENTS OF 1990 TRIM PACKAGES (IN ADDITION TO 1989 EQUIPMENT)

Cheyenne: Added to the 1990 Cheyenne package were all tinted windows, a deluxe heater, intermittent windshield wipers, a one-inch diameter front stabilizer bar, a 34-gallon fuel tank (on most models), halogen headlamps, a heavy-duty battery (with gas engines), a cigarette lighter, an AM radio with a fixed mast antenna, front towing hooks (on 4 x 4s) and voltmeter, temperature and oil pressure gauges.

Scottsdale: The Scottsdale package included items adding to or replacing Cheyenne equipment. It had several new features including a custom steering wheel, Rally wheels (on most models) and a deluxe front end appearance that included halogen headlamps, a dual-note horn and a specific grille.

Silverado: Silverado was the top trim level that started where Scottsdale left off and added or substituted numerous extras. New-for-1990 Silverado goodies were an optional bench seat with a center arm rest, special door trim panels, cloth fabric seats, swing-out rear quarter windows with Extended-Cab designs, floor mats, a Sport steering wheel, and an electronically-tuned AM/FM stereo radio with seek-and-scan and a digital clock. Other changes for the year included the availability of 60/40 seats in both regular- and Extended-Cab models.

The Onyx Black truck is a 1990 C1500 4 x 2 Fleetside with Sport Appearance package. The Flame Red rig is a K1500 4 x 4 Fleetside, also with the Sport Appearance package.
John A. Gunnell Collection

This view of a 1990 C/K Sportside pickup with Arizona tags shows it has EFI (electronic fuel injection). This unit also has the optional Z71 off-road package. Note the cargo bed light and slider rear window.
John A. Gunnell Collection

Johnny Parsons of Brownsburg, and Rich Volger of Indianapolis, the Fleetside short-box pickup truck was stock except for USAC-required safety modifications such as a five-point safety harness, roll cage, fire extinguisher, full instrumentation and a tonneau cover. Also, speed nuts were used on the wheels to facilitate use of air wrenches and a production bucket seat from a Chevrolet 454SS pickup was installed to clear the safety harness, In addition, the catalytic converter was removed to prevent excessive heat buildup.

The Chevy Sport was equipped with a production 350-cid V-8 engine with electronic fuel injection, a standard five-speed manual transmission, and original equipment P275/60R15 B.F. Goodrich Comp T/A radial tires.

The record and trophy added to Chevrolet's long tradition of victories at the Indianapolis Motor Speedway and complemented the then-current Chevrolet Indy V-8 used in the 1988 and 1989 race winning cars.

1991: MILLION-UNIT YEAR

There were no major changes in Chevrolet's full-size pickups for 1991. There were, however, significant technical advances to ensure their continued competitiveness in the light-duty truck sales battles with Ford and Dodge.

The big 7.4-liter "Mark V" V-8 engine had a new one-piece intake manifold with a relocated throttle-body injector, thus eliminating the previous TBI mounting adapters. Other new features included improved piston-to-cylinder tolerances, improved oil pan gaskets to help eliminate oil leaks, rigid cast iron rocker covers, and new engine oil cooler lines with improved bracketing. This engine also benefited from a new manufacturing process and updated tooling that Chevrolet noted was intended to improve the engine's overall reliability.

General Motors' all-new 4L80-E heavy-duty electronic control four-speed automatic overdrive transmission (RPO MXO) was available for all models rated at or above 8,600-pound GVWRs. This transmission delivered enhanced shifting precision and smoothness.

The 4L80-E nomenclature had the following significance 4 = four forward speeds, L = Longitudinal type, 80 = transmission gears based on relative torque capacity (this transmission could handle 885 lb.-ft. of gearbox torque, which represented 440 lb.-ft. of input torque), E = electronic controls. Aside from its four-speed overdrive configuration, this transmission also featured an aluminum case and a Power train Control Module (PCM) which combined engine and transmission functions on all gasoline engines and

This view gives you a good look at the '91 Chevrolet extended-cab short-box K2500 pickup. John A. Gunnell Collection

This is a 1991 C1500 (W/T 1500) "Work Truck" 4 x 4 in Summit White with black-finished grille, bumper, mirrors and hubcaps. Note the W/T badges on the lower section of the doors. John A. Gunnell Collection

It's hard to believe, but this huge-looking dump is based on the 1-ton K3500 four-wheel-drive pickup chassis. These still had the "old" sheet metal in '91, but that would soon change. John A. Gunnell Collection

This isn't the result of a collision, but you have to admit that the cabinet-style utility truck body is a rather awkward fit on the '91 Chevy R3500 Crew Cab chassis. John A. Gunnell Collection

From the rear you can see how the short 6-1/2-ft. cargo box fits on the chassis of the C/K extended-cab Sportside pickup. Buyers demanded bigger trucks with more features each passing year. John A. Gunnell Collection

compensated for variations in temperature, altitude and engine performance.

A Transmission Control Module (TCM) was used with the diesel V-8. A new dual-stator 310 mm torque converter was also included for increased low-speed torque. The 4L80-E was touted by Chevrolet as "one of the most technologically advanced transmissions ever offered in a Chevrolet truck."

Powertrain improvements on all C/K trucks included a new 220 Series throttle-body-injection system. A new SD 260 starter motor was used for the 4.3-liter V-6 and the 5.0-liter V-8. It was lighter in weight and more durable and reliable than the SD300 motor it replaced. The new TBI system was used on the 4.3-liter V-6, 5.0-liter V-8, 5.7-liter V-8 and 7.4-liter V-8 engines. It incorporated longer throttle shaft bearings, new throttle return springs, and improved fuel mixture distribution.

The 4.3-liter V-6 was also improved by the use of a revised air cleaner system and processing changes in manufacturing spark plugs. Both the 5.0-liter V-8 and 5.7-liter V-8 were upgraded with heavy-duty intake valves, powdered metal camshaft sprockets, and improved oil pan baffling on the heavy-duty 5.7-liter engine. Replacing the 12-SI-100 alternator was a lighter weight, more reliable CS130 alternator. A 100-ampere alternator was now standard on the C/K3500 pickup and chassis-and-cab models.

The Work Truck continued as Chevrolet's no-frills, basic pickup. Changes for 1991 included a new four-spoke steering wheel and larger outside rearview mirrors. A Custom urethane four-spoke steering wheel was standard.

Below-eye-line type exterior mirrors were now standard on all C/K pickups and chassis-and-cab models. These mirrors had adjustable heads in a black finish and measured 9.0 x 6.5-in. The standard AM/FM stereo radios were improved by increasing signal sensitivity and reducing signal interference and signal tracking. The RPO C60 air conditioning option for the C/K models included an HVAC climate control system incorporating new controls allowing for manual selection of the recirculation air inlet mode. In addition, revised display graphics provided clear readings in a dark cab. A computer software change provided an indication that the system required refrigerant servicing.

New options for 1991 included a bed liner for Fleetside and Extended-Cab models, high-back reclining front bucket seats and a gauge cluster with tachometer. The Cheyenne trim package had a new impact-resistant metal grille for 1991. Two new metallic colors, Brilliant Blue and Slate, brought the total number of exterior colors to 10. A light gray was added to the list of available interior colors.

An exciting option package was the 454SS high-performance truck. It included YE9 Silverado trim, a sliding rear window, Sport package equipment, air conditioning, a locking differential, an engine oil cooler, auxiliary lighting, cargo area lamp, an upgraded

The 1991 C2500 3/4-ton pickup was a sturdy unit for lots of those jobs where a "real" truck comes in handy. This one is done up in Flame Red, a color offered on '88-up C/K trucks, but not the old-style R/V models. *John A. Gunnell Collection*

Any type of excavating or mining operation could find a lot of chores to use this Chevy on. It's the '91 K3500 extended-cab model. This truck was base-priced at $16,855 and tipped the scales at 5,124 pounds.
John A. Gunnell Collection

The 454 SS had an improved 7.4-liter EFI V-8 and more horsepower. It used a four-speed electronic automatic. A tachometer was added to the '91 model. Included were dual exhausts and a 4.10:1 rear end. John A. Gunnell Collection

AM/FM ETR stereo with all the goodies, heavy-duty cooling, a Sport steering wheel, black body side moldings, power locks and windows, tilt steering, speed control, a Sport Handling chassis package, analog gauges with a tachometer and a 7.4-liter RPO L19 EFI V-8 linked to a four-speed overdrive automatic transmission.

C/K pickups were built in Fort Wayne, Indiana, Oshawa, Ontario, Canada, Pontiac, Michigan and Janesville, Wisconsin. Jim Perkins was general manager of Chevrolet Motor Division. J.N. Janowiak was national manager of truck merchandising and Mac Wisner was manager of truck advertising. Chevrolet calendar-year new-truck sales were: 404,763 C/K pickups. The big trucks contributed to total company sales of 1,065,794 units in the calendar-year. Chevrolet model-year new-truck sales included 402,539 C/K pickups. This represented a major portion of Chevy's total model-year sales of 1,084,847 units.

In 1992, this C1500 Sportside pickup carried a $13,495 window sticker, but that didn't include any options such as the sporty wheels and fat raised-white-letter tires. With no extras it weighed 3,735 pounds.
John A. Gunnell Collection

In the old days the term "Sport pickup" got you decals and badges, but this '92 Chevy K1500 Sport Pickup is very simple and clean looking. It has a slider-style rear window and a quad headlight grille design.
John A. Gunnell Collection

Offered again in 1992 was the hot-performing C1500 454SS Chevy pickup with its killer 7.4-liter (454-cid) big-block V-8 with 255 hp at 4000 rpm and 405 ft.-lbs. of torque at 2400 rpm. The power is routed through an automatic overdrive four-speed transmission. These trucks were in the $20,000 range new and bring $13,000-$20,000.
John A. Gunnell Collection

1992: CREW-CABS GET IMPROVEMENTS

Changes for 1992 in the Chevrolet trucks were lead by major developments in the four-door Crew-Cab models. The 1992 C/K3500 Crew-Cab pickup was the last Chevrolet pickup truck to take on the styling adopted by smaller models in 1988.

The all-new version of the big pickup had a four-inch longer wheelbase, nearly seven inches more rear-seat legroom and increased front leg and shoulder room. The Crew-Cab also had antilock brakes.

Standard engine in Crew-Cab trucks was a 5.7-

Chrome Rally wheels dress up the looks of this '92 C1500 Sportside extended-cab. 141.5-in. wheelbase extended-cabs were offered in Fleetside and Sportside styles, but the big 155.5-in. jobs were Fleetsides only. John A. Gunnell Collection

This 1992 Chevy C1500 full-size pickup has a standard grille with single rectangular headlights and parking lamps below the headlights. This Fleetside model, with no options of any type, listed for $13,095.
John A. Gunnell Collection

This 1992 Chevrolet K2500 extended-cab pickup must have been somebody's "pipe dream" judging from the background. With its two-tone finish and rally wheels, this is one good-looking stretched pickup. John A. Gunnell Collection

When surveying the pickup truck market in 1992, observers saw Chevrolet selling just over 450,000 full-size pickup trucks. This C2500 regular-cab long box pickup was one of them.
John A. Gunnell Collection

84 | Chevrolet Pickups 1973-1998

Seen here is the 1992 Chevrolet K2500 four-wheel-drive Sportside pickup with the extended cab. This year the bigger Chevy Crew Cab and Bonus Cab pickups (as well as Suburbans) took on the "1988" styling. John A. Gunnell Collection

As mentioned earlier, '92 was the year that the C/K styling adopted in 1988 was used on C3500 Crew Cabs. This model had a $17,047 base price, some $800 higher than the old-style trucks cost the year before. John A. Gunnell Collection

liter V-8 linked to a five-speed heavy-duty manual transmission with "deep low" and overdrive. Available for all trucks with a GVW rating of 8,600 lb. and up was a new 6.5-liter Turbo Diesel. This engine, built at the General Motors Moraine Engine Plant in Dayton, Ohio, had a special warranty of five years or 100,000 miles. Among its features were an all-new cylinder case design, and an optimized combustion chamber for totally smokeless performance.

The 1992 C/K pickups were built in Fort Wayne, Indiana; Oshawa, Canada; Pontiac, Michigan; and Janesville, Wisconsin. Added to the interior color availability for 1992 was beige. New exterior colors were Bright Red, and Beige Metallic.

Jim Perkins continued as general manager of Chevrolet Motor Division. J.N. Janowiak was national manager of truck merchandising and R.M. Wisner was manager of truck advertising. Chevrolet new-truck sales penetration included 450,650 C/K pickups which contributed to a company total of 1,163,368 light-duty truck sales. Chevy had 24.76 percent of the overall light-duty truck market in the United States.

John Gilbert, editor of **Custom & Classic Pickups**, calls the '88-'98 Chevys the "first Sport Trucks" and says they're popular in California where collecting trends start. This is a '92 C1500 extended-cab model. *John A. Gunnell Collection*

Finished in Chartreuse and Purple, the Highlander concept truck made the rounds of '93 auto shows. It was a vehicle that could easily be transformed from a pickup truck into an SUV and this concept would re-appear on full-size production models in the future. John A. Gunnell Collection

1993: POWER TO THE PICKUPS

Power train changes were the major developments for 1993 Chevy full-size pickups. The 4.3-liter Vortec V-6 got a new balance shaft to dampen vibrations in high rpm ranges. Other developments involved revised cylinder heads with improved flow characteristics, a revised throttle-body-injection unit for a smoother idle, a new quiet-fan drive to reduce engine noise (especially during cold starts), a new thermostat, a revised oil filter and a new dual-stud air cleaner.

Both the 5.0- and 5.7-liter V-8 engines were improved in the same areas. The 5.0-liter V-8 also had new low-tension piston pins for 1993. Beginning in 1993, a modified version of the 5.7-liter V-8 was available for conversion to compressed natural gas, propane or dual-fuel capability (with gasoline).

A large garage was needed if you wanted to keep your 1993 Chevrolet C3500 Crew Cab pickup indoors on a snowy night. Chevy made a total of 37,904 one-ton trucks for the model year. John A. Gunnell Collection

Chevrolet Pickups 1973-1998

As with the other V-8 engines, the 7.4-liter V-8 had a modified TBI unit and a larger radiator (midyear release). Other improvements included a one-piece dipstick, new spark plug shields, revised intake manifold, a machined water pump outlet, and a quiet fan drive. The 6.5-liter turbo diesel was now offered for Crew-Cab models and Extended-Cab Pickups with GVWRs over 8,500 lb. A new electronic four-speed automatic Hydramatic 4L60-E transmission was available for trucks under-8,500 lb. GVWR.

A new Sportside Sport Pickup for the 1500 series Regular-Cab included Silverado trim, Sport decals, a body-color Dura-Grille, a Sportside box, cast aluminum wheels, painted exterior mirrors and color-keyed front and rear bumpers. The Sportside Sport Pickup was offered in Summit White, Onyx Black or Victory Red.

All Chevy trucks had a new "Leading Edge" anti-chip coating applied to the leading edges of the hood, roof and A-pillars. Solar-Ray tinted glass was standard in all windows. Scotchguard fabric protector was applied to all cloth seat and door trim panels. The Extended-Cab was now available with two-passenger seating, giving customers a choice of two-, three-, five- or six-passenger seating. A 40/60- split-bench seat in cloth or vinyl, and low-back bucket seats in cloth or vinyl were available with the Cheyenne option. Previously, Scottsdale trim was required with these seats.

A seat-back recliner was added to the passenger side on the 40/60 split-bench seat and low-back bucket seats. Dual cup holders were now mounted on the instrument panel (this feature was not available with bucket seats). A steel sleeve steering column was

Chevrolet C/K pickups were built in Ft. Wayne, Indiana, Oshawa, Ontario, Canada, Pontiac, Michigan and Janesville, Wisconsin in 1994. This K1500 regular-cab long-box pickup was among them. *John A. Gunnell Collection*

The Sport package added to this C1500 Sportside "Shortie" pickup was an option with prices from $1,938-$2,460 depending upon specifics. It was definitely more than a couple of "signature" style decals on the side.
John A. Gunnell Collection

You could go up the down staircase and not find a better value for the money than this '93 Chevy 2500 full-size pickup. A deluxe grille and rally rims set off the appearance of an already-handsome pickup truck.
John A. Gunnell Collection

used with the Comfortilt steering wheel for improved security. The sun visors were now cloth-covered. The radio controls were revised with a new control panel and improved button operation. A full-cloth headliner was now optional for Regular-Cab Pickups. A cloth headliner continued as standard for the Silverado decor on pickups and Extended-Cab models.

A new electronic fuel shut-off automatically limited maximum engine speed to less than tire speed rating. A deluxe front appearance (RPO V22) was available as an option with Cheyenne models. The Cheyenne K3500 Chassis-Cab with Crew-Cab was also available with a new auxiliary lighting option.

Four new 1993 exterior colors were introduced: Light Quasar Blue Metallic, Teal Green Metallic, Indigo Blue Metallic and Dark Garnet Red Metallic. They replaced Brilliant Blue Metallic, Smoke Blue Metallic, Catalina Blue Metallic, and Crimson Red Metallic. The only new color offered for the Crew-Cab and chassis-and-cab models was Indigo Blue Metallic. The Scottsdale decor was canceled for 1993. Phased out during 1992, and not offered for 1993, was the special two-tone paint option.

Standard Chevy truck equipment included the 4.3-liter EFI V-6, power rear antilock brakes, a five-speed manual overdrive transmission and P225/75R15

Get out your checkbook if you want to buy this baby! The '93 K3500 extended-cab Dooley pickup came loaded with lots of extras before you even got down to details like radios and wheel options. John A. Gunnell Collection

Power train changes were the big development for '93 Chevy pickups like this K1500 regular-cab long-box pickup. Both the 5.0- and 5.7-liter V-8s had improvements to the air cleaner and the throttle body. John A. Gunnell Collection

steel-belted black sidewall tires. The high-performance 454SS package (PEG PSS1) was available. It included YE9 Silverado trim, a black grille with red bow tie, sliding rear window, 15-inch chrome-plated wheels, the Sport package, air conditioning, a locking differential, an oil cooler, auxiliary lighting, a cargo area lamp, an AM/FM ETR stereo system (with Seek-and-Scan, Search-and-Repeat cassette, graphic equalizer and digital clock), heavy-duty cooling system, Sport steering wheel, speed control, Sport Handling chassis package, analog gauges with tachometer and E63 body code.

C/K Pickups were built in Fort Wayne, Indiana; Oshawa, Ontario, Canada; Pontiac, Michigan; and Janesville, Wisconsin. Chevrolet new-truck sales (and market penetration) were 513,147 C/K Pickups. This helped Chevy achieve total light-duty truck sales of 1,309,879 units and capture 24.36 percent of the overall light-duty truck market.

Kurt Ritter was Chevrolet's marketing manager for trucks in 1994 and calendar-year sales of C/K models were 545,125 units This is the year's basic C1500 ½-ton rear-wheel-drive pickup
John A. Gunnell Collection

C/K pickups represented 38.8 percent of all Chevy trucks in 1994. One of the models aimed at younger, more active buyers was the K1500 Sportside Only 39.2 percent of the 1/2-ton pickups were 4 x 4s.
John A. Gunnell Collection

1994: SPORTSIDE BOWS

Chevrolet's full-size, rear-wheel-drive C Series pickups came in C1500 (half-ton), C2500 (3/4-ton), and C3500 (one-ton) lines. The four-wheel-drive K Series Pickups came in K1500 (1/2-ton), K2500 (3/4-ton), and K3500 (one-ton) lines. Buyers could choose from Regular-, Extended-, and Crew-Cabs. There was also a choice between the 6.5-foot short box and the 8-ft. long box. Fleetside and Sportside rear fender designs were offered. C/K Pickups were built in Fort Wayne, Indiana, Oshawa, Canada, Pontiac, Michigan and Janesville, Wisconsin.

The standard wheelbase for pickups was 117.5 in. Five different wheelbases were offered: 117.5 in. for Regular-Cab Short Box models, 131.5 in. for Regular-Cab Long Box models, 141.5 in. for Extended-Cab Short Box models, 155.5 in. for Extended-Cab Long Box models, and 168.5 in. for Crew-Cab Long Box models. Three-passenger bench seating was standard

This C2500 extended-cab pickup was one of 97,760 three-quarter-ton units made by Chevy in 1994. A V-8 was used in 98.7 percent of these and 65.1 percent used the popular 350-cid V-8. The truck 350 has 4-bolt mains. John A. Gunnell Collection

in all full-sized Chevrolet pickups, except Crew-Cab models, which came with twin three-passenger bench seats. Front bucket seats were optional for all models. Extended-Cab pickups could be optioned with a rear bench seat.

Standard equipment included a 4.3-liter EFI V-6, front disc/rear drum brakes with ABS, five-speed manual transmission with overdrive and P225/75R15 black sidewall ALSBR tires. A new 6.5-liter naturally-aspirated diesel was available. Another diesel option was the 6.5-liter Turbo Diesel V-8.

Of interest to collectors was the Sportside Sport model that had a "Stepside" short-box design and came in only three colors: Oynx Black, Teal Green Metallic or Victory Red. It included matching bumpers and mirrors, a new-design grille and aluminum wheel finish. Buyers could also add a Sport Handling package with chrome wheels, special springs and Bilstein gas shocks on 4 x 2 models or a Z71 off-road package on 4 x 4 versions.

EXTERIOR COLORS

Dark Autumnwood Metallic (#56)[1]

Teal Green Metallic (#38)

Light Autumnwood Metallic (#55)[1]

Quicksilver Metallic (#96)

Onyx Black (#41)

Burnt Red Metallic (#76)

Atlantic Blue Metallic (#30)[1]

Dark Garnet Red Metallic (#84)

Indigo Blue Metallic (#39)

Victory Red (#74)

Light Quasar Blue Metallic (#20)

Summit White (#50)

Teal Blue Metallic (#36)

A total of 13 colors were offered for 1994 Chevy C/K pickups. Blue colors were getting more popular and four were offered. John A. Gunnell Collection

Striving for a manly image with a truck having great masculine appeal, Chevrolet pictured a cowboy driving this 1995 K1500 extended-cab pickup. Improvements to 1995 C/Ks included a driver's airbag. John A. Gunnell Collection

1995: UNWANTED RECOGNITION

In December 1994, Chevrolet settled a controversy over older C/K pickup trucks with the U.S. Government. The government dropped its efforts to force a recall of older C/Ks in exchange for a multi-million dollar commitment, from GM, towards future auto safety efforts.

There were virtually no changes in Chevrolet pickups this year. The Sportside Sport model option with a "Stepside" Short-Box remained the most exciting model. This year it came in Summit White, as well as the carryover colors of Oynx Black and Victory Red. This model also had body-color bumpers and mirrors, a black air dam with fog lights (if a C1500) or tow hooks (if a K1500), a new-design body-color grille, aluminum wheels and a Chevrolet tailgate decal. The Sport Handling package returned, too.

Colors that 1995 C/K pickups came in besides the three also available on Sportside models were Teal Green Metallic, Light Autumnwood Metallic, Quicksilver Metallic, Dark Garnet Red Metallic, Indigo Blue Metallic, Light Quasar Blue Metallic, and Emerald Green Metallic. Chevy truck interiors came in beige, blue, gray or red. Vinyl, cloth, Custom cloth, and Custom leather trims are offered.

Handy for chores around the house or yard was this '95 Chevy C1500 Cheyenne regular-cab short-box Fleetside pickup. It's painted in Quicksilver Metallic and carries an optional chrome rear step bumper. John A. Gunnell Collection

Buyers of Chevrolet C/K models in 1995 could select from Conventional Two-Tones (accent color on bottom) or Deluxe Two-Tones (accent color in middle). John A. Gunnell Collection

Two-tone Onyx Black and Quicksilver Metallic finish sets off this 1995 Chevy C2500 two-wheel-drive Silverado long-box pickup. It seems to be up to the job of transporting a rather large boat to the water. *John A. Gunnell Collection*

The '95 C/K Silverado Custom Cloth interior had a richness to it. It included a 60/40 seating configuration and a center console with an armrest. Of course, there were lots of cupholders, a necessity in the '90s! *John A. Gunnell Collection*

Teal Green Metallic paint sets off the smooth, rounded lines of this 1995 Chevrolet K1500 Sportside Silverado pickup. This 4 x 4 could take fun lovers tout on the beach without getting stuck in the sand. John A. Gunnell Collection

Light Autumnwood Metallic (#55)

Teal Green Metallic (#38)[2]

Onyx Black (#41)[1]

Quicksilver Metallic (#96)

Indigo Blue Metallic (#39)

Dark Garnet Red Metallic (#84)[2]

Light Quasar Blue Metallic (#20)[2]

Victory Red (#74)[1]

Emerald Green Metallic (#43)[2, 3]

Summit White (#50)[1]

1 Available on C/K1500 Sportside Sport. **2** Not available on Crew-Cab. **3** New for '95.

Ten different colors could be selected for 1995 C/K pickup trucks, though some came on Sport models and others were not available on Crew Cabs. John A. Gunnell Collection

1996: HIGH-TECH HP

Chevrolet Truck had its best sales year ever in 1996 with a total of 1,496,624 Vehicles delivered. The success story of the Chevy pickups continued with the introduction of many new features.

For 1996, Chevrolet upgraded its V-6 and V-8 engines with Vortec technology for greater fuel economy, added performance, and longer maintenance intervals (spark plug life and coolant life were extended to 100,000 miles). The engines included the Vortec 4300 V-6, the Vortec 5000 V-8, the Vortec 5700 V-8 and the big-block Vortec 7400 V-8.

An example of the power improvement can be seen in the Vortec 5700 V-8, that was supplied as either standard equipment or an option on many full-size models. It gained 50 hp over its counterpart, the 5.7-liter V-8.

Other changes to C/K pickups included the introduction of standard Daytime Running Lamps (DRLs), a new clutch design for smoother and quicker gear changes in stick-shifted trucks, a new electro-chromatic rearview mirror for automatic nighttime glare reduction and a new electronic transfer case on K1500 and K 2500 4 x 4s for improved traction and quieter operation.

C/K Extended Cab and Crew Cab pickups were now fitted with an extra set of heat ducts for rear passengers. Passenger leg and foot room and

New Vortec 4300 V-6 and 5000, 5700 and 7400 V-8s were making news in the full-size pickup market in 1996. This C1500 regular-cab Fleetside pickup also added DRLs (Daytime Running Lights) as standard equipment. *John A. Gunnell Collection*

This shows the Chevy K1500 Silverado extended-cab interior in Neutral with optional Custom Leather seating surfaces, reclining high-back bucket seats and other options. We could get used to it, couldn't you?
John A. Gunnell Collection

Chevy made 338,604 full-size C/K pickups in 1996 and 42.9 percent of them had four-wheel drive. This is the K1500 1/2-ton Fleetside model carrying two cowboys through some rough terrain.
John A. Gunnell Collection

New for 1996 was the driver's side access panel or "third door" arrangement illustrated here. Chevrolet promoted this as its "Easy Access" system. It was available on C/K Silverados and S-Series LS models. John A. Gunnell Collection

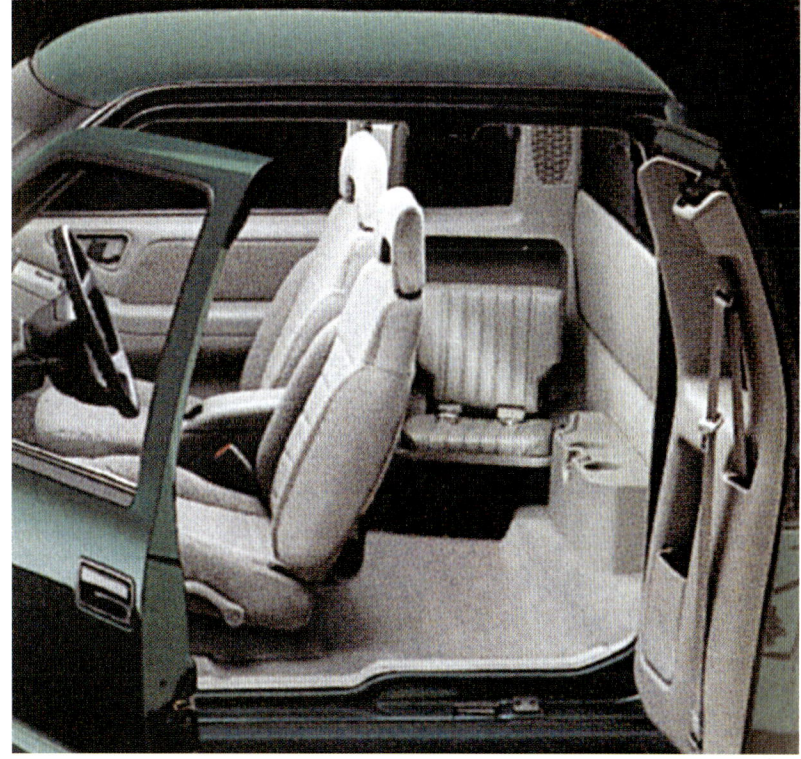

reducing the size of the engine cover.

The domestic auto industry celebrated its Centennial in 1996. In May, General Motors bought the Detroit Renaissance Center, originally built by Ford, for $72 million and renamed the building General Motors Global Headquarters.

At the 1996 Chicago Auto Show, it was announced that the full-size Chevrolet C/K pickups had copped four industry awards. *Consumers Digest* magazine gave them its "Best Buy" recommendation in the pickup category. *Popular Mechanics* picked the Chevy pickup's Easy Access third-door system for its Design & Engineering Award. *Popular Science* also honored the Easy Access System with a "100 Best of What's New" award. *Consumer Review* gave the new C/K a "Top Ten New Trucks" classification.

Based on the current Chevy C/K pickup, the '97 Craftsman Race Truck carried No. 16 on its side. Its dark blue paint reflected the fact that NAPA, an auto parts supplier with a blue-and-yellow logo, was its primary sponsor.
John A. Gunnell Collection

1997: HIGH-TECH HP

Chevrolet focused on three-door pickups in 1997, including the three-door version of the full-size C/K model, which had the third door on the passenger side. The front passenger seat in the C/K slid forward to allow easy access to the rear cab area, but could be returned to its original position without additional adjustment. Also in the extended-cab model was a three-passenger rear bench seat, rear cupholders and a rear seatback that folded down for added loading convenience. The lower portion also folded up for added storage room.

Elsewhere, technology dominated the changes for 1997. The four-speed electronic automatic transmission (4L60-E) supplied as standard equipment incorporated a more sophisticated engine/transmission computer that resulted in greater fuel economy and smoother shifts.

Chevy pegged the median C/K pickup buyers as a 45-year-old person, 90.5 percent male, with an average household income of $55,000 and probably (68.9 percent) married.

J. D. Power and Associates ranked the 1997 C/K models as the best full-sized pickup in initial quality reports. Chevy also bragged that a survey

Back for the second time in 1997 was the Easy-Access system available on trucks like this Chevrolet K1500 Silverado 4 x 4 extended-cab "Shortie" pickup. John A. Gunnell Collection

Gas prices and fuel economy were on everyone's mind in 1997 and Chevrolet's answer was a White '97 C/K Pickup that was factory-modified to operate on compressed natural gas. John A. Gunnell Collection

of 1989-1995 model-year pickup owners indicated that C/Ks had the highest owner satisfaction history of any full-size pickup truck. Going along with both of these positives, the C/Ks also had the best resale value. These were all good selling points.

On February 5, 1997, General Motors announced production plans for a fully certified $5,800 "factory" bi-fuel package for Chevy 2500 (and all GMC Sierra) pickup trucks starting in the 1997 model year. These trucks used a Vortec 5700 V-8 that was specially-modified to be gaseous fuel compatible.

"These natural gas pickup trucks have undergone an extensive and rigorous OEM development and validation process to operate on both gasoline and compressed natural gas," said Richard A. Moreau, program manager of alternative fuel vehicles for GM. "We wanted to be sure these trucks would exceed customer expectations for safety, quality, performance and durability." The CNG-compatible trucks, which were aimed at commercial buyers, came with a three-year/36,000-mile GM "Bumper to Bumper Plus" warranty.

Chevrolet Pickups 1973-1998

Though the building in the background is no more than a skeleton, this hardworking '98 Chevy K1500 Fleetside pickup has some "structure" to it. It has the base-level black-finished grille with single headlights. John A. Gunnell Collection

1998: HIGH-TECH HP

The *1998 Chevy Trucks* catalog described the C/K pickup as "The one you can depend on." The big pickups were promoted as powerful, tough, rugged and hardworking. To back up the claim of dependability, Chevy referenced light-duty truck registration figures for 1981-1996 that showed that Chevy came out tops in longevity.

There were no major changes in the full-size Chevrolet C/K pickups for 1998. Since a redesigned range of pickups and other models was due to take a bow in mid-1999. Prices climbed a bit, but the product offerings were essentially the same as the previous season.

Chevy again offered just seven basic configurations of the full-size pickup, while expanding the product range to over 300 variations of design, engine, drive train and payload. The seven basic offerings were the Regular-Cab Sportside, Extended-Cab Sportside, Regular-Cab Short Box, Regular-Cab Long Box, Extended-Cab Short Box, Extended-Cab Long Box and Crew-Cab Long Box. Each model came on one of five specified wheelbase lengths.

Buyers could select two- or four-wheel drive with 7 payload ranges for each, 6.5-ft. or 8-ft. boxes, six GVWR ranges, three towing capacities, a variety of seating options and two Vortec engines (4300 V-6 or 5700 V-8).

The Chevy C/K extended-cab pickup offered exceptional versatility for business or personal use. It had seats for six with breathing room and mucho storage space for tools and equipment. This one worked on the farm. John A. Gunnell Collection

This Chevy C/K Crew Cab with a cabinet-style utility body was the result of a semi-custom build on the Chassis-Cab platform. Chevy could whip up trucks like this with GVWRs up to 10,000 lbs. John A. Gunnell Collection

AVL North America used this base-level, regular cab C1500 Fleetside pickup to carry industrial equipment. John A. Gunnell Collection

F.H. Martin Construction Co. ordered its K1500 Cheyenne regular-cab Fleetside long-box pickup in Summit White and had it fitted out with large (and heavy) diamond plate tool boxes. John A. Gunnell Collection

Chevy adopted the practice of using classic pickups in ads for new ones and a '58 Apache was posed on top of a '98 rollback tow truck made from a C3500 Heavy-Duty Chassis-Cab configuration. John A. Gunnell Collection

One change was a Passlock theft deterrence system became available on C/K pickups and virtually all Chevrolet vans, trucks and SUVs. The system disabled the vehicle from starting for 10 minutes after an invalid key had been inserted in the ignition. Passlock theft deterrence was intended to fight thieves and to prevent dead batteries. It incorporated a battery-run-down-protection system that turned off interior lights (should the driver forget to do so) after the vehicle had been sitting with the ignition off for more than 20 minutes and cut all electrical power if the vehicle had been sitting ignition off for more than 24 days. One advantage was that trucks left at an airport would not have a dead battery.

In 1998, this 6.5-liter Turbo-Diesel V-8 was used in 0.4 percent of the 389,477 C/K1500s, 5.4 percent of 90,859 C/K2500s and 21 percent of 63,200 C/K3500s built that model year. John A. Gunnell Collection

As you can see, one of the cowpokes in this photo saddled up a new 1998 Chevrolet K1500 Fleetside Silverado extended-cab pickup with the Easy-Access system, but his friend was happy with a 1968 Chevy pickup. John A. Gunnell Collection

1973-87 El Camino

1973-1987 EL CAMINO COUPE-PICKUP

Australian farmer Slim Westman originated the idea for a vehicle that became known as the Ute and Chevrolet was not involved. Westman heard about pickup trucks that people in America were using on their farms. They did their chores with them during the week and drove them to church on Sunday.

Slim got in touch with Ford's Australian branch about making a cheap-to-operate, dual-purpose vehicle that combined the styling and comfort of a passenger car with the utility of a pickup. Lewis T. Bandt, chief designer at Ford in Geelong, Victoria, took the idea and created the 1934 Ford V-8 Model 302 UTE, which sold well and inspired Holden (GM's Australian branch) to develop one. The GM-H Ute was based on a 1934 Chevy from the United States, that came in CKD (completely-knocked-down) form and was assembled by local workers. This became the best-selling Ute. In 1951, a Ute based on the Holden 215 became the first Ute designed and manufactured in Australia.

The Conquista package shown here was a $128 option for the 1976 El Camino Classic. The Classic was the fancier version of the sedan-pickup, Model 1AD80. It listed for $4,468 and weighed 3,821 lbs. Gregg D. Merksamer Collection

This streamlined-looking, dealer-installed Hop Cap shell camper mounted on this 1975 El Camino SS had a built-in roof rack and rear air foil. It was one of many available factory options and dealer accessories. Gregg D. Merksamer Collection

Shown in an appropriately classic-looking setting is the last El Camino of 1987. The sales catalog noted," The end product makes a uniquely bold, personal statement." Three models were offered. Gregg D. Merksamer Collection

Utes never caught on in America, but the idea of a car-pickup was tried as early as the 1930s. Ford was first to bring the Ute concept to America in a high-volume way with the 1957 Ranchero. Seeing Ford's success with the Ranchero, General Motors decided to offer a car-based pickup. Chevy's 1959 El Camino was based on the big Chevy Impala. It had the gull-wing styling of the cars, but with a load box that could hold 34 cubic feet of cargo. El Caminos came in 13 solid colors and 10 two-tones and had a choice of one six-cylinder engine or two V8s. The model continued into 1960 and was then dropped.

In 1964, the El Camino re-appeared as a mid-sized Chevelle-based pickup. By 1967, it had a new grille and a new 396-cid "big-block" V-8. For 1968, a new SS 396 version greeted performance buffs and production topped 40,000 units. The '69 was a carryover model with nearly 50,000 built. Performance in the El Camino peaked in 1970 with a 454-cid 450-hp LS6 V-8. Tougher emissions laws and the elimination of leaded fuel in 1971, caused a drop in power ratings.

The 1973 El Camino received its first new body since 1968. It was a taller and some five inches longer.

This 1985 El Camino has the Z15 El Camino SS Sport Décor package. The SS included dual SS decal striping. A non-functional blister hood, dummy side pipes and pickup bed rails were optional. Gregg D. Merksamer Collection

The 1982 Conquista package, a $183 option, included dramatic two-tone paint, bright lower body side moldings, bright wheel opening moldings, a Conquista decal on the tailgate and a dash nameplate. Gregg D. Merksamer Collection

The 1980 El Camino had a very clean-looking appearance. "You won't believe you're in a pickup," the sales catalog said. A striking molding and paint treatment was part of the Conquista package shown here. Gregg D. Merksamer Collection

Like the C/K trucks, the El Camino was completely redesigned for 1973. The new style sedan-pickup was slightly taller and five inches longer. It boasted a few upgrades, including optional swivel bucket seats. Gregg D. Merksamer Collection

112 | Chevrolet Pickups 1973-1998

This '86 El Camino is getting to be a collector's item. Only 23,767 were sold that year, making survivors pretty rare. The '86 models were the 25th El Caminos, even though the first ones date from 1959. *Gregg D. Merksamer Collection*

If you collect El Camino sedan-pickups, look for the fancier versions in good condition. This is the 1979 version of the El Camino Royal Knight — a package that included a wild hood decal and more. Gregg D. Merksamer Collection

All models had impact-resistant front bumpers and were substantially improved in roadability, comfort and styling. Engines included a de-tuned 250-cid inline six, a 307-cid V-8 and two 350s. The base El Camino compared to a Chevelle Deluxe. The one-step-up Custom was like a Malibu and had an SS 454 option. Fancy Estate and Conquista packages were offered.

Modest El Camino styling revisions were seen in 1974 through 1977 models. A new Classic trim level was added in 1974. It included wide rocker panel moldings, an armrest seat and fancier trim. The SS package was a $215 option and the Conquista package for the Classic model was about $125. During this period, the base model had single headlights, while upscale versions used dual headlights. The grille and taillight designs changed annually and the SS became more of a lick-'em/stick 'em model than a true high-horsepower muscle truck.

Mid-size Chevys were down-sized in 1978. Chevy truck engineers felt that making the El Camino Classic Malibu-sized would have compromised its limited cargo capacity. Instead, the new wheelbase was made about an inch longer than the old one, although the body was several inches shorter and weight was reduced by 200 to 300 lbs. Interior head and legroom grew. The Conquista and SS options were carried over and were joined by a new Royal Knight package.

Full-frame construction was retained in the new El Camino. The base engine was now a thrifty V-6. Other top selling features included a standard front stabilizer bar, extensive corrosion-resistance treatments, the incorporation of 14 noise-insulating body mounts (for a quieter ride) and new double-panel door, hood and deck lid construction. After these revisions, the El Camino would stick around until 1987 with mostly minor updates and some engine changes.

A new 267-cid V-8 was introduced in 1979, though it wasn't available in California. A 3.3-liter V-6 was standard. A new lock-up automatic transmission arrived in 1980. Computer Command Control was new in 1981. That year a 3.8-liter V-6 became standard. Options included 4.4-liter and 5.0-liter V-8s. In California, a 3.8-liter V-6 was standard and a 5.0-liter V-8 was optional.

The 1982 El Camino used the Malibu's new Caprice-style grille and side-by-side dual rectangular headlamps. The seating and instrument panel were revised. A "Smart Switch" was added to the steering column. A 1983 option was a 5.7-liter diesel V-8.

Chevrolet dropped the mid-sized Malibu in 1983, but continued making El Caminos. The 1984 version was a luxurious vehicle with dual, side-by-side, rectangular headlights on either side of a cross-hatch grille and long, narrow parking lights directly below the headlights. The bumper was a simple, straight-across design. A 5.7-liter gas V-8 returned and the 5.7-liter diesel V-8 remained available. The '84 El Camino actually survived because its sales kept Chevy ahead of Ford as America's highest-volume producer of trucks.

The 1985 El Camino received a new 4.3-liter V-6 and a new instrument panel was added in 1986, but these changes didn't improve its sales figures. By this time, the sales of Chevrolet's new S-10 compact pickup truck were taking a toll on the El Camino, as buyers preferred the S-10's wider range of capabilities.

The 1987 El Camino catalog promised the utility of a pickup with the beauty of a Sport Coupe, but this combination was no longer in demand. Only 15,589 were made. After a few hundred more were built in the first four months of 1988, the El Camino was dropped.

Today there's speculation that GM might once again offer an El Camino in the not too distant future. This new El Camino would be based on GM's new Zeta rear-wheel-drive platform that serves as the platform for Holden Commodore Utes in Australia. It's actually the same vehicle architecture that will be used for the retro-styled 2009 Camaro. Strangely enough, this good-looking design proposal is like a revival of the Australian Ute and the El Camino all in one!

The 1989 Chevrolet XR2 concept vehicle represented a cross between the Camaro of that time and the El Camino. Although it never reached production, this truck had great styling lines. *Gregg D. Merksamer Collection*

1973-98 LUV AND S-10 PICKUPS

1973-1983 LIGHT UTILITY VEHICLE (LUV)

In the early 1970s, the Detroit automakers were blindsided by the popularity of small imported pickup trucks. While Ford, GM and Chrysler sold hundreds of thousands of big pickups annually, they ignored the fact that small, sporty, fun-to-drive pickups were catching on. As usually happens, a new wave of young buyers slapped them upside the head and they were caught napping. Finally, Ford took action and started selling the Mazda-made Courier — in big numbers!

Since car making is a copycat industry, Chevy soon wanted a mini pickup. Labor problems experienced in making Vegas had taught Chevy it was virtually impossible to build vehicles in the United States at a cost that would make them competitive in the marketplace with small Japanese vehicles. So, Chevy decided not to *produce* a mini-pickup truck. Instead, it purchased 34.2 percent of Isuzu Motors and modified a small Isuzu pickup to meet American emissions, safety and marketing standards. Then, Chevy dealers sold it as the LUV.

GENERATION ONE: LUV – 1973-1980

This so-called Light Utility Vehicle (thus the LUV name) initially went on sale during March 1972 at selected Chevy dealerships in the West Coast and Gulf Coast marketing areas. For power, it used a small overhead cam four-cylinder engine with a two-barrel carburetor linked to a four-speed gearbox. It had a

A long-box option was available for the two-wheel-drive LUV pickup and featured the biggest payload available on any small-sized pickup in 1978. It had a 7-1/2-ft. length and handled payloads up to 1,635 lbs. Old Cars Weekly Collection

*In addition to nabbing **Motor Trend's** "Truck of the Year" award, the Chevrolet LUV (light utility vehicle) came in a four-wheel-drive version with two-speed transfer case and a 6-foot cargo box.* Old Cars Weekly Collection

short wheelbase, a 6-ft. long "Fleetside" cargo bed and a 1/2-ton rating.

"As a truck, the Chevy entry is quite similar to the Ford entry," *Road & Track* said. "Just as the Ford-bought Toyo Kogyo (Mazda) truck is similar to the Datsun and Toyota trucks." The LUV was priced at $2,196 and though it was not an innovative product in any sense, a total of 21,098 were sold in the U.S.

The round-headlight LUV of 1972 was phased out and a version with rectangular headlights replaced it. The price went up slightly and production tapered. It is interesting to note that a unique feature of the Isuzu-made mini-truck was its crank-down spare — a system later adopted for full-size Chevy pickups. The LUV was promoted separately from other Chevy trucks and did not often appear in ads or literature, even though the Vega panel express truck did.

Vertical in-the-fender taillights and a sporty Mikado (or "Mike") trim package were new in 1974. The latter included striped upholstery, a fancier 3-spoke steering wheel, finer seat cloth, carpets and upgraded trim throughout. The 1975 model changed little. It was the last LUV to list for under $3,000.

Front disc brakes, new trimmings and a three-speed automatic transmission modernized the LUV in 1976 and raised the window sticker to $3,285. A chassis-only version was sold in 1977 and horsepower was upped to a bit thanks to carburetor improvements. As Americans got used to driving smaller vehicles in general, sales of the LUV (and other such trucks) soared. The LUV wore a Chevy bow-tie badge for the first time in '77. There was also a new "Mighty Mike" (translation "upgraded Mikado") kit with wide tape stripes, "color spectrum" paint treatments, white spoke wheels and raised-white-letter tires.

The imported LUV moved into its Series 8 mode in 1978, which provided a two-headlight design, a new grille) and another bed length. While the standard six-foot box rode on the carryover 102.4-inch wheelbase, a new 7.5-foot bed rode a 117.9-in.-wheelbase chassis. Inside the cab was a new instrument panel.

A four-wheel-drive LUV bowed in 1979 and helped win *Motor Trend's* second "Truck of the Year." The magazine liked the quiet-running four-speed transmission/two-speed transfer case housed in a single die-cast aluminum case. The 4 x 4 also had a torsion-bar independent front suspension. "The LUV handles like a small sports car," raved *Motor Trend.*

By 1980, the Gen I LUV was growing long in the tooth. Despite a new-and-needed 80-hp engine, a 16.5-second 0-to-60 time and a 20-second quarter-mile time revealed the truck was slow. A terrible review of the automatic-transmission-equipped 4 x 2 LUV in *Car and Driver* called it one of the "crudest rides this side of a farm wagon." Three colors – White, Yellow and Red – were removed from the palette to get the lead out. Mikado cloth trim came in blue, red or saddle. Sport package decals came in a light orange-orange-red combination or a light blue metallic-dark blue-medium blue alternative choice.

GENERATION TWO: LUV (1981-1982)

New aerodynamic styling was seen inside and outside the new Series 11 LUV. It had a smoother hood, more glass and a curved rear window. A new frame design grew the wheelbase some two inches and increased interior space. A larger Chevy bow tie graced the center of the egg-crate grille. The body sides were smoothly-curved and had a sculptured feature line near the bottom. The Mikado package was revised and a color-keyed floor console was standard with automatic transmission. Payloads increased and the standard suspension was improved. The LUV also had bigger brakes, an improved heating-and-ventilation system and a new electronic ignition system. *Car and Driver,* which was not a LUV fan, complained, "We're sorry a bigger engine was not on their list."

Chevrolet put less energy into promoting the 1981 LUV, since it was planning to introduce the S-10 in mid-1981. So, it was no surprise that sales dropped off. The model survived into 1982 with hardly any changes in that year's Series 12 models.

The LUV would live to see 1982 almost unchanged from the previous year and with almost no one caring. With its replacement already selling alongside it, sales dribbled down to just 22,304 trucks and some LUVs lingered on dealers' lots well into 1983. *Consumer Guide* gave the 1982 LUV 65 points out of a possible 100 points on its vehicle test rating.

The richer Mikado version of the LUV pickup was used to create this 1980 display unit. It was designed to exhibit the features of the small truck during major auto shows around the country. Old Cars Weekly Collection

The 1981 LUV featured a new aero exterior, a new interior and a 2.2-liter 118-hp OHV four with 118 hp. New options included SS equipment for the two-wheel-drive model and ZR2 content for the 4 x 4. John Gunnell Collection

Chevrolet Pickups 1973-1998 | 119

Chevrolet had to prove the sturdiness and reliability of the S-10 Durango pickup in its early years. Catalog art showing the little truck hauling a tractor didn't hurt. John Gunnell Collection

The S-10 Maxi-Cab offered two-plus-two seating in a small pickup truck. This 4 x 4 edition is finished in a neat combination of Desert Sand and Satin Black, with the darker accent color on the lower body perimeter. John Gunnell Collection

1982-1998 S-10/T-10 PICKUP

The S-10 was considered an important extension of the Chevrolet pickup line. The new truck was larger than the LUV, but smaller than a C/K model. It was aimed directly at the popular Toyota and Nissan pickups. Ford's Ranger mini-pickup would not arrive until early 1982. So the S-10 was a hot product. Chevy gave it a launch described as the "biggest ad campaign in history."

GENERATION ONE: S-10 (1982-1993)

Like other Chevy trucks, the S-10 was very conventional in design. It rode a ladder frame and used a double A-arm front suspension and solid axle on semi-elliptical leaf springs. It had front discs brakes and radial tires. Buyers could choose from a 2.0-liter 82-hp pushrod four with a two-barrel carburetor or the Citation-type 2.8-liter OHV with a two-barrel carburetor and 110 hp. A four-speed manual gearbox was standard and a three-speed automatic was optional.

Early S-10 were basic 4 x 2 trucks with regular cab styling on two wheelbases: 108.3- or 117.9-inches. The S-10's advantage over the LUV was primarily in interior room, as load capacities were similar. Trim levels for the new truck included standard, Sport ($775 extra) and Durango ($325 extra). A $550 Tahoe package included bucket seats and gauges. Two-tone paint was popular. Motor Trend tested the S-10 V-6 and got a 0-to-60-mph time of 12.7 seconds for its V6-powered, automatically shifted S-10 Tahoe long bed — this wasn't so great but it was still much better than any LUV. Throw in the S-10's soft ride, comfortable cabin and handsome appearance, and an instant hit was born.

The S-10 sold like hot cakes and earned improvements for 1983 including a 4 x 4 model, an unpopular diesel engine option and Chevy's first extended cab. The latter version had a 122.9-in. wheelbase and a 14.5-in. stretched cab with rear jump seats. The S-10 4 x 4 model — officially designated T-10 and picked to

Looking as if it has lost direction somewhere in the desert, this 1987 S-10 regular-cab pickup with the Tahoe package has optional four-wheel drive to help ensure traction on the dirt road it's traveling. John Gunnell Collection

All 1990 S-10 pickups, including this regular-cab edition, had a redesigned instrument cluster with improved legibility. This one has black-finished front-and-rear bumpers and plain-looking hubcaps. John Gunnell Collection

be "Four-Wheeler of the Year" by *Four-Wheeler* magazine — used a four-wheel-drive system similar to the LUV's with front A-arms and torsion bars.

By 1984 the LUV was gone (Chevy dealers sold a few in 1983). S-10/T-10 trucks got a new hydraulic clutch on stick shift models, an improved trip odometer and an optional Sport suspension for regular-cab 4 x 2 models. Equipment varied by trim level. Durangos had color-keyed floor mats, courtesy lights and Custom cloth-and-vinyl or special Custom cloth bench seats. The Tahoe package added carpeting, gauges and a right visor mirror. The 2.5-liter 92-hp "Iron Duke" OHV four became standard in 4 x 4s. The higher-priced Sport option included all Tahoe features, a Sport steering wheel, Sport cloth bucket seats and a console.

The easy way to spot a 1985 S-10 was by its larger, more stylized fender badges with no hyphen between the letter and number. At the rear there was a smaller Chevy name on the left of the tailgate. The 2.5-liter Iron Duke four became standard engine in 4 x 4s. Chevy stuck with the same four trim levels. Paint options included Custom two-tone (second color below the belt line), Sport two-tone (second color on the bottom below four-stripe decals or moldings) and Special two-tone (second color between the belt line and lower feature line).

Few styling or trim changes were enacted for 1986 S-10s, but the engines boasted improved performance, economy and durability. The Iron Duke was rated at 92 hp with a two-barrel carburetor. The 2.8-liter V-6 was updated with an optional TBI induction system that raised output to 125 hp. Also new was a high-tech instrument cluster and an electronically-engaged transfer case on 4 x 4s. Called "Insta-Trac," it allowed switches from two- to four-wheel drive on the fly.

Fuel injection and high-flow cylinder heads improved drivability of the 92-hp Iron Duke — now called the "Tech IV" — in 1987. Both engines got a serpentine-belt system. Chevy dropped the diesel. Emerald Green replaced Cinnamon Red on the color palette. Leather seats were optional in Tahoes.

The big news for 1988 was the optional 4.3-liter Vortec V-6 for all S-10s starting at midyear. The 160-hp motor was smoother and more powerful than both the Iron Duke four and the 2.8-liter V-6. It came attached to a four-speed automatic transmission. The front brakes had quiet new "SAS II" pads and redeveloped all-season tires were available. The instrument panel had changed styling details. A factory-installed tinted sun roof was one new option.

The S/T pickups (both said "S-10" on them) had mostly minor changes for 1989, except for the use of rear wheel antilock brakes as standard equipment. Also standard was a new electronic speedometer. An electronic instrument cluster was added to the options. S-10 buyers could pick the 2.5-liter four or 2.8-liter V-6 as standard engines, while T10s came with the 2.8-liter job. Supplies of the 4.3-liter V-6 (overdrive automatic only) were increased and models that used this engine had changes to the steering column and left exhaust manifold. The extended or "Maxi-Cab" models used the short box on a 122.9-in. wheelbase.

For 1990, the Vortec 4.3-liter V6 could be linked to a new Getrag-designed and Hydra-Matic-built five-speed manual transmission. This made that version of the S-10 the quickest ever. All models also had a more legible instrument cluster, front tow hooks and an electronically-tuned AM radio. The Maxi-Cab models came with reclining seat backs. New for the Tahoe were right- and left-hand black exterior mirrors, color-keyed floor mats and an engine compartment lamp. New colors included Garnet inside and out and Royal Blue on the outside only.

A new-for-1991 full-width grille incorporated square headlights into its design. There were also new nameplates, emblems, badges, bumper rub strips and body moldings. Revised striping and decals were seen, as were new wheels and wheel trim. Sky Blue and Mint Green replaced Woodlands Brown Metallic and Nevada Gold Metallic on the color spectrum. A Baja off-road package was based on Tahoe content, but had a charcoal interior with charcoal-and-red high-back bucket seats. The "Baja" name was stitched below the headrest and it had wide red body stripes, Baja graphics and a black decal surrounding the grille.

The Vortec 4.3-liter V-6 had an improved 220 series TBI setup with longer throttle shaft bearings, new return springs and improved fuel mixture distribution. It was said to improve starting, idling and durability. A new Thermac III modified air cleaner system and Quantum spark plugs were used to improve cold starting. The cylinder heads were modified, but output remained at 160 hp. With these and other improvements, as well as a longer-than-usual model year that started early, production for 1991 was very strong at 253,953 units versus 202,240 the prior year. Model-year sales, however, fell to 206,893 from 210,318 in 1990.

Changes for the 1992 S-10s assembled in GM's Pontiac, Michigan and Shreveport, Louisiana factories, were limited mostly to mechanical tweaks and trim

An attractive-looking truck was the 1991 Chevy S-10 EL pickup. As you can tell, a rear bumper was optional equipment. This model had a base retail price of $8,382 and weighed in at 2,671 lbs. John Gunnell Collection

Looking like a toy truck parked near an inventory of flexible exhaust pipes, this 1992 Chevrolet S-10 two-wheel-drive pickup has the long-box styling that came in useful for big jobs. John Gunnell Collection

revisions. The Tahoe LT option came out for two-door models in February.

Even though a brand new S-10 pickup was in the works, the 1993 models had many improvements shared with 1993 S-Series Blazers. This reflected the importance of the S-10 to Chevy, as its sales kept them in the race with Ford. Some upgrades included the addition of an internal balance shaft to the 4.3-liter V-6 and the use of Solar-Ray tinted glass in all windows. A single and more reliable controller was also used for the engine, transmission and anti-lock brakes. An improved O-ring seal on the intake manifold thermostat reduced coolant leaks. The V-6 also had revised spark plugs that improved idle quality. There was new color-keyed door trim, air conditioning and radio bezels. A dual-note horn became standard and the convenience tray now had a soft liner.

During calendar-year 1993, a new S-10 assembly line in GM's Linden, New Jersey assembly plant built 34,868 units. That was in addition to 94,146 units made in Shreveport, Louisiana and 51,381 made at Pontiac, Michigan.

The colors Dove Gray and Khaki replaced Aquamarine Green and Sky Blue and a revised high-solids enamel painting process was used for all colors starting in 1993. It involved the use of corrosion-resistant-steel, an eight-stage zinc-phosphate coating and the use of E-coat primer with anti-chip protection on body side panels and front sheet metal. A paint treatment featuring a middle break line with a blended stripe was available for the first time in 1993.

The pickup and extended-cab pickup with the Tahoe option had a redesigned chrome-and-gray grille, while the taillight bezels were black. A new electric, dual, remote-control mirror option was introduced. Also, a new electronic 4L60-E Hydra-Matic transmission was used. Trucks with it could also get a new optional heavy-duty cooling system. Additional upgrades were made to interior features, option packages and other equipment. Chevy obviously did not want sales of the "old" S-10 to slip in its last year. After 12 model years, it was hard to view the S-10 as less than a stellar product, although it usually ran behind the Ranger in the small pickup sales race. However, with the year's many improvements, it's hard to believe that a collector interested in a Gen I S-10 wouldn't be happy with one in its most refined state — as the '93 model was.

GENERATION TWO: S-10 (1994-1998)

The 1994 featured an all-new aerodynamic exterior, a restyled interior and a smaller standard engine (2.2-liter OHV four) with more juice (118 hp). New option packages included SS equipment for the two-wheel-drive model and ZR2 content for the 4 x 4 version. In calendar-year 1994, no S-10 were made at the Pontiac West assembly plant. Production at the other S-10 plants increased to 165,893 units in Shreveport and to 99,334 units in Linden. In January, a recall was issued for 53,000 early-build trucks (S-10s and Sonomas) to replace fuel-filler pipes that failed to meet federal safety standards.

This 1994 Chevrolet S-10 extended-cab four-wheel-drive pickup wears the perforated steel wheels that were standard on 4 x 4 models. It is finished in Midnight Black with Quick Silver Metallic accents. John Gunnell Collection

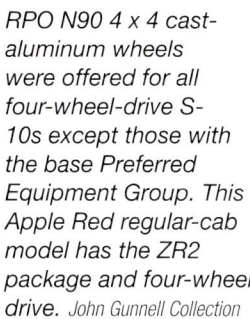

RPO N90 4 x 4 cast-aluminum wheels were offered for all four-wheel-drive S-10s except those with the base Preferred Equipment Group. This Apple Red regular-cab model has the ZR2 package and four-wheel drive. John Gunnell Collection

This two-wheel-drive '96 S-10 pickup features Sportside styling and white-finished 15-in. "Super Sport" cast-aluminum rims with bright center caps. The body is done in a popular Dark Teal Green Metallic hue. John Gunnell Collection

Metallic with Silver accents was a neat combination for the 1996 S-10 extended-cab pickup. This close up shows details of the "Easy Access" system with its "third door" arrangement. John Gunnell Collection

Chevrolet Trucks Market Manager K.L. Ritter said, "This redesign represents the most extensive use of customer input in GM history" and it was promoted as being "All new from the inside out with more power, more room, more precision and more safety enhancements than ever offered in this compact model." The buff magazines also gushed about the "all-new S-10 for 1994," but other than having 20 percent more glass area and a moved-forward windshield, the Chevy mini-pickup was pretty much the same as before in a basic sense.

A wraparound grille had wedge-shaped parking lights at each corner, deep-set rectangular headlights and a twin-slot grille with a big gold-finished bow tie emblem. The new S-10 offered regular or extended cabs, 6.1- or 7.4-foot load beds, and the same three wheelbases as before: 108.3 inches for the regular cab/short-bed, 117.9 inches for the regular cab/long-bed and 122.9 inches for the extended cab/short-bed. The body, depending on actual configuration,

The 1997 S-10 pickup line was composed of carryover models with few changes except new paint colors and ride-quality improvements. Fancy LS trim dresses up this Green 4 x 4 extended-cab model. John Gunnell Collection

The LS package seen on this extended-cab pickup was installed on only 24.7 percent of the 180,261 S-10s built during the '97 model year. This one also includes the optional Easy Access system. John Gunnell Collection

A 1997 Chevrolet S-10 served as the basis for this drag-racing pickup designed to compete in the National Hot Rod Association (NHRA)'s new Pro-Stock Truck racing series. John Gunnell Collection

was some 10 inches longer, three inches wider and two inches higher.

As before, S-10s had front A-arms and a leaf-spring rear suspension. Four-wheel antilock brakes were new. Tires, wheels and suspension tuning varied with three options for two-wheel-drive trucks and four for 4x4s. Besides the base four, 165- and 195-hp editions of the Vortec V-6 were offered. A high-tech fuel-injection system aided the hotter engine. All models were available a choice of five-speed manual or four-speed automatic transmission.

Regular-cab models in short- or long-box configuration were the entry level offerings. LS models included color-keyed door panels with cloth inserts, color-keyed carpeting, a rear bumper, dual mirrors, a lighted visor mirror, swing-out rear quarter windows in extended-cab models, a chrome grille (except on SS versions) and a 60/40 split bench seat with deluxe upholstery.

Motor Trend got it hands on a regular-cab Super Sport with the "Enhanced" Vortec V-6 and automatic. It pulled a 7.9-second 0-to-60 mph time and ran the quarter-mile in 16.1 seconds at 85.0 mph, but handling was so-so. "Chasing Porsches through back roads isn't what it's all about," said *Motor Trend.*

The 1995 Chevy S-10s had modest updates. A driver air bag was made standard equipment. ZRT heavy-duty components were offered for extended-cab models. The RPO L35 V-6 was equipped with OBD-Onboard diagnostics for lower emissions. The V-6 was offered with manual transmission in ZR2 four-wheel-drive models and all two-wheel-drive S-10s except the Super Sport.

A new "Easy Access System" gave S-10 Extended Cab models a third door on the driver's side. This option was a running addition, but ordering it meant giving up one of the folding rear jump seats that extended cab S-10s had. Also new was a Sportside cargo box, which was like the old Stepside style.

The base Vortec V-6 on four-wheel-drive models now came with sequential fuel injection, a reconfigured accessory-drive system and 175 hp. It was optional on two-wheel-drive trucks, which came standard with the 2.2-liter four and a five-speed gearbox. The trucks now featured a brake-transmission gearshift interlock and a new Sport suspension was available.

As a carryover model, the 1997 S-10 pickup had few changes except new paint colors and an improved ride. For fleet owners interested in saving gas (but not going fast or far) there was a new, electric-powered front-wheel-drive S-10 available. The improved ride came courtesy of the ZQ8 Sport suspension, which was now available for regular- and extended-cab models. Sixteen-inch five-spoke wheels and Goodyear high-performance tires. Smaller changes included a new automatic transmission fluid pump and a revised clutch plate for stick-shift trucks.

It is interesting to note that U.S. truck production exceeded passenger-car production for the first time ever in 1997. After two years of straight declines, the overall output of both cars and trucks marked a 2.5 percent increase at 12,130,486 units on a calendar-year basis. Trucks accounted for 51.1 percent of the total with 6,196,565 units built, a nice 7.8 percent increase from '96. Car output was 5,933,921 vehicles, down 2.5 percent for the year.

As it had always done to promote sales, Chevrolet hit the new-vehicle show circuit with "concept cars" — only some were trucks. This concept truck based on the 1997 S-10 pickup was called Xtreme Force. John Gunnell Collection

Xtreme Force was a standard S-10 Fleetside compact pickup with aftermarket goodies tacked on and Orange Glow PPG paint. It was shown at the Specialty Equipment Market Association's '97 SEMA Show. John Gunnell Collection

Although the S-10 story doesn't end in 1998, that's as far as we're tracing it in this book. Changes for the year included an "enhanced" Vortec 2200 (formerly referred to as 2.2-liter) four, an exterior front end facelift – with a new horizontal-bar grille and revised headlight design – and a revised instrument panel with a passenger airbag cut-off switch. Chevy also made the standard bench seat more comfy and added a retained-power feature and battery-run-down protection. Trucks with four-wheel-drive now had rear disc brakes and the enhanced Vortec V-6 was re-rated to 180 hp in two-wheel drives and 190 hp in four-wheel drives.

Truck Trend magazine liked the S-10 with the ZQ8 Sport package and noted, "For those of us who drive a truck every day and don't need the ultimate ability of a full-size hauler, the effortless grace of the compact S-10 is compelling." It did 0-to-60 mph in 8.7 seconds and turned in a 16.7-second quarter-mile at 81.5 mph.

Chevrolet Pickups 1973-1998 | 129

1973-98 OTHER CHEVROLET LIGHT-DUTY TRUCKS

We have looked at the history of Chevrolet's LUV, S10, El Camino and C/K pickup trucks for the years 1973-1998, so now let's take a glimpse at other types of light-duty trucks the company built in these years that collectors are starting to get interested in today.

Basically, this group includes the Suburban, the Blazer (which actually started as a big pickup with an open top and short wheelbase), the Vega Panel Express, the vans (Chevy Vans, G Vans, Luminas and Astros, which we're going to group together) and the Tahoe SUV (sport utility vehicle).

Since some enthusiasts are interested in these models and since these trucks have a family connection to the "Bow-Tie" pickups, we are going to present a capsule history of each model. Hopefully, it will paint a quick picture of other variations that might fit into a nice Chevy truck collection.

The Vega Panel Express was a low-production Chevy truck marketed between 1971-1975. Reminiscent of the popular sedan delivery of the '50s, the Vega Panel is catching on as a collector's item today. John Gunnell Collection

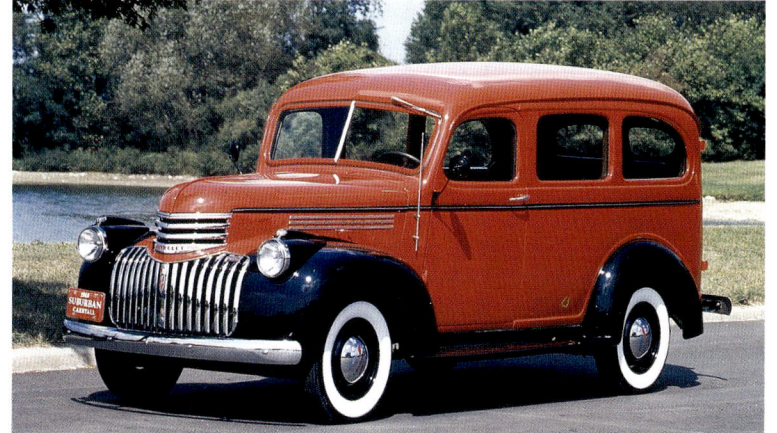

The history of the Suburban dated back to 1936, when it debuted as a truck-based station wagon. Seen here is a fully-restored 1946 model that today resides in the Chevrolet Historic Vehicle Collection.
John Gunnell Collection

1973-1998 SUBURBAN

Chevy's Suburban dates back to 1935. In the 1970s, 1980s and most of the 1990s, the Suburban was very much a Chevy exclusive and had little competition. Its styling changes reflected those of the pickups, as did its new features from engines and transmissions to stereos and air conditioning. Until 1988, if changes were made to the pickup, the Suburban usually got them.

A completely redesigned Suburban was introduced in 1973. It was boxy, but clean-looking and had four side doors replacing the unusual three-door configuration previously used. It came in half-, and 3/4-ton versions, the latter sharing the same body but having heavier-duty chassis, wheels and brakes. Both could be had with double doors at the rear or a station wagon style tailgate A full-time four-wheel-drive system was optional power plants ranged from a six to huge V-8s, with most collectors preferring a big-block and lots of options.

There were three trim levels for the popular mid-1970s Suburbans: Custom Deluxe, Scottsdale and Silverado. An Estate option with woodgrain trim was seen on upscale versions. The Suburban got the same changes outlined earlier for pickups like catalytic converters and a high-energy ignition (HEI) system.

By 1977, Chevy watched with a smile as demand for Suburbans grew to 60,000+ units annually. They were being built about as fast as the factory could crank them out. The new popularity was driven by a trend towards smaller station wagons in the passenger-car market. For many families, a Suburban replaced a big wagon. The *Old Cars Weekly* staff drove a 1978 Suburban for many years, criss-crossing the country to car shows and towing a trailer behind it. That truck went through several 454 V-8s and THM transmissions before being retired.

Aero restyling and a 300-lb. diet made the Suburban more modern, but it had some lean sales years in the early 1980s. By mid-decade, the base price jumped to five figures for the first time. Although 1988 Chevy pickups were completely redesigned, the Suburban continued with carryover looks, but renewed appeal. Production leaped to a record and rose the next year.

The styling and interior updates that C/K pickups got in 1988 were finally extended to Suburbans in 1992. Four-wheel antilock brakes became standard. 4 x 4 models featured a new independent front suspension and an Insta-Trac shift-on-the-fly system. Sales kept climbing, as did profits. By 1995, price range for Suburbans was $22,237 to $25,689 and by 1997 sales flirted with 100,000 units. By 1998, the Suburban was by all measures a sophisticated and successful luxury truck with high-tech features such as the OnStar satellite navigation system and a standard Autotrac electronically-controlled automatic transfer case on 4 x 4s.

Chevy truck enthusiasts have a special place in their hearts for Suburbans, whether they are the rare prewar models, fat-fender '50s trucks, the odd 1970s three-door models or accessory-loaded luxury trucks of more modern vintage. If they aren't collecting the 1990s models yet, at least they appreciate them as outstanding tow vehicles for their valuable vintage collector cars. I used to enjoy going the Classic Car Club of America shows and seeing all the fancy, highly-optioned Suburbans dressed up with aftermarket running boards, sun visors and even fender skirts. Suburbans are definitely collector trucks.

Chevy filled an exclusive market niche with the 1973-1998 Suburban. This model was usually in a class of its own. Seen here is the 1982 3/4-ton edition in two-tone colors of Midnight Blue and Light Blue. *John Gunnell Collection*

Suburbans were popular for pulling trailers, including some with restored Classic cars on them. This "tug" is an '89 R2500 Scottsdale. Note that the Suburban retained "old" styling after the '88 pickups were updated. *John Gunnell Collection*

In 1992, when this blue-and-white C1500 Suburban was put together, Chevy updated the Suburban to the same front end styling that pickups got earlier. The rest of the truck was restyled, too. *John Gunnell Collection*

1973-1994 K5 BLAZER

The full-size K5 Blazer was Chevy's answer to the rising popularity of Jeeps, IH Scouts and Ford's Bronco when the four-wheel-drive movement took off in the 1960s. It was introduced in 1969. The "big" Blazer really started off as a short-wheelbase, open-cab version of the full-size Chevy 4 x 4.

By teaming Jeep-like off-road capabilities with the convenience features of big pickups, the Blazer gained an immediate following. By 1970, a 4 x 2 version with independent front suspension was added and the Blazer outsold its rivals.

Blazer styling changes aped those of pickups,

The K-Series Blazer was essentially a short-wheelbase version of the K-Series pickup. In '73, it was a true "pickup" and came in soft- and hard-top models. Seen here is an '80 soft-top. It later became the Tahoe. John Gunnell Collection

Big K5 Blazers were popular with police departments in rural areas where their go-anywhere capabilities came in handy. This is a 1979 model that Chevy's promotional pros depicted as a Sheriff's Patrol truck. John Gunnell Collection

Chevrolet Pickups 1973-1998 | 133

Chevrolet got military contracts to produce specially-equipped Blazer-based military units like this 1983 model. These tough Chevys proved to be up to the demands of military service. John Gunnell Collection

The S-10 Blazer was a 1984 innovation inspired by America's increasing emphasis on fuel economy. By the time this '92 arrived, two- and four-door models were offered in a choice of 4 x 2 and 4 x 4 drive. John Gunnell Collection

which we've covered, so in 1973 it was redesigned along with other full-size Chevy trucks. A full-time four-wheel-drive system was adopted and a removable hardtop was also on the long list of optional equipment.

After 1976, a new body design was introduced. It featured a steel half-cab with an integral roll bar. A removable, fiberglass-reinforced plastic roof was optional. A Cheyenne package with simulated wood-grain trim was another extra.

The 350-powered K5 Blazer became the darling of off-roaders, who also like the early NP-205 gear-drive transfer case and 10- or 12-bolt axles. After 1980, the transfer case adopted a chain-drive design. Also popular with 4 x 4 enthusiasts is the M1009 CUCV military variant.

Over 20,200 K-Series Blazers were being built per year in 1993. This two-door, 4 x 4 example was one of them. It features two-tone red-and-brown paint. By this time, the big Blazer was a "wagon" rather than a pickup. John Gunnell Collection

Finished in black and tan, this '94 S-10 Blazer is a two-door, 4 x 4 wagon with upscale LT trim. The base price for this model was $16,583. John Gunnell Collection

Although Chevy introduced new GMT400 trucks for model-year 1988, the big K5 Blazer retained the previous appearance. A year later, the grille was changed to resemble that of the newer-design pickups, but the "old" body was used several more years. The K5 Blazer got updated to the GMT400 platform in 1992 and survived until 1994. In 1995, it actually evolved into the Tahoe.

The big Blazers are very popular with Chevy collectors, especially the "convertible" models with pickup boxes built early in the model's existence. The "classic" early Blazers have the advantage of appealing both to pickup truck collectors and four-wheel-drive buffs.

Chevrolet Pickups 1973-1998 | 135

Like its big Blazer predecessor, the K1500 Tahoe was a handy and hot-selling law-enforcement vehicle. This four-door version was placed in service by the Michigan State Police.
John Gunnell Collection

Starting in 1995, the S-10 Blazer became simply the Blazer, while the big K1500 Blazer became the Tahoe. Shown here is the 1996 K1500 Tahoe four-door LT wagon. John Gunnell Collection

1995-1998 TAHOE

In 1995, Chevrolet's full-size SUV (sport utility vehicle) was completely redesigned and given a new name. It became the Tahoe and the Blazer name was saved for the smaller S-Series SUVs. The initial Tahoe model was a three-door wagon. A five-door wagon was brought out at midyear.

The front end of the Tahoe looked like the front of the big C/K pickups, since it was based on that model. Rear-wheel-drive and all-wheel-drive versions were marketed. All Tahoe's came equipped with a driver's-side airbag in addition to a passenger-side airbag that the K-5 Blazer had before.

Standard engine in the Tahoe was a 200-hp 5.7-liter V-8. A 65.5-liter 180-hp turbo-diesel engine was optional. Gas-engined Tahoes featured a standard five-speed manual gearbox. An ETC (electronically-controlled) four-speed automatic was optional with gas and standard with diesel. The automatic transmission incorporated an interlock feature to prevent shifting if the brake was not applied. A 100,000-mile automatic transmission fluid was supplied.

The five-door Tahoe filled a marketing gap between the three-door model and the Suburban. It had a six-inch-longer wheelbase than the smaller Tahoe and 10 inches more length. The spare was under the floor to increase interior space. Insta-Trac was standard. There was an LS package that included

A/C, an ATC stereo cassette, a rear defogger and wiper/washer and a luggage carrier. The LT package added a power seat and remote keyless entry.

The rear-drive Tahoe (four doors only) listed for $26,385 and weighed 4769 pounds. The 4 x 4 version was $28,585 and 5124 pounds, respectively. The two-door model, which came only in 4 x 4 format, was base-priced at $21,830 and tipped the scale at 4,747 pounds.

For 1996, a rear-drive version of the two-door model was added to the line at $25,136. Also new was the powerfully advanced Vortec 5700 V-8 with Sequential Fuel Injection (SFI). It had 50 hp more than the '95 5.7-liter V-8. Shifting from two-wheel drive to 4 x 4 high and back again was made easier by the addition of n optional new electronic shift transfer case on 4 x 4 models.

For 1997, the Tahoe's center console had added features. Chevrolet also started supplying a quieter-running engine fan and an improved automatic transmission. Variable-orifice steering was also offered. Prices ranged from $24,147 up to $32,125.

The OnStar satellite navigation system was option in 1998 Tahoes and a new police package was introduced for law enforcement use. A new Comfort and Security package included heated seats, heated self-dimming mirrors, a HomeLink transmitter. A 6-way power passenger seat for four-door models was introduced. Also added was a "Premium Ride" suspension system.

Since the K-5 Blazer is already collectible and the 1995-up Tahoe is a K-5 Blazer with another name, you can bet that these trucks are going to be restored and collected, especially since they are more luxurious and better-performing vehicles than the early K-5s.

1982-1998 S-10/T-10 BLAZER

Smaller 4 x 2 and 4 x 4 Blazers were added to the S10 line in 1983. They immediately became strong sellers, especially the T10 four-wheel-drive version. The body style was described as a "hardtop with a tailgate," as they did not go the removable hardtop route. These two-door trucks had their own 100.5-inch wheelbase and 178.2-inch overall length. A 2.0-liter four (1.9-liter in California) was base engine and a 2.8 V-6 was available, as was a 2.2-liter Isuzu diesel.

Grille and taillight changes were the story through 1985. Then engines below 2.2 liters were replaced by a 2.5-liter four. The V-6 got throttle-body fuel injection for better performance and gas mileage. Production hit 232,000 units!

The late 1980s were a time of refinements from new dashes to high-tech engine tweaks to Insta-Trac. The "serpentine" drive belt was adopted in 1987.

In March 1990, an all-new "1991" S-10 Blazer with a 6.5-inch longer wheelbase and four doors arrived. It used a new one-piece grille with a black insert. The two-door kept the "old" body and three-piece grille. Snowflake alloy wheels in charcoal gray or argent silver were new. The '92s were similar to '91s and only a few changes were made in '93. They included an enhanced power train with 35 hp added, a higher console and a chrome-plated version of the painted S-10 pickup grille. Revised "S-Series" pickups arrived in 1994, but the S-10 Blazer continued with the major change being an added third brake light.

A new "S-Blazer" (not S-10) hit the showroom in 1995. It was derived from the Gen II S-10 pickup of '94. It was the only "Blazer" left in the lineup, as the full-size version became the Tahoe (a name that formerly identified a trim package for the smaller Blazer). The Blazer was the *Motor Trend* "Truck of the Year."

The 1998 Blazer got a redesigned front grille and stacked headlights that made it look similar to Chevy's big C/K pickups. The S-10/T-10-S-Series Blazers are popular trucks and will develop a larger and larger collector following as time goes on. This will certainly be a popular rig with a new generation of truck buffs.

1973-1975 VEGA PANEL EXPRESS

The word "Vega" means "brightest star in the constellation" and Chevy hoped that the sub-compact car it introduced in the '70s would live up to that standard. Though some people probably considered building one, Chevrolet did not make an El Camino-like pickup truck version of the Vega. However, it did offer the Vega Panel Express model starting in 1971. It made 7,800 of them that year and 4,114 the next year and continued to manufacture the sub-compact truck in 1973, 1974 and 1975.

The Vega Panel Express was Model (1971 and

In Chevy lingo, the designation APV stood for "all-purpose-vehicle." Shown here is the 1991 Lumina APV cargo van in white. Chevy merchandised this model as a minivan, but the government rated it like a truck. John Gunnell Collection

In 1993, Chevrolet stopped using the term APV and started referring to the Lumina as a "wagon." This is a 1994 model with Medium Adriatic Blue Metallic finish and LS trim. John Gunnell Collection

1972) 14105 or (1973 through 1975) 1HV05 in the 14000 Series Vega lineup. It was based on the Vega station wagon or Kammback model. The Vega Panel Express was classified as a half-ton truck with a 3,050 to 3,290-lb. gross vehicle weight for the early versions. Chevy promoted it as a "kinky way to haul around your surfboard."

It came only with the Vega's standard all-vinyl interior, less the passenger-side bucket seat. Limited upholstery color choices were available – in fact black or green were the options.

An aluminum overhead-cam four-cylinder engine was the power plant used. It had a 3.501 x 3.625-inch bore and stroke and 140 cubic inches of displacement. With an 8.0:1 compression ratio and a one-barrel carburetor, it produced 72 hp at 4200 rpm and 115 foot-pounds of torque at 2400 rpm. Also standard was a three-speed, floor-shifted manual transmission, front disk brakes and below-the-floor storage compartments.

The Vega Panel Express had a 97-inch wheelbase, a 176.5-inch overall length and a height of 51.8 inches. It was listed as a half-ton truck. With a 67.4-inch floor length and 42.6 inches between the wheel housings, it had 68.7 cubic feet of cargo space. Payload was 650 pounds.

There was very little change in the 1973 model, which said $2,106 on the bottom of the window sticker and tipped the scale at 2,303 pounds. The grille had slightly more of a horizontal design. Model-year production settled out at 3,886 units.

A revised frontal treatment graced the 1974

model. It featured a divided four-louver grille and recessed headlights. The parking lamps were relocated. Instead of being under the bumper, they moved to a spot between the headlights and the grille. They also changed from being round to tall rectangles. The front side marker lights were a bit higher and, at the rear, the license plate hung in the center of the tailgate. The front bumper, designed to meet five-mph barrier test standards, was fatter than before, but not unattractive. You could get the Panel Express in all 14 standard Vega color combinations. A larger 16-gallon fuel tank was supplied this year.

Though it was a neat little rig, Chevy did not spend a ton of money promoting the Vega Panel Express. In fact, even though the '74 model had a bunch of changes, the company used the same illustration of a truck operated by the fictitious "T. Tonies Bakery" in its sales catalog and simply airbrushed the design changes in. Talk about cheap, but production picked up a bit to 4,289.

For its final appearance in 1975, the Vega Panel Express had its Gross Vehicle Weight rating raised to 3,283 to 3,552 lbs. Apparently, the springs or shocks were up-rated, although the little truck looked just the same as before. The price for the 2,401-lbs. mini-truck went up to $2,822, but production went the other way and bottomed out at 1,525 units.

Vegas were very popular with the car-buying public in the early 1970s and the car models sold well despite problems that the earliest editions had with head gaskets and other things. Most of the problems were eventually corrected. In total, 2,154,434 Vegas (and badge-engineered Pontiac Astres) were built from 1971 through 1977. Most were produced at the Lordstown, Ohio, GM assembly plant, but some were also built at Saint Thérèse Assembly in Quebec, Canada. These trucks are rare to find today, but the popularity of survivors is increasing as gas prices climb. After all, for a 1970s car, the Vega gets pretty good gas mileage — even the Panel Express version.

1989-1998 TRACKER

The Tracker started as a Geo model and later became a Chevrolet. It is a small sports utility vehicle made by Suzuki plants around the world, the Tracker model succeeded the SJ410/LJ80 model. It has been produced and sold throughout the world under various names like Sunrunner, Sidekick and Vitara.

Features of the Gen I Tracker included a 1.6-liter 95-hp inline four-cylinder engine, a five-speed manual gearbox and a choice of two body configurations. The two-door rode an 86.6-inch wheelbase and the four-door had an 11-inch longer stance. Three- and four-speed automatic transmissions were optional after the first year. Buyers also could buy a rear-wheel-drive ragtop after 1991.

Chevrolet's Suzuki-designed Tracker 4 x 4 sport utility vehicle entered North America production, at CAMI Automotive in Canada, for the 1990 model year. This '93 edition had few significant changes.
John Gunnell Collection

A total of 47,591 Geo Trackers were built in North America in model-year 1994. This Hardtop model is finished in white and carries the optional LSi package.
John Gunnell Collection

The Tracker bowed as a companion to the Geo Metro and Geo Spectrum when the Geo brand was introduced in 1989. In 1990, the Tracker LSI convertible arrived and an automatic transmission became available. Aluminum wheels became an option in 1992. There were no changes in 1993.

As before, the 1994 Tracker convertible came in two-wheel-drive and 4 x 4 versions, while the hardtop came only with drive at all corners. New aluminum wheels and all-season tires debuted. A new easily-retractable convertible top and Multi Port Fuel Injection (MFI) system were added in 1995.

A four-door Tracker 4 x 4 was new for 1996. The tiny SUV's outer skin was also restyled. Front airbags and a 1.6-liter SOHC engine were now standard and four-wheel anti-lock brakes were available. The hardtop was dropped.

In 1998, GM dropped the Geo brand and made the Tracker a Chevy. The two-door rear-drive model and the four-door LSi hardtop were dropped from the U.S. model lineup, although they were still marketed elsewhere.

The Tracker is a neat vehicle. I took my first ride in one back in the late 1980s, when my son Jesse and I visited the headquarters of the Kruse International collector-car auction company in Auburn, Indiana. At that time Dean V. Kruse was constructing his huge new facility there and Mitchell Kruse took us for a ride over some tough terrain in a new Tracker. Its performance was impressive. We liked that truck very much and I have little doubt that Trackers will be collected more and more as time goes by.

1973-1998 CHEVY VANS

In mid-1964, a compact forward-control Chevy Van was phased in as a replacement for the Corvair truck. Available in a G10 half-ton series only, it was offered in Carryall (window van) and Panel (commercial van) models that used the Chevy II four-cylinder engine as standard equipment and an in-line six as an option. As vans caught on as people-movers in the freewheeling 1960s, the Chevy Van turned into a cultural icon and the line grew to include fancier and sportier versions of the window-van model. By 1966, the four vanished. A year later, the original 90-inch wheelbase model was still available, but a longer-bodied G10 Chevy Van with a 108-inch wheelbase was added. A matching line of ¾-ton G20 models arrived as well. The six was standard and a 307-cid V-8 was optional.

By the 1970s, buyers wanted more room and G-vans were attractively restyled in 1971. They now had a mini hood up in front and the wheelbases grew to 110 inches and 125 inches, respectively. The 12-passenger Sportvan Deluxe model adopted the Beauville name once used on fancy mid-'50s Chevy station wagons. The commercial version was the Chevy Van and the Sportvan was the window model. Sixes and V-8s were available. Also a G-30 one-ton line was added. There were minor alterations in 1972 and 1973. Chevy concocted some new two-tone paint schemes for 1975. There was a new instrument panel and A/C system.

The 1970s were the age of the van and especially the "customized" van. The Chevy Van/Sportvan/

The big, full-sized Chevy Van has underwent numerous changes since it first arrived back in the "hippie '60s." It's a solid part of the Chevy truck lineup, but not a real big collector's item. This is a '94 Sportvan.
John Gunnell Collection

Beauville line was a popular one. In 1975, a total of nearly 109,000 vans left the assembly lines. By 1976, the number was 153,000. In 1977, it climbed to 191,000. By 1978, the number was at 247,077. Chevrolet reported an all-time record of 1.34 million truck sales in 1978 and the G Vans or Chevy Vans were a big contributor to that type of performance.

The gas crunch of 1979 leveled off van sales. In 1980, they headed down for the first time in years. Only 99,000 were built in both 1981 and 1982.

By 1983 there were 12 models left in five series. The G10 half-ton 110-inch-wheelbase series offered a commercial panel van and windowed Sportvan. The counterpart 125-inch-wheelbase series offered the Bonaventure travel van and the fancy Beauville. All of these models were duplicated in the G20 ¾-ton series and there was also a G20 125-inch-wheelbase Sportvan. G30 one-ton models came only on the longer wheelbase and all four models were available. This was the only line that offered a long-wheelbase commercial panel van. New for 1983 were a 6.2-liter diesel engine and a four-speed overdrive automatic transmission.

A bi-level grille came into use in 1984 and the name "Chevy Van" got renewed promotional emphasis. Halogen headlights were available as an option, but little changed in a basic sense. Van sales did pick up again, climbing to the 175,000 to 200,000 units per year range. The model count climbed to 13 and a cutaway version of the G van platform was also used for Hi-Cube van and motor home conversions. A 146-inch wheelbase option was added.

Seen for the first time in 1985 was the Astro, Chevy's all-new rear-wheel-drive compact van. It came in cargo and passenger van styles and the people-moving models were offered in CS sporty trim and CL luxury trim. Nearly 60,000 were made and the total leaped to 140,000 in 1986. By 1987, the Astro added base and LT Wagon models and hit 170,000 production. This did take some wind out of the big G vans, which slid to production of 129,000, which still wasn't bad.

This was more or less the program throughout the 1980s, with production of both the small and large rear-wheel-drive vans holding steady at a very nice pace. Naturally, there were refinements to styling and interior design and consistent improvements in technology, but nothing changed drastically.

In 1990, the Astro became the first U.S.-built minivan to be offered with full-time all-wheel-drive. Extended (10-inch-longer) versions of both the two- and all-wheel-drive Astros were new. That same year, the Chevy Lumina APV (All Purpose Vehicle) arrived on the scene. It was a front-wheel-drive minivan with

As a rear-wheel-drive minivan, the long-lasting Astro has some unique handling characteristics and "personality traits." This is the 1988 model in Deep Red Metallic color. John Gunnell Collection

a 109.8-inch wheelbase and a standard 3.1-liter V-6 engine. A Cargo Van model was offered at $12,895. The windowed wagon was $13,995 or $15,745 with CL trim. The Lumina netted Chevy nearly 80,000 production with only a slight impact on the production of G Vans or Astros. It was another coup for Chevrolet.

Only relatively modest changes were made in the three types of Chevrolet vans in the early '90s. Passenger comfort and convenience features were improved almost annually. Safety increased (more airbags, etc.) and technology upgrades like Vortec engines were phased in each year. In 1995, the Astro's regular body was replaced with an extended-body design and both Astros and Luminas got improved engines. The Beauville was given more standard features and all the big vans were made quieter.

In 1996 Chevy restyled the Astro's interior and refined its Vortec 4300 V-6 and 4L60-E automatic transmission. It was the last season for the Lumina APV, which got a 3400 V-6 and standard seven-passenger seating. As for the big G vans, all-new models with longer 135- and 155-inch wheelbases were launched in the spring of 1996. The Sportvan became the Express and a Vortec 4300 V-6 with 195 hp was made standard, Vortec 5000, 5700 and 7400 V-8s were optional.

Big news in 1997 was the Venture, an all-new replacement for the Lumina APV. It was promoted as GM's first "global" minivan. The $20,000 Opel-created Venture featured a 180-hp 3400 V-6 and a choice of short- and extended-wheelbase models. This front driver was positioned to compete with the Ford Windstar and Dodge Caravan and had more interior room than the Lumina. Astros and the G-series Chevy Vans got refinements and new colors. There were no major changes in any vans for 1998, but the Venture did get the OnStar communications system as an option and the short-wheelbase model was now available with an optional power passenger-side sliding door.

In general, Chevy vans are not as collectible as pickups, Vega panels and various 4 x 4 models, although some of the fancier custom travel van conversions show up from time to time in collector-vehicle auctions. There are also some people who collect "hippie" style vans to go along with their interested in the cultural revolution of the late 1960s and early 1970s in America. However, if you want to invest in a collectible Chevrolet truck, go with the pickups first.

Factory Factors

A. 1973-1981 El Camino Vehicle Identification Numbers

1973: First symbol indicates manufacturer, 1=Chevrolet. Second symbol indicates car-line/series: C=El Camino, D=El Camino Custom. Third and fourth symbols indicate body type: 80=Sedan-Pickup. Fifth symbol indicates engine: H=350-cid/145-hp two-barrel V-8, L=350-cid/160-hp four-barrel V-8, R=400-cid/150-hp two-barrel V-8, U=402-cid/180-hp four-barrel V-8, Y=454-cid/235-hp four-barrel V-8. Sixth symbol indicates model-year: 3=1973. Seventh symbol indicates assembly plant. Symbols 8-13 indicate the production sequence number starting at 100,001. Ending numbers not available.

1974: First symbol indicates manufacturer, 1=Chevrolet. Second symbol indicates car-line/series: C=El Camino, D=El Camino Custom. Third and fourth symbols indicate body type: 80=Sedan-Pickup. Fifth symbol indicates engine: 1[El Camino] H=350-cid/145-hp two-barrel V-8, L=350-cid/160-hp four-barrel V-8, R=400-cid/150-hp two-barrel V-8, U=402-cid/180-hp four-barrel V-8, Y=454-cid/235-hp four-barrel V-8. Sixth symbol indicates model-year: 4=1974. Seventh symbol indicates assembly plant. Symbols 8-13 indicate the production sequence number starting at 100,001. Ending numbers not available.

1975: First symbol indicates manufacturer, 1=Chevrolet. Second symbol indicates car-line/series: C=El Camino, D=El Camino Custom. Third and fourth symbols indicate body type: 80=Sedan-Pickup. Fifth symbol indicates engine: [El Camino] H=350-cid/145-hp two-barrel V-8, L=350-cid/160-hp four-barrel V-8, U=402-cid/175-hp four-barrel V-8, Y=454-cid/235-hp four-barrel V-8. Sixth symbol indicates model-year: 5=1975. Seventh symbol indicates assembly plant. Symbols 8-13 indicate the production sequence number starting at 100,001. Ending numbers not available.

1976: First symbol indicates manufacturer, 1=Chevrolet. Second symbol indicates car-line/series: C=El Camino, D=El Camino Classic. Third and fourth symbols indicate body type: 80=Sedan-Pickup. Fifth symbol indicates engine: [El Camino] D=250-cid/105-hp one-barrel L6, Q=305-cid/140-hp two-barrel V-8 (except Calif.), H=350-cid/145-hp two-barrel V-8 (except Calif.), L=350-cid/165-hp four-barrel V-8, U=400-cid/175-hp four-barrel V-8. Sixth symbol indicates model-year: 6=1976. Seventh symbol indicates assembly plant. Symbols 8-13 indicate the production sequence number starting at 100,001. Ending numbers not available.

1977: First symbol indicates manufacturer, 1=Chevrolet. Second symbol indicates car-line/series: C=El Camino, D=El Camino Classic. Third and fourth symbols indicate body type: 80=Sedan-Pickup. Fifth symbol indicates engine: [El Camino] D=250-cid/110-hp one-barrel L6, U=305-cid/145-hp two-barrel V-8, L=350-cid/170-hp four-barrel V-8. Sixth symbol indicates model-year: 7=1977. Seventh symbol indicates assembly plant. Symbols 8-13 indicate the production sequence number starting at 100,001. Ending numbers not available.

1978: First symbol indicates manufacturer, 1=Chevrolet. Second symbol indicates car-line/series: W=El Camino. Third and fourth symbols indicate body type: 80=Sedan-Pickup. Fifth symbol indicates engine: [El Camino] A=231-cid/105-hp two-barrel V-6, D=250-cid/105-hp one-barrel L6, H=305-cid/140-hp two-barrel V-8, L=350-cid/170-hp four-barrel V-8. Sixth symbol indicates model-year: 8=1978. Seventh symbol indicates assembly plant. Symbols 8-13 indicate the production sequence number starting at 100,001. Ending numbers not available.

1979: First symbol indicates manufacturer, 1=Chevrolet. Second symbol indicates car-line/series: W=El Camino. Third and fourth symbols indicate body type: 80=Sedan-Pickup. Fifth symbol indicates engine: [El Camino] A=231-cid (3.8 liter)/115-hp two-barrel V-6, J=267-cid (4.4 liter)/125-hp two-barrel V-8, L=350-cid (5.7 liter)/170-hp four-barrel V-8, M=200-cid (3.3 liter)/94-hp two-barrel, V-6. Sixth symbol indicates model-year: 9=1979. Seventh symbol indicates assembly plant. Symbols 8-13 indicate the production sequence number starting at 100,001. Ending numbers not available.

1980: First symbol indicates manufacturer, 1=Chevrolet. Second symbol indicates car-line/series: W=El Camino. Third and fourth symbols indicate body type: 80=Sedan-Pickup. Fifth symbol indicates engine: [El Camino] A=229-cid (3.8-liter)/115-hp two-barrel V-6, J=267-cid (4.4-liter)/120-hp two-barrel V-8, M=305-cid (5.0-liter)/155-hp four-barrel V-8. Sixth symbol indicates model-year: A=1980. Seventh symbol indicates assembly plant. Symbols 8-13 indicate the production sequence number starting at 100,001. Ending numbers not available.

1981: New system for all Light-Duty and Medium-Duty models including El Camino. See below.

B. 1973-1998 Light Truck Vehicle Identification Numbers

1973: The first symbol indicates manufacturer: 1=Chevrolet Motor Division. The second symbol indicates chassis type: C=96 in. or 106 in. Conventional Cab, G=Sportvan, H=92 in. Conventional Cab, J=92 in. Conventional Cab with tandem, K=4 x 4, L=Light-Utility, M=96 in. or 114 in. Conventional Cab with tandem, P=Forward-Control, Z=Motorhome. The third symbol indicates engine as follows: L=454-cid/245-hp four-barrel V-8, N=110-cid/75-hp two-barrel L4, Q=250-cid/100-hp one-barrel L-6, S=292-cid L-6 with LPG conversion, T=292-cid/120-hp one-barrel L-6, X=307-cid/120-hp two-barrel V-8, Y=350-cid/145-hp two-barrel V-8, W=350-cid V-8 with LPG conversion, Y=350-cid/160-hp four-barrel V-8, Z=454-cid/235-hp four-barrel V-8. The fourth symbol indicates series and tonnage: 1=1/2-ton, 2=3/4-ton, 3=1-ton. The fifth symbol indicates body type: 2=Chassis-and-Cowl, 3=Chassis-and-Cab or Motorhome Chassis, 4=Cab with pickup box, 5=Panel or Panel Van, 6=Sportvan, 7=Motorhome, 8=Blazer. The sixth symbol indicated model-year: 3=1973. The seventh symbol indicates the assembly plant: A=Lakewood, Ga., B=Baltimore, Md., F=Flint, Mich., J=Janesville, Wis., K=Leeds, Mo., U=Lordstown, Ohio, V=Pontiac, Mich., Z=Fremont, Calif., 1=Oshawa, Canada, 3=GMAD, Detroit, Mich., 8=Fujisawa, Japan. Symbols 8-13 are the production sequence number. Starting number: 10001.

1974: The first symbol indicates manufacturer: 1=Chevrolet Motor Div. The second symbol indicates chassis type: C=96 in. or 106 in. Conventional Cab, G=Sportvan, H=92 in. Conventional Cab, J=92 in. Conventional Cab with tandem, K=4 x 4, L=Light-Utility, M=96 in. or 114 in. Conventional Cab with tandem, P=Forward-Control, Z=Motorhome. The third symbol indicates engine as follows: L=454-cid/245-hp four-barrel V-8, N=110-cid/75-np two-barrel L4, Q=250-cid/100-hp one-barrel L-6, S=292-cid L-6 with LPG conversion, T=292-cid/120-hp one-barrel L-6, X=307-cid/120-hp two-barrel V-8, Y=350-cid/145-hp two-barrel V-8, W=350-cid V-8 with LPG conversion, Y=350-cid/160-hp four-barrel V-8, Z=454-cid/235-hp four-barrel V-8. The fourth symbol indicates series and tonnage: 1-1/2-ton, 2=3/4-ton, 3=1-ton. The fifth symbol indicates body type: 2=Chassis & Cowl, 3=Chassis-and-Cab or Motorhome Chassis, 4=Cab with pickup box, 5=Panel or Panel Van, 6=Sportvan, 7=Motorhome, 8=Blazer. The sixth symbol indicated model-year: 4=1974. The seventh symbol indicates the assembly plant: A=Lakewood, Ga., B=Baltimore, Md., F=Flint, Mich., J=Janesville, Wis., K=Leeds, Mo., U=Lordstown, Ohio, V=Pontiac, Mich., , Z=Fremont, Calif., 1=Oshawa, Canada, 3=GMAD, Detroit, Mich., 8=Fujisawa, Japan. Symbols 8-13 are the production sequence number. Starting number: 10001.

1975: The first symbol indicates manufacturer: 1=Chevrolet Motor Div. The second symbol indicates chassis type: C=96 in. or 106 in. Conventional Cab including Blazer, G=Chevy Van or Sportvan, K=106-in. wheelbase Conventional cab 4 x 4, P= Forward-Control. The third symbol indicates engine as follows: L=454-cid/245-hp four-barrel V-8 (P-Series only), M=400-cid/175-hp four-barrel V-8, N=110-cid/75-hp two-barrel L4, P=250-cid/105-hp one-barrel six, Q=250-cid/100-hp one-barrel L-6, R=292-cid/120-hp one-barrel L-6, T=292-cid/150-hp one-barrel L-6, U=350-cid four-barrel V-8, V=350-cid/145-hp two-barrel V-8, Y=350-cid/160-hp four-barrel V-8, Z=454-cid/230-hp four-barrel V-8. The fourth symbol indicates series and tonnage: 1=1/2-ton, 2=3/4-ton, 3=1-ton. The fifth symbol indicates body type: 2=Chassis & Cowl, 3=Chassis-and-Cab or

Motorhome Chassis, 4=Cab with pickup box, 5=Panel or Panel Van, 6=Sportvan, Carryall Suburban (doors) 7=Motorhome chassis, 8=Blazer. The sixth symbol indicates model-year: 5=1975. The seventh symbol indicates the assembly plant: A=Lakewood, Ga., B=Baltimore, Md., D=Doraville, Ga., F=Flint, Mich., J=Janesville, Wis., K=Leeds, Mo., S=St. Louis, Mo., R=Arlington, Texas, U=Lordstown, Ohio, V=Pontiac, Mich. GMAD, Z=Fremont, Calif., 1=Oshawa, Canada, 3=GMAD, Detroit, Mich., 4=Scarborough, Ontario, Canada, 8=Fujisawa, Japan. Symbols 8-13 are the production sequence number. Starting number: 10001 Ending numbers not available.

1976: The first symbol indicates manufacturer: 1=Chevrolet Motor Div. The second symbol indicates chassis type: C=96 in. or 106 in. Conventional Cab including Blazer, G=Chevy Van or Sportvan, K=106 in. Conventional cab 4 x 4, P= Forward-Control. The third symbol indicates engine as follows: D=250-cid/105-hp one-barrel L6, L=350-cid/160-hp four-barrel V-8, N=110-cid/75-hp two-barrel L4 (LUV), Q=305-cid/130-hp two-barrel V-8 (except Calif.), S=454-cid/240-hp four-barrel V-8 (C models only), T=292-cid/120-hp one-barrel L-6, U=400-cid/175-hp four-barrel V-8, V=350-cid/145-hp two-barrel V-8, Y=454-cid/245-hp four-barrel V-8 (P models only). The fourth symbol indicates series and tonnage: 1=1/2-ton, 2=3/4-ton, 3=1-ton. The fifth symbol indicates body type: 2=Chassis & Cowl, 3=Chassis-and-Cab, 4=Cab with pickup box, 5=Panel or Panel Van, 6=Sportvan, Carryall Suburban (doors) 7=Motorhome chassis, 8=Blazer. The sixth symbol indicates model-year: 6=1976. The seventh symbol indicates the assembly plant: A=Lakewood, Ga., B=Baltimore, Md., F=Flint, Mich., J=Janesville, Wis., S=St. Louis, Mo., U=Lordstown, Ohio, V=Pontiac, Mich. GMAD, Z=Fremont, Calif., 1=Oshawa, Canada, 3=GMAD, Detroit, Mich., 4=Scarborough, Ontario, Canada, 8=Fujisawa, Japan. Symbols 8-13 are the production sequence number. Starting number: 10001 Ending numbers not available.

1977: The first symbol indicates manufacturer: 1=Chevrolet Motor Div. The second symbol indicates chassis type: C=96 in. or 106 in. Conventional Cab including Blazer, G=Chevy Van or Sportvan, K=106 in. Conventional cab 4 x 4, P=Forward-Control, L=Light Utility. The third symbol indicates engine as follows: D=250-cid/110-hp one-barrel L6, L=350-cid/165-hp four-barrel V-8, N=110-cid/80-hp two-barrel L4 (LUV), S=454-cid/245-hp four-barrel V-8 (C models only), T=292-cid/120-hp one-barrel L-6, U=305-cid/145-hp two-barrel V-8, Y=454-cid/240-hp four-barrel V-8 (P models only). The fourth symbol indicates series and tonnage: 1=1/2-ton, 2=3/4-ton, 3=1-ton. The fifth symbol indicates body type: 2=Chassis & Cowl, 3=Chassis-and-Cab, 4=Cab with pickup box or Hi-Cube van, 5=Panel or Panel Van, 6=Sportvan, Carryall Suburban (doors) 7=Motorhome chassis, 8=Utility. The sixth symbol indicates model-year: 7=1977 The seventh symbol indicates the assembly plant: A=Lakewood, Ga., B=Baltimore, Md., F=Flint, Mich., J=Janesville, Wis., S=St. Louis, Mo., U=Lordstown, Ohio, V=Pontiac, Mich. GMAD, Z=Fremont, Calif., 1=Oshawa, Canada, 3=GMAD, Detroit, Mich., 4=Scarborough, Ontario, Canada, 8=Fujisawa, Japan. Symbols 8-13 are the production sequence number. Starting number: 10001 Ending numbers not available.

1978: The first symbol indicates manufacturer: 1=Chevrolet Motor Div. The second symbol indicates chassis type: C=96 in. or 106 in. Conventional Cab including Blazer, G=Chevy Van or Sportvan, K=106 in. Conventional cab 4 x 4, P=Forward-Control, L=Light Utility. The third symbol indicates engine as follows: D=250-cid/one-barrel L6 (horsepower rated 115 for models with GVW under 6,000 lb., 100 for models with GVWs over 6,000 lb.), L=350-cid/165-hp four-barrel V-8, N=110-cid/80-hp two-barrel L4 (LUV), R=400-cid/175-hp four-barrel V-8, S=454-cid-hp four-barrel V-8 for C models only (horsepower rated 205 for models with GVW under 6,000 lb., 240 for models with GVWs over 6,000 lb.), T=292-cid/120-hp one-barrel L-6, U=305-cid two-barrel V-8 (horsepower rated 145 for models with GVW under 6,000 lb., 140 for models with GVWs over 6,000 lb.), Z=5.7 liter LF9 350-cid/120-hp diesel V-8. The fourth symbol indicates series and tonnage: 1=1/2-ton, 2=3/4-ton, 3=1-ton, 4=1/2-ton with heavy-duty suspension. The fifth symbol indicates body type: 2=Chassis-and-Cowl, 3=Chassis-and-Cab, 4=Cab with pickup box or van with Hi-Cube box, 5=Panel or Panel Van, 6=Sportvan, Carryall Suburban (doors) 7=Motorhome chassis, 8=Utility (Blazer). The sixth symbol indicates model-year: 8=1978. The seventh symbol indicates the assembly plant: A=Lakewood, Ga., B=Baltimore, Md., F=Flint, Mich., J=Janesville, Wis., S=St. Louis, Mo., U=Lordstown, Ohio, V=Pontiac, Mich. GMAD, Z=Fremont, Calif., 0=Pontiac (GMC) Michigan,

1=Oshawa or London, Ontario, Canada, 3=GMAD, Detroit, Mich., 4=Scarborough, Ontario, Canada, 8=Fujisawa, Japan. Symbols 8-13 are the production sequence number. Starting number: 10001 Ending numbers not available.

1979: The first symbol indicates manufacturer: 1=Chevrolet Motor Div. The second symbol indicates chassis type: C=106 in. Conventional Cab including Blazer, G=Chevy Van or Sportvan, K=106 in. Conventional cab 4 x 4, P=Forward-Control, L=LUV, R=LUV (4 x 4). The third symbol indicates engine as follows: D=250-cid (4.1 liter)/one-barrel L6 (horsepower rated 115 for models with GVW under 6,000 lb., 100 for models with GVWs over 6,000 lb.), L=350-cid (5.7 liter)/165-hp four-barrel V-8, M=350-cid (5.7 liter)/145-hp two-barrel V-8, N=110-cid (1.8 liter)/80-hp two-barrel L4 (LUV), R=400-cid (6.6 liter)/175-hp four-barrel V-8, S=454-cid (7.4 liter) four-barrel V-8 for C models only (horsepower rated 205 for models with GVW under 6,000 lb., 245 for models with GVWs over 6,000 lb.), T=292-cid (4.8 liter)/120-hp one-barrel L-6, U=305-cid (5.0 liter) two-barrel V-8 (horsepower rated 145 for models with GVW under 6,000 lb., 140 for models with GVWs over 6,000 lb.), Z=5.7 liter LF9 350-cid/120-hp diesel V-8. The fourth symbol indicates series and tonnage: 1=1/2-ton, 2=3/4-ton, 3=1-ton, 4=1/2-ton with heavy-duty suspension. The fifth symbol indicates body type: 2=Chassis & Cowl, 3=Chassis-and-Cab, 4=Cab with pickup box or van with Hi-Cube box, 5=Panel or Panel Van, 6=Sportvan, Carryall Suburban (doors) 7=Motorhome chassis, 8=Utility (Blazer). The sixth symbol indicates model-year: 9=1979. The seventh symbol indicates the assembly plant: A=Lakewood, Ga., B=Baltimore, Md., F=Flint, Mich., J=Janesville, Wis., S=St. Louis, Mo., U=Lordstown, Ohio, V=Pontiac, Mich. GMAD, Z=Fremont, Calif., 0=Pontiac (GMC) Michigan, 1=Oshawa or London, Ontario, Canada, 3=GMAD, Detroit, Mich., 4=Scarborough, Ontario, Canada, 8=Fujisawa, Japan. Symbols 8-13 are the production sequence number. Starting number: 10001 Ending numbers not available.

1980: The first symbol indicates manufacturer: 1=Chevrolet Motor Div. The second symbol indicates chassis type: C=106-in. Conventional Cab including Blazer, G=Chevy Van or Sportvan, K=106-in. Conventional cab 4 x 4, P=Forward-Control, L=LUV, R=LUV (4 x 4). The third symbol indicates engine as follows: D=250-cid (4.1-liter)/one-barrel L6 (horsepower rated 115 hp for models with GVW under 6,000 lb., 100 hp for models with GVWs over 6,000 lb.), G=305-cid (5.0-liter)/140-hp two-barrel V-8, L=350-cid (5.7-liter)/165-hp four-barrel V-8, M=350-cid (5.7-liter)/145-hp two-barrel V-8, N=110-cid (1.8-liter)/80-hp two-barrel L4 (LUV), P=350-cid (5.7-liter) 120-hp two-barrel V-8, R=400-cid (6.6-liter)/175-hp four-barrel V-8, S=454-cid (7.4-liter) four-barrel V-8 for C models only (horsepower rated 205 for models with GVW under 6,000 lb., 245 for models with GVWs over 6,000 lb.), T=292-cid (4.8-liter)/120-hp one-barrel L-6, W=454-cid (7.4-liter)/245-hp four-barrel V-8, X=400-cid (6.6-liter) 180-hp four-barrel V-8, Z=350-cid (5.7-liter)/120-hp diesel V-8. The fourth symbol indicates series and tonnage: 1=1/2-ton, 2=3/4-ton, 3=1-ton, 4=1/2-ton with heavy-duty suspension. The fifth symbol indicates body type: 2=Chassis-and-Cowl, 3=Chassis-and-Cab, 4=Cab with pickup box or van with Hi-Cube box, 5=Panel or Panel Van, 6=Sportvan, Suburban (doors) 7=Motorhome chassis, 8=Utility (Blazer). The sixth symbol indicates model year: A=1980. The seventh symbol indicates the assembly plant: A=Lakewood, Ga., B=Baltimore, Md., F=Flint, Mich., J=Janesville, Wis., S=St. Louis, Mo., U=Lordstown, Ohio, V=Pontiac, Mich. GMAD, Z=Fremont, Calif., 0=Pontiac (GMC) Michigan, 1=Oshawa or London, Ontario, Canada, 3=GMAD, Detroit, Mich., 4=Scarborough, Ontario, Canada, 8=Fujisawa, Japan. Symbols 8-13 are the production sequence number. Starting number: 10001 Ending numbers not available.

1981: The first symbol indicates country of origin: 1=U.S.A., 2=Canada, J=Japan. The second symbol indicates manufacturer: 8=Isuzu, G=General Motors Chevrolet Motor Div. The third symbol indicates brand: C=Chevrolet Truck, 8=Chevrolet MPV, A=Chevy Van with fourth seat, Z=LUV. The fourth symbol indicates GVWR and brake system: B=3,001-4,000 lb. (hydraulic brakes), C=4,001-5,000 lb. (hydraulic brakes), etc. The fifth symbol indicates line and chassis type: C=106-in. Conventional Cab 4 x 2 including Blazer, G=Chevy Van or Sportvan, K=106-in. Conventional cab 4 x 4 including Blazer, P=Forward-Control 4 x 2 , L=LUV 4 x 2 , R=LUV 4 x 4 , W=El Camino, Z=Special body. The sixth symbol indicates series: 1=1/2-ton, 2=3/4-ton, 3=1-ton, 8=1/2-ton El Camino, 9=Chassis-and-Short Sill Cowl. The seventh symbol indicates body type: 0=El Camino, 1=Hi-Cube and Cut-away Van, 2=Forward-Control, 3=Four-door

Cab, 4=Two-door cab, 5=Van, 6=Suburban (doors), 7=Motorhome chassis, 8=Utility (Blazer), 9=Stake. The eighth symbol indicates engine as follows: D=250-cid (4.1-liter)/one-barrel L6 (horsepower rated 115 for models with GVW under 6,000 lb., 100 for models with GVWs over 6,000 lb.), F/H=305-cid (5.0-liter) four-barrel V-8, G=305-cid (5.0-liter)/140-hp two-barrel V-8, L=350-cid (5.7-liter)/165-hp four-barrel V-8, M=350-cid (5.7-liter)/145-hp two-barrel V-8, N=110-cid (1.8-liter)/80-hp two-barrel L4 (LUV), P=350-cid (5.7-liter) 120 -hp two-barrel V-8, T=292-cid (4.8-liter)/120-hp one-barrel L-6, W=454-cid (7.4-liter)/245-hp four-barrel V-8, Z=350-cid (5.7-liter)/120-hp diesel V-8. The ninth symbol indicates model-year: B=1981. The tenth symbol indicates the assembly plant: A=Lakewood, Ga., B=Baltimore, Md., F=Flint, Mich., J=Janesville, Wis., S=St. Louis, Mo., U=Lordstown, Ohio, V=Pontiac, Mich. GMAD, Z=Fremont, Calif., 0=Pontiac (GMC) Michigan, 1=Oshawa or London, Ontario, Canada, 3=GMAD, Detroit, Mich., 4=Scarborough, Ontario, Canada, 8=Fujisawa, Japan. Symbols 11-17 are the production sequence number. Starting number: 10001 Ending numbers not available.

1982: The first symbol indicates country of origin: 1=U.S., 2=Canada, J=Japan. The second symbol indicates manufacturer: G=General Motors, 8=Isuzu. The third symbol indicates make: A=Chevrolet bus, B=Chevrolet (incomplete), C=Chevrolet truck, Y=LUV (incomplete), Z=LUV truck, 8=Chevy MPV. The fourth symbol indicates GVW rating (and brake system), B=3,001 lb.-4,000 lb. (hydraulic), C=4,001 lb.-5,000 lb. (hydraulic), etc. through K for hydraulic brakes. The fifth symbol indicates line and chassis type: C=Conventional cab (including Blazer and Suburban) 4 x 2, G=Chevy Van and Sportvan 4 x 2, K=Conventional cab (including Blazer and Suburban) 4 x 4, L=LUV 4 x 2, R=LUV 4 x 4, P=Forward-Control, S=Conventional cab 4 x 2, W=El Camino 4 x 2, Z=Special body 4 x 2. The sixth symbol indicates series: 1=1/2-ton, 2=3/4-ton, 3=1-ton, 8=El Camino. The seventh symbol indicates body type: 0=El Camino Pickup-Delivery, 1=Hi-Cube and Cutaway Vans, 2-Forward-Control, 3=Four-door cab, 4=Two-door cab, 5=Van, 6=Suburban, 7=Motorhome chassis, 8=Blazer Utility, 9=Stake. The eighth symbol indicated engine: [El Camino] A=231-cid (3.8-liter)/110-hp two-barrel V-6), K=229-cid (3.8-liter)/110-hp two-barrel V-6 for California, J=267-cid (4.4-liter)/115-hp two-barrel V-8, H=305-cid (5.0-liter)/145-hp four-barrel V-8, T=262-cid (4.3-liter)/85-hp diesel V-8. [Trucks] A=119-cid (1.9-liter)/82-hp two-barrel Isuzu four-cylinder, B=173-cid (2.8-liter)/110-hp two-barrel V-6, C or J=379-cid (6.2-liter)/110-hp diesel V-8, D=250-cid (4.1-liter)/105-hp two-barrel inline six-cylinder, F or H=305-cid (5.0-liter)/140-hp two-barrel V-8, L or M=350-cid (5.7-liter)/160-hp four-barrel V-8, N=110.8-cid (1.8-liter) two-barrel Isuzu four-cylinder, P=350-cid (5.7-liter)/145-hp two-barrel V-8, S=136.6-cid (2.2-liter)/58-hp Isuzu four-cylinder diesel, T=292-cid (4.8-liter)/120-hp one-barrel inline six-cylinder, W=454-cid (7.5-liter)/245-hp four-barrel V-8. The ninth symbol was a check digit. The 10th symbol indicated model-year: C=1982. The 11th symbol indicated the assembly plant: A=Lakewood, Ga., B=Baltimore, Md., C=Southgate, Calif., D=Doraville, Ga., E=Linden, N.J., F=Flint, Mich., G=Framingham, Mass., H=Flint, Mich., J=Janesville, Wis., K=Leeds, Mo., L=Van Nuys, Calif., M=Lansing, Mich., N=Norwood, Ohio, P=Pontiac, Mich., R=Arlington, Texas, S=St. Louis, Mo., T=Tarrytown, N.Y., V=GMC, Pontiac, Mich., W=Willow Run, Mich., X=Fairfax, Va., Y=Wilmington, Dela., Z=Fremont, Calif., 0=GMAD, Pontiac, Mich., 1=Oshawa, Canada, 2=Moraine, Ohio, 2=Ste. Therese, Quebec, Canada, 3=Chevrolet-Detroit, Mich., 3=St. Eustache, Quebec, Canada, 4=Orion Plant, Pontiac, Mich., 4=Scarborough, Ontario, Canada, 5=Bowling Green, Ken., 5=London, Ontario, Canada, 6=Oklahoma City, Okla., 7=Lordstown, Ohio, 8=Shreveport, La., 8=Fujisawa, Japan, 9=Cadillac, Detroit, Mich. (Note: Trucks were not built at all factories). Symbols 12-17 were the production sequence number starting at 100001. Ending numbers not available.

1983: The first symbol indicates country of origin: 1=U.S., 2=Canada, J=Japan. The second symbol indicates manufacturer: G=General Motors, 8=Isuzu. The third symbol indicates make: A=Chevrolet bus, B=Chevrolet (incomplete), C=Chevrolet truck, Y=LUV (incomplete), Z=LUV truck, 8=Chevy MPV. The fourth symbol indicates GVW rating (and brake system): B=3,001 lb.-4,000 lb. (hydraulic), C=4,001 lb.-5,000 lb. (hydraulic), etc. through K for models with hydraulic brakes. The fifth symbol indicates line and chassis type: C=Conventional cab (including Blazer and Suburban) 4 x 2, G=Chevy Van and Sportvan 4 x 2, K=Conventional cab (including Blazer and Suburban) 4 x 4, L=LUV 4 x 2, R=LUV 4 x 4, P=Forward-Control,

S=Conventional Cab 4 x 2, W=El Camino 4 x 2, Z=Special body 4 x 2. The sixth symbol indicates series: 1=1/2-ton, 2=3/4-ton, 3=1-ton, 8=El Camino. The seventh symbol indicates body type: 0=El Camino Pickup-Delivery, 1=Hi-Cube and Cutaway Vans, 2-Forward-Control, 3=Four-door cab, 4=Two-door cab, 5=Van, 6=Suburban, 7=Motorhome chassis, 8=Blazer Utility, 9=Stake. The eighth symbol indicates engine: [El Camino] A=231-cid (3.8-liter)/110-hp two-barrel V-6), K=229-cid (3.8-liter)/110-hp two-barrel V-6 for California, H=305-cid (5.0-liter)/145-hp four-barrel V-8, T=262-cid (4.3-liter)/85-hp diesel V-8, N=350-cid (5.7-liter)/105-hp diesel V-8. [Trucks] A=119-cid (1.9-liter)/82-hp two-barrel Isuzu four-cylinder, B=173-cid (2.8-liter)/110-hp two-barrel V-6, C or J=379-cid (6.2-liter)/110-hp diesel V-8, D=250-cid (4.1-liter)/105-hp two-barrel inline six-cylinder, F or H=305-cid (5.0-liter)/140-hp two-barrel V-8, L or M=350-cid (5.7-liter)/160-hp four-barrel V-8, P=350-cid (5.7-liter)/145-hp two-barrel V-8, S=136.6-cid (2.2-liter)/58-hp Isuzu four-cylinder diesel, T=292-cid (4.8-liter)/120-hp one-barrel inline six-cylinder, W=454-cid (7.5-liter)/245-hp four-barrel V-8. The ninth symbol was a check digit. The 10th symbol indicated model-year: D=1983. The 11th symbol indicated the assembly plant: A=Lakewood, Ga., B=Baltimore, Md., C=Southgate, Calif., D=Doraville, Ga., E=Linden, N.J., F=Flint, Mich., G=Framingham, Mass., H=Flint, Mich., J=Janesville, Wis., K=Leeds, Mo., L=Van Nuys, Calif., M=Lansing, Mich., N=Norwood, Ohio, P=Pontiac, Mich., R=Arlington, Texas, S=St. Louis, Mo., T=Tarrytown, N.Y., V=GMC, Pontiac, Mich., W=Willow Run, Mich., X=Fairfax, Va., Y=Wilmington, Dela., Z=Fremont, Calif., O=GMAD, Pontiac, Mich., 1=Oshawa, Canada, 2=Moraine, Ohio, 2=Ste. Therese, Quebec, Canada, 3=Chevrolet-Detroit, Mich., 3=St. Eustache, Quebec, Canada, 4=Orion Plant, Pontiac, Mich., 4=Scarborough, Ontario, Canada, 5=Bowling Green, Ken., 5=London, Ontario, Canada, 6=Oklahoma City, Okla., 7=Lordstown, Ohio, 8=Shreveport, La., 8=Fujisawa, Japan, 9=Cadillac, Detroit, Mich. (Note: Trucks were not built at all factories). Symbols 12-17 were the production sequence number starting at 100001. Ending numbers not available.

1984: The first symbol indicates country of origin: 1=U.S., 2=Canada, J=Japan. The second symbol indicates manufacturer: G=General Motors, 8=Isuzu. The third symbol indicates make: A=Chevrolet bus, B=Chevrolet (incomplete), C=Chevrolet truck, Y=LUV (incomplete), Z=LUV truck, 8=Chevy MPV. The fourth symbol indicates GVW rating (and brake system), B=3,001 lb.-4,000 lb. (hydraulic), C=4,001 lb.-5,000 lb. (hydraulic), etc. through K for hydraulic brakes. The fifth symbol indicates line and chassis type: C=Conventional cab (including Blazer and Suburban) 4 x 2, G=Chevy Van and Sportvan 4 x 2, K=Conventional cab (including Blazer and Suburban) 4 x 4, L=LUV 4 x 2, R=LUV 4 x 4, P=Forward-Control, S=Conventional Cab 4 x 2, W=El Camino 4 x 2, Z=Special body 4 x 2. The sixth symbol indicates series: 1=1/2-ton, 2=3/4-ton, 3=1-ton, 8=El Camino. The seventh symbol indicates body type: 0=El Camino Pickup-Delivery, 1=Hi-Cube and Cutaway Vans, 2-Forward-Control, 3=Four-door cab, 4=Two-door cab, 5=Van, 6=Suburban, 7=Motorhome chassis, 8=Blazer Utility, 9=Stake. The eighth symbol indicates engine: [El Camino] A=231-cid (3.8-liter)/110-hp two-barrel V-6), K=229-cid (3.8-liter)/110-hp two-barrel V-6 for California, H=305-cid (5.0-liter)/145-hp four-barrel V-8, T=262-cid (4.3-liter)/85-hp diesel V-8, N=350-cid (5.7-liter)/105-hp diesel V-8. [Trucks] A=119-cid (1.9-liter)/82-hp two-barrel Isuzu four-cylinder, B=173-cid (2.8-liter)/110-hp two-barrel V-6, C or J=379-cid (6.2-liter)/110-hp diesel V-8, D=250-cid (4.1-liter)/105-hp two-barrel inline six-cylinder, F or H=305-cid (5.0-liter)/140-hp two-barrel V-8, L or M=350-cid (5.7-liter)/160-hp four-barrel V-8, P=350-cid (5.7-liter)/145-hp two-barrel V-8, S=136.6-cid (2.2-liter)/58-hp Isuzu four-cylinder diesel, T=292-cid (4.8-liter)/120-hp one-barrel inline six-cylinder, W=454-cid (7.5-liter)/245-hp four-barrel V-8. The ninth symbol was a check digit. The 10th symbol indicated model-year: E=1984. The 11th symbol indicated the assembly plant: A=Lakewood, Ga., B=Baltimore, Md., C=Southgate, Calif., D=Doraville, Ga., E=Linden, N.J., F=Flint, Mich., G=Framingham, Mass., H=Flint, Mich., J=Janesville, Wis., K=Leeds, Mo., L=Van Nuys, Calif., M=Lansing, Mich., N=Norwood, Ohio, P=Pontiac, Mich., R=Arlington, Texas, S=St. Louis, Mo., T=Tarrytown, N.Y., V=GMC, Pontiac, Mich., W=Willow Run, Mich., X=Fairfax, Va., Y=Wilmington, Dela., Z=Fremont, Calif., O=GMAD, Pontiac, Mich., 1=Oshawa, Canada, 2=Moraine, Ohio, 2=Ste. Therese, Quebec, Canada, 3=Chevrolet-Detroit, Mich., 3=St. Eustache, Quebec, Canada, 4=Orion Plant, Pontiac, Mich., 4=Scarborough, Ontario, Canada, 5=Bowling Green, Ken., 5=London, Ontario, Canada, 6=Oklahoma City, Okla., 7=Lordstown, Ohio, 8=Shreveport, La., 8=Fujisawa, Japan, 9=Cadillac, Detroit, Mich. (Note:

Trucks were not built at all factories). Symbols 12-17 were the production sequence number starting at 100001. Ending numbers not available.

1985: The first symbol indicates country of origin: 1=U.S., 2=Canada, J=Japan. The second symbol indicates manufacturer: G=General Motors, 8=Isuzu. The third symbol indicates make: A=Chevrolet bus, B=Chevrolet (incomplete), C=Chevrolet truck, Y=LUV (incomplete), Z=LUV truck, 8=Chevy MPV. The fourth symbol indicates GVW rating (and brake system), B=3,001 lb.-4,000 lb. (hydraulic), C=4,001 lb.-5,000 lb. (hydraulic), etc. through K for models with hydraulic brakes. The fifth symbol indicates line, and chassis type: C=Conventional cab (including Blazer, and Suburban) 4 x 2, G=Chevy Van, and Sportvan 4 x 2, K=Conventional cab (including Blazer, and Suburban) 4 x 4, L=LUV 4 x 2, R=LUV 4 x 4, P=Forward-Control, S=Conventional Cab 4 x 2, W=El Camino 4 x 2, Z=Special body 4 x 2. The sixth symbol indicates series: 1=1/2-ton, 2=3/4-ton, 3=1-ton, 8=El Camino. The seventh symbol indicates body type: 0=El Camino Pickup-Delivery, 1=Hi-Cube, and Cutaway Vans, 2-Forward-Control, 3=Four-door cab, 4=Two-door cab, 5=Van, 6=Suburban, 7=Motorhome chassis, 8=Blazer Utility, 9=Stake. The eighth symbol indicated the engine. Engine codes were generally the same as 1983. The ninth symbol was a check digit. The 10th symbol indicated model-year: F=1985. The 11th symbol indicated the assembly plant: A=Lakewood, Ga., B=Baltimore, Md., C=Southgate, Calif., D=Doraville, Ga., E=Linden, N.J., F=Flint, Mich., G=Framingham, Mass., H=Flint, Mich., J=Janesville, Wis., K=Leeds, Mo., L=Van Nuys, Calif., M=Lansing, Mich., N=Norwood, Ohio, P=Pontiac, Mich., R=Arlington, Texas, S=St. Louis, Mo., T=Tarrytown, N.Y., V=GMC, Pontiac, Mich., W=Willow Run, Mich., X=Fairfax, Va., Y=Wilmington, Dela., Z=Fremont, Calif., O=GMAD, Pontiac, Mich., 1=Oshawa, Canada, 2=Moraine, Ohio, 2=Ste. Therese, Quebec, Canada, 3=Chevrolet-Detroit, Mich., 3=St. Eustache, Quebec, Canada, 4=Orion Plant, Pontiac, Mich., 4=Scarborough, Ontario, Canada, 5=Bowling Green, Ken., 5=London, Ontario, Canada, 6=Oklahoma City, Okla., 7=Lordstown, Ohio, 8=Shreveport, La., 8=Fujisawa, Japan, 9=Cadillac, Detroit, Mich. (Note: Trucks were not built at all factories). Symbols 12-17 were the production sequence number starting at 100001. Ending numbers not available.

1986: The first symbol indicates country of origin: 1=U.S., 2=Canada, J=Japan. The second symbol indicates manufacturer: G=General Motors, 8=Isuzu. The third symbol indicates make: A=Chevrolet bus, B=Chevrolet (incomplete), C=Chevrolet truck, Y=LUV (incomplete), Z=LUV truck, 8=Chevy MPV. The fourth symbol indicates GVW rating (and brake system), B=3,001 lb.-4,000 lb. (hydraulic), C=4,001 lb.-5,000 lb. (hydraulic), etc. through K for hydraulic brakes. The fifth symbol indicates line and chassis type: C=Conventional cab (including Blazer and Suburban) 4 x 2, G=Chevy Van and Sportvan 4 x 2, K=Conventional cab (including Blazer and Suburban) 4 x 4, L=LUV 4 x 2, R=LUV 4 x 4, P=Forward-Control, S=Conventional cab 4 x 2, W=El Camino 4 x 2, Z=Special body 4 x 2. The sixth symbol indicates series: 1=1/2-ton, 2=3/4-ton, 3=1-ton, 8=El Camino. The seventh symbol indicates body type: 0=El Camino Pickup-Delivery, 1=Hi-Cube and Cutaway Vans, 2-Forward-Control, 3=Four-door cab, 4=Two-door cab, 5=Van, 6=Suburban, 7=Motorhome chassis, 8=Blazer Utility, 9=Stake. The eighth symbol indicated engine. Engine codes (all light trucks) C=6.2-liter diesel V-8, J=6.2-liter diesel V-8, E=2.5-liter fuel-injected I4, H=5.0-liter four-barrel V-8, K=5.7-liter throttle body injected V-8, M=5.7-liet four-barrel V-8, N=7.4-liter throttle body injected V-8, R=2.8-liter fuel-injected V-6, W=7.4-liter four-barrel V-8 and Z=4.3-liter throttle body injected four. The ninth symbol was a check digit, The 10th symbol indicated model year: G=1986. The 11th symbol indicated the assembly plant: A=Lakewood, Ga., B=Baltimore, Md. C=Southgate, Calif., D=Doraville, Ga., E=Linden, N.J., F=Flint, Mich., G=Framingham, Mass., H=Flint, Mich., J=Janesville, Wis., K=Leeds, Mo., L=Van Nuys, Calif., M=Lansing, Mich., N=Norwood, Ohio, P=Pontiac, Mich., R=Arlington, Texas, S=St. Louis, Mo., T=Tarrytown, N.Y., V=GMC, Pontiac, Mich., W=Willow Run, Mich., X=Fairfax, Va., Y=Wilmington, Dela., Z=Fremont, Calif., O=GMAD, Pontiac, Mich., 1=Oshawa, Canada, 2=Moraine, Ohio, 2=Ste. Therese, Quebec, Canada, 3=Chevrolet-Detroit, Mich., 3=St. Eustache, Quebec, Canada, 4=Orion Plant, Pontiac, Mich., 4=Scarborough, Ontario, Canada, 5=Bowling Green, Ken., 5=London, Ontario, Canada, 6=Oklahoma City, Okla., 7=Lordstown, Ohio, 8=Shreveport, La., 8=Fujisawa, Japan, 9=Cadillac, Detroit, Mich. (Note: Trucks were not built at all factories). Symbols 12-17 were the production sequence number starting at 100001. Ending numbers not available.

1987: The first symbol indicates country of origin: 1=U.S., 2=Canada, J=Japan. The second symbol indicates manufacturer: G=General Motors, 8=Isuzu. The third symbol indicates make: C=Chevrolet truck, 8=Chevy MPV. The fourth symbol indicates GVW rating and brake system: B=3,001 lb.-4,000 lb. hydraulic, C=4,001 lb.-5,000 lb. hydraulic, etc. through K for hydraulic brakes. The fifth symbol indicates line and chassis type: C/R=Conventional cab (including Blazer and Suburban) 4 x 2, G=Chevy Van and Sportvan 4 x 2, K/V=Conventional cab (including Blazer and Suburban) 4 x 4, P=Forward-Control, S=Conventional Cab 4 x 2, W=El Camino 4 x 2, Z=Special body 4 x 2. The sixth symbol indicates series: 1=1/2-ton, 2=3/4-ton, 3=1-ton, 8=El Camino. The seventh symbol indicates body type: 0=El Camino Pickup-Delivery, 1=Hi-Cube and Cutaway Vans, 2-Forward-Control, 3=Four-door cab, 4=Two-door cab, 5=Van, 6=Suburban, 7=Motorhome chassis, 8=Blazer Utility, 9=Stake. The eighth symbol identifies the engine [Chevrolet engines] C=6.2-liter/130 hp diesel V-8, H=5.0-liter V-8, J=6.2-liter/148 hp diesel V-8, K=5.7-liter V-8, M=5.7-liter V-8, N=7.4-liter V-8, R=2.8-liter V-6, T=4.3-liter V-6, W=7.4-liter V-8, Z=4.3-liter V-6. [GM engines] A=5.7-liter V-8, [Pontiac engine] E=2.5-liter L4. The ninth symbol was a check digit. The 10th symbol indicated model year: H=1987. The 11th symbol indicated the assembly plant: A=Lakewood, Ga., B=Baltimore, Md., C=Southgate, Calif., D=Doraville, Ga., E=Linden, N.J., F=Flint, Mich., G=Framingham, Mass., H=Flint, Mich., J=Janesville, Wis., K=Leeds, Mo., L=Van Nuys, Calif., M=Lansing, Mich., N=Norwood, Ohio, P=Pontiac, Mich., R=Arlington, Texas, S=St. Louis, Mo., T=Tarrytown, N.Y., V=GMC, Pontiac, Mich., W=Willow Run, Mich., X=Fairfax, Va., Y=Wilmington, Dela., Z=Fremont, Calif., O=GMAD, Pontiac, Mich., 1=Oshawa, Canada, 2=Moraine, Ohio, 2=Ste. Therese, Quebec, Canada, 3=Chevrolet-Detroit, Mich., 3=St. Eustache, Quebec, Canada, 4=Orion Plant, Pontiac, Mich., 4=Scarborough, Ontario, Canada, 5=Bowling Green, Ken., 5=London, Ontario, Canada, 6=Oklahoma City, Okla., 7=Lordstown, Ohio, 8=Shreveport, La., 8=Fujisawa, Japan, 9=Cadillac, Detroit, Mich. Note: Trucks were not built at all factories. Symbols 12-17 were the production sequence number starting at 100001. Ending numbers not available.

1988: The first symbol indicates country of origin: 1=U.S., 2=Canada, 3=Mexico. The second symbol indicates manufacturer: G=General Motors. The third symbol indicates make: A=Chevy Bus, B=Chevy Incomplete, C=Chevrolet truck, 8=Chevy MPV. The fourth symbol indicates GVW rating and brake system: B=3,001 lb.-4,000 lb. hydraulic, C=4,001 lb.-5,000 lb. hydraulic, etc. through K for hydraulic brakes. The fifth symbol indicates line and chassis type: C/R=Conventional cab GMT-400 4 x 2, D=Military Truck 4 x 4, G=Chevy Van and Sportvan 4 x 2, K/V=Conventional cab GMT-400 4 x 4, P=Forward-Control 4 x 2, S=Small Conventional Cab 4 x 2, T=Small Conventional Cab 4 x 2, Z=Special body 4 x 2. The sixth symbol indicates series: 1=1/2-ton, 2=3/4-ton, 3=1-ton. The seventh symbol indicates body type: 0=Chassis only, 1=Hi-Cube and Cutaway Vans, 2-Forward-Control, 3=Four-door cab, 4=Two-door cab, 5=Van, 6=Suburban, 7=Motorhome chassis, 8=Blazer Utility, 9=Extended cab. The eighth symbol identifies the engine [Chevrolet engines] C=6.2-liter/130 hp diesel V-8, E=2.5-liter fuel-injected I4, H=5.0-liter fuel-injected V-8, J=6.2-liter/148 hp diesel V-8, K=5.7-liter fuel-injected V-8, M=5.7-liter four-barrel V-8, N=7.4-liter fuel-injected V-8, R=2.8-liter fuel-injected V-6, T=4.3-liter one-barrel V-6, W=7.4-liter four-barrel V-8, Z=4.3-liter fuel-injected V-6, 5=4.5-liter fuel-injected V-8. The ninth symbol was a check digit. The 10th symbol indicated model year: I=1988. The 11th symbol indicated the assembly plant: A=Lakewood, Ga., B=Baltimore, Md., C=Lansing, Mich. D=Doraville, Ga., E=Linden, N.J., F=Flint, Mich., G=Framingham, Mass., H=Flint, Mich., J=Janesville, Wis., K=Leeds, Mo., L=Van Nuys, Calif., M=Lansing, Mich., N=Norwood, Ohio, P=Pontiac, Mich., R=Arlington, Texas, S=St. Louis, Mo., T=Terrytown, N.Y., V=GMC, Pontiac, Mich., W=Willow Run, Mich., X=Fairfax, Va., Y=Wilmington, Dela., Z=Fremont, Calif., O=GMAD, Pontiac, Mich., 1=Oshawa, Canada, 2=Moraine, Ohio, 2=Moraine, Ohio, 3=Detroit Truck & Coach, Mich., 3=St. Eustache, Quebec, Canada, 4=Orion Plant, Pontiac, Mich., 4=Scarborough, Ontario, Canada, 5=Bowling Green, Ken., 5=London, Ontario, Canada, 6=Oklahoma City, Okla., 7=Lordstown, Ohio, 8=Shreveport, La., 9=Cadillac, Detroit, Mich. Note: Trucks were not built at all factories. Symbols 12-17 were the production sequence number starting at 100001. Ending numbers not available.

1989: The first symbol indicates country of origin: 1=U.S., 2=Canada, 4=U.S. The second symbol indicates manufacturer: G=General Motors, G=Suzuki. The third symbol indicates make: A=Chevy Bus, B=Chevy Incomplete, C=Chevrolet truck, H=Chevy MPV. The fourth symbol indicates GVW rating and brake system: B=3,001 lb.-4,000 lb. hydraulic, C=4,001 lb.-5,000 lb. hydraulic, etc. through K for hydraulic brakes. The fifth symbol indicates line and chassis type: B=Special Body, C/R=Conventional cab GMT-400 4 x 2, D=Military Truck 4 x 4, G=Chevy Van and Sportvan 4 x 2, K/V=Conventional cab GMT-400 4 x 4, M=Small van 4 x 2, P=Forward-Control 4 x 2, S=Small Conventional Cab 4 x 2, T=Small Conventional Cab 4 x 2, Z=Special body 4 x 2. The sixth symbol indicates series: 1=1/2-ton, 2=3/4-ton, 3=1-ton. The seventh symbol indicates body type: 0=Chassis only, 1=Hi-Cube and Cutaway Vans, 2-Forward-Control, 3=Four-door cab, 4=Two-door cab, 5=Van, 6=Suburban, 7=Motorhome chassis, 8=Blazer Utility, 9=Extended cab. The eighth symbol identifies the engine [Chevrolet engines] C=6.2-liter/130 hp diesel V-8, E=2.5-liter fuel-injected I4, H=5.0-liter fuel-injected V-8, J=6.2-liter/148 hp diesel V-8, K=5.7-liter fuel-injected V-8, N=7.4-liter fuel-injected V-8, R=2.8-liter fuel-injected V-6, T=4.8-liter one-barrel V-6, U=I-6, W=7.4-liter four-barrel V-8, Y=5.0-liter V-8 four-barrel, Z=4.3-liter fuel-injected V-6, 5=4.5-liter fuel-injected V-8. The ninth symbol was a check digit. The 10th symbol indicated model year: K=1989. The 11th symbol indicated the assembly plant: A=Lakewood, Ga., B=Baltimore, Md., C=Lansing, Mich. D=Doraville, Ga., E=Linden, N.J., F=Flint, Mich., G=Framingham, Mass., H=Flint, Mich., J=Janesville, Wis., K–Leeds, Mo., L=Van Nuys, Calif., M=Lansing, Mich., N=Norwood, Ohio, P=Pontiac, Mich., R=Arlington, Texas, S=St. Louis, Mo., T=Terrytown, N.Y., V=GMC, Pontiac, Mich., W=Willow Run, Mich., X=Fairfax, Va., Y=Wilmington, Dela., Z=Fremont, Calif., O=GMAD, Pontiac, Mich., 1=Oshawa, Canada, 2=Moraine, Ohio, 2=Moraine, Ohio, 3=Detroit Truck & Coach, Mich., 3=St. Eustache, Quebec, Canada, 4=Orion Plant, Pontiac, Mich., 4=Scarborough, Ontario, Canada, 5=Bowling Green, Ken., 5=London, Ontario, Canada, 6=Oklahoma City, Okla., 7=Lordstown, Ohio, 8=Shreveport, La., 9=Cadillac, Detroit, Mich. Note: Trucks were not built at all factories. Symbols 12-17 were the production sequence number starting at 100001. Ending numbers not available.

1990: The first symbol indicates country of origin: 1=U.S., 2=Canada, 4=U.S. The second symbol indicates manufacturer: G=General Motors, G=Suzuki. The third symbol indicates make: A=Chevy Bus, B=Chevy Incomplete, C=Chevrolet truck, H=Chevy MPV. The fourth symbol indicates GVW rating and brake system: B=3,001 lb.-4,000 lb. hydraulic, C=4,001 lb.-5,000 lb. hydraulic, etc. through K for hydraulic brakes. The fifth symbol indicates line and chassis type: B=Special Body, C/R=Conventional cab GMT-400 4 x 2, D=Military Truck 4 x 4, G=Chevy Van and Sportvan 4 x 2, K/V=Conventional cab GMT-400 4 x 4, M=Small van 4 x 2, P=Forward-Control 4 x 2, S=Small Conventional Cab 4 x 2, T=Small Conventional Cab 4 x 2, Z=Special body 4 x 2. The sixth symbol indicates series: 1=1/2-ton, 2=3/4-ton, 3=1-ton. The seventh symbol indicates body type: 0=Chassis only, 1=Hi-Cube and Cutaway Vans, 2-Forward-Control, 3=Four-door cab, 4=Two-door cab, 5=Van, 6=Suburban, 7=Motorhome chassis, 8=Blazer Utility, 9=Extended cab. The eighth symbol identifies the engine [Chevrolet engines] C=6.2-liter/130 hp diesel V-8, H=5.0-liter V-8, J=6.2-liter/148 hp diesel V-8, K=5.7-liter V-8, N=7.4-liter V-8, R=2.8-liter V-6, Z=4.3-liter V-6. [GM engines] A=2.5-liter L4, B=4.3-liter V-6, D=3.1-liter V-6, M=7.0-liter V-8. [Pontiac engine] E=2.5-liter L4. The ninth symbol was a check digit. The 10th symbol indicated model year: L=1990. The 11th symbol indicated the assembly plant: A=Lakewood, Ga., B=Baltimore, Md., C=Lansing, Mich. D=Doraville, Ga., E=Linden, N.J., F=Flint, Mich., G=Framingham, Mass., H=Flint, Mich., J=Janesville, Wis., K=Leeds, Mo., L=Van Nuys, Calif., M=Lansing, Mich., N=Norwood, Ohio, P=Pontiac, Mich., R=Arlington, Texas, S=St. Louis, Mo., T=Terrytown, N.Y., V=GMC, Pontiac, Mich., W=Willow Run, Mich., X=Fairfax, Va., Y=Wilmington, Dela., Z=Fremont, Calif., O=GMAD, Pontiac, Mich., 1=Oshawa, Canada, 2=Moraine, Ohio, 2=Moraine, Ohio, 3=Detroit Truck & Coach, Mich., 3=St. Eustache, Quebec, Canada, 4=Orion Plant, Pontiac, Mich., 4=Scarborough, Ontario, Canada, 5=Bowling Green, Ken., 5=London, Ontario, Canada, 6=Oklahoma City, Okla., 7=Lordstown, Ohio, 8=Shreveport, La., 9=Cadillac, Detroit, Mich. Note: Trucks were not built at all factories. Symbols 12-17 were the production sequence number starting at 100001. Ending numbers not available.

1991: The first symbol indicates country of origin: 1=U.S., 2=Canada, 4=U.S. The second symbol indicates manufacturer: G=General Motors, G=Suzuki.

The third symbol indicates make: A=Chevy Bus, B=Chevy Incomplete, C=Chevrolet truck, H=Chevy MPV. The fourth symbol indicates GVW rating and brake system: B=3,001 lb.-4,000 lb. hydraulic, C=4,001 lb.-5,000 lb. hydraulic, etc. through K for hydraulic brakes. The fifth symbol indicates line and chassis type: B=Special Body, C/R=Conventional cab GMT-400 4 x 2, D=Military Truck 4 x 4, G=Chevy Van and Sportvan 4 x 2, K/V=Conventional cab GMT-400 4 x 4, M=Small van 4 x 2, P=Forward-Control 4 x 2, S=Small Conventional Cab 4 x 2, T=Small Conventional Cab 4 x 2, Z=Special body 4 x 2. The sixth symbol indicates series: 1=1/2-ton, 2=3/4-ton, 3=1-ton. The seventh symbol indicates body type: 0=Chassis only, 1=Hi-Cube and Cutaway Vans, 2-Forward-Control, 3=Four-door cab, 4=Two-door cab, 5=Van, 6=Suburban, 7=Motorhome chassis, 8=Blazer Utility, 9=Extended cab. The eighth symbol identifies the engine [Chevrolet engines] C=6.2-liter/130 hp diesel V-8, H=5.0-liter V-8, J=6.2-liter/148 hp diesel V-8, K=5.7-liter V-8, N=7.4-liter V-8, R=2.8-liter V-6, Z=4.3-liter V-6. The ninth symbol was a check digit. The 10th symbol indicated model year: M=1991. The 11th symbol indicated the assembly plant: A=Lakewood, Ga., B=Baltimore, Md., C=Lansing, Mich. D=Doraville, Ga., E=Linden, N.J., F=Flint, Mich., F=Fairfax II, Va., H=Flint, Mich., J=Janesville, Wis., K=Kosai, Japan, L=Van Nuys, Calif., M=Lansing, Mich., R=Arlington, Texas, R=Ramos, T=Terrytown, N.Y., U=Hamtramck, W=Willow Run, Mich., Y=Wilmington, Dela., Z=Fremont, Calif., O=GMAD, Pontiac, Mich., 1=Oshawa, Canada, 2=Moraine, Ohio, 2=Moraine, Ohio, 3=Detroit Truck & Coach, Mich., 3=St. Eustache, Quebec, Canada, 4=Orion Plant, Pontiac, Mich., 4=Scarborough, Ontario, Canada, 5=Bowling Green, Ken., 5=London, Ontario, Canada, 6=Oklahoma City, Okla., 7=Lordstown, Ohio, 8=Shreveport, La., 9=Cadillac, Detroit, Mich. Note: Trucks were not built at all factories. Symbols 12-17 were the production sequence number starting at 100001. Ending numbers not available.

1992: The first symbol indicates country of origin: 1=U.S., 2=Canada, 3=Mexican built, 4=U.S. and 5=Japan built. The second symbol indicates manufacturer: C=Cami GM of Canada or Suzuki, G=General Motors, G=Suzuki and 8-Isuzu. The third symbol indicates make: A=Chevy Bus, B=Chevy Incomplete, C=Chevrolet truck, N=Chevy MPV. The fourth symbol indicates GVW rating and brake system: B=3,001 lb.-4,000 lb. hydraulic, C=4,001 lb.-5,000 lb. hydraulic, etc. through K for hydraulic brakes. The fifth symbol indicates line and chassis type: B=Special Body, C/R=Conventional cab GMT-400 4 x 2, D=Military Truck 4 x 4, E=Compact cab, G=Chevy Van and Sportvan 4 x 2, K/V=Conventional cab GMT-400 4 x 4, L=Small van 4 x 4, M=Small van 4 x 2, P=Forward-Control 4 x 2, S=Small Conventional Cab 4 x 2, T=Small Conventional Cab 4 x 2, U=All-Purpose Vehicle (APV) 4 x 2, Z=Special body 4 x 2. The sixth symbol indicates series: 1=1/2-ton, 2=3/4-ton, 3=1-ton, O=All-Purpose Vehicle.. The seventh symbol indicates body type: 0=Chassis only, 1=Hi-Cube and Cutaway Vans, 2-Forward-Control, 3=Four-door cab, 4=Two-door cab, 5=Van, 6=Suburban, 7=Motorhome chassis, 8=Blazer Utility, 9=Extended cab. The eighth symbol identifies the engine [Chevrolet engines] A=2.5-liter L4, B=4.9-liter V-8, C=6.2-liter/130 hp diesel V-8, D=3.1-liter V-6, E=5.0-liter V-8, F=6.5-liter V-8, H=5.0-liter V-8, J=6.2-liter/148 hp diesel V-8, K=5.7-liter V-8, L=3.8-liter V-6, N=7.4-liter V-8, R=2.8-liter V-6, U=1.6-liyter L4, W=4.3-liter V-6, Z=4.3-liter V-6. The ninth symbol was a check digit. The 10th symbol indicated model year: N=1992. The 11th symbol indicated the assembly plant: A=Lakewood, Ga., B=Baltimore, Md., C=Lansing, Mich. D=Doraville, Ga., E=Linden, N.J., F=Flint, Mich., F=Fairfax II, Va., H=Flint, Mich., J=Janesville, Wis., K=Kosai, Japan, L=Van Nuys, Calif., M=Lansing, Mich., R=Arlington, Texas, R=Ramos, T=Terrytown, N.Y., U=Hamtramck, W=Willow Run, Mich., Y=Wilmington, Dela., Z=Fremont, Calif., O=GMAD, Pontiac, Mich., 1=Oshawa, Canada, 2=Moraine, Ohio, 2=Moraine, Ohio, 3=Detroit Truck & Coach, Mich., 3=St. Eustache, Quebec, Canada, 4=Orion Plant, Pontiac, Mich., 4=Scarborough, Ontario, Canada, 5=Bowling Green, Ken., 5=London, Ontario, Canada, 6=Oklahoma City, Okla., 7=Lordstown, Ohio, 8=Shreveport, La., 9=Cadillac, Detroit, Mich. Note: Trucks were not built at all factories. Symbols 12-17 were the production sequence number starting at 100001. Ending numbers not available.

1993: The first symbol indicates country of origin: 1=U.S., 2=Canada, 3=Mexican built, 4=U.S. and 5=Japan built. The second symbol indicates manufacturer: C=Cami GM of Canada or Suzuki, G=General Motors, G=Suzuki and 8-Isuzu. The third symbol indicates make: A=Chevy Bus, B=Chevy Incomplete, C=Chevrolet truck, N=Chevy MPV.

The fourth symbol indicates GVW rating and brake system: B=3,001 lb.-4,000 lb. hydraulic, C=4,001 lb.-5,000 lb. hydraulic, etc. through K for hydraulic brakes. The fifth symbol indicates line and chassis type: B=Special Body, C/R=Conventional cab GMT-400 4 x 2, D=Military Truck 4 x 4, E=Compact cab, G=Chevy Van and Sportvan 4 x 2, K/V=Conventional cab GMT-400 4 x 4, L=Small van 4 x 4, M=Small van 4 x 2, P=Forward-Control 4 x 2, S=Small Conventional Cab 4 x 2, T=Small Conventional Cab 4 x 2, U=All-Purpose Vehicle (APV) 4 x 2, Z=Special body 4 x 2. The sixth symbol indicates series: 1=1/2-ton, 2=3/4-ton, 3=1-ton, O=All-Purpose Vehicle.. The seventh symbol indicates body type: 0=Chassis only, 1=Hi-Cube and Cutaway Vans, 2-Forward-Control, 3=Four-door cab, 4=Two-door cab, 5=Van, 6=Suburban, 7=Motorhome chassis, 8=Blazer Utility, 9=Extended cab. The eighth symbol identifies the engine [Chevrolet engines] C=6.2-liter/130 hp diesel V-8, H=5.0-liter V-8, J=6.2-liter/148 hp diesel V-8, K=5.7-liter V-8, N=7.4-liter V-8, R=2.8-liter V-6, Z=4.3-liter V-6. [GM engines] A= 5.7-liter V-8 or 2.5-liter L4, D=3.1-liter V-6, F=6.5-liter diesel V-8, L=3.8-liter V-6, W=4.3-liter V-6. The ninth symbol was a check digit. The 10th symbol indicated model year: P=1993. The 11th symbol indicated the assembly plant: A=Lakewood, Ga., B=Baltimore, Md., C=Lansing, Mich. D=Doraville, Ga., E=Linden, N.J., F=Flint, Mich., F=Fairfax II, Va., H=Flint, Mich., J=Janesville, Wis., K=Kosai, Japan, L=Van Nuys, Calif., M=Lansing, Mich., R=Arlington, Texas, R=Ramos, T=Terrytown, N.Y., U=Hamtramck, W=Willow Run, Mich., Y=Wilmington, Dela., Z=Fremont, Calif., O=GMAD, Pontiac, Mich., 1=Oshawa, Canada, 2=Moraine, Ohio, 2=Moraine, Ohio, 3=Detroit Truck & Coach, Mich., 3=St. Eustache, Quebec, Canada, 4=Orion Plant, Pontiac, Mich., 4=Scarborough, Ontario, Canada, 5=Bowling Green, Ken., 5=London, Ontario, Canada, 6=Oklahoma City, Okla., 7=Lordstown, Ohio, 8=Shreveport, La., 9=Cadillac, Detroit, Mich. Note: Trucks were not built at all factories. Symbols 12-17 were the production sequence number starting at 100001. Ending numbers not available.

1994: The first symbol indicates country of origin: 1=U.S., 2=Canada, 3=Mexican built, 4=U.S. and 5=Japan built. The second symbol indicates manufacturer: C=Cami GM of Canada or Suzuki, G=General Motors, G=Suzuki and 8-Isuzu. The third symbol indicates make: A=Chevy Bus, B=Chevy Incomplete, C=Chevrolet truck, N=Chevy MPV. The fourth symbol indicates GVW rating and brake system: B=3,001 lb.-4,000 lb. hydraulic, C=4,001 lb.-5,000 lb. hydraulic, etc. through K for hydraulic brakes. The fifth symbol indicates line and chassis type: B=Special Body, C/R=Conventional cab GMT-400 4 x 2, D=Military Truck 4 x 4, E=Compact cab, G=Chevy Van and Sportvan 4 x 2, K/V=Conventional cab GMT-400 4 x 4, L=Small van 4 x 4, M=Small van 4 x 2, P=Forward-Control 4 x 2, S=Small Conventional Cab 4 x 2, T=Small Conventional Cab 4 x 2, U=All-Purpose Vehicle (APV) 4 x 2, Z=Special body 4 x 2. The sixth symbol indicates series: 1=1/2-ton, 2=3/4-ton, 3=1-ton, O=All-Purpose Vehicle.. The seventh symbol indicates body type: 0=Chassis only, 1=Hi-Cube and Cutaway Vans, 2-Forward-Control, 3=Four-door cab, 4=Two-door cab, 5=Van, 6=Suburban, 7=Motorhome chassis, 8=Blazer Utility, 9=Extended cab. The eighth symbol identifies the engine: [Chevrolet engines] H=5.0-liter V-8, K=5.7-liter V-8, N=7.4-liter V-8, Z=4.3-liter V-6. [GM engines] A= 5.7-liter V-8, D=3.1-liter V-6, F=6.5-liter diesel V-8 (190 hp), L=3.8-liter V-6, M=7.0-liter V-8, P=6.5-liter diesel (155 hp), S=6.5-liter diesel V-8 (180 hp), W=4.3-liter V-6, 4=2.2-liter L4. The ninth symbol is the check digit. The 10th symbol indicated model year: R=1994. The 11th symbol indicated the assembly plant: A=Lakewood, Ga., B=Baltimore, Md., C=Lansing, Mich. D=Doraville, Ga., E=Linden, N.J., F=Flint, Mich., F=Fairfax II, Va., H=Flint, Mich., J=Janesville, Wis., K=Kosai, Japan, L=Van Nuys, Calif., M=Lansing, Mich., R−Arlington, Texas, R=Ramos, T=Terrytown, N.Y., U=Hamtramck, W=Willow Run, Mich., Y=Wilmington, Dela., Z=Fremont, Calif., O=GMAD, Pontiac, Mich., 1=Oshawa, Canada, 2=Moraine, Ohio, 2=Moraine, Ohio, 3=Detroit Truck & Coach, Mich., 3=St. Eustache, Quebec, Canada, 4=Orion Plant, Pontiac, Mich., 4=Scarborough, Ontario, Canada, 5=Bowling Green, Ken., 5=London, Ontario, Canada, 6=Oklahoma City, Okla., 7=Lordstown, Ohio, 8=Shreveport, La., 9=Cadillac, Detroit, Mich. Note: Trucks were not built at all factories. Symbols 12-17 were the production sequence number starting at 100001. Ending numbers not available.

1995: The first symbol indicates country of origin: 1=U.S., 2=Canada, 3=Mexican built, 4=U.S. and 5=Japan built. The second symbol indicates manufacturer: C=Cami GM of Canada or Suzuki, G=General Motors. The third symbol indicates make:

A=Chevy Bus, B=Chevy Incomplete, C=Chevrolet truck, N=Chevy MPV. The fourth symbol indicates GVW rating and brake system: B=3,001 lb.-4,000 lb. hydraulic, C=4,001 lb.-5,000 lb. hydraulic, etc. through K for hydraulic brakes. The fifth symbol indicates line and chassis type: B=Special Body, C/R=Conventional cab GMT-400 4 x 2, D=Military Truck 4 x 4, E=Compact cab, J=Compact Cab 4 x 4, G=Chevy Van and Sportvan 4 x 2, K/V=Conventional cab GMT-400 4 x 4, L=Small van 4 x 4, M=Small van 4 x 2, P=Forward-Control 4 x 2, S=Small Conventional Cab 4 x 2, T=Small Conventional Cab 4 x 2, U=All-Purpose Vehicle (APV) 4 x 2. The sixth symbol indicates series: 1=1/2-ton, 2=3/4-ton, 3=1-ton, O=All-Purpose Vehicle.. The seventh symbol indicates body type: 0=Chassis only, 1=Hi-Cube and Cutaway Vans, 2-Forward-Control, 3=Four-door cab/utility, 4=Two-door cab, 5=Van, 6=All-Purpose Vehicle, 6=Suburban, 7=Motorhome chassis, 8=two-door Utility, 9=Extended cab/Van. The eighth symbol identifies the engine: [Chevrolet engines] H=5.0-liter V-8, K=5.7-liter V-8, N=7.4-liter V-8, Y=6.5-liter V-8, Z=4.3-liter V-6. [GM engines] A= 5.7-liter V-8, D=3.1-liter V-6, F=6.5-liter diesel V-8 (190 hp), L=3.8-liter V-6, M=7.0-liter V-8, P=6.5-liter diesel (155 hp), P=5.7-liter diesel, S=6.5-liter diesel V-8 (180 hp), U=1.6-liter four, W=4.3-liter V-6, 4=2.2-liter L4 and 6=1.6-liter L4. The ninth symbol is the check digit. The 10th symbol indicated model year: S=1995. The 11th symbol indicated the assembly plant: B=Baltimore, Md., C=Lansing, Mich. D=Doraville, Ga., E=Pontiac East Truck & Bus, Pontiac, Mich., F=Flint, Mich., F=Fairfax II, Va., G=Silo, Mexico, H=Flint, Mich., J=Janesville, Wis., K=Linden Truck & Bus, Linden, N.J., M=Lansing, Mich., M-Mexico City, Mexico, R=Arlington, Texas, R=Ramos Arise, Mexico, T=Terrytown, N.Y., U=Hamtramck, Y=Wilmington, Dela., Z=Springhill, Tenn., Z=Ft. Wayne Truck & Bus, Ft. Wayne, Ind., 1=Oshawa, Canada, 1=Oshawa Truck & Bus, Oshawa, Canada, 2=Moraine Truck & Bus, Moraine, Ohio, 2=St. Therese, Canada, 3=Detroit Truck & Coach, Mich., 3=Kawasaki, Japan, 4=Orion Plant, Pontiac, Mich., 5=Bowling Green, Ken., 6=Ingersoll, Ontario, Canada, 6=Oklahoma City, Okla., 7=Lordstown, Ohio, 7=Fujisawa, Japan, 8=Shreveport Truck & Bus, Shreveport, 8=Tillsonburg, Ontario, Canada, 9=Oshawa #1, Ontario, Canada. Trucks were not built at all factories. Symbols 12-17 were the production sequence number starting at 100001. Ending numbers not available.

C. 1973-1998 Chevrolet Pickup Engine Options

1973

[LUV] Inline. OHV. Four-cylinder. Cast iron block. **Bore & stroke:** 3.31 in. x 3.23 in. Displacement: 110.8 cid. Compression ratio: 8.5:1. Net horsepower: 75 at 5000 rpm. Maximum torque: 88 lb.-ft. at 3000 rpm. Five main bearings. Hydraulic valve lifters. Carburetor: two-barrel.

[Standard: all, except El Camino/LUV/K20/K30/C20] Inline. OHV. Six-cylinder. Cast iron block. Bore & stroke: 3-7/8 in. x 3-1/2 in. Displacement: 250 cid. Compression ratio: 8.25:1. Net horsepower: 100 at 3600 rpm. Maximum torque: 175 lb.-ft. at 2000 rpm. Seven main bearings. Hydraulic valve lifters. Carburetor: Rochester one-barrel.

[Optional: C/K Series] Inline. OHV. Six-cylinder. Cast iron block. Bore & stroke: 3-7/8 in. x 4-1/8 in. Displacement: 292 cid. Compression ratio: 8.0:1. Net horsepower: 120 at 3600 rpm. Maximum torque: 225 lb.-ft. at 2000 rpm. Seven main bearings. Hydraulic valve lifters. Carburetor: one-barrel.

[Optional: C10/Blazer, Standard El Camino] V-block. OHV. Eight-cylinder. Cast iron block. Bore & stroke: 3-7/8 in. x 3-1/4 in. Displacement: 307 cid. Compression ratio: 8.5:1. Net horsepower: 115 at 3600 rpm. Maximum torque: 205 lb.-ft. at 2000 rpm. Five main bearings. Hydraulic valve lifters. Carburetor: two-barrel.

[Standard: C20/K20/K30/El Camino] V-block. OHV. Eight-cylinder. Cast iron block. Bore & stroke: 4 in. x 3.48 in. Displacement: 350 cid. Compression ratio: 8.5:1. Net horsepower: 155 at 4000 rpm. Maximum torque: 225 lb.-ft. at 2400 rpm. Five main bearings. Hydraulic valve lifters. Carburetor: two-barrel.

[Optional: El Camino] V-block. OHV. Eight-cylinder. Cast iron block. Bore & stroke: 4 in. x 3.48 in. Displacement: 350 cid. Compression ratio: 8.5:1. Net horsepower: 175 at 4000 rpm. Maximum torque: 260 lb.-ft. at 2800 rpm. Five main bearings. Hydraulic valve lifters. Carburetor: Rochester model Quadra-Jet, four-barrel.

[Optional: El Camino/C20/C30] V-block. OHV. Eight-cylinder. Cast iron block. Bore & stroke: 4.251 in. x 4.0 in. Displacement: 454 cid. Compression ratio: 8.25:1. Net horsepower: 240 at 4000 rpm. Maximum torque: 355 lb.-ft. at 2800 rpm. Five main bearings. Hydraulic valve lifters. Carburetor: Rochester model Quadra-Jet, four-barrel.

1974

[Standard LUV] Inline. OHV. Four-cylinder. Cast iron block. Bore & stroke: 3.31 in. x 3.23 in. Displacement: 110.8 cid. Compression ratio: 8.5:1. Net horsepower: 75 at 5000 rpm. Maximum torque: 88 lb.-ft at 3000 rpm. Five main bearings. Hydraulic valve lifters. Carburetor: two-barrel.

[Standard all except El Camino/LUV] Inline. OHV. Six-cylinder. Cast iron block. Bore & stroke: 3-7/8 in. x 3-1/2 in. Displacement: 250 cid. Compression ratio: 8.25:1. Net horsepower: 100 at 3600 rpm. Maximum torque: 175 lb.-ft. at 1800 rpm. Seven main bearings. Hydraulic valve lifters. Carburetor: one-barrel.

[Optional C20/C30/K20, Standard G20/G30] Inline. OHV. Six-cylinder. Cast iron block. Bore & stroke: 3-7/8 in. x 4.12 in. Displacement: 292 cid. Compression ratio: 8.0. Net horsepower: 120 at 3600 rpm. Maximum torque: 215 lb.-ft. at 2000 rpm. Seven main bearings. Hydraulic valve lifters. Carburetor: one-barrel. (An LPG conversion was available).

[Optional C10, Standard El Camino] Inline. OHV. Eight-cylinder. Cast iron block. Bore & stroke: 4 in. x 3.48 in. Displacement: 350 cid. Compression ratio: 8.5. Brake horsepower: 145 at 3800 rpm. Net horsepower: 145 at 3600 rpm. Maximum torque: 250 lb.-ft. at 2200 rpm. Five main bearings. Hydraulic valve lifters. Carburetor: two-barrel. (An LPG conversion was available).

[Optional C30/K10/K20/El Camino] Inline. OHV. Eight-cylinder. Cast iron block. Bore & stroke: 4 in. x 3.48 in. Displacement: 350 cid. Compression ratio: 8.5. Brake horsepower: 245 at 3800 rpm. Net horsepower: 160 at 3800 rpm. Maximum torque: 255 lb.-ft. at 2400 rpm. Five main bearings. Hydraulic valve lifters. Carburetor: four-barrel.

[Optional: El Camino] V-block. OHV. Eight-cylinder. Cast iron block. Bore & stroke: 4.126 in. x 3.76 in. Displacement: 400 cid. Compression ratio: 8.5:1. Net horsepower: 150. Five main bearings. Hydraulic valve lifters. Carburetor: Rochester four-barrel.

[Optional: El Camino] V-block. OHV. Eight-cylinder. Cast iron block. Bore & stroke: 4.125 in. x 3.75 in. Displacement: 400 cid. Compression ratio: 8.5:1. Net horsepower: 180. Five main bearings. Hydraulic valve lifters. Carburetor: Rochester four-barrel.

[Optional C10/C20/C30/El Camino] Inline. OHV. Eight-cylinder. Cast iron block. Bore & stroke: 1-1/4 in. x 4 in. Displacement: 454 cid. Compression ratio: 8.5. Net horsepower: 220. Five main bearings. Hydraulic valve lifters. Carburetor: Rochester four-barrel model Quadra-Jet.

[El Camino] Inline. OHV. Eight-cylinder. Cast iron block. Bore & stroke: 1-1/4 in. x 4 in. Displacement: 454 cid. Compression ratio: 8.5. Net horsepower: 235 at 4000 rpm. Five main bearings. Hydraulic valve lifters. Carburetor: Rochester four-barrel model Quadra-Jet.

[Optional C10/C20/C30] Inline. OHV. Eight-cylinder. Cast iron block. Bore & stroke: 1-1/4 in. x 4 in. Displacement: 454 cid. Compression ratio: 8.5. Brake horsepower: 5. Net horsepower: 245 at 4000 rpm. Maximum torque: 365 lb.-ft. at 2800 rpm. Five main bearings. Hydraulic valve lifters. Carburetor: Rochester four-barrel model Quadra-Jet.

1975

[LUV] Inline. OHV. Four-cylinder. Cast iron block. Bore & stroke: 3.31 in. x 3.23 in. Displacement: 110.8 cid. Compression ratio: 8.5:1. Net horsepower: 75 at 5000 rpm. Maximum torque: 88 lb.-ft. at 3000 rpm. Five main bearings. Hydraulic valve lifters. Carburetor: two-barrel.

[Standard C10/K10/Blazer/El Camino] Inline. Gasoline. Six-cylinder. Cast iron block. Bore & stroke: 3-7/8 in. x 3-1/2 in. Displacement: 250 cid. Compression ratio: 8.25:1. Net horsepower: 105 at 3800 rpm. Maximum torque: 185 lb.-ft. at 1200 rpm. Seven main bearings. Hydraulic valve lifters. Carburetor: one-barrel.

[Optional C10/El Camino] V-block. Gasoline. Eight-cylinder. Cast iron block. Bore & stroke: 4 in. x 3-1/2 in. Displacement: 350 cid. Compression ratio: 8.5:1. Net horsepower: 145 at 3800 rpm.

Maximum torque: 250 lb.-ft. at 2200 rpm. Five main bearings. Hydraulic valve lifters. Carburetor: two-barrel.

[Standard C20/C30/K20] Inline. OHV. Six-cylinder. Cast iron block. Bore & stroke: 3-7/8 in. x 4-1/8 in. Displacement: 292 cid. Compression ratio: 8.0:1. Net horsepower: 120 at 3600 rpm. Maximum torque: 215 lb.-ft. at 2000 rpm. Seven main bearings. Hydraulic valve lifters. Carburetor: one-barrel.

[Optional C10, Standard El Camino] Inline. OHV. Eight-cylinder. Cast iron block. Bore & stroke: 4 in. x 3.48 in. Displacement: 350 cid. Compression ratio: 8.5. Brake horsepower: 145 at 3800 rpm. Net horsepower: 145 at 3600 rpm. Maximum torque: 250 lb.-ft. at 2200 rpm. Five main bearings. Hydraulic valve lifters. Carburetor: two-barrel. (An LPG conversion was available).

[Optional all except LUV] V-block. Gasoline. Eight-cylinder. Cast iron block. Bore & stroke: 4 in. x 3-1/2 in. Displacement: 350 cid. Net horsepower: 160 at 3800 rpm. Maximum torque: 250 lb.-ft. at 2400 rpm. Five main bearings. Hydraulic valve lifters. Carburetor: four-barrel.

[Optional K10/K20/El Camino] V-block. OHV. Eight-cylinder. Cast iron block. Bore & stroke: 4-1/8 in. x 4 in. Displacement: 400 cid. Compression ratio: 8.5:1. Net horsepower: 175 at 3600 rpm. Five main bearings. Hydraulic valve lifters. Carburetor: four-barrel.

[Optional C10/C20/C30] V-block. OHV. Eight-cylinder. Cast iron block. Bore & stroke: 4-1/8 in. x 4 in. Displacement: 454 cid. Compression ratio: 8.25:1. Net horsepower: 230 at 3800 rpm. Five main bearings. Hydraulic valve lifters. Carburetor: Rochester four-barrel Quadra-Jet.

[El Camino] V-block. OHV. Eight-cylinder. Cast iron block. Bore & stroke: 4-1/8 in. x 4 in. Displacement: 454 cid. Compression ratio: 8.25:1. Net horsepower: 235 at 3800 rpm. Five main bearings. Hydraulic valve lifters. Carburetor: Rochester four-barrel Quadra-Jet.

1976

[Standard LUV] Inline. OHV. Four-cylinder. Cast iron block. Bore & stroke: 3.31 in. x 3.23 in. Displacement: 110.8 cid. Compression ratio: 8.5:1. Net horsepower: 75 at 5000 rpm. Maximum torque: 88 lb.-ft. at 3000 rpm. Five main bearings. Hydraulic valve lifters. Carburetor: Rochester Quadra-Jet four-barrel.

[Standard C10/K10/El Camino/Blazer] Inline. OHV. Six-cylinder. Cast iron block. Bore & stroke: 3-7/8 in. x 3-1/2 in. Displacement: 250 cid. Compression ratio: 8.25:1. Net horsepower: 100 at 3600 rpm. Maximum torque: 175 lb.-ft. at 1800 rpm. Seven main bearings. Hydraulic valve lifters. Carburetor: one-barrel.

[Standard C20/C30/K20] Inline. OHV. Six-cylinder. Cast iron block. Bore & stroke: 3-7/8 in. x 4-1/8 in. Displacement: 292 cid. Compression ratio: 8.0:1. Net horsepower: 120 at 3600 rpm. Maximum torque: 215 lb.-ft. at 2000 rpm. Seven main bearings. Hydraulic valve lifters. Carburetor: one-barrel.

[Optional El Camino] V-block. OHV. Eight-cylinder. Cast iron block. Bore and stroke: 3.736 x 3.48 in. Displacement: 305 cid. Net horsepower: 140. Taxable horsepower: 44.66. Five main bearings. Hydraulic lifters. Carburetor: two-barrel.

[Optional C Series] V-block. OHV. Eight-cylinder. Cast iron block. Bore and stroke: 3.736 x 3.48 in. Displacement: 305 cid. Net horsepower: 130. Taxable horsepower: 44.66. Five main bearings. Hydraulic lifters. Carburetor: two-barrel.

[Optional C10/El Camino] V-block. OHV. Eight-cylinder. Cast iron block. Bore & stroke: 4 in. x 3-1/2 in. Displacement: 350 cid. Compression ratio: 8.5:1. Net horsepower: 145 at 3800 rpm. Maximum torque: 250 lb.-ft. at 2200 rpm. Five main bearings. Hydraulic valve lifters. Carburetor: two-barrel.

[Optional: Except LUV/El Camino] V-block. OHV. Eight-cylinder. Cast iron block. Bore & stroke: 4 in. x 3-1/2 in. Displacement: 350 cid. Compression ratio: 8.5:1. Net horsepower: 160 at 3800 rpm. Maximum torque: 255 lb.-ft. at 2800 rpm. Five main bearings. Hydraulic valve lifters. Carburetor: Rochester Quadra-Jet four-barrel.

[Optional: El Camino] V-block. OHV. Eight-cylinder. Cast iron block. Bore & stroke: 4 in. x 3-1/2 in. Displacement: 350 cid. Compression ratio: 8.5:1. Net horsepower: 165 at 3800 rpm. Maximum torque: 255 lb.-ft. at 2800 rpm. Five main bearings. Hydraulic valve lifters. Carburetor: Rochester Quadra-Jet four-barrel.

[Optional K10/K20/Blazer/El Camino] V-block. OHV. Eight-cylinder. Cast iron block. Bore & stroke: 4-1/8 in. x 4 in. Displacement: 400 cid. Compression ratio: 8.5:1. Net horsepower: 175 at

3600 rpm. Maximum torque: 290 lb.-ft. at 2800 rpm. Five main bearings. Hydraulic valve lifters. Carburetor: Rochester four-barrel Quadra-Jet.

[Optional C10/C20/C30] V-block. OHV. Eight-cylinder. Cast iron block. Bore & stroke: 4-1/4 in. x 4 in. Displacement: 454 cid. Compression ratio: 8.25:1. Net horsepower: 240 at 3800 rpm. Maximum torque: 370 lb.-ft. at 2800 rpm. Five main bearings. Hydraulic valve lifters. Carburetor: Rochester Quadra-Jet four-barrel.

1977

[Standard LUV] Inline. OHV. Four-cylinder. Cast iron block. Bore & stroke: 3.31 in. x 3.23 in. Displacement: 110.8 cid. Compression ratio: 8.5:1. Net horsepower: 80 at 5000 rpm. Maximum torque: 88 lb.-ft. at 3000 rpm. Five main bearings. Hydraulic valve lifters. Carburetor: Rochester Quadra-Jet four-barrel.

[Standard C10/K10/El Camino/Blazer] Inline. OHV. Six-cylinder. Cast iron block. Bore & stroke: 3-7/8 in. x 3-1/2 in. Displacement: 250 cid. Compression ratio: 8.25:1. Net horsepower: 110 at 4800 rpm. Maximum torque: 175 lb.-ft. at 1800 rpm. Seven main bearings. Hydraulic valve lifters. Carburetor: one-barrel.

[Standard C20/C30/K20] Inline. OHV. Six-cylinder. Cast iron block. Bore & stroke: 3-7/8 in. x 4-1/8 in. Displacement: 292 cid. Compression ratio: 8.0:1. Net horsepower: 120 at 3600 rpm. Maximum torque: 215 lb.-ft. at 2000 rpm. Seven main bearings. Hydraulic valve lifters. Carburetor: one-barrel.

[Optional El Camino] V-block. OHV. Eight-cylinder. Cast iron block. Bore and stroke: 3.736 x 3.48 in. Displacement: 305 cid. Net horsepower: 145. Taxable horsepower: 44.66. Five main bearings. Hydraulic lifters. Carburetor: two-barrel.

[Optional C Series] V-block. OHV. Eight-cylinder. Cast iron block. Bore and stroke: 3.736 x 3.48 in. Displacement: 305 cid. Net horsepower: 130. Taxable horsepower: 44.66. Five main bearings. Hydraulic lifters. Carburetor: two-barrel.

[Optional C Series] V-block. OHV. Eight-cylinder. Cast iron block. Bore & stroke: 4 in. x 3-1/2 in. Displacement: 350 cid. Compression ratio: 8.5:1. Net horsepower: 145 at 3800 rpm. Maximum torque: 250 lb.-ft. at 2200 rpm. Five main bearings. Hydraulic valve lifters. Carburetor: two-barrel.

[Optional El Camino] V-block. OHV. Eight-cylinder. Cast iron block. Bore & stroke: 4 in. x 3-1/2 in. Displacement: 350 cid. Compression ratio: 8.5:1. Net horsepower: 170 at 3800 rpm. Maximum torque: 255 lb.-ft. at 2800 rpm. Five main bearings. Hydraulic valve lifters. Carburetor: Rochester Quadra-Jet four-barrel.

[Optional K10/K20/Blazer] V-block. OHV. Eight-cylinder. Cast iron block. Bore & stroke: 4-1/8 in. x 4 in. Displacement: 400 cid. Compression ratio: 8.5:1. Net horsepower: 175 at 3600 rpm. Maximum torque: 290 lb.-ft. at 2800 rpm. Five main bearings. Hydraulic valve lifters. Carburetor: Rochester four-barrel Quadra-Jet.

1978

[Standard LUV] Inline. OHV. Four-cylinder. Cast iron block. Bore & stroke: 3.31 x 3.23 in. Displacement: 110.8 cid. Compression ratio: 8.5:1. Net horsepower: 80 at 4800 rpm. Maximum torque: 95 lb.-ft at 3000 rpm. Five main bearings. Hydraulic valve lifters. Carburetor: One-barrel.

[Standard El Camino] V-block. OHV. Six-cylinder. Cast iron block. Bore & stroke: 3.50 x 3.48 in. Displacement: 200 cid. Compression ratio: 8.2:1. Net horsepower: 95 at 3800 rpm. Maximum torque: 160 lb.-ft at 2000 rpm. Hydraulic valve lifters. Carburetor: Rochester two-barrel.

[Optional El Camino] (Standard for California delivery) Available only automatic transmission. V-type. OHV. Six-cylinder. Cast iron block. Bore & stroke: 3.80 x 3.40 in. Displacement: 231 cid. Compression ratio: 8.0:1. Net horsepower: 105 at 3400 rpm. Net torque: 185 lb.-ft at 2000 rpm. Carburetor: Rochester two-barrel.

[Standard C10/Big 10/K10] Inline. OHV. Six-cylinder. Cast iron block. Bore & stroke: 3.876 x 3.530 in. Displacement: 250 cid. Compression ratio: 8.25:1. Net horsepower: 115 at 3800 rpm. Torque: 195 lb.-ft. at 1800 rpm. Seven main bearings. Hydraulic valve lifters. Carburetor: Mono-jet model 1ME. RPO Code: LD4.

[Standard C20/C30/K20/K30] Inline. OHV. Six-cylinder. Cast iron block. Bore & stroke: 3.8764 x 4.120 in. Displacement: 292 cid. Compression ratio: 8.0:1. Net horsepower: 120 at 3600 rpm. Net torque: 215 lb.-ft. at 2000 rpm. Seven main bearings. Hydraulic valve lifters. Carburetor: One-barrel. RPO Code: L25.

[Optional C10/El Camino] V--block. OHV. Eight-cylinder. Cast iron block. **Bore & stroke:** 3.736 x 3.480 in. Displacement: 305 cid. Compression ratio: 8.5:1. Net horsepower: 145 at 3800 rpm. Net torque: 245 lb.-ft. at 2400 rpm. Five main bearings. Hydraulic valve lifters. Carburetor: Two-barrel model 2GC. RPO Code: LG9.

[Optional all models] V-type. OHV. Eight-cylinder. Cast iron block. **Bore & stroke:** 4.0 x 3.480 in. Displacement: 350 cid. Compression ratio: 8.5:1. Net horsepower: 165 at 3800 rpm. Net torque: 260 lb.-ft. at 2400 rpm. Five main bearings. Hydraulic valve lifters. Carburetor: Four-barrel model M4MC/MV. RPO Code: LS9.

[Optional K10/K20/K30] V-type. OHV. Eight-cylinder. Cast iron block. **Bore & stroke:** 4.125 x 3.750 in. Displacement: 400 cid. Compression ratio: 8.5:1. Net horsepower: 175 at 3600 rpm. Net torque: 290 lb.-ft. at 2800 rpm. Five main bearings. Hydraulic valve lifters. Carburetor: Four-barrel model M4MC/MV. RPO Code: LF4.

[Optional C1500/C2500/C3500] V-type. OHV. Eight-cylinder. Cast iron block. **Bore & stroke:** 4.250 x 4.0 in. Displacement: 454 cid. Compression ratio: 8.5:1 Net horsepower: 205 at 3600 rpm. Net torque: 355 lb.-ft. at 2800 rpm. Five main bearings. Hydraulic valve lifters. Carburetor: Four-barrel model M4MC/MV. RPO Code: LF8.

[Optional C10/Big 10] V-type. OHV diesel. Eight-cylinder. Cast iron block. **Bore & stroke:** 4.057 x 3.385 in. Displacement: 350 cid. Compression ratio: 20.5:1. Net horsepower: 120 at 3600 rpm. Net torque: 222 lb.-ft. at 1900 rpm. Five main bearings. Hydraulic valve lifters. RPO Code: LF9.

1979

[Standard LUV] Inline. OHV overhead camshaft. Four-cylinder. Cast iron block. **Bore & stroke:** 3.31 x 3.23 in. Displacement: 110.8 cid. Compression ratio: 8.5:1. Net horsepower: 80 at 4800 rpm. Maximum torque: 95 lb.-ft. at 3000 rpm. Five main bearings. Hydraulic valve lifters. Carburetor: One-barrel.

[Standard El Camino] V-type. OHV. Six-cylinder. Cast iron block. **Bore & stroke:** 3.5 x 3.48 in. Displacement: 200 cid. Compression ratio: 8.2:1. Net horsepower: 95. Four main bearings. Hydraulic valve lifters. Carburetor: Rochester two-barrel model 210.

[Optional El Camino] V-type. OHV. Six-cylinder. Cast iron block. **Bore & stroke:** 3.8 x 3.4 in. Displacement: 231 cid. Compression ratio: 8.0:1. Net horsepower: 105. Four main bearings. Hydraulic valve lifters. Carburetor: Rochester two-barrel model 2GC.

[Standard C10/Big 10/K10] Inline. OHV. Six-cylinder. Cast iron block. **Bore & stroke:** 3.876 x 3.530 in. Displacement: 250 cid. Compression ratio: 8.3:1. Net horsepower: 130 at 3800 rpm. Torque: 210 lb.-ft. at 2400 rpm. Seven main bearings. Hydraulic valve lifters. Carburetor: Two-barrel. NOTE: Base engine in California had 125 horsepower at 4000 rpm/ Torque: 205 lb.-ft. at 2000 rpm.

[Optional El Camino] V-type. OHV. Eight-cylinder. Cast iron block. **Bore & stroke:** 3.5 x 3.48 in. Displacement: 267 cid. Five main bearings. Hydraulic valve lifters. Carburetor: two-barrel.

[Standard C20/C30/K20/K30] Inline. OHV. Six-cylinder. Cast iron block. **Bore & stroke:** 3.876 x 4.120 in. Displacement: 292 cid. Compression ratio: 8.0:1. Net horsepower: 115 at 3400 rpm. Net torque: 215 lb.-ft. at 3400 rpm. Seven main bearings. Hydraulic valve lifters. Carburetor: Rochester one-barrel.

[Optional C10] V-type. OHV. Eight-cylinder. Cast iron block. **Bore & stroke:** 3.736 x 3.480 in. Displacement: 305 cid. Compression ratio: 8.4:1. Net horsepower: 140 at 4000 rpm. Net torque: 235 lb.-ft. at 2000 rpm. Five main bearings. Hydraulic valve lifters. Carburetor: Rochester two-barrel model 2GC. NOTE: Base engine in California had 155 horsepower at 3600 rpm/Torque: 260 lb.-ft. at 2000 rpm. (Four-barrel California engine) 155 horsepower at 4000 rpm. Torque: 260 lb.-ft. at 2000 rpm.

[Optional El Camino] V-type. OHV. Eight-cylinder. Cast iron block. **Bore & stroke:** 3.736 x 3.480 in. Displacement: 305 cid. Compression ratio: 8.4:1. Net horsepower: 145/135. Five main bearings. Hydraulic valve lifters. Carburetor: Rochester two-barrel model 2GC. NOTE: 135 is California rating.

[Optional El Camino] V-type. OHV. Eight-cylinder. Cast iron block. **Bore & stroke:** 4.0 x 3.48 in. Displacement: 350 cid. Compression ratio: 8.2:1. Net horsepower: 170/160 at 3800 rpm. Maximum torque: 270 lb.-ft. at 2400 rpm. Five main bearings. Hydraulic valve lifters. Carburetor: Rochester four-barrel model M4 MC/MV. NOTE : 160 is California rating.

[Optional C10/Big 10] V-type. OHV diesel. Eight-cylinder. Cast iron block. Bore & stroke: 4.057 x 3.385 in. Displacement: 350 cid. Compression ratio: 20.5:1. Net horsepower: 120 at 3600 rpm. Net torque: 222 lb.-ft. at 1900 rpm. Five main bearings. Hydraulic valve lifters.

[Optional all models except LUV] V-type. OHV. Eight-cylinder. Cast iron block. Bore & stroke: 4.0 x 3.48 in. Displacement: 350 cid. Compression ratio: 8.2:1. Net horsepower: 165 at 3600 rpm. Net torque: 270 lb.-ft. at 2700 rpm. Five main bearings. Hydraulic valve lifters. Carburetor: Rochester four-barrel model M4 MC/MV.

[Optional K10/K20/K30] V-type. OHV. Eight-cylinder. Cast iron block. Bore & stroke: 4.125 x 3.750 in. Displacement: 400 cid. Compression ratio: 8.5:1. Net horsepower: 185 at 3600 rpm. Net torque: 300 lb.-ft. at 2400 rpm. Five main bearings. Hydraulic valve lifters. Carburetor: Rochester four-barrel model M4 MC/MV.

[Optional All models except Blazer/El Camino/LUV] V-type. OHV. Eight-cylinder. Cast iron block. Bore & stroke: 4.250 x 4.0 in. Displacement: 454 cid. Compression ratio: 7.6:1. Net horsepower: 245 at 4000 rpm. Net torque: 380 lb.-ft. at 2500 rpm. Five main bearings. Hydraulic valve lifters. Carburetor: Rochester four-barrel model M4 MC/MV.

1980

[Standard LUV] Inline. OHV. OHC. Four-cylinder. Cast iron block. Bore & stroke: 3.31 x 3.23 in. Displacement: 110.8 cid. Compression ratio: 8.5:1. Net horsepower: 80 at 4800 rpm. Maximum torque: 95 lb.-ft at 3000 rpm. Five main bearings. Hydraulic valve lifters. Carburetor: One-barrel.

[Standard El Camino] V-block. OHV. Six-cylinder. Cast iron block. Bore & stroke: 3.5 x 3.48 in. Displacement: 200 cid. Compression ratio: 8.2:1. Net horsepower: 95. Four main bearings. Hydraulic valve lifters. Carburetor: Rochester two-barrel model 210.V-block. OHV. Six-cylinder. Cast iron block. Bore & stroke: 3.8 x 3.4 in. Displacement: 231 cid. Compression ratio: 8.0:1. Net horsepower: 105. Four main bearings. Hydraulic valve lifters. Carburetor: Rochester two-barrel model 2GC.

[Standard C10/Big 10/K10] Inline. OHV. Six-cylinder. Cast iron block. Bore & stroke: 3.876 x 3.530 in. Displacement: 250 cid. Compression ratio: 8.3:1. Net horsepower: 130 at 3800 rpm. Torque: 210 lb.-ft. at 2400 rpm. Seven main bearings. Hydraulic valve lifters. Carburetor: Two-barrel model Rochester.

[Optional El Camino] V-block. Eight-cylinder. Cast iron block. Bore & stroke: 3.5 x 3.48 in. Displacement: 267 cid. Five main bearings. Hydraulic valve lifters. Carburetor: two-barrel.

[Standard C20/C30/K20/K30] Inline. OHV. Six-cylinder. Cast iron block. Bore & stroke: 3.876 x 4.120 in. Displacement: 292 cid. Compression ratio: 8.0:1. Net horsepower: 115 at 3400 rpm. Torque: 215 lb.-ft. at 3400 rpm. Seven main bearings. Hydraulic valve lifters. Carburetor: Rochester model one-barrel.

[Optional C10] V-block. OHV. Eight-cylinder. Cast iron block. Bore & stroke: 3.736 x 3.480 in. Displacement: 305 cid. Compression ratio: 8.4:1. Net horsepower: 140 at 4000 rpm. Net torque: 235 lb.-ft. at 2000 rpm. Five main bearings. Hydraulic valve lifters. Carburetor: Rochester two-barrel model 2GC.

[Optional El Camino] V-block. OHV. Eight-cylinder. Cast iron block. Bore & stroke: 3.736 x 3.480 in. Displacement: 305 cid. Compression ratio: 8.4:1. Net horsepower: 145/135*. Five main bearings. Hydraulic valve lifters. Carburetor: Rochester two-barrel model 2GC. NOTE: California rating.

[Optional C10/Big 10] V-type. OHV Diesel. Eight-cylinder. Cast iron block. Bore & stroke: 4.057 x 3.385 in. Displacement: 350 cid. Compression ratio: 20.5:1. Net horsepower: 120 at 3600 rpm. Net torque: 222 lb.-ft. at 1900 rpm. Five main bearings. Hydraulic valve lifters.

[Optional all models except LUV] V-block. OHV. Eight-cylinder. Cast iron block. Bore & stroke: 4.0 x 3.48 in. Displacement: 350 cid. Compression ratio: 8.2:1. Net horsepower: 165 at 3600 rpm. Net torque: 270 lb.-ft. at 2700 rpm. Five main bearings. Hydraulic valve lifters. Carburetor: Rochester four-barrel model M4 MC/MV.

[Optional all models except LUV] V-type. OHV. Eight-cylinder. Cast iron block. Bore & stroke: 4.0 x 3.48 in. Displacement: 350 cid. Compression ratio: 8.2:1. Net horsepower: 170/160 at 3800 rpm. Maximum torque: 270 lb.-ft. at 2400 rpm. Five main bearings. Hydraulic valve lifters. Carburetor: Rochester four-barrel model M4 MC/MV.

[Optional K10/K20/K30] V-block. OHV. Eight-cylinder. Cast iron block. Bore & stroke: 4.125 x 3.750 in. Displacement: 400 cid. Compression ratio: 8.5:1. Net horsepower: 185 at 3600 rpm. Net torque: 300 lb.-ft. at 2400 rpm. Five main bearings. Hydraulic valve lifters. Carburetor: Rochester four-barrel model M4 MC/MV.

[Optional all models except Blazer, El Camino, LUV] V-block. OHV. Eight-cylinder. Cast iron block. Bore & stroke: 4.250 x 4.0 in. Displacement: 454 cid. Compression ratio: 7.6:1. Net horsepower: 245 at 4000 rpm. Net torque: 380 lb.-ft. at 2500 rpm. Five main bearings. Hydraulic valve lifters. Carburetor: Rochester four-barrel model M4 MC/MV.

NOTE: On all 1980 engines horsepower and torque can vary on vehicles sold in California.

1981

[Standard LUV] Inline. OHV. OHC. Four-cylinder. Cast iron block. Bore & stroke: 3.31 x 3.23 in. Displacement: 110.8 cid. Compression ratio: 8.5:1. Net horsepower: 80 at 4800 rpm. Maximum torque: 95 lb.-ft. at 3000 rpm. Five main bearings. Hydraulic valve lifters. Carburetor: Single one-barrel.

[Standard El Camino, except in California] V-block. OHV. Six-cylinder. Cast iron block. Bore & stroke: 3.7 x 3.48 in. Displacement: 229 cid. Compression ratio: 8.6:1. Net horsepower: 110 at 4200 rpm. Maximum torque: 170 lb.-ft. at 2000 rpm. Four main bearings. Hydraulic valve lifters. Order Code LC3(A).

[Standard El Camino, California only] V-block. OHV. Eight-cylinder. Cast iron block. Bore & stroke: 3.8 x 3.4 in. Displacement: 231 cid. Compression ratio: 8.0:1. Net horsepower: 110 at 3800 rpm. Maximum torque: 190 lb.-ft. at 1600 rpm. Four main bearings. Hydraulic valve lifters. Order Code LD5(C).

[Standard C10/C20/K10/Blazer] Inline. OHV. Six-cylinder. Cast iron block. Bore & stroke: 3.9 x 4.5 in. Displacement: 250 cid. Compression ratio: 8.3:1. Net horsepower: 115 at 3600 rpm. Torque: 200 lb.-ft. at 2000 rpm. Seven main bearings. Hydraulic valve lifters. Carburetor: Rochester model staged two-barrel. Order Code LE3(A).

[Optional El Camino, except in California] V-block. OHV. Eight-cylinder. Cast iron block. Bore & stroke: 3.5 x 3.48 in. Displacement: 267 cid. Compression ratio: 8.3:1. Net horsepower: 115 at 4000 rpm. Maximum torque: 200 lb.-ft. at 2400 rpm. Five main bearings. Hydraulic valve lifters. Carburetor: Rochester model staged two-barrel. Order Code L39(B).

[StandardC20 HD (C6P)/C20 Bonus and Crew-Cab/ C30/C30 Bonus and Crew-Cab/K20 HD] Inline. OHV. Six-cylinder. Cast iron block. Bore & stroke: 3.876 x 4.12 in. Displacement: 292 cid. Compression ratio: 7.8:1. Net horsepower: 115 at 3400 rpm. Maximum torque: 215 lb.-ft. at 1600 rpm. Five main bearings. Hydraulic valve lifters. Carburetor: Rochester model one-barrel. Order Code L25(B).

[Optional C10/C20/K10/Blazer] V-block. OHV. Eight-cylinder. Cast iron block. Bore & stroke: 3.736 x 3.480 in. Displacement: 305 cid. Compression ratio: 8.5:1. Net horsepower: 130 at 4000 rpm. Maximum torque: 240 lb.-ft. at 2000 rpm. Five main bearings. Hydraulic valve lifters. Carburetor: Rochester model staged two-barrel. Order Code LG9(C).

[Optional C10/C20/K10/Blazer] V-block. OHV. Eight-cylinder. Cast iron block. Bore & stroke: 3.736 x 3.480 in. Displacement: 305 cid. Compression ratio: 9.2:1. Net horsepower: 160 at 4400 rpm. Maximum torque: 235 lb.-ft. at 2000 rpm. Five main bearings. Hydraulic valve lifters. Carburetor: Rochester model staged four-barrel with Electronic Spark Control. Order Code LE9(C). Not available for California.

[Optional El Camino] V-block. OHV. Eight-cylinder. Cast iron block. Bore & stroke: 3.7 x 3.48 in. Displacement: 305 cid. Compression ratio: 8.6:1. Net horsepower: 145 at 3800 rpm. Maximum torque: 248 lb.-ft. at 2400 rpm. Five main bearings. Hydraulic valve lifters. Carburetor: Rochester model staged four-barrel. Order Code LG4(B).

[Optional C10/C20/K10] V-block. OHV. Eight-cylinder. Cast iron block. Bore & stroke: 3.736 x 3.480 in. Displacement: 305 cid. Compression ratio: 8.6:1. Net horsepower: 150 at 4200. Maximum torque: 240 lb.-ft. at 2000 rpm. Five main bearings. Hydraulic valve lifters. Carburetor: Rochester model staged four-barrel. Order Code LF3(C).

[Standard C20/K10/K20, OptionalC20/K20/K20 HD (CP6)/K30] V-block. OHV. Eight-cylinder. Cast iron block. Bore & stroke: 4.3 x 3.5 in. Displacement: 350 cid. Compression ratio: 8.2:1.

Five main bearings. Hydraulic valve lifters. Carburetor: Rochester model four-barrel. Order Code L59(A).

[Optional C10] V-block. OHV Diesel. Eight-cylinder. Cast iron block. Bore & stroke: 4.06 x 3.38 in. Displacement: 350 cid. Compression ratio: 22.5:1. Net horsepower: 125 at 3600 rpm. Maximum torque: 225 lb.-ft. at 1600 rpm. Five main bearings. Hydraulic valve lifters. Carburetor: Fuel injection. Order Code LS9(A).

[OptionalC20/C20 HD/CP6/C30] V-block. OHV. Eight-cylinder. Cast iron block. Bore & stroke: 4.250 x 4.0 in. Displacement: 454 cid. Compression ratio: 7.9:1. Net horsepower: 210 at 3800 rpm. Maximum torque: 340 lb.-ft at 2800 rpm. Five main bearings. Hydraulic valve lifters. Carburetor: Rochester model four-barrel. Order Code LE8(A).

NOTE: Versions of some engines used in trucks for California sale have different horsepower and torque ratings.

1982

[Standard S-10] Inline. OHV. OHC. Four-cylinder. Cast iron block. Bore & stroke: 3.42 x 3.23 in. Displacement: 119 cid. Compression ratio: 8.4:1. Net horsepower: 82 at 4600 rpm. Maximum torque: 101 lb.-ft. at 3000 rpm. Hydraulic valve lifters. Order Code LR1.

[Standard 4 x 4 LUV] Inline. OHV. OHC. Four-cylinder. Cast iron block. Bore & stroke: 3.31 x 3.23 in. Displacement: 110.8 cid. Compression ratio: 8.5:1. Net horsepower: 80 at 4800 rpm. Maximum torque: 95 lb.-ft at 3000 rpm. Five main bearings. Hydraulic valve lifters. Carburetor: one-barrel. Order Code L10.

[Standard 4 x 2 LUV models, Optional: LUV 4 x 4] Inline. OHV Diesel. Four-cylinder. Cast iron block. Displacement: 136.6 cid. Compression ratio: 21:1. Net horsepower: 58 at 4300 rpm. Maximum torque: 93 lb.-ft. at 2200 rpm. Hydraulic valve lifters. Order Code LQ7.

[Optional S-10] V-block. OHV. Six-cylinder. Cast iron block. Bore & stroke: 3.50 x 2.99 in. Displacement: 173 cid. Compression ratio: 8.5:1. Net horsepower: 110 at 4800 rpm. Maximum torque: 148 lb.-ft. at 2000 rpm. Hydraulic valve lifters. Order Code LR2.

[Standard El Camino, except California] V-block. OHV. Six-cylinder. Cast iron block. Bore & stroke: 3.7 x 3.48 in. Displacement: 229 cid. Compression ratio: 8.6:1. Net horsepower: 110 at 4200 rpm. Maximum torque: 170 lb.-ft. at 2000 rpm. Four main bearings. Hydraulic valve lifters. Code LC3(A).

[Optional El Camino, California only] V-block. OHV. Six-cylinder. Cast iron block. Bore & stroke: 3.8 x 3.4 in. Displacement: 231 cid. Compression ratio: 8.0:1. Net horsepower: 110 at 3800 rpm. Maximum torque: 190 lb.-ft. at 1600 rpm. Five main bearings. Hydraulic valve lifters. Carburetor: Rochester two-barrel. Order Code LO5(C).

[Standard C10/C20/K10] Inline. OHV. Six-cylinder. Cast iron block. Bore & stroke: 3.9 x 4.5 in. Displacement: 250 cid. Compression ratio: 8.3:1. Net horsepower: 110 at 3600 rpm. Torque: 195 lb.-ft. at 2000 rpm. Seven main bearings. Hydraulic valve lifters. Carburetor: Rochester staged two-barrel. Order Code LE3(A).

[Optional El Camino, except California] V-block. OHV. Eight-cylinder. Cast iron block. Bore & stroke: 3.5 x 3.48 in. Displacement: 267 cid. Compression ratio: 8.3:1. Net horsepower: 115 at 4000 rpm. Maximum torque: 200 lb.-ft. at 2400 rpm. Five main bearings. Hydraulic valve lifters. Carburetor: Rochester staged two-barrel. Order Code L39(B).

[Standard C20 HD (C6P)/C20/C30/K20 HD (C6P)/K30] Inline. OHV. Six-cylinder. Cast iron block. Bore & stroke: 3.876 x 4.12 in. Displacement: 292 cid. Compression ratio: 7.8:1. Net horsepower: 115 at 3400 rpm. Maximum torque: 215 lb.-ft. at 1600 rpm. Seven main bearings. Hydraulic valve lifters. Carburetor: Rochester one-barrel. Order Code L25(B).

[Optional El Camino] V-block. OHV. Eight-cylinder. Cast iron block. Bore & stroke: 3.7 x 3.48 in. Displacement: 305 cid. Compression ratio: 8.6:1. Net horsepower: 150 at 3800 rpm. Maximum torque: 240 lb.-ft. at 2400 rpm. Five main bearings. Hydraulic valve lifters. Carburetor: Rochester staged four-barrel. Order Code LG4(B).

[Optional C10/C20/K10] V-block. OHV. Eight-cylinder. Cast iron block. Bore & stroke: 3.736 x 3.480 in. Displacement: 305 cid. Compression ratio: 9.2:1. Net horsepower: 160 at 4400 rpm. Maximum torque: 235 lb.-ft. at 2000 rpm. Five main bearings. Hydraulic valve lifters. Carburetor: Rochester staged four-barrel with Electronic Spark Control. Order Code LE9(C). Not available in California.

[Optional C20/C20 HD (C6P)/C30/K20 HD (C6P)/K30] V-block. OHV. Eight-cylinder. Cast iron block. **Bore & stroke:** 4.0 x 3.5 in. Displacement: 350 cid. Compression ratio: 8.2:1. Net horsepower: 165 at 3800 rpm. Maximum torque: 275 lb.-ft. at 1600 rpm. Five main bearings. Hydraulic valve lifters. Carburetor: Rochester four-barrel. Order Code LS9(A). Not available in California.

[Optional C10/C20/C30/K10/K20/K30/C20 HD (C6P)/K20 HD (C6P)] V-block. OHV. Diesel. Eight-cylinder. Cast iron block. **Bore & stroke:** 3.98 x 3.80 in. Displacement: 379 cid. Compression ratio: 21.5:1. Net horsepower: 130 at 3600 rpm. Maximum torque: 240 lb.-ft. at 2000 rpm. Hydraulic valve lifters. Carburetor: fuel-injection. Order Code LH6(A).

[Optional C20 HD (C6P)/C20/C30/K30] V-block. OHV. Eight-cylinder. Cast iron block. **Bore & stroke:** 4.25 x 4 in. Displacement: 454 cid. Compression ratio: 7.9:1. Net horsepower: 210 at 3800 rpm. Maximum torque: 340 lb.-ft. at 2800 rpm. Five main bearings. Hydraulic valve lifters. Carburetor: Rochester four-barrel. Order Code LE8(A).

1983

[Standard S-10] Inline. OHV. OHC. Four-cylinder. Cast iron block. **Bore & stroke:** 3.42 x 3.23 in. Displacement: 119 cid. Compression ratio: 8.4:1. Net horsepower: 82 at 4600 rpm. Maximum torque: 101 lb.-ft. at 3000 rpm. Hydraulic valve lifters. Order Code LR1.

[Standard S-10 Blazer/optional Extended-Cab S-10 models] Inline. OHV. Four-cylinder. Cast iron block. **Bore & stroke:** 3.50 x 3.15 in. Displacement: 121 cid. Compression ratio: 9.3:1. Net horsepower: 83 at 4000 rpm. Maximum torque: 108 lb.-ft. at 2400 rpm. Hydraulic valve lifters. Carburetor: Rochester two-barrel. Order Code LQ2.

[Optional S-10/S-10 Blazer] Inline. OHV. Diesel. Four-cylinder. Cast iron block. **Bore & stroke:** 3.46 x 3.62 in. Displacement: 136.6 cid. Net horsepower: 62 at 4300 rpm. Maximum torque: 96 lb.-ft. at 2200 rpm. Hydraulic valve lifters. Order Code LQ7.

[Optional S-10/S-10 Blazer] V-block. OHV. Six-cylinder. Cast iron block. **Bore & stroke:** 3.50 x 2.99 in. Displacement: 173 cid. Compression ratio: 8.5:1. Net horsepower: 110 at 4800 rpm. Maximum torque: 145 lb.-ft. at 2100 rpm. Hydraulic valve lifters.

[Standard El Camino] V-block. OHV. Six-cylinder. Cast iron block. **Bore & stroke:** 3.7 x 3.48 in. Displacement: 229 cid. Compression ratio: 8.6:1. Net horsepower: 110 at 4200 rpm. Torque: 170 lb.-ft. at 2000 rpm. Four main bearings. Hydraulic valve lifters. Carburetor: Rochester two-barrel.

[Standard C10/C20/K10]. Inline. OHV. Six-cylinder. Cast iron block. **Bore & stroke:** 3.9 x 3.5 in. Displacement: 4.1-liter (250 cid). Compression ratio: 8.3:1. Net horsepower: [C10] 120 at 4000 rpm. Torque 205 lb.-ft. at 2000 rpm. Seven main bearings. Hydraulic valve lifters. Carburetor: Rochester two-barrel. Order Code LE3(A).

[Optional C20 HD/C20/C30/K20 HD/K301] Inline. OHV. Six-cylinder. Cast iron block. **Bore & stroke:** 3.9 x 4.1 in. Displacement: 4.8-liters (292 cid). Compression ratio: 7.8:1. Net horsepower: 115 at 3600 rpm. Net torque: 215 lb.-ft. at 1600 rpm. Five main bearings. Hydraulic valve lifters. Carburetor: Rochester one-barrel. Order Code L25(B).

[Optional C10/C20 K10/El Camino]. V-block. OHV. Eight-cylinder. Cast iron block. **Bore & stroke:** 3.74 x 3.48 in. Displacement: 5-liters (305 cid). Compression ratio: 9.2:1. Net horsepower: [C10] 165 at 4400 rpm. Torque: 240 lb.-ft. at 2000 rpm. Five main bearings. Hydraulic valve lifters. Carburetor: Rochester four-barrel. Order Code LE9(C).

[Optional: El Camino] V-block. OHV. Diesel. Eight-cylinder. Cast iron block. **Bore & stroke:** 4.0 x 3.5 in. Displacement: 350 cid. Net horsepower: 105 rpm. Five main bearings. Fuel-injected.

[Optional C20/C20 HD/C30/K10/K20/K20 HD/K30] V-block. OHV. Eight-cylinder. Cast iron block. **Bore & stroke:** 4.0 x 3.5 in. Displacement: 5.7-liters (350 cid). Compression ratio: 8.2:1. Net horsepower: 165 at 3800 rpm. Torque: 275 lb.-ft. at 1600 rpm. Five main bearings. Hydraulic valve lifters. Carburetor: Rochester four-barrel. Order Code LS9(A).

[Optional C10/C20/C20 HD/C30/K10/K20/K20 HD/K30] V-block. OHV. Diesel. Eight-cylinder. Cast iron block. **Bore & stroke:** 3.98 x 3.80 in. Displacement: 6.2-liters (379 cid). Compression ratio: 21.3:1. Net horsepower: 130 at 3600 rpm. Torque: 240 lb.-ft. at 2000 rpm. Order Code LH6(D).

[Optional C20 HD/C20/C30/K30] V-block. OHV. Eight-cylinder. Cast iron block. **Bore & stroke:** 4.3 x 4.0 in. Displacement: 7.4-liters (454 cid).

Compression ratio: 7.9:1. Net horsepower: 230 at 3800 rpm. Net. Torque: 360 lb.-ft. at 2800 rpm. Five main bearings. Hydraulic valve lifters. Carburetor: four-barrel. Order Code LE8(A).

1984

[Standard 108.3-in. wheelbase Regular-Cab S-10 models and all models with California emissions] Inline. OHV. OHC. Four-cylinder. Cast iron block. Bore & stroke: 3.42 x 3.23 in. Displacement: 119 cid. Compression ratio: 8.4:1. Net horsepower: 82 at 4000 rpm. Maximum torque: 101 lb.-ft. at 3000 rpm. Order Code LR1(A).

[Standard All S-10 models except short wheelbase Regular-Cab models. Not available in California] Inline. OHV. Four-cylinder. Cast iron block. Bore & stroke: 3.50 x 3.15 in. Displacement: 121 cid. Compression ratio: 9.3:1. Net horsepower: 83 at 4600 rpm. Maximum torque: 108 lb.-ft. at 2400 rpm. Order Code LQ2(B).

[Optional S-10 4 x 2 regular and Maxi-Cab models] Inline. OHV. Diesel. Four-cylinder. Cast iron block. Bore & stroke: 3.46 x 3.62 in. Displacement: 137 cid. Compression ratio: 21:1. Net horsepower: 62 at 4300 rpm. Maximum torque: 96 lb.-ft. at 2200 rpm. Order Code LQ7(A).

[Optional All S-10 models] V-block. OHV. Six-cylinder. Cast iron block. Bore & stroke: 3.50 x 2.99 in. Displacement: 173 cid. Compression ratio: 8.5:1. Net horsepower: 110 at 4800 rpm. Maximum torque: 145 lb.-ft. at 2100 rpm. Order Code LR2(B).

[Standard El Camino] V-block. OHV. Six-cylinder. Cast iron block. Bore & stroke: 3.7 x 3.48 in. Displacement: 229 cid. Net horsepower: 110 at 4000 rpm. Torque: 190 lb.-ft. at 1600 rpm. Four main bearings. Hydraulic valve lifters. Carburetor: Two-barrel.

[Standard C10/C20/K10] Inline. OHV. Six-cylinder. Cast iron block. Bore & stroke: 3.9 x 3.5 in. Displacement: 250 cid. Compression ratio: 8.3:1. Net horsepower: 115 at 3600 rpm. Maximum torque: 200 lb.-ft. at 2000 rpm. Seven main bearings. Hydraulic valve lifters. Carburetor: Rochester staged two-barrel. Order Code LE3(A).

[Standard C20 HD (C6P)/C20 Bonus/Crew/C30/K20 HD (C6P)/K30] Inline. OHV. Six-cylinder. Cast iron block. Bore & stroke: 3.876 x 4.12 in. Displacement: 292 cid. Compression ratio: 7.8:1. Net horsepower: 115 at 3600 rpm. Maximum torque: 215 lb.-ft. at 1600 rpm. Five main bearings. Hydraulic valve lifters. Carburetor: Rochester one-barrel. Order Code L25(B).

[Optional C10/C20 K10, Standard K10 Blazer] V-block. OHV. Eight-cylinder. Cast iron block. Bore & stroke: 3.736 x 3.480 in. Displacement: 305 cid. Compression ratio: 9.2:1. Net horsepower: 160 at 4400 rpm. Maximum torque: 235 lb.-ft. at 2000 rpm. Five main bearings. Hydraulic valve lifters. Carburetor: Rochester staged four-barrel (Electronic spark control). Order Code LE9(C).

[Optional El Camino] V-block. OHV. Eight-cylinder. Cast iron block. Bore & stroke: 3.7 x 3.48 in. Displacement: 305 cid. Compression ratio: 9.2:1. Net horsepower: 160 at 4400 rpm., 235 lb.-ft. at 2000 rpm. Five main bearings. Hydraulic valve lifters. Carburetor: Rochester model four-barrel.

[Optional El Camino] V-block. OHV. Diesel. Eight-cylinder. Cast iron block. Bore & stroke: 4.0 x 3.5 in. Displacement: 350 cid. Net horsepower: 105. Five main bearings. Hydraulic valve lifters. Fuel-injection.

[Optional in specific 10/20/30 models] V-8. OHV. Eight-cylinder. Cast iron block. Bore & stroke: 4.0 x 3.5 in. Displacement: 350 cid. Compression ratio: 8.2:1. Net horsepower: 165 at 3800 rpm. Maximum torque: 275 lb.-ft. at 1600 rpm. Five main bearings. Hydraulic valve lifters. Carburetor: Rochester four-barrel. Order Code LS9(A).

[Optional All 4 x 2 /4 x 4 /Full Size Pickups/K10 Blazer] V-block. OHV. Diesel. Eight-cylinder. Cast iron block. Bore & stroke: 3.98 x 3.80 in. Displacement: 379 cid. Compression ratio: 21.3:1. Net horsepower: 130 at 3600 rpm. Maximum torque: 240 lb.-ft. at 2000 rpm. Hydraulic valve lifters. Order Code LH6(D).

[Optional C20 HD (C6P)/C20/C30/K30] V-block. OHV. Eight-cylinder. Cast iron block. Bore & stroke: 4.250 x 4 in. Displacement: 454 cid. Compression ratio: 7.9:1. Net horsepower: 230 at 3800 rpm. Maximum torque: 360 lb.-ft. at 2800 rpm. Five main bearings. Hydraulic valve lifters. Carburetor: Rochester four-barrel. Order Code LE8(A).

1985

Inline. OHV. Four-cylinder. Cast iron block. Bore & stroke: 3.42 x 3.23 in. Displacement: 119 cid.

Compression ratio: 8.4:1. Net horsepower: 82 at 4600 rpm. Net torque: 101 lb.-ft. at 3000 rpm. Ordering code LR1.

Inline. OHV. Diesel Four-cylinder. Cast iron block. Bore & stroke: 3.46 x 3.62 in. Displacement: 137 cid. Compression ratio: 21:1. Net horsepower: 62 at 4300 rpm. Net torque: 96 lb.-ft. at 2200 rpm. Ordering code LQ7.

Inline. OHV. Four-cylinder. Cast iron block. Bore & stroke: 4 x 3.00 in. Displacement: 151 cid. Compression ratio: 9.0:1. Net horsepower: 92 at 4400 rpm. Net torque: 132 lb.-ft. at 2800 rpm. Electronic fuel injection. Ordering code LN8.

V-block. OHV. Six-cylinder. Cast iron block. Bore & stroke: 3.50 x 2.99 in. Displacement: 173 cid. Compression ratio: 8.5:1. Net horsepower: 110 at 4800 rpm. Net torque: 145 lb.-ft. at 2100 rpm. Electronic fuel injection.

V-block. OHV. Six-cylinder. Cast iron block. Bore & stroke: 4.0 x 3.48 in. Displacement: 262 cid. Compression ratio: 9.3:1. Net horsepower: 155 at 4000 rpm. Torque: 230 lb.-ft. at 2400 rpm. Hydraulic valve lifters. Carburetor: Single four-barrel. Ordering code LB1.

V-block. OHV. Six-cylinder. Cast iron block. Bore & stroke: 4.0 x 3.48 in. Displacement: 202 cid. Compression ratio: 9.3:1. Net horsepower: 130 at 3600 rpm. 210 lb.-ft. at 2000 rpm. Hydraulic valve lifters. Electronic fuel injection. Ordering code LB4.

Inline. OHV. Six-cylinder. Cast iron block. Bore & stroke: 3.9 x 4.1 in. Displacement: 292 cid. Compression ratio: 7.8:1. Net horsepower: 115 at 3600 rpm. Net torque: 215 lb.-ft. at 1600 rpm. Seven main bearings. Hydraulic valve lifters. Carburetor: Rochester single one-barrel. Ordering code L25.

V-block. OHV. Eight-cylinder. Cast iron block. Bore & stroke: 3.74 x 3.48 in. Displacement: 305 cid. Compression ratio: 9.5:1. Net horsepower: 150 at 4000 rpm. Net torque: 240 lb.-ft. at 2000 rpm. Five main bearings. Hydraulic valve lifters. Carburetor: Single four-barrel. Ordering code LG4.

V-block. OHV. Eight-cylinder. Cast iron block. Bore & stroke: 3.74 x 3.48 in. Displacement: 305 cid. Compression ratio: 9.2:1. Net horsepower: 160 at 4400 rpm. Net torque: 235 lb.-ft. at 2000 rpm. Four main bearings. Hydraulic valve lifters. Carburetor: Rochester single four-barrel. Ordering code LE9.

V-block. OHV. Eight-cylinder. Cast iron block. Bore & stroke: 4.0 x 3.5 Displacement: 350 cid. Compression ratio: 8.3:1. Net horsepower: 160 at 3800 rpm. Net torque: 250 lb.-ft. at 2800 rpm. Five main bearings. Hydraulic valve lifters. Carburetor: Rochester four-barrel. Ordering code LT9.

V-block. OHV. Eight-cylinder. Cast iron block. Bore & stroke: 4.0 x 3.48 in. Displacement: 350 cid. Compression ratio: 8.2:1. Net horsepower: 165 at 3800 rpm. Net torque: 275 lb.-ft. at 1600 rpm. Carburetor: Rochester single four-barrel. Ordering code LS9.

V-block. OHV. Diesel eight-cylinder. Cast iron block. Bore & stroke: 3.98 x 3.82 in. Displacement: 379 cid. Compression ratio: 21.3:1. Net horsepower: 130 at 3600 rpm. Net torque: 240 lb.-ft. at 2000 rpm. Hydraulic valve lifters. Fuel-injection. Ordering code LH6.

Inline. Diesel. OHV. Eight-cylinder. Cast iron block. Bore & stroke: 3.98 x 3.80 in. Displacement: 379 cid. Compression ratio: 21.3:1. Net horsepower: 151 at 3600 rpm. Net torque: 248 lb.-ft at 2000 rpm. Hydraulic valve lifters. Fuel-injection. Ordering code LL4.

V-block. OHV. Eight-cylinder. Cast iron block. Bore & stroke: 4.3 x 4.0 in.

V-block. OHV. Displacement: 454 cid. Compression ratio: 7.9:1. Net horsepower: 230 at 3800 rpm. Net torque: 360 lb.-ft. at 2800 rpm. Five main bearings. Carburetor: Rochester single four-barrel. Ordering code LE8.

1986

[Optional S-10 Pickup, S-10 Blazer] (Diesel). Inline. OHV. Four-cylinder. Cast iron block. Bore & stroke: 3.46 x 3.62 in. Displacement: 137 cid (2.2 liter). Brake horsepower: 62 at 4300 rpm. Taxable horsepower: 19.50. Torque: 96 lb.-ft. at 2200 rpm. Hydraulic valve lifters. VIN code S. Manufactured by Isuzu of Japan.

[Standard S-10 Pickup, S-10 Blazer] (Gas). Inline. OHV. Four-cylinder. Cast iron block. Bore & stroke: 4.0 x 3.0 in. Displacement: 151 cid (2.5 liter). Compression ratio: 9.0:1. Brake horsepower: 92 at 4400 rpm. Taxable horsepower: 25.6. Torque: 134 lb.-ft. at 2800 rpm. Hydraulic valve lifters. Carburetor: Two-barrel. VIN code E, manufactured by Pontiac.

[Optional S-10 Pickup, S-10 Blazer] (Gas). V-block. OHV. Six-cylinder. Cast iron block. **Bore & stroke:** 3.5 x 2.99 in. Displacement: 173 cid (2.8 liter). Compression ratio: 8.5:1. Brake horsepower: 125 at 4800 rpm. Taxable horsepower: 29.4. Torque: 150 lb.-ft. at 2200 rpm. Hydraulic valve lifters. Induction system: TBI. VIN code B. Manufactured by Chevrolet.

[Standard El Camino] (Gas). V-block. OHV. Six-cylinder. Cast iron block. **Bore & stroke:** 4.0 x 3.48 in. Displacement: 262 cid (4.3 liter). Compression ratio: 9.3:1. Brake horsepower: 140 at 4000 rpm. Taxable horsepower: 38.4. Torque: 225 lb.-ft. at 2000 rpm. Hydraulic valve lifters. Carburetor: Two-barrel. VIN code Z.

[Standard C/K10, C/K20, C/K30, K Blazer] (Gas). V-block. OHV. Six-cylinder. Cast iron block. **Bore & stroke:** 4.0 x 3.48 in. Displacement: 262 cid (4.3 liter). Compression ratio: 9.5:1. Brake horsepower: 155 at 4000 rpm. Taxable horsepower: 38.4. Torque: 230 lb.-ft at 2400 rpm. Hydraulic valve lifters. Induction system: TBI. VIN code N.

[Standard Crew-Cab Pickup, Bonus Cab Pickup] (Gas). Inline. OHV. Six-cylinder. Cast iron block. **Bore & stroke:** 3.88 x 4.12 in. Displacement: 292 cid (4.8 liter). Brake horsepower: 115 at 4000 rpm. Taxable horsepower: 36.13. Torque: 210 lb.-ft. at 2800 rpm. Hydraulic valve lifters. Carburetor: Two-barrel. VIN code T. Manufactured by Chevrolet. Standard in Step-Vans and Crew Cab/Bonus Cab Pickups.

[Optional C/K10, C/K20, C/K30, K Blazer, El Camino] (Gas). V-block. OHV. Eight-cylinder. Cast iron block. **Bore & stroke:** 3.74 x 3.48 in. Displacement: 305 cid (5.0 liter). Compression ratio: 8.6:1. Brake horsepower: 155 at 4000 rpm. Taxable horsepower: 44.76. Torque: 245 lb.-ft. at 1600 rpm. Hydraulic valve lifters. Carburetor: Four-barrel. VIN code F.

[Optional C/K10, C/K20, C/K30, K Blazer, El Camino] (Gas). V-block. OHV. Eight-cylinder. Cast iron block. **Bore & stroke:** 3.74 x 3.48 in. Displacement: 305 cid (5.0 liter). Brake horsepower: 160 at 4400 rpm. Taxable horsepower: 44.76. Torque: 235 lb.-ft. at 2000 rpm. Hydraulic valve lifters. Carburetor: Four-barrel. VIN code H. Manufactured by Chevrolet.

[Optional C/K10, C/K20, C/K30, K Blazer with heavy-duty emissions] (Gas). V-block. OHV. Eight-cylinder. Cast iron block. **Bore & stroke:** 4.0 x 3.48 in. Displacement: 350 cid (5.7 liter). Compression ratio: 8.3:1. Brake horsepower: 160 at 3800 rpm. Taxable horsepower: 51.2. Torque: 275 lb.-ft. at 2400 rpm. Hydraulic valve lifters. Carburetor: Four-barrel. VIN code A. This engine manufactured by various GM divisions.

[Optional C/K10, C/K20, C/K30, K Blazer] (Gas). V-block. OHV. Eight-cylinder. Cast iron block. **Bore & stroke:** 4.0 x 3.48 in. Displacement: 350 cid (5.7 liter). Compression ratio: 8.2:1. Brake horsepower: 165 at 3800 rpm. Taxable horsepower: 51.2. Torque: 275 lb.-ft. at 1600 rpm. Hydraulic valve lifters. Carburetor: Four-barrel. VIN code L. Manufactured by Chevrolet.

[Optional C/K10, C/K20, C/K30, K Blazer] (Gas). V-block. OHV. Eight-cylinder. Cast iron block. **Bore & stroke:** 4.0 x 3.48 in. Displacement: 350 cid (5.7 liter). Brake horsepower: 185 at 4000 rpm. Taxable horsepower: 51.2. Torque: 285 lb.-ft. at 2400 rpm. Hydraulic valve lifters. Carburetor: Four-barrel. VIN code M. Manufactured by Chevrolet.

[Diesel Option] (Diesel). V-block. OHV. Eight-cylinder. Cast iron block. **Bore & stroke:** 3.98 x 3.82 in. Displacement: 379 cid (6.2 liter). Brake horsepower: 130 at 3600 rpm. Taxable horsepower: 50.69. Torque: 240 lb.-ft. at 2000 rpm. Hydraulic valve lifters. Carburetor: Four-barrel. VIN code C. Manufactured by Chevrolet. Diesel option.

[Diesel Option] (Diesel). V-block. OHV. Eight-cylinder. Cast iron block. **Bore & stroke:** 3.98 x 3.82 in. Displacement: 379 cid (6.2 liter). Brake horsepower: 148 at 3600 rpm. Taxable horsepower: 50.69. Torque: 246 lb.-ft. at 2000 rpm. Hydraulic valve lifters. Carburetor: Four-barrel. VIN code J. Manufactured by Chevrolet. Diesel option.

1987

[Standard in S10/T10, S-Series Blazer (all)] Inline. Tech IV four-cylinder. **Bore & stroke:** 4.00 x 3.00 in. Displacement: 2.5-liter 151 cid. Brake horsepower: 92 at 4400 rpm. Torque: 130 lb.-ft. at 2300 rpm. Compression ratio: 8.3:1. EFI/Throttle-body-injection. VIN Code E. GM-built.

[Optional in S10, optional in S-Series Blazers] V-block. Six-cylinder. **Bore & stroke:** 3.52 x 2.99 in. Displacement: 2.8-liter 173 cid. Brake horsepower: 125 at 4800 rpm. Torque: 150 lb.-ft. at 2400 rpm.

Compression ratio: 8.9:1. EFI/Throttle-body-injection. VIN Code R. Chevrolet-built.

[Standard in El Camino] V-block. Six-cylinder. Bore & stroke: 4.0 x 3.48 in. Displacement: 4.3-liter 262 cid. Brake horsepower: 145 at 4200 rpm. Torque: 225 lb.-ft. at 2000 rpm. Compression ratio: 9.3:1. EFI/Throttle-body-injection. VIN Code n.a. GM-built.

[Standard in R/V10 and R20 pickups, standard in C/K 1500/2500, optional in S10/T10 pickups, optional in all S-Blazers] V-block. Six-cylinder. Bore & stroke: 4.0 x 3.48 in. Displacement: 4.3-liter 262 cid. Brake horsepower: 160 at 4000 rpm. Torque: 235 lb.-ft. at 2400 rpm. Compression ratio: 9.1:1. EFI/Throttle-body-injection. VIN Code Z. Chevrolet-built.

[Standard in El Camino] V-block. Eight-cylinder. Bore & stroke: 3.74 x 3.48 in. Displacement: 5.0-liter 305 cid. Brake horsepower: 150 at 4000 rpm. Torque: 240 lb.-ft. at 2400 rpm. EFI/Throttle-body-injection. VIN Code n.a. Chevrolet-built.

[Optional in R/V10, R/V20,] V-block. Eight-cylinder. Bore & stroke: 3.74 x 3.48 in. Displacement: 5.0-liter 305 cid. Brake horsepower: 170 at 4000 rpm. Torque: 255 lb.-ft. at 2400 rpm. EFI/Throttle-body-injection. VIN Code H. Chevrolet-built.

[Standard in heavy-duty R/V30, optional in R/V and C/K pickups] V-block. Eight-cylinder. Bore & stroke: 4.0 x 3.48 in. Displacement: 5.7-liter 350 cid. Brake horsepower: 190 at 4000 rpm. Torque: 300 lb.-ft. at 2400 rpm. Compression ratio: 8.6:1. EFI/Throttle-body-injection. VIN Code A. GM-built.

[Standard in R/V Blazer] V-block. Eight-cylinder. Bore & stroke: 4.0 x 3.48 in. Displacement: 5.7-liter 350 cid. Brake horsepower: 210 at 4000 rpm. Compression ratio: 9.3:1. Torque: 300 lb.-ft. at 2800 rpm. EFI/Throttle-body-injection. VIN Code K. Chevrolet-built.

[Optional in R/V30 pickup] Diesel. V-block. Light-duty. Eight-cylinder. Bore & stroke: 3.98 x 3.82 in. Displacement: 6.2-liter 379 cid. Brake horsepower: 148 at 3600 rpm. Torque: 248 lb.-ft. at 2000 rpm. VIN Code J. GM-built.

[Optional in R/V30 pickup] Diesel. V-block. Heavy-duty. Eight-cylinder. Bore & stroke: 3.98 x 3.82 in. Displacement: 6.2-liter 379 cid. Brake horsepower: 130 at 3600 rpm. Torque: 240 lb.-ft. at 2000 rpm. VIN Code C. GM-built.

1988

[Standard in S-10/T-10, S-Series Blazer 4 x 2] Inline. Four-cylinder. Bore & stroke: 4.00 x 3.00 in. Displacement: 2.5-liter (151 cid). Brake horsepower: 92 at 4400 rpm. Torque: 130 lb.-ft. at 2300 rpm. Compression ratio: 8.3:1. EFI/Throttle-body-injection. VIN Code E. GM-built.

[Standard in S-Series Blazer 4 x 4 s, optional in S-10] V-block. Six-cylinder. Bore & stroke: 3.52 x 2.99 in. Displacement: 2.8-liter (173 cid). Brake horsepower: 125 at 4800 rpm. Torque: 150 lb.-ft. at 2400 rpm. Compression ratio: 8.9:1. EFI/Throttle-body-injection. VIN Code R. Chevrolet-built.

[Standard in C/K 1500/2500, optional in S-10/T-10 pickups, optional in all S-Blazers] V-block. Six-cylinder. Bore & stroke: 4.0 x 3.48 in. Displacement: 4.3-liter (262 cid). Brake horsepower: 160 at 4000 rpm. Torque: 235 lb.-ft. at 2400 rpm. Compression ratio: 9.1:1. EFI/Throttle-body-injection. VIN Code Z. Chevrolet-built. [

[Standard in C/K, R3500] Inline. Six-cylinder. Bore & stroke: 3.88 x 4.12 in. Displacement: 4.8-liter (292 cid). Brake horsepower: 115 at 4000 rpm. Torque: 210 lb.-ft. at 800 rpm. Compression ratio: 7.8:1, Carburetor: 1V. VIN Code T. Chevrolet-built.

[Optional in C/K 1500, C/K 2500] V-block. Eight-cylinder. Bore & stroke: 3.74 x 3.48 in. Displacement: 5.0-liter (305 cid). Brake horsepower: 170 at 4000 rpm. Torque: 255 lb.-ft. at 2400 rpm. EFI/Throttle-body-injection. VIN Code H. Chevrolet-built.

[Standard in heavy-duty C/K 3500, optional in R/V pickups] V-block. Eight-cylinder. Bore & stroke: 4.0 x 3.48 in. Displacement: 5.7-liter (350 cid). Brake horsepower: 190 at 4000 rpm. Torque: 300 lb.-ft. at 2400 rpm. Compression ratio: 8.6:1. EFI/Throttle-body-injection. VIN Code A. GM-built.

[Standard in C/K Blazer, optional] V-block. Eight-cylinder. Bore & stroke: 4.0 x 3.48 in. Displacement: 5.7-liter (350 cid). Brake horsepower: 210 at 4000 rpm. Compression ratio: 9.3:1. Torque: 300 lb.-ft. at 2800 rpm. EFI/Throttle-body-injection. VIN Code K. Chevrolet-built.

[Optional in C/K 3500 pickup] Diesel. V-block. Light-duty. Eight-cylinder. Bore & stroke: 3.98

x 3.82 in. Displacement: 6.2-liter (379 cid). Brake horsepower: 148 at 3600 rpm. Torque: 248 lb.-ft. at 2000 rpm. VIN Code J. GM-built.

[Optional in C/K 3500 pickup] Diesel. V-block. Heavy-duty. Eight-cylinder. Bore & stroke: 3.98 x 3.82 in. Displacement: 6.2-liter (379 cid). Brake horsepower: 130 at 3600 rpm. Torque: 240 lb.-ft. at 2000 rpm. VIN Code C. GM-built.

1989

[Standard in S-10/T-10] Inline. Four-cylinder. Bore & stroke: 4.00 x 3.00 in. Displacement: 2.5-liter (151 cid). Brake horsepower: 92 at 4400 rpm. Torque: 130 lb.-ft. at 2300 rpm. Compression ratio: 8.3:1. EFI/Throttle-body-injection. VIN Code E. GM-built.

[Standard in S-Series Blazer, optional in S-10] V-block. Six-cylinder. Bore & stroke: 3.52 x 2.99 in. Displacement: 2.8-liter (173 cid). Brake horsepower: 125 at 4800 rpm. Torque: 150 lb.-ft. at 2400 rpm. Compression ratio: 8.9:1. EFI/Throttle-body-injection. VIN Code R. Chevrolet-built.

[Standard in C/K 1500/2500, optional in S-10/T-10 pickups] V-block. Six-cylinder. Bore & stroke: 4.0 x 3.48 in. Displacement: 4.3-liter (262 cid). Brake horsepower: 160 at 4000 rpm. Torque: 235 lb.-ft. at 2400 rpm. Compression ratio: 9.1:1. EFI/Throttle-body-injection. VIN Code Z. Chevrolet-built.

[Optional in C/K1500, C/K2500] V-block. Eight-cylinder. Bore & stroke: 3.74 x 3.48 in. Displacement: 5.0-liter (305 cid). Brake horsepower: 170 at 4000 rpm. Torque: 255 lb.-ft. at 2400 rpm. EFI/Throttle-body-injection. VIN Code H. Chevrolet-built.

[Standard in heavy-duty C/K3500, optional in C/K pickups] V-block. Eight-cylinder. Bore & stroke: 4.0 x 3.48 in. Displacement: 5.7-liter (350 cid). Brake horsepower: 190 at 4000 rpm. Torque: 300 lb.-ft. at 2400 rpm. Compression ratio: 8.6:1. EFI/Throttle-body-injection. VIN Code A. GM-built.

[Standard in C/K Blazer] V-block. Eight-cylinder. Bore & stroke: 4.0 x 3.48 in. Displacement: 5.7-liter (350 cid). Brake horsepower: 210 at 4000 rpm. Compression ratio: 9.3:1. Torque: 300 lb.-ft. at 2800 rpm. EFI/Throttle-body-injection. VIN Code K. Chevrolet-built

[Optional in C/K3500 pickup] Diesel. V-block. Light-duty. Eight-cylinder. Bore & stroke: 3.98 x 3.82 in. Displacement: 6.2-liter (379 cid). Brake horsepower: 148 at 3600 rpm. Torque: 248 lb.-ft. at 2000 rpm. VIN Code J. GM-built.

[Optional in C/K3500 pickup] Diesel. V-block. Heavy-duty. Eight-cylinder. Bore & stroke: 3.98 x 3.82 in. Displacement: 6.2-liter (379 cid). Brake horsepower: 130 at 3600 rpm. Torque: 240 lb.-ft. at 2000 rpm. VIN Code C. GM-built.

1990

[Standard in S10] Inline. Four-cylinder. Bore & stroke: 4.00 x 3.00 in. Displacement: 2.5-liter (151 cid). Brake horsepower: 105 at 4800 rpm. Torque: 135 lb.-ft. at 3200 rpm. Compression ratio: 8.3:1. EFI/Throttle-body-injection. VIN Code A. GM-built.

[Optional in S10] V-block. Six-cylinder. Bore & stroke: 3.52 x 2.99 in. Displacement: 2.8-liter (173 cid). Brake horsepower: 125 at 4800 rpm. Torque: 150 lb.-ft. at 2400 rpm. Compression ratio: 8.9:1. EFI/Throttle-body-injection. VIN Code R. Chevrolet-built.

[Standard in C/K2500 Extended-Cab long-box pickups] V-block. Heavy-duty. Six-cylinder. Bore & stroke: 4.0 x 3.48 in. Displacement: 4.3-liter (262 cid). Brake horsepower: 155 at 4000 rpm. Torque: 230 lb.-ft. at 2400 rpm. Compression ratio: 8.6:1. EFI/Throttle-body-injection. VIN Code B. GM-built.

[Standard in S/T-series Blazer, standard in C/K 1500/2500, standard in T10 pickups, optional in S10 pickups] V-block. Six-cylinder. Bore & stroke: 4.0 x 3.48 in. Displacement: 4.3-liter (262 cid). Brake horsepower: 160 at 4000 rpm. Torque: 235 lb.-ft. at 2400 rpm. Compression ratio: 9.1:1. EFI/Throttle-body-injection. VIN Code Z. Chevrolet-built.

[Optional in C/K1500, C/K2500] V-block. Eight-cylinder. Bore & stroke: 3.74 x 3.48 in. Displacement: 5.0-liter (305 cid). Brake horsepower: 170 at 4000 rpm. Torque: 255 lb.-ft. at 2400 rpm. EFI/Throttle-body-injection. VIN Code H. Chevrolet-built.

[Standard in C/K3500, optional in C/K pickups] V-block. Eight-cylinder. Bore & stroke: 4.0 x 3.48 in. Displacement: 5.7-liter (350 cid). Brake horsepower: 190 at 4000 rpm. Torque: 300 lb.-ft. at 2400 rpm. Compression ratio: 8.6:1. EFI/Throttle-body-injection. VIN Code A. GM-built.

[Standard in C/K Blazer] V-block. Eight-cylinder. Bore & stroke: 4.0 x 3.48 in. Displacement: 5.7-liter (350 cid). Brake horsepower: 210 at 4000 rpm. Compression ratio: 9.3:1. Torque: 300 lb.-ft. at

2800 rpm. EFI/Throttle-body-injection. VIN Code K. Chevrolet-built.

[Standard in 454SS, Optional in C/K1500, C/K2500, C/K3500] V-block. Eight-cylinder. Bore & stroke: 4.25 x 4.00 in. Displacement: 7.4-liter (454 cid). Brake horsepower: 230 at 3600 rpm. Torque: 385 lb.-ft. at 1600 rpm. Throttle-body- fuel-injection. VIN Code N. Chevrolet-built.

[Optional in C/K3500 pickup] Diesel. V-block. Light-duty. Eight-cylinder. Bore & stroke: 3.98 x 3.82 in. Displacement: 6.2-liter (379 cid). Brake horsepower: 148 at 3600 rpm. Torque: 248 lb.-ft. at 2000 rpm. VIN Code J. GM-built.

[Optional in C/K3500 pickup] Diesel. V-block. Heavy-duty. Eight-cylinder. Bore & stroke: 3.98 x 3.82 in. Displacement: 6.2-liter (379 cid). Brake horsepower: 130 at 3600 rpm. Torque: 240 lb.-ft. at 2000 rpm. VIN Code C. GM-built.

1991

[Standard in S10] Inline. Four-cylinder. Bore & stroke: 4.00 x 3.00 in. Displacement: 2.5-liter (151 cid). Brake horsepower: 105 at 4800 rpm. Torque: 135 lb.-ft. at 3200 rpm. Compression ratio: 8.3:1. Throttle-body-injection. VIN Code A. GM-built.

[Optional in S10] V-block. Six-cylinder. Bore & stroke: 3.52 x 2.99 in. Displacement: 2.8-liter (173 cid). Brake horsepower: 125 at 4800 rpm. Torque: 150 lb.-ft. at 2400 rpm. Compression ratio: 8.9:1. Throttle-body-injection. VIN Code R. Chevrolet-built.

[Standard in C/K1500/2500 pickups] V-block. Six-cylinder. Bore & stroke: 4.0 x 3.48 in. Displacement: 4.3-liter (262 cid). Brake horsepower: 155 at 4000 rpm. Torque: 230 lb.-ft. at 2400 rpm. Compression ratio: 8.6:1. Throttle-body-injection. VIN Code B. GM-built.

[Standard in S-Series Blazer, optional in S-Series pickups, optional in C/K 1500/2500] V-block. Six-cylinder. Bore & stroke: 4.0 x 3.48 in. Displacement: 4.3-liter (262 cid). Brake horsepower: 160 at 4000 rpm. Torque: 235 lb.-ft. at 2400 rpm. Compression ratio: 9.:11. Throttle-body-injection. VIN Code Z. Chevrolet-built.

[Optional in C/K1500, C/K2500] V-block. Eight-cylinder. Bore & stroke: 3.74 x 3.48 in. Displacement: 5.0-liter (305 cid). Brake horsepower: 170-175 at 4000 rpm. Torque: 255-270 lb.-ft. at 2400 rpm. Throttle-body-injection. VIN Code H. Chevrolet-built.

[Standard in C/K3500, optional in C/K pickups] V-block. Eight-cylinder. Bore & stroke: 4.0 x 3.48 in. Displacement: 5.7-liter (350 cid). Brake horsepower: 190 at 4000 rpm. Torque: 300 lb.-ft. at 2400 rpm. Compression ratio: 8.6:1. Throttle-body-injection. VIN Code A. GM-built.

[Standard in C/K Blazer, optional in C/K1500/2500/3500] V-block. Eight-cylinder. Bore & stroke: 4.0 x 3.48 in. Displacement: 5.7-liter (350 cid). Brake horsepower: 210 at 4000 rpm. Compression ratio: 9.3:1. Torque: 300 lb.-ft. at 2800 rpm. Throttle-body-injection. VIN Code K. Chevrolet-built.

[Optional in C/K1500, C/K2500, C/K3500] V-block. Eight-cylinder. Bore & stroke: 4.25 x 4.00 in. Displacement: 7.4-liter (454 cid). Brake horsepower: 230 at 3600 rpm. Torque: 385 lb.-ft. at 1600 rpm. Throttle-body- fuel-injection. VIN Code N. Chevrolet-built.

[Optional in C/K3500 pickup] Diesel. V-block. Eight-cylinder. Bore & stroke: 3.98 x 3.82 in. Displacement: 6.2-liter (379 cid). Brake horsepower: 130 at 3600 rpm. Torque: 240 lb.-ft. at 2000 rpm. VIN Code C. GM-built.

1992

[Standard in S10] Inline. Four-cylinder. Bore & stroke: 4.00 x 3.00 in. Displacement: 2.5-liter (151 cid). Brake horsepower: 105 at 4800 rpm. Torque: 135 lb.-ft. at 3200 rpm. Compression ratio: 8.3:1. EFI/Throttle-body-injection. VIN Code A. GM-built.

[Optional in S10 (4 x 2) only] V-block. Six-cylinder. Bore & stroke: 3.52 x 2.99 in. Displacement: 2.8-liter (173 cid). Brake horsepower: 125 at 4800 rpm. Torque: 150 lb.-ft. at 2400 rpm. Compression ratio: 8.9:1. EFI/Throttle-body-injection. VIN Code R. Chevrolet-built.

[Standard early-1992 S-Series Blazer] V-block. Vortec six-cylinder. Bore & stroke: 4.0 x 3.48 in. Displacement: 4.3-liter (262 cid). Brake horsepower: 155 at 4000 rpm. Torque: 230 lb.-ft. at 2400 rpm. Compression ratio: 9.1:1. EFI/Throttle-body-injection. VIN Code B. Chevrolet-built.

[Standard in T10, standard in late-1992 S-Series Blazer, optional in S10, standard in C/K 1500/2500] V-block. Vortec six-cylinder. Bore &

stroke: 4.0 x 3.48 in. Displacement: 4.3-liter (262 cid). Brake horsepower: 160 at 4000 rpm. Torque: 235 lb.-ft. at 2400 rpm. Compression ratio: 9.1:1. EFI/Throttle-body-injection. VIN Code Z. Chevrolet-built.

[Optional in S-Series Blazer] V-block. Enhanced Vortec six-cylinder. Bore & stroke: 4.0 x 3.48 in. Displacement: 4.3-liter (262 cid). Brake horsepower: 200 at 4400 rpm. Torque: 260 lb.-ft. at 3600 rpm. Compression ratio 9.3:1: Central-point-injected. VIN Code W. GM-built.

[Optional in C/K1500, C/K2500] V-block. Eight-cylinder. Bore & stroke: 3.74 x 3.48 in. Displacement: 5.0-liter (305 cid). Brake horsepower: 170-175 at 4000 rpm. Torque: 255-270 lb.-ft. at 2400 rpm. EFI/Throttle-body-injection. VIN Code H. Chevrolet-built.

[Optional in C/K1500/2500 pickups] V-block. Eight-cylinder. Bore & stroke: 4.0 x 3.48 in. Displacement: 5.7-liter (350 cid). Brake horsepower: 190 at 4000 rpm. Torque: 300 lb.-ft. at 2400 rpm. Compression ratio: 8.6:1. EFI/Throttle-body-injection. VIN Code A. GM-built.

[Standard in C/K Blazer, standard in C/K3500, optional in C/K1500/2500] V-block. Eight-cylinder. Bore & stroke: 4.0 x 3.48 in. Displacement: 5.7-liter (350 cid). Brake horsepower: 210 at 4000 rpm. Compression ratio: 9.3:1. Torque: 300 lb.-ft. at 2800 rpm. EFI/Throttle-body-injection. VIN Code K. Chevrolet-built

[Optional in C/K1500, C/K2500, C/K3500] V-block. Eight-cylinder. Bore & stroke: 4.25 x 4.00 in. Displacement: 7.4-liter (454 cid). Brake horsepower: 230 at 3600 rpm. Torque: 385 lb.-ft. at 1600 rpm. Throttle-body-fuel-injection. VIN Code N. Chevrolet-built.

[Optional in C/K3500 pickup] Diesel. V-block. Eight-cylinder. Bore & stroke: 3.98 x 3.82 in. Displacement: 6.2-liter (379 cid). Brake horsepower: 130 at 3600 rpm. Torque: 240 lb.-ft. at 2000 rpm. VIN Code C. GM-built.

[Optional in C/K3500 pickup] Diesel. V-block. Eight-cylinder. Turbo Diesel. Bore & stroke: 4.06 x 3.82 in. Displacement: 6.5-liter (400 cid). Brake horsepower: 190 at 3400 rpm. Torque: 380 lb.-ft. at 1700 rpm. VIN Code F. GM-built.

[Optional in all C/K2500 pickups and C/K3500 Crew-Cabs] Diesel. V-block. Eight-cylinder. Turbocharged. Bore & stroke: 4.06 x 3.82 in. Displacement: 6.5-liter (400 cid). Brake horsepower: 190 at 3400 rpm. Torque: 240 lb.-ft. at 2000 rpm. VIN Code F. GM-built.

1993

[Standard in S10] Inline. Four-cylinder. Bore & stroke: 4.00 x 3.00 in. Displacement: 2.5-liter (151 cid). BHP: 105 at 4800 rpm. Torque: 135 lb.-ft. at 3200 rpm. Compression ratio: 8.3:1. EFI/Throttle-body-injection. VIN Code A. GM-built.

[Optional in S10] V-block. Six-cylinder. Bore & stroke: 3.52 x 2.99 in. Displacement: 2.8-liter (173 cid). BHP: 125 at 4800 rpm. Torque: 150 lb.-ft. at 2400 rpm. EFI/Throttle-body-injection. VIN Code R. Chevrolet-built.

[Standard C/K1500, C/K2500, T10, S-Blazer, optional in S10] V-block. Six-cylinder. Bore & stroke: 4.0 x 3.48 in. Displacement: 4.3-liter (262 cid). BHP: 165 at 4000 rpm. Torque: 235 lb.-ft. at 2400 rpm. Compression ratio: 9.1:1. EFI/Throttle-body-injection. VIN Code Z. Chevrolet-built.

[Optional in C/K1500, C/K2500] V-block. Eight-cylinder. Bore & stroke: 3.74 x 3.48 in. Displacement: 5.0-liter (305 cid). BHP: 170 at 4000 rpm. Torque: 255 lb.-ft. at 2400 rpm. EFI/Throttle-body-injection. VIN Code H. Chevrolet-built.

[Standard in C/K Blazer, C/K3500] V-block. Eight-cylinder. Bore & stroke: 4.0 x 3.48 in. Displacement: 5.7-liter (350 cid). BHP: 210 at 4000 rpm. Compression ratio: 9.1:1. Torque: 300 lb.-ft. at 2800 rpm. EFI/Throttle-body-injection. VIN Code K. Chevrolet-built

[Optional in C/K1500, C/K2500, C/K3500] V-block. Eight-cylinder. Bore & stroke: 4.25 x 4.00 in. Displacement: 7.4-liter (454 cid). BHP: 230 at 3600 rpm. Torque: 385 lb.-ft. at 1600 rpm. Throttle-body-fuel-injection. VIN Code N. Chevrolet-built.

[Optional in C/K2500 Pickup, optional in C/K3500 Pickup] Diesel. V-block. Heavy-duty. Diesel. Eight-cylinder. Bore & stroke: 3.98 x 3.82 in. Displacement: 6.2-liter (379 cid). BHP: 130 at 3600 rpm. Torque: 240 lb.-ft. at 2000 rpm. VIN Code C. Chevrolet-built.

[Optional in all C/K2500 Pickups and C/K3500 Crew-Cabs] Diesel. V-block. Eight-cylinder. Turbocharged. Bore & stroke: 4.06 x 3.82 in. Displacement: 6.5-liter (400 cid). BHP: 190 at 3400

1994

[Standard in S10] Inline. Four-cylinder. Bore & stroke: 3.5 x 3.46 in. Displacement: 2.2-liter (133 cid). BHP: 118 at 5200 rpm. Torque: 130 lb.-ft. at 2800 rpm. EFI/Throttle-body-injection. VIN Code 4. GM-built.

{Standard in C/K1500, C/K2500, T10/S10 Extended-Cab, S-Blazer, G10] V-block. Vortec six-cylinder. Bore & stroke: 4.0 x 3.48 in. Displacement: 4.3-liter (262 cid). BHP: 155-165 at 4000 rpm. Torque: 230-235 lb.-ft. at 2400 rpm. EFI/Throttle-body-injection. VIN Code Z. Chevrolet-built.

[Optional in C/K Pickups with GVWR less than 8,600 lb] V-block. Eight-cylinder. Bore & stroke: 3.74 x 3.48 in. Displacement: 5.0-liter (305 cid). BHP: 170-175 at 4200 rpm. Torque: 255-265 lb.-ft. at 2800 rpm. EFI/Throttle-body-injection. VIN Code H. GM-built.

[Standard in C/K Blazer, C/K3500] V-block. Light-Duty. Eight-cylinder. Bore & stroke: 4.0 x 3.48 in. Displacement: 5.7-liter (350 cid). BHP: 200-210 at 4000 rpm. Torque: 300 lb.-ft. at 2800 rpm. EFI/Throttle-body-injection. VIN Code K. Chevrolet-built.

[Optional in C/K3500] V-block. Eight-cylinder. Bore & stroke: 4.25 x 4.00 in. Displacement: 7.4-liter (454 cid). BHP: 230 at 3600 rpm. Torque: 385 lb.-ft. at 1600 rpm. Throttle-body- fuel-injection. VIN Code N. Chevrolet-built.

[Optional in C/K1500/2500] Diesel. V-block. Light-duty. Eight-cylinder. Bore & stroke: 4.06 x 3.82 in. Displacement: 6.5-liter (400 cid). BHP: 155 at 3600 rpm. Torque: 275 lb.-ft. at 1700 rpm. VIN Code P. GM-built.

[Optional in C/K3500 Crew-Cab] Diesel. V-block. Heavy-duty. Eight-cylinder. Bore & stroke: 4.06 x 3.82 in. Displacement: 6.5-liter (400 cid). BHP: 180 at 3400 rpm. Torque: 360 lb.-ft. at 1700 rpm. VIN Code S. GM-built.

[Optional in all C/K Pickups with GVWRs (automatic) 11,000 to 14,500 lb., (manual) 9,000 to 12,000 lb.] Diesel. V-block. Eight-cylinder. Turbocharged. Bore & stroke: 4.06 x 3.82 in. Displacement: 6.5-liter (400 cid). BHP: 190 at 3400 rpm. Torque: 240 lb.-ft. at 2000 rpm. VIN Code F. GM-built.

1995

[Standard in S10] Inline. Four-cylinder. Bore & stroke: 3.5 x 3.46 in. Displacement: 2.2-liter (133 cid). BHP: 118 at 5200 rpm. Torque: 130 lb.-ft. at 2800 rpm. EFI/Throttle-body-injection. VIN Code 4. GM-built.

[Standard in C/K1500, C/K2500, T10, S10 Extended-Cab, Blazer] V-block. Vortec six-cylinder. Bore & stroke: 4.0 x 3.48 in. Displacement: 4.3-liter (262 cid). BHP: 155-165 at 4000 rpm. Torque: 230-235 lb.-ft. at 2400 rpm. EFI/Throttle-body-injection. VIN Code Z. Chevrolet-built.

[Optional in S10] V-block. Enhanced Vortec six-cylinder. Bore & stroke: 4.0 x 3.48 in. Displacement: 4.3-liter (262 cid). BHP: 200 at 4400 rpm. Torque: 260 lb.-ft. at 3600 rpm. Central-point-injected. VIN Code W. GM-built.

[Optional in C/K pickups with GVWR less than 8,600-lb] V-block. Eight-cylinder. Bore & stroke: 3.74 x 3.48 in. Displacement: 5.0-liter (305 cid). BHP: 170-175 at 4200 rpm. Torque: 255-265 lb.-ft. at 2800 rpm. EFI/Throttle-body-injection. VIN Code H. GM-built.

[Standard in C/K3500] V-block. Light-Duty. Eight-cylinder. Bore & stroke: 4.0 x 3.48 in. Displacement: 5.7-liter (350 cid). BHP: 200-210 at 4000 rpm. Torque: 300 lb.-ft. at 2800 rpm. EFI/Throttle-body-injection. VIN Code K. Chevrolet-built

[Optional in C/K3500] V-block. Eight-cylinder. Bore & stroke: 4.25 x 4.00 in. Displacement: 7.4-liter (454 cid). BHP: 230 at 3600 rpm. Torque: 385 lb.-ft. at 1600 rpm. Throttle-body-fuel-injection. VIN Code N. Chevrolet-built.

[Optional in C/K1500/2500] Diesel. V-block. Light-duty. Eight-cylinder. Bore & stroke: 4.06 x 3.82 in. Displacement: 6.5-liter (400 cid). BHP: 155 at 3600 rpm. Torque: 275 lb.-ft. at 1700 rpm. VIN Code P. GM-built.

[Optional in C/K3500 Crew-cab] V-block. Heavy-duty. Eight-cylinder. Bore & stroke: 4.06 x 3.82 in. Displacement: 6.5-liter (400 cid). BHP: 180 at 3400 rpm. Torque: 360 lb.-ft. at 1700 rpm. VIN Code S. GM-built.

[Optional in all C/K pickups with GVWRs (automatic) 11,000 to 14,500-lb., (manual) 9,000 to 12,000-lb.] V-block. Eight-cylinder.

Turbocharged. **Bore & stroke:** 4.06 x 3.82 in. Displacement: 6.5-liter (400 cid). BHP: 190 at 3400 rpm. Torque: 240 lb.-ft. at 2000 rpm. VIN Code F. GM-built.

1996

[Standard in S10] Inline. Four-cylinder. **Bore & stroke 3.50 x 3.46 in. Displacement:** 2.2-liter (134 cid). Brake horsepower: 118 at 5200 rpm. Torque: 130 lb-ft at 2800 rpm. Sequential fuel injection (SFI). VIN code 4; engine code LN2.

[Standard in T10; Optional in S10] V-block. **Vortec six-cylinder. Bore & stroke 4.00 x 3.48 in. Displacement:** 4.3-liter (262 cid). Brake horsepower: 170 at 4400 rpm (2WD), 180 at 4400 rpm (4WD). Torque: 235 lb-ft at 2800 rpm. Sequential fuel injection (SFI). VIN code X; engine code LF6.

[Standard in C/K1500; Standard in Blazer; Standard in T10; Optional in S10: V-block. Vortec six-cylinder. Bore & stroke 4.00 x 3.48 in. Displacement: 4.3-liter (262 cid). Brake horsepower: 190 at 4400 rpm. Torque: 250 lb-ft at 2800 rpm. Sequential fuel injection (SFI). VIN code W; engine code L35.

[Standard in C/K2500 Extended-Cab; Optional in C/K Regular Cab]: V-block. Vortec eight-cylinder. Bore & stroke 3.74 x 3.48 in. Displacement: 5.0-liter (305 cid). Brake horsepower: 220 at 4600 rpm. Torque: 285 lb-ft at 2800 rpm. Sequential fuel injection (SFI). VIN code M; engine code L30.

[Standard in C/K3500: Optional C/K2500]: V-block. Vortec eight-cylinder. Bore & stroke 4.00 x 3.48 in. Displacement: 5.7-liter (350 cid). Brake horsepower: 250 at 4600 rpm below 8600-lb GVWR; 245 at 4200 rpm at 8600-lb and above GVWR. Torque: 330 lb-ft at 2800 rpm below 8600-lb GVR; 330 lb-ft at 2800 rpm at 8600-lb and above GVWR. Sequential fuel injection (SFI). VIN code R; engine code L31.

[Optional in C/K with 8600-lb. and Higher GVRW]: V-block. Vortec eight-cylinder. Bore & stroke 4.25 x 4.00 in. Displacement: 7.4-liter (454 cid). Brake horsepower: 290 at 4600 rpm. Torque: 410 lb-ft at 3200 rpm. Sequential fuel injection (SFI). VIN code J; engine code L29.

DIESEI:

[Optional in K10 and in C/K2500 and C/K3500]: V-block. Turbo-diesel eight-cylinder. Bore & stroke 4.06 x 3.82 in. Displacement: 6.5-liter (395 cid). Brake horsepower: 180 at 3400 rpm. Torque: 360 lb-ft at 1800 rpm. Indirect electronic fuel injection with turbo. VIN code F; engine code L65.

1997

[Standard in S10]: Inline. Four-cylinder. Bore & stroke 3.50 x 3.46 in. Displacement: 2.2-liter (134 cid). Brake horsepower: 118 at 5200 rpm. Torque: 130 lb-ft at 2800 rpm. Sequential fuel injection (SFI). VIN code 4; engine code LN2

[Standard in T10; Optional S10]: V-block. Vortec six-cylinder. Bore & stroke 4.00 x 3.48 in. Displacement: 4.3-liter (262 cid). Brake horsepower: 170 at 4400 rpm (2WD), 180 at 4400 rpm (4WD). Torque: 235 lb-ft at 2800 rpm. Sequential fuel injection (SFI). VIN code X; engine code LF6.

[Standard C/K1500 and C/K2500 Regular-Cab; Optional S-10]: V-block. Vortec six-cylinder. Bore & stroke 4.00 x 3.48 in. Displacement: 4.3-liter (262 cid). Brake horsepower: 190 at 4400 rpm. Torque: 250 lb-ft at 2800 rpm. Sequential fuel injection (SFI). VIN code W; engine code L35.

[Standard C/K2500 Extended-Cab; Optional C/K1500 Regular-Cab]: V-block. Vortec eight-cylinder. Bore & stroke 3.74 x 3.48 in. Displacement: 5.0-liter (305 cid). Brake horsepower: 220 at 4600 rpm. Torque: 285 lb-ft at 2800 rpm. Sequential fuel injection (SFI). VIN code M; engine code L30.

[Standard in C/K3500: Optional C/K1500 and C/K2500]: V-block. Vortec eight-cylinder. Bore & stroke 4.00 x 3.48 in. Displacement: 5.7-liter (350 cid). Brake horsepower: 250 at 4600 rpm below 8600-lb. GVWR; 245 at 4200 rpm at 8600-lb and above GVWR. Torque: 330 lb-ft at 2800 rpm below 8600-lb GVR; 330 lb-ft at 2800 rpm at 8600-lb and above GVWR. Sequential fuel injection (SFI). VIN code R; engine code L31.

[Optional in C/K with 8600-lb. and Higher GVRW]: V-block. Vortec eight-cylinder. Bore & stroke 4.25 x 4.00 in. Displacement: 7.4-liter (454 cid). Brake horsepower: 290 at 4600 rpm. Torque: 410 lb-ft at

3200 rpm. Sequential fuel injection (SFI). VIN code J; engine code L29.

DIESEL:

[Optional in K10 and in C/K2500 and C/K3500]: V-block. Turbo-diesel eight-cylinder. Bore & stroke 4.06 x 3.82 in. Displacement: 6.5-liter (395 cid). Brake horsepower: 180 at 3400 rpm. Torque: 360 lb-ft at 1800 rpm. Indirect electronic fuel injection with turbo. VIN code F; engine code L65.

1998

[Standard in S10]: Inline. Four-cylinder. Bore & stroke 3.50 x 3.46 in. Displacement: 2.2-liter (134 cid). Brake horsepower: 120 at 5000 rpm. Torque: 130 lb-ft at 2800 rpm. Sequential fuel injection (SFI). VIN code 4; engine code LN2.

[Standard in T10; Optional in S10]: V-block. Vortec six-cylinder. Bore & stroke 4.00 x 3.48 in. Displacement: 4.3-liter (262 cid). Brake horsepower: 175 at 4400 rpm (2WD), 180 at 4400 rpm (4WD). Torque: (2WD) 240 lb-ft at 2800 rpm, (4WD) 245 lb-ft at 2800 rpm. Sequential fuel injection (SFI). VIN code X; engine code LF6.

[Standard in Regular-Cab C/K1500 and C/K2500; Optional in S10]: V-block. Vortec six-cylinder. Bore & stroke 4.00 x 3.48 in. Displacement: 4.3-liter (262 cid). Brake horsepower: 200 at 4400 rpm. Torque: 255 lb-ft at 2800 rpm. Sequential fuel injection (SFI). VIN code W; engine code L35.

[Standard C/K2500 Extended-Cab; Optional C/K1500 Regular-Cab]: V-block. Vortec eight-cylinder. Bore & stroke 3.74 x 3.48 in. Displacement: 5.0-liter (305 cid). Brake horsepower: 230 at 4600 rpm. Torque: 285 lb-ft at 2800 rpm. Sequential fuel injection (SFI). VIN code M; engine code L30.

[Standard in C/K3500: Optional C/K1500 and C/K2500]: V-block. Vortec eight-cylinder. Bore & stroke 4.00 x 3.48 in. Displacement: 5.7-liter (350 cid). Brake horsepower: 255 at 4600 rpm below 8600-lb. GVWR; 250 at 4200 rpm at 8600-lb and above GVWR. Torque: 330 lb-ft at 2800 rpm below 8600-lb GVR; 330 lb-ft at 2800 rpm at 8600-lb and above GVWR. Sequential fuel injection (SFI). VIN code R; engine code L31.

[Optional in C/K with 8600-lb. and Higher GVRW]: V-block. Vortec eight-cylinder. Bore & stroke 4.25 x 4.00 in. Displacement: 7.4-liter (454 cid). Brake horsepower: 290 at 4000 rpm. Torque: 410 lb-ft at 3200 rpm. Sequential fuel injection (SFI). VIN code J; engine code L29.

DIESEL:

[Optional in K10 and in C/K2500 and C/K3500]: V-block. Turbo-diesel eight-cylinder. Bore & stroke 4.06 x 3.82 in. Displacement: 6.5-liter (395 cid). Brake horsepower: 180 at 3400 rpm. Torque: 360 lb-ft at 1800 rpm. Indirect electronic fuel injection with turbo. VIN code F; engine code L65.

D. 1970-1998 Chevrolet Full-Size Pickup Color Options

1970-1974 Chevrolet Truck Color Options

Name	Ditzler Code	Model-Year(s)					
Acanthus Blue (Dark) [L]	14448		74	73	72		
Adonis Yellow [L]	82025		74	73	72		
Argent Silver (Interior)	8568				72	71	
Avocado (Interior)	44738		74	73			
Avocado (Interior)	44742		74	73			
Black (Exterior & Interior) [L]	9000		74	73	72	71	70
Black (Interior)	9248		74				
Black (Interior-flat)	9317		74		72	71	70
Black (Interior)	9387		74				
Blue [V]	2329				72		
Blue	14715			73			
Blue Gray Poly (Interior) [L]	33041			73	72		
Bright Green Poly	2676		74				
Bright Red	2258		74				
Bright Yellow Poly	2570			73			
Bright Yellow	2681		74				
Burnt Orange Poly	2565			73			
Bronze	2671		74				
Charcoal (Interior)	33048		74	73			
Charcoal (Interior)	33049		74	73			
Clematis Blue (Light) [L]	14449	75	74	73	72		
Copper Poly	2202				72	71	70
Crimson Red [L]	72096	75	74				
Dark Argent [L]	33042			73	72		
Dark Blue	2366			73			
Dark Blue	2169						70
Dark Blue (Exterior/Interior)	2366			73	72	71	
Dark Blue	12409						70
Dark Blue (Interior)	13823		74				
Dark Blue Poly (Exterior/Interior)	2169						70
Dark Blue-Green Poly	2206						70
Dark Bright Blue Poly	2564			73			
Dark Bright Blue Poly	2672		74				
Dark Bronze [V]	2451				72		

Name	Ditzler Code	Model-Year(s)
Dark Bronze Poly	2203	70
Dark Gold Poly	2204	70
Dark Green [V]	2439	72
Flat Dark Green (Interior)	44224	70
Dark Green (Interior)	44392	72 71
Dark Green Poly (Interior)	2206	70
Dark Green Poly	2207	72 70
Flat Dark Olive (Interior)	44225	70
Dark Olive (Interior)	44384	71
Dark Olive (Interior)	44390	71
Dark Olive Poly (Exterior/Interior)	2207	72 71 70
Dark Saddle (Interior)	23453	72 71
Dark Saddle (Interior)	23519	72 71
Dark Sandalwood	2368	70
Dark Sandalwood (Interior)	23374	72 71 70
Flat Dark Sandalwood (Interior)	23375	72 71 70
Flat Dark Red (Interior)	71809	74 70
Dark Red	2673	74
Dark Yellow [V]	2463	72
Desert Sand	2568	74 73
Flame Red	2258	73 70
Gold [V]	2448	72
Horizon Blue [L]	14719	74
Hugger Orange	2212	72 71 70
Ivory	8290	74
Jasmine Yellow [L]	82162	74
Light Blue	2563	74 73
Light Green [V]	2437	72
Light Olive	2571	74 73
Light Sandalwood	2370	70
Light Turquoise Poly	2572	73
Lime Poly	2674	74
Madder Red [L]	71993	74 73 72
Matte Black [L]	9222	73 72
Matte Black [L]	9396	73 72

Name	Ditzler Code	Model-Year(s)			
Matte Black [L]	9371		73	72	
Meadow Green	2208	74			
Medium Blue (Exterior/Interior)	2188	74		72	71	70
Medium Blue Poly (Exterior/Int.)	2163					70
Medium Blue-Green Poly	2205					70
Medium Gold Poly	2176			72		70
Medium Green (Exterior/Interior)	2208			72	71	70
Medium Green	2369					70
Medium Olive Poly	2097			72	71	
Midnight Black [L]	9000	74			
New Saddle (Interior)	23825	74	73		
New Saddle (Interior)	23820	74	73		
Ochre	2323	74	73	72	71
Ochre [L]	82056		73	72	
Orange [V]	2450			72	
Orange	61056			72	71	70
Palm Green [L]	44935	74			
Parchment (Interior)	23128			72	71
Pearl (Interior)	33047	74	73		
Red [V]	2189			72	
Red (Interior)	2209					70
Red (Exterior/Interior)	70704	74		72	71	70
Red-Orange	2212					70
Sandalwood (Interior)	23373					70
Silver [V]	2429			72	
Silver [L]	8593		73	72	
Silver Poly (Exterior/Interior)	32537	74	73		
Slate Blue (Exterior/Interior)	14520	74	73		
Slate Blue (Exterior/Interior)	14523	74	73		
Slate Green (Exterior/Interior)	44737	74	73		
Strato White [L]	0883	74			
Tan	2569		73		
Walnut Beige [L]	23735	74	73	72	71
Weldenia White [L]	0831	74			
Westway Tan [L]	24003	74			

Name	Ditzler Code	Model-Year(s)				
Wheatland Yellow	81348	74				
White [L]	0844		73	72		
White [V]	2058			72		
White	2185	74	73	72	71	70
Yellow	2324			72	71	
Yellow	81348			72	71	70
Yellow Gold	2567	74	73			
Yellow Green Poly	2097					70

Specify DQE for alkyd enamel, DDL for acrylic lacquer, DAR for acrylic enamel, DL or DIA for interior.
[L] = LUV Mini-Pickup truck color.
[V] = Vega Panel Express color

1975-1978 CHEVROLET COLOR OPTIONS

Name	Ditzler Code	Model-Year(s)			
Acanthus Blue (Dark) [L]	14448				75
Adonis Yellow [L]	82025				75
Black (Exterior & Interior) [L]	9000	78	77	76	75
Black (Interior)	9248	78	77	76	75
Black (Interior-flat)	9317	78	77	76	75
Black (Interior)	9387	78	77	76	75
Black (Interior)	9396	78	77	76	75
Blue (4061-P) [L]	15174	78			
Blue Gray Poly (Interior) [L]	33041	78	77	76	75
Brown Poly	2947	78	77		
Buckskin	2829	78	77		
Cardinal Red	70704			76	
Catalina Blue Poly	2672			76	75
Clematis Blue Light {L}	14449				75
Crimson Red [L]	72096	78	77	76	75
Dark Argent [L]	33042	78	77	76	75
Dark Blue	2904	78	77		
Dark Blue (Interior)	14783				75
Dark Blue (Interior)	14796				75
Dark Blue (Interior)	15070	78	77		
Flat Dark Blue (Interior)	15072	78	77		
Dark Blue Green (Interior)	45064	78	77		
Flat Dark Blue Green (Interior)	45092	78	77		

Name	Ditzler Code	Model-Year(s)			
Dark Brown (Interior)	24407	78	77		
Flat Dark Brown (Interior)	24408	78	77		
Dark Firethorn (Interior)	72145	78	77		
Flat Dark Firethorn (Interior)	72158	78	77		
Dark Gold Poly	2779			76	75
Dark Graystone (Interior)	33154				75
Dark Graystone (Interior)	33156				75
Dark Green	2951	78	77		
Dark Green (Interior)	44863				75
Dark Green (Interior)	44898				75
Dark Green Poly	2781			76	75
Dark Mandarin (Interior)	60764	78	77		
Flat Dark Mandarin (Interior)	60783	78	77		
Dark Oxblood (Interior)	72007				75
Dark Oxblood Poly (Interior)	72008				75
Dark Saddle (Interior)	23942	78	77		
Flat Dark Saddle (Interior)	23988	78	77		
Dark Saddle (Interior)	23774				75
Dark Saddle (Interior)	23778				75
Dark Sandstone (Interior)	24106				75
Dark Sandstone (Interior)	24123				75
Desert Tan [L]	24310	78	77	76	
Glenwood Green	42850			76	75
Grecian Bronze	2671			76	75
Hawaiian Blue	2188			76	75
Horizon Blue [L]	14719	78	77	76	75
Jasmine Yellow [L]	82162	78	77		75
Light Blue	2892	78	77		
Light Buckskin (Interior)	24174	78	77		
Light Graystone	2780			76	75
Light Green	2775			76	75
Light Green Poly	2905	78	77		
Light Saddle	2778			76	75
Light Smoke Gray (Interior)	33187	78	77		
Madder Red [L]	71993				75
Mahogany	2948	78	77		

Name	Ditzler Code	Model-Year(s)			
Mandarin Orange (Interior)	60761	78	77		
Matte Black [L]	9222	78	77	76	75
Matte Black [L]	9396	78	77	76	75
Matte Black [L]	9371	78	77	76	75
Medium Blue (Exterior/Interior)	2188	78	77		
Medium Gold Poly	2176			76	75
Medium Graystone (Interior)	33155				75
Medium Graystone Poly	2773	78	77	76	75
Medium Green (Interior)	44862				75
Medium Lime Poly	2774			76	75
Medium Red (Interior)	72054				75
Medium Saddle (Interior)	23797	78	77		
Medium Sandstone (Interior)	24107				75
Midnight Black [L]	9000	78	77	76	75
Midnight Blue (Interior)	15071	78	77		
Flat Midnight Blue (Interior)	15073	78	77		
Neutral	2777	78	77	76	75
Ochre [L]	82056	78	77	76	75
Palm Green [L]	44935				75
Polar White	2680	78	77	76	75
Red	2932	78	77		
Red-Brown Poly [L]	24188				75
Red Poly	2933	78	77		
Rosedale Red	2673			76	75
Russet Poly	2926	78	77		
Saddle Poly	2783			76	75
School Bus Yellow	2785				75
Shannon Green [L]	45199	78	77	76	
Silver [L]	8593	78	77	76	75
Silver Gray Poly	2860	78	77	76	
Silver Poly	8982	78	77		
Sky Blue [L]	14965	78	77	76	
Skyline Blue	2563			76	75
Strato White [L]	0883	78	77	76	75
Tangier Orange	60156	78	77	76	75
Walnut Beige [L]	23735				75

Name	Ditzler Code	Model-Year(s)			
Weldenia White	0831	78	77	76	75
Westway Tan [L]	24003				75
Wheatland Yellow	2785	78	77	76	
White [L]	2185	78	77	76	
Yellow	2929	78	77		

Specify DQE for alkyd enamel, DDL for acrylic lacquer, DAR for acrylic enamel, DL or DIA for interior.
[L] = LUV Mini-Pickup truck color.
[V] = Vega Panel Express color

1979-1998 Chevrolet Colors

1979

Silver Metallic, White, Dark Bright Blue, Medium Blue, Dark Blue, Medium Green Metallic, Bright Green Metallic, Dark Green, Yellow, Neutral, Carmel Metallic, Dark Carmine, Bright Red, Russet Metallic, Dark Brown Metallic, Dark Yellow, Charcoal and Black.

1980

Frost White, Medium Blue, Dark Blue, Light Blue Metallic, Nordic Blue Metallic, Emerald Green, Santa Fe Tan, Carmine Red, Cardinal Red, Midnight Black and Burnt Orange Metallic.

1981

Frost White, Nordic Blue Metallic, Carmine Red, Light Blue Metallic, (New) Dark Chestnut Metallic, Medium Blue, Santa Fe Tan, Midnight Black, (New) Colonial Yellow, Cardinal Red, (New) Charcoal Metallic, Dark Carmine Red, (New) Light Silver Metallic, Emerald Green and Burnt Orange Metallic. Tan, Carmine Red, Cardinal Red, Midnight Black and Burnt Orange Metallic.

1982

Frost White, (New) Light Blue Metallic, (New) Almond, (New) Mahogany Metallic, (New) Silver Metallic), (New) Midnight Blue, Carmine Red, Midnight Black, Colonial Yellow, Light Bronze Metallic. Tan, Carmine Red, Cardinal Red, Midnight Black and Burnt Orange Metallic.

1983

Almond, Silver Metallic, Light Blue Metallic, Midnight Blue, Midnight Black, Mahogany Metallic, Carmine Red, Frost White, Colonial Yellow and Light Bronze Metallic.

1984

Doeskin Tan, Desert Sand Metallic, Indian Bronze Metallic, Apple Red, Frost White, Silver Metallic, Midnight Black, Light Blue Metallic, Midnight Blue and Colonial White.

1985

Frost White, Silver Metallic, Midnight Black, Light Blue Metallic, Midnight Blue, Colonial Yellow, Doeskin Tan, Desert Sand Metallic, Indian Bronze Metallic and Apple Red.

1986

Frost White, Steel Gray Metallic, Light Blue Metallic, Midnight Blue, Canyon Copper Metallic. Doeskin Tan, Nevada Gold Metallic, Indian Bronze Metallic and Apple Red.

1987

Steel Gray Metallic, Frost White, Midnight Black, Light Blue Metallic, Galaxy Blue Metallic, Doeskin Tan, Indian Bronze Metallic, Nevada Gold Metallic, Apple Red, Emerald Metallic and Silver Metallic.

1988

Brandywine Metallic, Sandstone Metallic, Pacific Blue Metallic, Adobe Gold Metallic, Sable Black Metallic, Quicksilver Metallic, Spice Brown Metallic, Summit White, Flame Red and Iced Blue.

1989

Regular Pickups: Brandywine Metallic, Sandstone Metallic, Adobe Gold Metallic, Sable Black Metallic, Quicksilver Metallic, Summit White, Flame Red, Smoke Blue Metallic, Carmel Brown Metallic and Midnight Blue Metallic.

Bonus Cab/Crew Cab Pickups: Midnight Black, Midnight Blue, Steel Gray Metallic, Apple Red, Wheat and Frost White.

Note: *The Bonus Cab and Crew Cab models were still of the old R/V style. They were built on different assembly lines and came in different colors.*

1990

Regular Pickups: Onyx Black, Catalina Blue Metallic, Crimson Red, Sandstone Metallic, Adobe Gold Metallic, Quicksilver Metallic, Summit White, Flame Red, Smoke Blue Metallic and Carmel Brown Metallic.

Bonus Cab/Crew Cab Pickups: Midnight Black, Midnight Blue, Steel Gray Metallic, Apple Red, Wheat and Frost White.

Note: *The Bonus Cab and Crew Cab models were still of the old R/V style. They were built on different assembly lines and came in different colors.*

1991

Onyx Black, Catalina Blue Metallic, Crimson Red, Sandstone Metallic, Adobe Gold Metallic, Quicksilver Metallic, Summit White, Flame Red, Smoke Blue Metallic, Carmel Brown Metallic, Brilliant Blue and Slate.

1992

Bright Red, Beige Metallic, Brilliant Blue, Slate, Black Onyx, Catalina Blue Metallic, Crimson Red, Brandywine Metallic, Sandstone Metallic, Adobe Gold Metallic, Sable Black Metallic, Quicksilver Metallic, Summit White, Flame Red, Smoke Blue Metallic, Carmel Brown Metallic and Midnight Blue Metallic.

1993

Light Quasar Blue Metallic, Teal Green Metallic, Indigo Blue Metallic, Dark Garnet Red Metallic, Bright Red, Beige Metallic, Slate, Black Onyx, Brandywine Metallic, Sandstone Metallic, Adobe Gold Metallic, Sable Black Metallic, Quicksilver Metallic, Summit White, Flame Red, Carmel Brown Metallic and Midnight Blue Metallic.

1994

Dark Autumnwood Metallic (#56), Teal Green Metallic (#38), Onyx Black (#41), Light Autumnwood Metallic (#55), Quicksilver Metallic (#96), Burnt Red Metallic (#76), Atlantic Blue Metallic (#30), Dark Garnet Red Metallic (#84), Indigo Blue Metallic (#39), Victory Red (#754), Light Quasar Blue Metallic (#20), Summit White (#50), and Teal Blue Metallic (#36). Interiors came in vinyl, custom cloth and cloth.

1995

Teal Green Metallic (No. 38), Onyx Black (No. 41), Light Autumnwood Metallic (No. 55), Quicksilver Metallic (No. 96), Dark Garnet Red Metallic (No. 84), Indigo Blue Metallic (No. 39), Victory Red (No. 74), Light Quasar Blue Metallic (No. 20), Summit White (No. 50), and Emerald Green Metallic (No. 43). Interiors came in beige, blue, gray or red. Vinyl, cloth, Custom cloth, and Custom leather trims are offered.

1996

Teal Green Metallic (No. 38), Onyx Black (No. 41), Light Autumnwood Metallic (No. 55), Quicksilver Metallic (No. 96), Dark Garnet Red Metallic (No. 84), Indigo Blue Metallic (No. 39), Victory Red (No. 74), Light Quasar Blue Metallic (No. 20), Summit White (No. 50), and Emerald Green Metallic (No. 43). Interiors came in beige, blue, gray or red. Vinyl, cloth, Custom cloth, and Custom leather trims are offered.

1997

Teal Green Metallic (No. 38), Onyx Black (No. 41), Light Autumnwood Metallic (No. 55), Quicksilver Metallic (No. 96), Dark Garnet Red Metallic (No. 84), Indigo Blue Metallic (No. 39), Victory Red (No. 74), Light Quasar Blue Metallic (No. 20), Summit White (No. 50), and Emerald Green Metallic (No. 43). Interiors came in beige, blue, gray or red. Vinyl, cloth, Custom cloth, and Custom leather trims are offered.

1998

Teal Green Metallic (No. 38), Onyx Black (No. 41), Light Autumnwood Metallic (No. 55), Quicksilver Metallic (No. 96), Dark Garnet Red Metallic (No. 84), Indigo Blue Metallic (No. 39), Victory Red (No. 74), Light Quasar Blue Metallic (No. 20), Summit White (No. 50), and Emerald Green Metallic (No. 43). Interiors came in beige, blue, gray or red. Vinyl, cloth, Custom cloth, and Custom leather trims are offered.

CUSTOMIZING AND RESTYLING

CUSTOMIZING AND RESTYLING CHEVY PICKUPS

Twenty years ago, *Chevrolet Pickups 1946-1972* noted that enthusiasts had started "improving" the engines, bodies and interiors of those trucks, before they started giving them the "find-and-fix-to-original" treatment. Today, the same is true of 1973-1998 models. Collectors are beginning to "restore" them, but it is common to go to a cruise or car show and see the trucks lowered, jacked-up, wearing flame paint jobs or belching smoke in burn-out contests.

What goes around comes around, but with differences. In 1988, the in thing was to drop a V-8 in a six-cylinder Advance-Design pickup. Today's engine mods are more along the lines of a turbo or new computer chip. In a similar vein, trucks of the '70s-'90s are now "restyled," rather than "customized." When it comes to a trimmer who modernizes interiors, the terms have also changed. Twenty years ago, it was "reupholstery," but now it's called "building" an interior.

THEN AND NOW

When vehicles are modified now, there are things to think about that didn't seem important years ago. Even though you own a truck, you cannot modify it in ways that flaunt safety or pollution laws. In addition, if modifications that you make cause injuries or damage, you could be legally responsible. It is important to check applicable laws before making any motor vehicle modifications.

When trucks are modified, equipment "installs" must be done *right*. In many instances, professional labor is a good idea, particularly when special equipment is required. Shop safety should be a primary concern. Alterations made to a vehicle should be reported to motor vehicle agencies and insurers, to guarantee that your modified truck is legal to use and properly insured.

The information in this book is a guide to popular modifications, but the book does not cover step-by-step procedures for making alterations. We recommend that you contact the parts or equipment suppliers for how-to information or hire professionals to do installs on your truck. For legal advice, you can also contact the Specialty Vehicle Market Association at www.SEMA.org.

PERSONALIZATION

Remember when Laverne and Shirley had their names embroidered on their sweaters? Today, everyone is into *personalization*. You can purchase a T-shirt with your name or picture on it. If you buy a certain dog book, you can send an insert card to 24/7 and for $15 they will make a dust jacket for the book with your own dog pictured on it. In the auto world, where manufacturers clone successful ideas, "cookie cutter" cars and trucks are common.

By nature, older-vehicle enthusiasts are different. They drive cars and trucks that went out of style 10, 15, 20, 30 — even 50 — years ago. Those who like modified older vehicles are even more individualistic. They start with "wheels" that are out of the ordinary and do things to make them even more extraordinary.

In the 1950s, people who did mechanical modifications were "hot rodders." Those who changed a car's looks were "customizers." These terms are still used, of course, but newer ones are coming on-line. Those who hot rod computer-era vehicles are often referred to as "tuners." Modern customizes are often called "restylers." In general, they alter the looks of a vehicle with add-on body panels or decals, rather than lead body filler or "20 coats of hand-rubbed lacquer."

STARTING POINT

One thing that hasn't changed in 20 years is the fact that a restyler (customizer) can usually start with a vehicle that is cheaper because it is missing pieces and needs work. The collector/restorer will pay more to buy a "cherry" truck that has all its parts and is in pristine condition. The restyler does not have to do this, since he or she is going to completely redo the vehicle and change things from factory-stock. That doesn't mean that buying a rust bucket is a good idea, but it does mean that a truck with a relatively solid cab and frame is OK.

Many modifieds will wind up with a replacement engine, an updated and upgraded suspension, modern tires and wheels, a custom interior and a home-built cargo box and load floor. The majority of restylers save abused trucks, instead of ruining good ones. No wonder they get along so well with restorers. It's hard to fault a restyler who turns a "sow's ear" pickup into a "silk purse" truck.

ENGINE ENHANCEMENTS

Twenty years ago, engine swapping was the heartbeat of the modified truck sport. The enthusiast with a Model A Ford four-banger or a Chevy Advance-Design with a straight six wanted to upgrade to Chevy V-8 power (either small-block or big-block). Likewise, the owner of a 1960s or early 1970s truck with a carbureted V-8 was probably anxious to switch to a fuel-injected 350.

Compare this with today's enthusiast who is restyling a 1973 through 1998 Chevy pickup and wants a little more "snort" under the hood. Most likely, the truck already has a 350-, 400- or 454-cid Chevy V-8 so the motivation to make an engine swap is lower than it used to be. Swaps are still done, of course, but there are better and easier ways to gain a few "ponies" without doing a transplant.

Some of the simplest, bolt-on ways to boost horsepower quickly are the installation of high-performance aftermarket air cleaners, headers, cat-back (catalytic converter rearwards) exhaust systems and hotter-than-stock coils and plug wires. On carbureted trucks built through the mid-1980s, bigger carbs and other fuel system upgrades will also pay off in increased performance. If your mid-1970s or later truck has breaker points, it's time to add electronic ignition.

With the Computer Controlled Command system introduced in 1980, GM (and Chevy) started moving towards high-tech engine-management systems that upped factory performance levels. Naturally, there are aftermarket electronic ignition systems, control boxes and timing controllers that can boost things from that starting point. The "trick" thing these days is to swap computer chips to gain performance. This will also allow you to tune (reprogram) your truck's engine-management software using your laptop computer. Talk about cool!

More mechanically-inclined Chevy pickup lovers will not stop there. Why not rework the heads, modify the valve train or change to a more radical cam grind? Induction systems that will increase airflow to your "air pump" (engine) can be purchased readily in the aftermarket. If you want to go all out (price and performance wise) you can add a supercharger or a blower.

Naturally, when you get to the point where your once-meek little engine is breathing fire, you'll want to dress it up with such goodies as a chrome air cleaner and finned valve covers. Then you can brighten (and protect) the plug wires, vacuum lines and other hoses and tubing with colorful plastic or braided metal covers. Those who want to go "all out" will travel to a powder coating shop to have their engine "painted for life." If you do this, talk to the powder coater first. Often, he will have to work hand in hand with your machine shop to insure that the everlasting finish is applied in the right places at the right time.

If your Chevy pickup is a 1988 through 1998 model, don't be surprised if your 305- or 350-cid V-8 looks cool just the way it came from the factory. At the 1988 Chicago Auto Show, the author talked to the man who was responsible for the under hood "design" of this generation of Chevy tricks. He was a true enthusiast and a big fan of the classic V-16 Cadillac engine of the 1930s. This was one of the prettiest power plants that Detroit ever created and this man used the V-16's black-finished finned valve covers as the theme for his Chevy V-8 work. We always thought he did a marvelous job of "nailing" it.

SUSPENSION OF DISBELIEF

Truck restylers "go both ways" and that is not a lifestyle comment. We're talking about raising a truck high or "slamming" it closer to the ground. Raising or lower a pickup makes an immediate and obvious statement that the truck is no longer "stock." Raising a truck gives it a "macho" look and can increase obstacle clearance for off-road use. Lowering a truck makes it look more sophisticated and streamlined and makes it handle like a bobsled.

If you want your truck reaching for the sky, you can install one of the many body-lift kits available in the aftermarket. These require a bit more work than bolt-on accessories and it's a good idea to have some degree of mechanical skill to do this type of install. Buy a quality kit and you'll find it comes with complete (and very helpful) step-by-step instructions. You will have to remove some suspension components, so special heavy-duty tools will be required. Also, you will need to install brake line extensions so that the "juice" will get to the brakes after the wheels have been moved further from the frame than they are on a stock truck.

Lowering a truck involves different procedures front and rear. Up front, the Chevy pickup features an independent coil-spring suspension (with torsion bars on some 4 x 4 models). The front end can safely be lowered by installing shorter coil springs, deeper lower control arms or lowered spindles. Aftermarket suppliers sell all of these parts. Some enthusiasts simply adapt the sub-frame from another vehicle to the Chevy pickup, but this takes special skills.

At the rear end, Chevy pickups use a solid rear axle. The rear can be safely lowered by the use of lowering blocks or by changing the axle and leaf-spring mountings so that the axle winds up above the springs. Also available in the aftermarket are custom-designed 4-link suspensions. Some truck builders have adapted a Jaguar independent rear suspension setup to their Chevy pickups. Others have gone the route of welding in a different sub frame.

For truck owners less inclined to tear their suspensions apart, there are bolt-on upgrades ranging from air suspensions to stabilizer bars available in the aftermarket. High-performance shocks, multiple-shock setups and air shocks are other alternatives that suppliers offer for improved ride quality and handling.

This customized 1978 Chevrolet C-10 pickup was for sale at Highway 31 Auto Sales in McHenry, Illinois, when we spotted it. The truck's cab has been "chopped." It has the "slammed" look that's popular today. Note the horizontal-bars grille and the round bumper lights. John Gunnell photo

The custom pickup at Highway 31 Auto sales featured a rolled rear pan and a Step-Side box that appeared to have come from a more modern truck. The license plate was nestled into a custom recess and oblong back-up lights decorated the rear bumper. John Gunnell photo

Chevrolet Pickups 1973-1998

RETIREMENT PLAN

After making drive train and chassis modifications, many truck restylers will turn their attention to tires and wheels. Mag wheels were the trick way to go 20 years ago, but today there are lots of other options. Aftermarket wheel manufacturers offer thousands of custom designs and bright chrome spoke wheels seem to be the "hot ticket" item. Wheels with spokes that keep turning when a vehicle comes to a stop are very eye catching, though not everyone's cup of tea. In 2003, Krause Publication's released the *Complete Wheel and Tire Buyer's Guide* by Brad Bowling, a book that covers every aspect of "shodding" your truck properly. Look for it in bookstores or online. You won't find a better source of information about wheels and tires than this $21.99 book.

A wide range of truck tires will fit on most Chevy pickups without interfering with fender or frame clearance. There's usually plenty of room in those large wheel wells to fit extra-large or extra-wide tires. Most hobby truckers seem to prefer black sidewall tires or raised-white letter (RWL) styles. White sidewall designs look good on some of the fancier late-1970s models, such as those with exterior woodgrain panels. Local tire stores are very helpful in selecting tires.

Don Coonen, of Appleton, Wisconsin, owns this fully-customized 1974 Chevy C10 Fleetside long-box pickup, which actually represents a combined total of 28 years of restoration and modification work. The trucks has been updated outside, inside and under the hood. John Gunnell photo

The flared wheel wells on the custom truck circle 6-spoke chrome wheel rims. Decorative bright metal panels have been added along the bottom of the cargo box. This truck had 120,000 miles of use and was for sales at $8,500 or best offer. John Gunnell photo

Don Coonen started this "build" with the concept of a nice "street truck" in his head. He wanted to have an eye-catching everyday runner, but says "I got carried away." The first owner of the truck was his brother. Now, his wife loves it and won't let him sell the truck. John Gunnell photo

Don Coonen's truck has been lowered and fitted with custom wheels. A quick-change rear end was installed for drag racing. The headlamp lens features a "smoked glass" black-out treatment. Wisconsin "Hobbyist" plates decorate the body-color bumper and grille. *John Gunnell photo*

OUTSIDE OPPORTUNITIES

If you're interested in modifying the exterior of your pickup, there are companies willing to help. Many enthusiasts begin by taking stuff *off* their truck to give it a cleaner look. The removal of badges, nameplates and moldings is easy if you go slow. On 1970s trucks and early 1980s trucks, trim removal may require bodywork, since holes were drilled in the body, at the factory, to hold the trim in place. On 1980s and 1990s trucks, most trim and moldings are stuck on with glue.

A heat gun and scraper will remove glued trim. Specialty tool companies, such as Eastwood, make plastic tools that do a good job of taking off trim. Often, a piece of fishing line can be used to cut through adhesives that are softened with heat. Decals and vinyl graphics can also be removed with a heat gun.

Many pickup owners change outside mirrors. Bolt-on replacements are available with factory-style mountings. In some cases, chrome-plated mirrors are installed in place of black ones. Sometimes, a black or body-color mirror replaces a chrome one. There are also custom mirror with flames or other designs.

Custom headlights or headlight covers are another popular modification today. For the later model trucks, you will need a screwdriver with different types of bits to remove Allen screws or Torx fasteners. Custom taillight assemblies and covers to dress up stock taillights are other bolt-on items available from truck accessory suppliers. Cool-looking billet aluminum grilles are available for 1990s models. Stainless steel bar grilles with applications back to 1988 are another hot item. Of course, if you spend a bunch on aftermarket headlights and grilles, you'll want to add painted or stainless steel grille guards to protect your investment.

The parts mentioned so far can usually be installed by truck owners without being concerned about bodywork or paint. Other bolt-on items like bumper covers, running boards, side skirts, wheel flare, sun visors, side bars, louvers, air deflectors and hood scoops or power blisters may require color-matching. The same is true for aero side skirts, hard tonneau covers and some running boards, although chrome or matte black running boards are popular, too.

Accessories such as bed mats, plastic bed liners and slider-style rear cab windows are seen on both stock trucks and those that have been restyled. In certain climates (but not here in Wisconsin) carpeted cargo beds are popular. Some owners prefer spray-on bed liners to the plastic slide-in type.

We spotted this custom 1998 Chevy Silverado for sale in a parking lot in Stevens Point, Wisconsin and thought that the restyler's "1957 Chevy" theme for this project was a nice nod to Chevy's long legacy of building classic vehicles. John Gunnell photo

Although we didn't get to peek under the hood of the custom Chevy pickup in Stevens Point, the hood-mounted air scoop suggests that a few tweaks to the engine may have been part of this restyling project. John Gunnell photo

FINISHING TOUCHES

What most of us think of as "paint" is actually known as "finish" to an auto-body technician. Since truck enthusiasts are very interested in personalizing their vehicles, an eye-catching finish is an absolute must on a restyled truck. In some cases, the intention is to apply better-looking paint that's glossier, shinier or more distinctive than the factory finish. In other cases, the goal is to go for the wild look with unique custom color combinations, painted-on or vinyl body graphics and specials finishes like "chameleon" paint that changes color in different light. Those wild flame paint jobs that were used by 1950s hot rodders are now an "in thing" among restylers. Thanks to modern computer graphics programs, all kinds of personalized decals and decorations can easily be made up for trucks today.

INSIDE STORY

The next step in restyling or customizing a Chevy pickup is the "trim" work. This is the proper term for repairs and upgrades to the upholstery, door panels, dashboard, headliner, floor coverings and other interior items. As we mentioned earlier, the real experts in this field today — like Randy and Tina Sharpe of Deluxe Automotive Interior Stylists — talk about "building" interiors.

Chevrolet Pickups 1946-1972 suggested that in most projects, the truck restyler "may want to replace the stock bench seats with a set of bucket seats from a donor car or truck." That was probably true when that book first hit in 1988, but you have to remember that most trucks of that era had rather plain cloth or vinyl bench seats. From 1973 on, factory-supplied Chevy pickup truck interiors grew increasingly richer

This truck was first customized around 1979, when it was only five years old. In 1982 or 1983, after an interior fire, the original red color was changed to the current hue. The last time the truck was on the road, prior to the latest "build," was in 1991. John Gunnell photo

and more stylish. The plainest factory interior offered in 1980s and 1990s models probably looks fancier and more personalized than most custom interiors did two decades ago.

Due to this general upgrading of pickup truck interiors, custom trim trends have also changed. The in thing today is custom leather seat covers. These are often crafted in "sculpted" designs with different-shaped panels done in various bright colors. For example, the seats may have scallops or flames sculpted into them with the shape of the flames done in yellow, red or orange leather, while the background is in a different color. The dashboard and door panels can be trimmed to match either with film or fabric paints.

Most interior restylers strive to achieve an integrated look. They want their seat designs to "go with" their sun visors, headrests, consoles, carpets and headliner. Suppliers also offer customized gauge faces, custom steering wheel rims, pedal covers, leather shift covers, color-coordinated air conditioning vents, speaker grille covers, custom door pulls, special window cranks, design-coordinated door sill plates, pedal covers and custom dashboard inserts. The design of the various covers and inserts can range from a simulated woodgrained pattern to bright-colors to the satin-silver metallic "billet" look. Designer steering wheels in a myriad of colors are another trendy item.

MUSIC, MUSIC, MUSIC

Sound systems — as well as DVD players, video systems, satellite radios — are a big part of restyling a car or truck today. It's no wonder that "Mobile Electronics and Technology" is one of the 11 Show Sections of the SEMA Show held each fall in Las Vegas. In fact, the Specialty Equipment Marketers Association (SEMA) trade group also includes remote-mounted cameras, auxiliary lighting and security systems in this category.

Truck restylers are interested in all of these features, because they are passionate about creating a relaxing, enjoyable environment in their customized pickups. These enthusiasts use their trucks for both work and play and mobile electronics play a big part in adding to driver comfort and convenience.

The goal is to load the restyled truck up with all the "right" electronic gadgets and install them in such a way that everything looks like the factory designed it to fit. The "bolt-on" look is out when it comes to interior alterations. Today's enthusiast would rather hide an electronic device under a custom center console than have it hanging from under the dashboard. If a stereo face plate can be color-coded to match an instrument panel insert or if a video screen can be incorporated into a headrest, it's all the better. And don't forget incorporating a flip-down computer screen where the factory glove box used to be. How else are you going to "dial-in" your truck's computer chip for top performance?

100 Sources

ACCESSORIES

Advantage Truck Accessories
PO Box 1747
Elkhart, IN 46515
(574) 522-2853
www.advantagetruckaccessories.com

American Force Wheels, Inc.
3500 NW 77 Ct.
Miami, FL 33122
(800) 620-6259
www.americanforcewheels.com

Bully Dog Technologies
604 Pershing Ste B
Pocatello, ID 83210
(208) 397-3200
www.bullydog.com

Carriage Works Billet Accessories
4303 E. 140th St.
PO Box 858
Grandview, MO 64030
(816) 966-1405
www.carriageworksinc.com

Century Truck Caps
1131 D.I. Dr.
Elkhart, IN 46514
(800) 828-2277
www.centurycaps.com

Crazyfish Graphics & Accessories
2996 S. Archer Ave.
Chicago, IL 60608
(773) 254-3500
www.crazyfishgraphics.com

Smittybilt
1550 Magnolia Ave.
Corona, CA 92879
(888) 717-5797
www.smittybilt.com

Street Scene Equipment
365 McCormick Ave.
Costa Mesa, CA 92626
(888) 477-0707
www.streetsceneeq.com

TJM Products
2510 Quality Lane
Knoxville, TN 37931
(865) 670-1012
www.tjmbullbars.com

Truck Accessories Group
28858 Ventura Dr.
Elkhart, IN 46517
(800) 755-5337
www.leer.com

Warn Industries
12900 SE Capps Rd.
Clackamas, OR 97015-8903
(800) 543-9276
www.warn.com

AXLE

Lokar, Inc.
10924 Murdock Dr.
Knoxville, TN 37942
(865) 966-2269
www.lokar.com

BED LINERS

ArmorThane USA, Inc.
310 S. Union Ave.
Springfield, MO 65802
(800) 227-2905
www.sprayedonbedliners.com

Bedliner.com/Superwraps.com
PO Box 270130
Austin, TX 78727
(512) 990-8808
www.bedliner.com

BedSlide – IFW, Inc.
6451 Crater Lake Hwy
Central Point, OR 97502
(888) 807-0099
www.bedslide.com

Dual Comp
2030 Constitution Ave.
Hartland, WI 53027
(800) 992-1949
www.dualcomp.com

In addition to looking like a Wilem DeKooning artwork on wheels, this S-10 pickup featured an up-to-date tire and wheel treatment with oversized chrome rims and low-profile tires that gave it a "slammed" (lower-to-the-ground) appearance.
John Gunnell photo

BODY

American Products Company
11324 Temescal Canyon Rd.
Corona, CA 92883
(909) 898-9840

ATS Design
11110 Business Circle
Cerritos, CA 90703
(866) 213-2873
www.zex.com

Bell Powder Coating
4747 McGrath St.
Ventura, CA 93006
(805) 658-2233

Billet Specialties
500 Shawmut Ave.
LaGrange, IL 60526
(708) 588-0505
www.billetspecialties.com

C.R. Laurence Co., Inc.
2503 E. Vernon Ave.
Los Angeles, CA 90058
(800) 412-6144
www.crlaurence.com

Dash Designs, Inc.
6014 S. Ash Ave.
Tempe, AZ 85283
(480) 967-7829
www.dashdesigns.com

Dashtop
5980 Alpha Ave.
Reno, NV 89506
(800) 349-3274
www.dashtop.com

Dawn Enterprises, Inc.
9155 Sweet Valley Dr.
Cleveland, OH 44125-4223
(216) 447-1777
www.dawn-ent.com

Empire Motorsports
9261 Bally Ct.
Rancho Cucamonga, CA 91730
(909) 980-8922
www.empiremotorsports.com

Gaylord's
13538 Excelsior Dr.
Santa Fe Springs, CA 90670
(562) 529-7543
www.GaylordsLids.com

Grillcraft Custom Products
11651 Prairie Ave.
Hawthorne, CA 90250
(310) 970-0300
www.grillcraft.com

J.C. Whitney
225 N. Michigan Ave.
Chicago, IL 60601-7601
(800) 529-4486
www.jcwhitney.com

Lund International
911 Lund Blvd.
Suite 100
Noka, MN 55303
(763) 576-4200
www.lundinternational.com

Universal Products
521 Industrial St.
Goddard, KS 67052
(316) 794-8601
www.u-p.com

Wise Industries, Inc.
PO Box 149
Old Hickory, TN 37138-0149
(800) 462-8435
www.wiseindustries.com

BRAKES

Baer Brake Systems
3108 W. Thomas Rd. #1201
Phoenix, AZ 85017
(602) 233-1411
www.baer.com

Brembo North American Snowmobiler
1585 Sunflower Ave.
Costa Mesa, CA 92628
(714) 641-5831
www.brembo.com

Drive Train
Advance Adaptors
PO Box 247
Paso Robles, CA 93447
(805) 238-7000
www.advance adapters.com

ELECTRONICS

Accele Electronics
17900 Crusader Ave.
Cerritos, CA 90703
(562) 809-5090
www.accele.com

ORCA Design & Mfg.
1531 Lookout Dr.
Agoura, CA 91310
(818) 707-1629
www.focal-america.com

ENGINE

Airaid/Poweraids
14840 N. 74th St.
Scottsdale, AZ 85260
(800) 498-6951
www.airaid.com

BBK Performance Parts
1871 Delilah St.
Corona, CA 92879
(909) 735-2400
www.blingzwheels.com

Blueprint Engines
404 W. 8th St.
Kearney, NE 68845
(800) 483-4263
www.blueprintengines.com

Classic Tube (stainless lines)
80 Rotech Dr.
Lancaster, NY 14086
(800) 882-3711
www.classictube.com

Competition Cams
3406 Democrat Rd.
Memphis, TN 38118
(888) 817-1008
www.zex.com

DoneRite Automotive Performance
999 Happy Hollow Rd.
Mosinee, WI 54455-8404
(715) 693-5740
www.doneriteautomotive.com

DUB Air
18239 S. Figueroa St.
Gardena, CA 90248
(310) 532-6617
www.dub-air.com

Gale Banks Engineering
546 Duggan Ave.
Azusa, CA 9702
(800) 601-8072
www.bankspower.com

Holley Performance Products
1801 Russellville Rd.
PO Box 10360
Bowling Green, KY 42102-7360
(800) Holley-1
www.holley.com

Jet Performance
17491 Apex Circle
Huntington Beach, CA 92647
(800) 736-9578
www.jetchip.com

K & N Engineering
PO Box 1329
Riverside, CA 92502
(888) 949-1832
www.knfilters.com

Magnuson Products
3172 Bunsen Ave.
Ventura, CA 93003
(805) 289-0044
www.magnacharger.com

Dan Coonen's truck originally had a two-barrel version of the popular Chevy 350 V-8. Today it runs a blown small-block. Note the MSD ignition and wires, braided lines and cool details like the powder-coated master cylinder and heater blower. There's chrome everywhere. *John Gunnell photo*

MSD Ignition
1490 Henry Brennan Dr.
El Paso, TX 79936
(915) 857-5200
www.msdignition.com

Painless Performance
2501 Ludelle St.
Ft. Worth, TX 76105-1036
(817) 244-6212
www.painlessperformance.com

Powerdyne
104-C East Ave K-4
Lancaster, CA 93535
(661) 723-2800
www.powerdyne.com

Smeding Performance
3340 Sunrise Blvd. Unit E
Rancho Cordova, CA 95742
(916) 638-0899
www.smedingperformance.com

Superchips
1790 E. Airport Blvd.
Sanford, FL 32773
(407) 585-7000
www.superchips.com

Whipple Superchargers
3292 N. Weber
Fresno, CA 93722
(559) 442-1261

EXHAUST

Bassani Xhaust
2900 E. La Jolla Ave.
Anaheim, CA 92806
866-782-3283
www.bassani.com

Billy Boat Performance Exhaust
23045 N. 15th Ave.
Phoenix, AZ 85027
(623) 518-7600
www.bbexhaust.com

Borla USA
5901 Edison Dr.
Oxnard, CA 93033
Ph: 805-986-8600
www.borla.com

Corsa Performance
140 Blaze Parkway
Berea, OH 44017
(800) 486-0999
www.corsaperformance.com

Dynatech Competition Exhausts
PO Box 608
Booneville, IN 47601
(800) 848-5850
www.dynayechheaders.com

Doug Thawley Headers
1180 W. Railroad St.
Corona, CA 92882
(951) 739-5900
www.dougthawleyheaders.com

Pypes Performance Exhaust
2880 Bergey Rd. Unit E
Hatfield, PA 19440
(800) 421-3890
www.pypesexhaust.com

SLP Performance Parts
1501 Industrial Way North
Toms River, NJ 08755
732-240-3696
www.slponline.com

INTERIOR

Deluxe Automotive Interior Styling
960 S. Lay Ave.
St. Clair, MO 63077
www.deluxeautointerior.com

Grant Products
700 Allen Ave.
Glendale, CA 91201
(818) 247-2910
www.grantproducts.com

Katzkin Leather
6868 Acco St.
Montebello, CA 90640
(800) 842-0590
www.katzskin.com

Woodview Interior Kits
5670 Timberlea Blvd.
Mississauga, Ontario, Canada L4W 4M6
(800) 797-DASH
www.woodcorp.com

PAINT

DuPont Hot Hues
4417 Lancaster Pike
Wilmington, DE 19805
(302) 992-2959
www.hothues.dupont.com

House of Kolor
210 Crosby St.
Picayune, MS 39466
(800) 845-2500
www.houseofkolor.com

READING

Auto Trim & Restyling News
3520 Challenger St.
Torrance, CA 90503
(951) 371-8519
www.bobit.com

Krause Publications
700 E. State St.
Iola, WI 54990
(715) 445-2214
www.krausebooks.com

SHOWS

Carlisle All-Truck Nationals
1000 Bryn-Mawr Rd.
Carlisle, PA 17013-1588
(717) 243-7855
www.carsatcarlisle.com

Iola Military Vehicle and Work Truck Show
PO Box 1
Iola, WI 54945
(715) 445-4000
www.iolaoldcarshow.com

SOUND

Audiovox Corp.
150 Matcus Blvd.
Hauppaugue, NY 11788
(800) 645-4994
www.audiovox.com

J. L. Audio
10369 N. Commerce Parkway
Miramar, FL 33025
(954) 443-1100
www.jlaudio.com

Scosche
1550 Pacific Ave.
Oxnard, CA 93033
(800) 621-3695
www.sc0sche.com

Street Sound Plus
2751 Thousand Oaks Blvd
Thousand Oaks, CA 91362
(805) 557-1054

SUSPENSION

Air Lift Co.
PO Box 80167
Lansing, MI 48908
(800) 248-0892
www.airliftcompany.com

Air Ride Technologies
350 S. St. Charles St.
Jasper, IN 47546
(812) 481-4712
www.ridetech.com

Bilstein Shock Absorbers
14102 Stowe Dr.
Poway, CA 92064
(858) 386-5903
www.bilstein.com

Eaton Detroit Springs
1555 Michigan Ave.
Detroit, MI 48216
(313) 963-3839
www.eatonsprings.com

Edelbrock Corp.
2700 California St.
Torrance, CA 90503
(310) 781-2222
www.edelbrock.com

Full-Force Suspension, Inc.
1914 Bon View Ave. #8
Ontario, CA 91761
(909) 673-0000
www.zex.com

Race Car Dynamics
11433 Woodside Ave.
Santee, CA 92071
(619) 566-4723
www.redsuspension.com

SporTrucks by Dean
619 Fitch Ave. No. 1
Moorpark, CA 93021
(805) 529-3844

Trailmaster Suspension
1550 Magnolia Ave.
No. 101
Corona, CA 92879-2073
(908) 736-8686
www.trailmastersuspension.com

TIRES

Bridgestone/Firestone
535 Marriott Dr.
Nashville, TN 37214-2428
(615) 937-1000
www.bridgestone-firestone.com

Continental Tire North
1800 Continental Blvd.
Charlotte, NC 28202
(704) 583-8900
www.continentaltire.com

TONNEAU COVERS

A.R.E.
PO Box 1100
Massillon, OH 44648
(330) 830-7800
www.4are.com

Snugtop
1711 Harbor Ave.
Long Beach, CA 90813
(562) 432-5454
www.snugtop.com

Truck Covers USA
6875 Nancy Rides Dr., Ste C
San Diego, CA 92121
(858) 622-9135
www.truckcoversusa.com

TOOLS

The Eastwood Company
263 Shoemaker Rd.
Pottstown, PA 19464
(610) 323-2200
www.eastwood.com

WHEELS

AKA Motoring Accessories Corp.
1500 S. Milliken Ave. Ste D
Ontario, CA 91761
(909) 390-7228
www.akamotoringus.com

ALT Wheels
705 Challenger St.
Brea, CA 92821
(714) 255-9099
www.altwheels.com

BBH Luxury Motorsports
390 Camarillo Ranch Rd.
Camarillo, CA 93012
(866) 541-5412

Blingz, Inc.
390 Camarillo Ranch Rd.
Camarillo, CA 93012
(866) 541-5412
www.blingzwheels.com

Centerline Wheels
PO Box 321187
Detroit, MI 48232-1187
(519) 734-8464
www.centerline.com

Dayton Wire Wheel
115 Compark Rd.
Dayton, OH 45459
(800) 862-6000
www.daytonwirewheel.com

Diablo Wheels
4315 Marine Ave.
Baldwin Park, CA 91706
(626) 813-2500
www.diablousa.com

Echelon Wheels
1428 E. 6th St.
Corona, CA 92879
(951) 549-8671
www.echelonwheels.com

Eco Wheel Corp.
15619 S. Blackburn Ave.
Norwalk, CA 90650
(562) 921-9888
www.ecowheel.com

Wheel Concepts
1103 Lawrence Dr.
Newbury Park, CA 91320
(805) 376-2113

A view from the left-hand rear of this sano-looking '98 Silverado exhibits other nods to the iconic '57 Chevy, such as the "Chevrolet"-over-V tailgate emblems and the stylized anodized Bel-Air-tailfin-shaped decorations on the sides of the cargo box. John Gunnell photo

COLLECTING AND RESTORING

A THEORY ABOUT COLLECTING

Classic-car auctioneer Dean Kruse, of Auburn, Ind., has sold thousands of collector vehicles, from modestly-priced Model Ts to $1 million dollar Duesenbergs. Years ago — around the same time that I was writing my earlier book about 1946-1972 Chevy pickups. Dean told me his theory on what motivates vintage-vehicle collectors. The auctioneer stated his opinion that cars and trucks start to become collectible when they reach 20 years of age.

According to Kruse, 20 years was also the point at which people who admired those vehicles when they were new were finding that they had *discretionary* income to spend on things they wanted years ago. Up to that point, most of their money went towards things they needed. Then, the kids moved out, the mortgage got paid and they suddenly had money to spend on their dreams.

This theory did seem to more or less "fit" my book, since it was being written in 1988 and Chevy trucks of the 1967-1972 style were starting to get very popular. Although the '72 models weren't quite 20 years old, they were basically part of a series that was introduced in 1967, about two decades before the book was published. As a collector, you should keep this 20-year rule in mind as you build your collection. However, it is also important to keep up with newer trends.

THE NEW REALITY

The book you hold in your hands covers Chevy trucks up to 1998 models and you're probably asking, if the 20-year theory works, why didn't I stop at 1988? That's a logical question, but a couple of factors have come into play since the earlier book was done. First, there's the fact that 1998 Chevy pickups are essentially the same as 1988 models — or are improved versions of '88s. On top of that is the fact that everything in modern life seems speeded up. Consumers are used to changing computers every 3-4 years or buying the latest cell phone as soon as it hits the market. Therefore, it's reasonable to assume that today's collectors will start collecting 10- or 15-year-old trucks. The truth is, most young people today think that a 1998 car or truck is a real "antique."

I'm going to stick my neck out and predict the trucks covered in this book are going to start increasing in collector value soon. So, don't wait until they hit 20 years old to buy your favorite. If you follow the theory of trucks becoming collectible when they turn 20 years old, you might get left out in the cold.

HOW TO FIND VINTAGE TRUCKS

The first place to look for these trucks is everywhere: streets, driveways, alleys, body shops, junkyards and church parking lots on Sunday morning. You may find the best bargain right under your nose — but don't count on it. Non-collectors sometimes over-value their older pickups. They may watch re-runs of the Barrett-Jackson auction on TV and set their prices accordingly.

Keep in mind that every old truck is for sale if you're willing to cough up enough cash. You don't want to overpay, but don't low-ball everything either. The trick is buying the "right" truck at the "right" price, but that doesn't mean you should only do bargain-basement buying. If you buy everything on the cheap, the treasure you're after may turn out to be "fool's gold." Pay a fair price for a good truck and remember — if a deal seems too good to be true, it probably is.

"NATIONWIDE" IS ON YOUR SIDE

By the 1970s, a Chevy pickup was a $3,000+ vehicle with a smooth ride, a long list of options and some rich interior decorations. The basic bare-bones truck of the 1950s and 1960s gave way to a powerful, stylish and well-equipped rig that had just about everything going for it, except a tendency to rust quickly. But a rust-free 1973-1998 pickup is a comfortable vehicle that's a pleasure to drive.

Because of inherent rust problems, the best

survivors today show up in the Sunbelt states or on the West Coast. Trucks used in the snow belt — where roads are salted in winter — had higher junkyard scrappage rates from day one. Remember that the collector-truck market is nationwide in scope. Many California trucks wind up in Wisconsin. In fact, when we swapped engines on my 1988 Chevy pickup, we discovered it had the plumbing for a "California" smog system. It had practically no rust when I bought it eight years ago, but it suffered a serious attack of the "tin worm" after several years of winter use in the Badger State.

If you don't find the 1973-1998 Chevy pickup you want in the area you live in, start looking for one online or in the classifieds ads in collector-car publications. These range from club newsletters and magazines to regional shoppers to national trader magazines. Such publications also include a calendar of events that will carry listings for shows. Check the "Information Department" in this book for listings of such magazines. They can help you find a good truck.

Newspapers, estate or farm auctions, even parades, are other places to keep your eyes open. Hundreds of collector-vehicle-specific auctions are also held each year. And there are nearly 5,000 full-time or part-time collector-vehicle dealers throughout the country. Check the free bulletin board in your local supermarket for postings of old trucks. A great place to look for nice buys on old trucks is in the magazines and newsletters published by the clubs in that hobby niche. Or put the shoe on the other foot and write an ad saying that you want to buy an old truck. This works well for some people. The listing of magazines, clubs, auction companies and dealers in our "Information Department" chapter will help get you pointed in the right direction for contacting such sources.

HOW TO BUY VINTAGE TRUCKS

There's some good buying advice that veteran collectors give, but novice collectors sometimes have trouble following: Pass over buying a truck that needs any kind of major work, either body repair or mechanical rebuilding. Don't buy into any opinions that it's worth buying a truck with a bad engine because the body is nice — or vise-versa. These days it costs a *LOT* to fix anything on a vehicle and with these relatively modern trucks, you shouldn't have any problems finding a good one somewhere in the country. So buy the most perfect truck you can find and put your money into buying it and getting it home.

The pickups built from 1973-1988 are not all that rare, so why get into an expensive restoration? It costs a fortune to buy parts and fix trucks up today. In 90 percent of all cases, you'll be better off paying a premium to get a truck that doesn't need any significant amount of repair. So what if the truck is in California and will cost you $2,000 to ship or drive home? You will easily put that much money into a good-quality engine rebuild or a fresh coat of paint.

Let's say you see a truck that looks like new for $4,000 and you see another that needs body repair and paint for $1,000. You buy the cheaper truck and take it to a body shop where they work on it for 10 hours at $75 an hour. Then, you have nice new paint squirted on it for the bargain price of $2,500. When it is done, you have $4,250 in the truck you fixed. With its new paint, it may even look a little shinier than the $4,000 original. However, it is not worth more to a collector who wants the most original truck available. The bottom line is you would have been far better off spending $4,000 for a nice original truck.

There are many good books available on buying and selling vehicles. Most libraries carry a few. They explain how to inspect and road test trucks, how to use price guides to estimate value and how to arrange financing and insurance. Instead of repeating the advice in such buyer's guides, let's concentrate on the specialty factors involved in collector-vehicle deals.

ODOMETER READINGS

Used-vehicle buying guides may reflect a $1,000 value difference between similar trucks with 30,000 and 70,000 miles. In the collector-truck marketplace, condition would count more than mileage and both of those trucks could be of equal value or even reversed. Collectors know that there are 70,000-mile trucks that look and run like new and 30,000-mile trucks that have many problems.

That doesn't mean odometer readings don't count to truck collectors. Nothing could be further than the truth. Documented instances of very low mileage can multiply the value of a vintage truck may times over.

Let's take the case of two 1987 GMC trucks owned by John Ernst, of Brandon, Florida, as an example. I corresponded with John when I was writing my book *GMC: The First 100 Years* back in 2002. It seems that John liked 1987 GM trucks and knew that series was going to end. So he visited Hunt Truck Sales in Tampa and purchased a C3500 pickup that was built in St. Louis on May 12, 1987 and decided to keep it and not drive it. In 2002, the truck had 3.7 miles of use. On the last day that anyone could order 1987 models, John purchased a second 1987 C3500 that was identical to his first one, but Blue and White instead of Red and White and diesel powered. The salesman convinced John to get the diesel, because ordering the same 454-cid gas V-8 the first truck had could have negated the late-year order. His second truck was built on July 15, 1987 and had 5.7 miles on the odometer in 2002.

Both of John Ernst's "new" 1987 pickups would be of particular interest to collectors because they have never really been used. They are perfect 1987 trucks — just the way the factory built them. However, if they had been used for 30,000 miles or 70,000 miles or 100,000 miles, collectors would then be more interested in the condition that they are in, than their odometer reading. In general, you could say that the aging of a vehicle diminishes the importance of odometer readings, unless the readings are so low as to be out of the ordinary.

Collectors' reactions to low mileage readings will also vary with the age of a vehicle. For instance, if both units were in equal physical condition, a 1973 Chevy pickup with 5,000 documented original miles would probably command more of a premium in price than a 1993 pickup with only 5,000 original miles.

The level and quality of restoration work is another factor that goes hand in hand with the significance of odometer readings and their effect on value. If you have a truck that traveled 300,000 miles before undergoing a thorough and correct restoration to factory condition, why worry about mileage at all? In this case, you essentially have a "new" 300,000-mile vehicle. In fact, some restorers set odometers back to "0" after they have completely restored a car or truck. I personally feel that this is a misleading — and probably illegal — practice, but it is being done and it does help the new owner figure when to change oil.

CONDITION RATINGS

Instead of odometer readings, collectors rely on grading systems to rate an old truck's condition. One such system is based on concours judging and uses a 100-point scale with point deductions for flaws. A 98-point truck would be near perfect. A simpler system is the one we adapted from *Old Cars Price Guide* for use it this book. It uses six condition classes with trucks at the bottom of the scale being No. 6 parts trucks and those at the top being No. 1 show trucks. This condition code system, developed in 1977 by *Old Cars Weekly*, looks like this:

1) EXCELLENT: restored to current maximum professional standards of quality in every area; or perfect original with all components operating and appearing as new.

2) FINE: well-restored or a combination of superior restoration and excellent original; or an extremely well-maintained original showing very minimal wear.

3) VERY GOOD: completely operable original or older restoration showing wear; or amateur restoration; all presentable and serviceable inside and out. Also combinations of well-done restoration and good operable components; or partially restored car with all parts necessary to complete or valuable new-old-stock (NOS) parts.

4) GOOD: a driveable vehicle needing no or only minor work to be functional; or a deteriorated restoration; or a very poor amateur restoration. All components may need restoration to be Excellent, but mostly usable "as is."

5) RESTORABLE: needs complete restoration of body, chassis and interior. May or may not run, but isn't weathered, wrecked or stripped to the point of being useful only for parts salvage.

6) PARTS CAR: may or may not be running, but is weathered, wrecked or stripped of parts to the point of being useful primarily for parts.

PRICING

Once you've inspected an old pickup and determined its condition class, the next step in the buying process is arriving at a price. "Tex" Smith, a publisher *of Old Cars Weekly* in the early 1980s, used to tell me "The price of an older vehicle is someplace between what a seller wants and a buyer wants to pay." Over the years, I have come to believe his viewpoint on this is the best.

Unfortunately, our hobby seems to have progressed to the point where everyone uses printed price guides and TV auction coverage to evaluate vintage vehicles as if they had set prices. The old-time art of "haggling" seems to be falling by the wayside, but if you want to get the most truck for the least amount of money, haggling is the game you'll want to play.

I recommend using books like Old Cars Price Guide to establish a very rough idea of value. You really want to have some idea whether that old truck is worth $400 or $4,000. Beyond that, set the book aside and use your head. When you look at the truck, what do you think it's worth? What's your first impression? There's a good chance your impression is very close to what you're willing to pay

At this point you know what the seller wants (the asking price) and what the buyer (you) is willing to pay. If the two numbers are close, start haggling. If the two are far apart, walk away. When haggling, you will want to avoid criticizing the seller's car or restoration work. Don't nit pick. Instead, you should inspect the vehicle for things you will honestly need to fix and figure out a cost on each one. If the car needs new tires, that a cost of $400 to $600 that you are going to incur. Point this out to the owner. If he or she knows the truck, they know its problems, too. It's possible that the asking price reflects a consideration for problems, but don't take this for granted. The owner may have used Old Cars Price Guide to set the price and may not have considered restoration costs.

When I deal on a car or truck, I set a price I want to pay in my mind. Ideally, I will stick to that ceiling and wind-up buying the vehicle for less. If the owner shows me a receipt for new tires and they cost $200 more than I guessed, then I may go up $100. However, in most cases my top price is my top price and nothing will push me past it. If you can, bring your top price with you in cash and show the money when you make your offer. One of the best buys I ever got was on a nice Chevy with a $4,500 asking price. I waved $2,800 in cash and the owner said, "Let me go talk to my wife." Now, what lady is going to tell her husband, "Keep that truck you've been spending so much money on and turn down the offer." It took the seller's wife about two seconds to take my offer.

A great place to buy an old truck is at a swap meet that takes place late in the year, such as the Antique Automobile Club of America's Hawkeye Downs Swap Meet in Iowa. It is held in late-October and is always filled with trucks that have been for sale all summer and didn't sell. With the winter approaching, sellers have the choice of storing the car or dropping their price. Since vehicle storage often has a cost attached to it, quite a few prices get lowered.

CLOSING THE DEAL

Don't be afraid to make an offer on a car that is priced more than you want to pay. Just put the offer in writing and tell the seller how to contact you. Many sellers will hold a vehicle because someone talked to them about paying more than you were willing to. However, if the first party doesn't come up with the cash in a few days, the seller may want to contact you about taking your offer.

No matter how you close the deal, make sure that you get a valid title and don't stop there. Check to see that the title matches the car. I purchased a vehicle last year that had a valid title, but when I researched it, the features of the car did not agree with what the title said. The seller had obtained a data plate from a similar car, but a different model. He took that to the licensing folks and told them he had removed it while painting the car. For some reason, they believed him and gave him a valid title that was incorrect for the actual car. Sorting out his mess was no fun, although I did get the problem corrected.

In most states (if not all) you have an obligation to title the car and pay sales tax on it within a certain time period (usually 48 hours from purchase). You do not have to register for license plates, but you need to do the title work to prove you legally own the car. Some collectors sell vehicles on an "open title" to avoid paying taxes, but this is illegal and makes you libel for a stiff fine. With an open title, you leave the truck in the original seller's name, then resell it.

If you license your old truck and start driving it right away, it will have to be insured. There are a number of specialized insurers (see our "Information Department) who offer reasonably-priced collector-vehicle insurance plans.

RESTORING OLD TRUCKS

Restoring a vintage pickup truck is an expensive, time-consuming process. A complete body-off-frame restoration entails totally (and very carefully) disassembling the vehicle, tagging and storing (and cleaning) all parts removed, repairing/replacing and refinishing all worn-out parts, painting and upholstering the truck, re-wiring the vehicle, reassembling all pieces, installing new tires and spark plugs, etc., making all necessary final adjustments and taking care of finish details. It takes far longer to rebuild a vehicle than it does to build it at the factory.

The cost of restoring a truck could be as much as two or three times the market value it will have when restored! "The best way to make $1 million in the old truck hobby is to start with $2 million," is a standing joke. That may be an exaggeration, but the only logical reason to completely restore an old truck is that you want a particular model and you can't find a good original or restored one.

If you locate a pretty good truck that's rust free, a partial or "rolling" restoration is possible. In a partial you do mechanical repairs, body and paint work and trim replacement without a complete disassembly. In a rolling restoration, you keep driving the car while restoring it piece by piece. Both techniques should reduce your restoration costs considerably.

Numerous books, including our own *Collector Car Restoration Bible* by Matt Joseph, offer complete, step-by-step restoration advice. In a chapter this size, we cannot cover it all, but we are going to outline the process and then the listings in our "Information Department" chapter will help you locate the services, parts, tools and books you will need to do a complete restoration.

The first phase of a restoration starts before you even pick up a tool. It involves planning and preparation. To restore a truck, you are going o have to play general contractor and supervise the job. You will need to plan for a place to do the work. You will have to determine what work is required. You'll have to order parts and have them shipped to you. You'll need to hire services that you're unable to do yourself, like a welder or painter. Taking pictures of each phase of the work may be a good idea. You'll want to keep records, so you don't misplace anything or forget to do something. How about paying the bills in a timely manner? You might have to buy or rent tools and equipment you don't have.

RESTORATION CONSIDERATIONS

Generally speaking, a place large enough for two or three trucks is required for a complete restoration. One space will hold the chassis, the second is for the body parts and the third is for storing the small parts removed as well as for use as a work area. It is possible to get by in a 2-car garage is the small parts can be stored on shelves or if you are only doing a partial restoration.

Many books recommend photographing all parts removed. Years ago, very few veteran restorers did this, because film and photo developing was too expensive. Today, however, many shops are using digital cameras to restore each restoration on a separate memory card. If you don't take pictures, you can color code, label, tag or box up the parts you remove. Make drawings of assemblies showing the relationship of parts so that they can be reassembled.

You will need factory service manuals or at least aftermarket service manuals to help you rebuild sub-assemblies and assemblies of parts. Helm, Inc., of Highland Park, Michigan, produces service manuals for all major U.S. automakers. These days, Helm sells these books direct to do-it-yourselfers via the Internet. In some cases. CDs are also available. The company has five pages of listing for Chevrolet trucks from 1985 up. The products listed include service manuals, CDs, factory repair manuals, body repair manuals and collision manuals (known as "crash" books). Typical prices include $75 for the *1985 Chevrolet Light Truck Service Manual,* $105 for the *1988 C/K Pickup Shop Manual Set* and $23 for a *Do-It-Yourself Guide to 1988-1998 Chevrolet pickups.*

EBay auctions are a great place to find used factory repair manuals at even more attractive prices. In a quick check, we found the *1973 Chevrolet Light Truck Shop Manual* offered with a $30 buy-it-now and the 1976 version at $25. The 1978, 1980 and 1981 manuals were listed with varying starting bids but a uniform $60 buy-it-now price. Many other manuals for Chevy trucks were offered.

Sources such as LMC Truck and Auto Zone sell the Chevrolet & GMC Pickups repair manuals published by Haynes and the *Repair Manual for General Motors Full-Size Trucks* published by Chilton. You will want both of these books in your restoration library, plus whatever factory service manuals you can afford. Crash books and Factory Assembly Manuals are particularly handy references.

Some of these manuals will provide step-by-step disassembly instructions for your truck. Taking things apart sounds easy, but it tends to get harder the newer the truck is. Remember, too, that you want to disassemble as many parts as you can without breaking fasteners, plastic clips, trim holders, etc.

You will need some special tools (like Torx bits) and equipment (like a 20-ton press) to take modern trucks apart. A hoist will be required to lift the cab and cargo box from the frame. Be prepared to mount the body securely on sawhorses or jack stands. Our friends at Backyard Buddy now make special Easy Access body supports that are essentially jack stands on wheels. They allow you to safely move a vehicle's body while it's supported off the ground.

One snag that novice restorers encounter with factory shop manuals is when they call for the use of special tools. Many of these were manufactured by a company called Kent-Moore and some will be found listed on eBay. However, it doesn't pay to put off a job because you can't find a Kent-Moore tool. Just track down a mechanic (active or retired) who worked on these Chevy trucks when they were new. He'll be able to tell you how common tools were used to get certain jobs done. In a few cases, you may need the help of a machine shop.

With the cab and pickup box removed, you can get at the rolling chassis (frame, front and rear suspensions, drive train and wheel parts) to work on the various mechanical components. Usually, the rolling chassis will be the last thing you uncover when doing disassembly and the first thing you start restoring.

With the help of local suppliers, you should be able to rebuild most of the chassis parts. I would recommend sending the brake cylinders to Brake & Equipment Warehouse, Apple Hydraulics or White Post Restorations to have them sleeved with brass or stainless. Rebuild all cylinders and link them using stainless steel lines from Classic Tube or Inline tube. Then rebuild the hydraulic system, have the drums turned, put the brakes together and fill the system with silicone brake fluid. After that, you should never have to do your brakes again.

The first antilock braking system used on Chevy pickups seems to be somewhat problematic. Brakes disassembled after 100,000 miles of use, sometimes look hardly used. On the other hand, front brakes tend to be overused and wear out prematurely. John Gunnell photo

During a night-school bodywork course, the author used an air-powered cut-off wheel to remove rusted portion of the left-hand rear wheel arch on his '88 Chevy C10 Fleetside pickup. Rust in this area is very familiar to restorers of 1988-1998 full-size Chevy pickups. *John Gunnell photo*

Rusted sheet metal sections must be cut back to the point where good metal is found. This allows the restorer to attach the aftermarket repair panel to a solid foundation, either by welding or "gluing" the so-called "patch panel" in place. *John Gunnell photo*

Dave Stencil used his air grinder to rough out an area on the author's pickup where a new repair panel sourced from LMC Truck would be attached. Some restorers cut the patch panels to fit the repair, but Stencil preferred to use the whole repair panel and cut the fender. *John Gunnell photo*

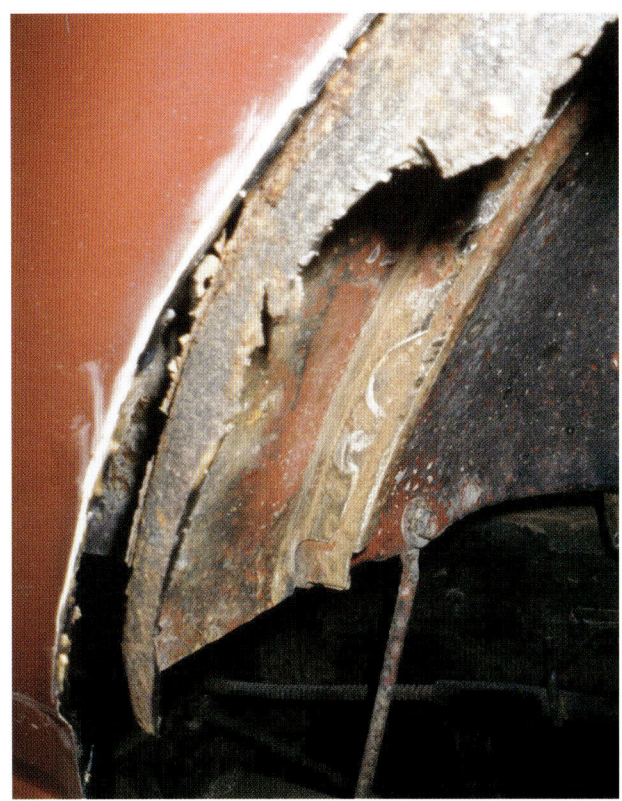

The wheel arch on a 1988-'98 Chevy pickup actually consists of inner and outer panels that were welded together and to the body at the Chevy factory. A rod-type brace is bolted in place to keep the fender from flexing. Only the outer arch on my truck had to be replaced. John Gunnell photo

For engine rebuilding parts, before going anywhere else, try Tim S. Archer at J & C Enterprises in Fairmont, WV. A quick scan of the *LMC Truck Catalog* we have at home shows nearly all electrical, brake, suspension and rear axle parts being available through mail order. LMC is just one of many suppliers, so check out our "Information Department" chapter, then contact them all and compare products and prices. These companies also stock engine-modification parts to help you up power and performance. The catalog shows new leaf springs available for 1988-1998 Chevy pickups. For older trucks, you can visit a local spring shop to have the originals rebuilt. Spring steel in truck styles and sizes is still available, in case any leaves are broken and need to be replaced.

Some hobbyists like to farm out work on mechanical sub-assemblies to machine shops. The drawback is extra expense going into the restoration. Also remember most of these shops won't clean or paint parts unless you pay extra. You will have to plan how to refinish various parts around the work other people are doing. This is a particular problem when restorers want to have engine parts powder coated. Often, the shop will need to do some powder coating, then have the machining done, before the parts come

There is nothing like a plasma cutter to slice easily through automotive-gauge sheet metal. It took Dave Stencil only a few minutes to remove the section of the truck's rear "fender" that he had roughed out with the grinder marks. John Gunnell photo

After cutting the old, rust-damaged panel off the truck, Dave Stencil used his air grinder to remove the factory finish from the edges of the cut-out section so that the aftermarket repair panel could be attached to "clean" metal. John Gunnell photo

Chevrolet Pickups 1973-1998 | 203

In addition to cleaning the edges of the cut-out he made on the side of the truck, Dave Stencil used his air grinder to clean the black factory primer off the inside edges of the repair panel. This allowed him to attach clean metal to clean metal. John Gunnell photo

Here we see Dave Stencil using applying a special epoxy used to "glue" the right-hand repair panel to the truck. In this project, the concept was to glue one side and weld the other to test which system worked best. Gluing was easier and sealed rust out better. John Gunnell photo

back for final powder coating. If the shops are far from your home, you'll have extra running to do.

When it comes to engine detailing, it is nice to see the parts catalogers already stocking reproduction engine compartment decals for 1988-1998 pickups. Another nice thing is that modern sales catalog show the engines in the correct colors, so they can be used as a guide for getting colors right and for applying labels and decals. The Eastwood Company, of Pottstown, Pennsylvania, markets an engine compartment detailing kit for restorers.

RESTORING BODY PARTS

If you are completely restoring your truck, you will need to remove all of the old paint from the body before you can squirt on new paint. The easiest way to accomplish this is to take all parts you plan to paint to a commercial stripper where they have large tanks the parts can be dipped into. If you go this route, you'll need to put the body on a trailer and take it to the stripping shop.

I am not talented in body work, so I'd probably just keep going and take the stripped body parts to a body shop for painting. However, if you are talented enough or brave enough to attempt your own bodywork, keep in mind that collectors prefer a vehicle restored with lead body filler to one done with plastic filler. A good way to learn how to work with lead filler is to get a copy of the book *Automobile Sheet Metal Repair* by Robert L. Sargent. It will teach you about lead filler, the use of body repair tools and the way to fabricate patch panels.

Several companies, like Eastwood, sell body repair tools and lead body solder (see Information Department). Fabricating patch panels is a essential skill for restorers, since repair panels for many older vehicles are either not made or not made very well. However, in the case of Chevrolet pickup trucks, you can get just about any panel you'll need and sometimes in several designs or sizes. The available parts include cab corners, cowl panels, rocker panels, front bed panels, cab front floors and reinforcements, rear bed sills, angle strip covers, tailgates, inner fender liners, firewall covers and bed strips.

Installing such parts involves cutting away corroded metal, welding or riveting patches in place and using filler to smooth the seams. To make patch panels that fit snugly, attach sturdily and require minimal filling, the edges need to be flanged so that the surface of the patch panel winds up flush with the surface of the panel being patched. Eastwood makes special flanging pliers designed to help home restorers do this job.

Today, patch panels can be glued or welded in place and based on a test we did using my 1988 Chevy pickup, I would recommend gluing the panels on. The glue is easier to use and there is no problem with heat warping, plus, the glued seam resists corrosion and simply looks smoother and nicer. We attached 60-inch wheel opening panels made by LMC

Truck to both sides of the truck using glue on one side and welding the other side. We sprayed on primer but no other finish and drove the truck through one winter. The seams on both sides started to form rust, but it was much, much heavier on the welded seam. With proper painting, we would not worry too much about a glued seam rusting.

When the body is patched and ready, you can start reassembling it by mounting the cab on the chassis. All body parts should be painted with the same batch of paint to ensure that you get the same paint mix. But you will probably want to leave at least the cargo box off the frame until it is painted. How else can you paint the rear of the cab and front of the cargo box? The parts usually needed to mount everything back on the frame are available through catalogs.

With the unpainted cab mounted and the running gear restored, your Chevy pickup should be starting to look like a truck again, although it is still far from being finished. Luckily, unlike trucks of the '40s-'60s, most '70s-'90s pickups will not require replacement of the electrical wiring harness.

With the truck semi-assembled, you'll need to make final adjustments, grease the chassis, tune the ignition, tweak the carburetor (if it has one) and have the wheels aligned if the truck can be towed to a front-end shop. Go over all nuts and bolts with a torque wrench. Put in oil, coolant and gas. Check all vacuum hoses and electrical connectors to be sure every switch, sensor and solenoid is working. On late-model GM vehicles, each electrical connection is made using a unique socket and clip, so it's hard to make improper connections.

You can start your rebuilt engine (it will smoke quite a bit at first as the fluids burn off) and let the truck run for 10-15 minutes. Then, shut it down and re-torque the cylinder head bolts. You may find that you have to put some very heavy pressure on the brake pedal to make the red brake-on light go off.

REFINISHING

Painting is one of the most important steps in the job of restoring your Chevy pickup. Whether you do this work yourself or farm it out to an expert, it pays to prep the vehicle at home. I'm assuming you still have the bumpers, grille and bright metal trim off the vehicle. On some models, it may be factory correct to paint the bumper or grille, but you'll still want them off the truck so you can finish them separately. You may want to keep the fenders, hood and doors off well. Most restorers like to paint all panels while disassembled. Others think this leads to scratches on new paint during re-assembly and prefer to paint the entire front end and cab as a unit, then mount the (painted) cargo box later.

Application of a prime coat comes first. Prime coats help prepare the surface for paint and promote better paint adherence. Wash the body parts with water and treat them with a solvent to eliminate all

On the left-hand side, Dave Stencil used a stitch welding technique to attach the LMC Truck repair panel. To avoid warping the metal, Dave made wide-spaced "stiches" first, then went back to add more "stitches" between the first ones he did. *John Gunnell photo*

Dave Stencil – who operates Stencil's Body Shop in Scandinavia, Wisconsin – took a couple of manual swings with his trusty old pick hammer to flatten the panel fit just a bit. The panel on the "welded" side required much more work than the one on the "glued-on" side. *John Gunnell photo*

traces of wax, grease, dirt and road tar. Next, use newspaper and masking tape to protect the glass and any non-removable trim. Automotive primers come in different colors. A red primer will work best under dark earth colors. Dark gray primer is recommended for black paint. Light gray primer works well under whites and yellows.

Before priming, use course 80-grit sandpaper to scuff up the body for better paint adhesion. Also apply a metal-prep, then clean it off and apply a synthetic primer-sealer. Next, apply the actual primer working top to bottom. Primer should be applied with a quality air gun hooked to an air compressor that can maintain a steady 30 psi at the nozzle of the spray gun. For safety purposes, you should wear a respirator when spraying automotive finishes.

After application of the primer, the body parts should be sanded with fine-grit #320 paper. Blow away sanding residue with the air compressor and apply a second primer coat. Re-sand with even finer #400 sandpaper. When the primer is smooth and residue-free, it will be time to think about the color and whether you want to spray it yourself or leave the painting to a professional.

After stitch welding the panel onto the truck and pick hammering the high spots, Dave Stencil used his air grinder to level off the "stitches" and get the edges of the repaired section as clean looking as possible. *John Gunnell photo*

With the higher standards of restoration evident in restoration work today, many hobbyists are having their vehicles painted by professionals who have the equipment and skills to do factory-quality refinishing. For those who own only one collector car or truck, this is probably the most economical way to go simply because of the cost of paint spraying equipment. The investment in equipment can be considerable. Many hobbyists feel that it pays for them to prep their own vehicles, but to hire a professional to complete the job.

This is probably true. The car owner has more time to spend on minor preparation tasks like removal of trim and the masking of glass and can be meticulous about such tasks. The hobbyist does not have to worry about rolling the next job into the shop or balancing the needs of numerous customers. That's why I recommend doing the prep work yourself.

Unlike the laborious job of body surface preparation, the application of color coats moves fast. At this stage, professional experience will help. An amateur paint job will look like an amateur paint job, unless the amateur gets some expert training. Of course, many hobbyists enjoy the feeling of pride and personal accomplishment that comes with painting one's own car or truck. If you fall into this group, there are books and videos you can get or adult-education classes you can sign up for to learn the basics of painting a vehicle.

One class at Marquette University in Milwaukee, Wisconsin, was taught by Classic Car restorer Beaver Culver who explained that paint manufacturers now market, "complete refinishing systems." Culver recommended always sticking to one line of products to get good results. "There's enough of a problem choosing different lacquers and enamels," he said. "Why use different brands of paint?" Culver also recommended using a brand that other restorers had luck with.

Culver pointed out that the "days of 30 coats of hand-rubbed lacquer are gone." He explained that refinements in paint technology have created refinishing products requiring only a few coats to give good results. According to Culver, novices usually found lacquer easiest to spray, followed by acrylics and the enamels. But today's base-coat clear-coat finishes are the easiest yet to use.

Good painters, like Culver, learn how to mix just the right combination of thinner, following the manufacturer's recommendations. They stir it and select the proper spray-gun head, adjusting the spray so that it has a fan pattern about eight inches wide and 12 inches from the gun head. After making a few practice passes on a piece of cardboard, the painter is ready to squirt. He keeps the gun parallel to the surface being painted and swings it back and forth, horizontally, overlapping his last coat of paint on each pass. There's a real rhythm to it.

When paint is correctly applied, it will appear smooth and wet for a short time after application. Graininess indicates the paint is too thick or the painter is holding the gun too far away from the truck. If the paint runs, it's too thin or the gun is being held too close. Another problem is spraying in one spot for too long.

You should spray just one panel – hood, fender, door – at a time and try to use a spraying technique that seems "natural." This will result in coatings that are consistent in texture, thickness and depth of color. Beginners sometimes have luck first making horizontal strokes across a panel, then directly following with vertical strokes. Everyone develops his or her own style of applying paint. Years ago, when paint was hand-sprayed on auto assembly lines, operators were matched in technique so that both sides of a vehicle would look the same.

Paint-spraying techniques have to vary for different kinds of paint. Lacquer is easiest to apply. With acrylics, the paint had to "flash" or harden on its surface before a second coat could be applied. Enamel dries slowly, so it cannot be applied all at once. Enamel actually requires a tack coat, a color coat and a finish coat. Enamel should only be sprayed in a moisture-free environment. The absence of dust is required in all types of painting

If runs develop in your paint, adjust the gun to make the spray lighter and, when the first color coat has been sprayed, dip a tiny brush in a can of thinner. Use it to remove any excess paint. Then, simply "fog" the area lightly on the finish coat. Do not try moving your truck until the paint is completely dry.

After spraying the body parts, allow the paint to dry while keeping the truck stored indoors overnight. After three days, wash the pickup with clean water and then color sand the entire truck, by hand, with 600-grit sandpaper. Next, buff it lightly with an electric buffer and suitable rubbing compound. Then clean up.

Instructions like these make painting sound easy, but it's not. There's no substitute for hands-on experience. You should constantly practice your spraying technique on pieces of scrap metal. An if you find night-school classes in your area, sign up for them. Classes will give you the hands-on experience you need.

WRAP-UP

At this stage, you'll be installing upholstery, door panels, chrome trim, accessories, floor mats and carpeting. A new set of tires in the authentic style and size is another neat wrap-up touch.

The long-term test will be whether the glued-on or welded-on panel holds up better over several "corrosive" Wisconsin winters. Welding tends to promote rusting, while the special epoxy tends to make a cleaner repair and also seals the rust out to a certain degree. John Gunnell photo

TRUCKOMOBILIA

HOW THINGS HAVE CHANGED

"Truckomobilia" is a word I coined 20 years ago to describe truck memorabilia. A lot has taken place since my 1988 book *Chevrolet Pickups 1946-1972* surveyed memorabilia that truck enthusiasts were collecting in the late '80s.

One change is that the number of trucks built each year has increased immensely, so more of some types of collectibles have been made. Conversely, the cost of making sales aids is up. Dealers have to purchase sales catalogs from the manufacturer, so many are giving away less in order to hold costs down.

There seem to be fewer plastic "dealer promo" models of trucks today than there were years ago. However, more die-cast metal models are being made in the aftermarket. In addition, eBay and other online auctions have made real promos more accessible to collectors and lowered the prices on newer ones. We would guess that the number of toy trucks being made has gone up overall, but there are probably fewer toys that resemble a real Chevrolet truck, which is what collectors like. Toy makers always strive to make their products look wild.

The dealer films and film strips that Chevy truck enthusiasts collected in 1988 were first replaced by tapes and then by floppy discs and CDs. In 1988, collectors were anxious to get their hands on a press kit with printed descriptions of different trucks and nice black-and-white glossy photos. By the early '90s the photos were color slides, by the mid '90s the printed sheets were put on a floppy disc and by the late 1990s, many press kits consisted of little more than a CD

As they have with factory sales literature, car and truck dealers have also tried to cut back on the gimmicks and premiums they once liberally gave out to try to sell vehicles. Dealer postcards, key chains, rulers, cigarette lighters, playing cards and other items designed to help push sales of newer trucks are not common items to find. By the mid-1980s, auto manufacturers were printing mail order catalogs designed to sell these items to the public, rather than give them away. Only some very common items — like cheap ball pens — can still be found at car shows and other venues where dealers set up booths.

Factory maintenance and service literature like owner's manuals and service manuals still exist, but things have changed here, too. At one point, manufacturers started using cassette tapes in the glove box to try to replace or at least water down the content of owner's manuals. Service manuals (now often produced in sets of several "phonebook-sized" volumes) have been simplified to the point where you really need some GM factory training to understand the repairs. And if you take your Chevy truck to a dealer for service, it's likely that the technician will look up the parts and repair steps on a computer, rather than open a service manual. There may even be new pickups that only have service CDs.

Although the things that truck enthusiasts collect have changed, that hardly means there are no collectible items to be had. So let's review what truckomobilia is and see what really neat items are out there today to look for.

WHAT IS "TRUCKOMOBILIA?"

Memorabilia is anything worthy of remembrance. The manufacturing and marketing of Chevy pickups and other trucks led to the creation of many items, both large and small, that are related to the full-size trucks, such as literature and toys. As this "truckomobilia" ages, it increases in historical interest and value.

Such items can be special-interest or general in nature. Special-interest truck memorabilia fits into established collecting categories such as models, toys, sales catalogs, license plates, etc. General-interest items are anything else a hobbyist can link to his or her truck, such as Chevrolet key chains, ballpoint pens that dealers gave out, showroom banners, promotional paper weights and so on.

Although a lot of the memorabilia that truck hobbyists collect is "factory" material made by Chevrolet, this isn't always the source. Toy makers, oil companies, auto-parts suppliers, calendar produces and even hobby clubs have made other items that are of interest to truckomobilia buffs.

Some enthusiasts collect everything related to Chevrolet trucks. Others collect only a certain type of memorabilia — say models — or memorabilia related to only one type of truck — for example, *1972 Chevy* pickup memorabilia. Whether your interests are narrow or broad, memorabilia is fun to look for.

Years ago, the best place to find truckomobilia was at automotive swap meets or flea markets. These are still fun to attend, but anybody with a computer can now shop for memorabilia without leaving home or waiting for weekend shows. Websites like eBay, Parts123 and Craig's List have made in possible to go "swapping" in your own home via online auctions

Truckomobilia can also turn up at garage sales, flea markets, antique shops, estate auctions and dozens of other places. Sometimes you'll be able to attend other types of collecting shows and leave with truckomobilia. For instance, you may stumble on Chevy dealer postcards at a postcard show or license plates at a license plate-collector's show. Magazines for other types of collectibles – such as *Toy Cars & Models* or even *Coin Prices* will sometimes carry classified ads listing truck-related memorabilia for sale.

A great way to build up your collection of truckomobilia is to put your own "want ad" out in the various collector publications. Collectors are "pack rats" by nature and tend to hoard all types of neat things. Maybe you can trade a postcard you picked up for a truck item that some postcard collector has.

One advantage of collecting general items is that you can build a valuable collection without being pinpointed as a "sucker for this or that." Some items you add to the collection might have very little intrinsic value, but as they become part of a collection, the value of the items goes up. In other words, the value of the total collection is often greater than the sum of its parts.

Value appreciation is one reason for building a collection, but certainly not the only one. Many people are motivated more by nostalgia. They may be looking for the toy Chevy truck they had when they were a child or literature covering the first year, make and model of truck they ever owned. Recently, I met a man who restored his grandfather's car as a keepsake. There are all kinds of reasons for being a collector and you'll usually enjoy it more if you're doing it more for fun than money.

Keep in mind that anything related to your vintage Chevrolet pickup can be added to a truckomobilia collection. Maybe you always kept a 1975 road map in the glove box of the '75 C10 Fleetside pickup you owned years ago. If you buy a similar truck to restore, it wouldn't be the same without an old road map in the glove box.

In the next few pages, we're going to take a closer look at a few of the more popular categories that truck collectibles fall into. However, don't feel you have to limit your collection to these categories. The sky is the limit when it comes to collecting neat truck stuff.

Models & Toys

Miniature cars and trucks have been around since the early days of car making. Models are scaled miniatures of real vehicles and most are accurate in terms of colors and details. Toys resemble the full-size trucks, but are not necessarily done to scale and they are usually less detailed then models.

For the 1973-1998 Chevy truck buff, the most important type of miniature is the dealer "promo" model. These are exact-scale models (usually 1/25 the size of the real truck) that Chevy dealers use to illustrate the appearance of new vehicles to customers. They are supplied through Chevy's parts department.

The earliest die-cast aluminum Chevy "promos" were produced in 1947. Soon, plastic models replaced them. Early plastic promos warp. Later versions are better, although heat can still damage them. The promos cost about .98 when new. Some rare ones are worth thousands, but most range from $20-$200.

Ron Pittman, a collector who has over 3,000 Chevy promos, once told the editors of *Friends* magazine why prices are high. "Collectors place the highest value on the promo because they offer the closest link to the real thing," he explained. "Like advertisements and sales literature, they have nostalgic value."

Companies like JoHan Plastic Company, AMT (SMP), Hubley, Master Caster, Product Miniatures and National Products, Inc. built promo models. In recent years, AMT has produced the Chevy factory promos.

Some of the handsomest pickup promos were those replicating late-'50s Chevrolet Apaches, which came in very attractive two-tone color combinations. Models of the early 1959-1960 full-size El Caminos are very desirable, too. A survey of several swap meets and a scan of eBay listings indicates booming interest in promos, with prices all over the ballpark. You will see small vendors at shows selling promos they picked up for under $10, but full-time promo dealers will make considerable mark ups. One advantage to buying at shows is you pay no shipping, which can be a big expense with the new postal rates.

Some nice Chevy pickup promos of the '60s and '70s are available in the $100-$125 range. Some very desirable or rare models will bring even more. Prices tend to follow the history and popularity of the real trucks, which supports Ron Pittman's views of why promos are popular. For instance, a promo of the first-of-its-style '73 C/K pickup is probably worth more than a '74 C/K promo.

As you move up to the 1980s and 1990s trucks, prices level off considerably. For instance, one eBay listing offered a "hard-to-find" 1988 Chevy Silverado C1500 promo in a brandywine color. It had opening doors, but cost only $8.97, plus $8,00 for shipping. The listing noted that '88 was "the first year for the newly-designed truck, so Chevy decided to include

Features of the 1988 Chevy Silverado promotional model include a fully-detailed chassis, a drop-down tailgate, rally wheels, chrome bumpers, a detailed bucket seat interior, rubber "Goodyear" tires, a deluxe grille and Crimson Red Metallic finish. John Gunnell photo

This factory promotional model No. 7082 is a very authentic replica of the 1988 Chevrolet C10 Silverado Fleetside pickup. This truck was purchased through an eBay auction, by the author, for $8.97 plus $8.00 shipping. It resembles the author's '88 Cheyenne pickup. John Gunnell photo

it with the year's promo cars." It further suggested, "Everyone is looking for the (1988) Camaro and Corvette promo cars, but you need this truck to make your collection complete for 1988."

Chevy promos of 1990 pickups, made by AMT, are also reasonably priced on eBay. A 1993 Bonus Cab long-bed pickup in green in mint condition, but without the box, was listed with a $15 buy-it-now price and a $7 shipping charge. It seemed like a buy for $22 delivered to your door. Pricing was about the same for a red 1995 C1500 Chevy extended-cab pickup model. It had an opening bid of $12.95 and a $7.95 shipping cost for a total of $20.90.

An interesting promo, also from 1995, is a white and blue C1500 regular-cab Brickyard 500 pace truck. A bunch of these are listed on eBay at prices in the $10 range with shipping costs around $7. Apparently, a lot of these were made and that's keeping the model affordable. Who knows what this one will bring years from now, as it seems to offer some good investment potential?

Another 1995 Chevy truck promo available is a 4 x 4 version of the S-10 done in red with a tan interior and a black bumper and grille. This model has a lot of eye appeal, but was listed with a $9 buy-it-now price and $4.50 shipping cost. It seems hard to go wrong buying promo models at prices like that.

Not all pickup truck promo models are 1:25th-scale AMT products made for Chevrolet factory dealers. Hot Wheels produced a smaller-sized white Chevy C3500 Bonus Cab pickup for the big auto-parts cataloger J. C. Whitney. This one was available on eBay, brand new in the box, for less than $4. If you're into Chevy trucks as a hobby and want to make some good investments, it would be hard to beat buying up a bunch of the lower-priced promos at current prices.

In addition to promo models, built-it-yourself model kits of some 1973-1998 Chevy pickups are available. Kits of the early 1970s trucks sell for $15-$125 and prices will most likely keep climbing. When nicely painted and properly assembled, kits provide the same link with real trucks that promos do — the hobbyist ends up with a replica of his truck.

Another type of model is the metal die-cast version. These range in price from under $10 to upwards of $200. They are generally made in smaller scale than promos and are often highly detailed. In general, the more accurately detailed they are, the more die-cast models will bring in the collector market.

In addition to models, there were numerous "toy" trucks produced between 1973 and 1998 that copied or resembled Chevrolet pickup trucks. *Toy Cars & Models,* 700 E. State St., Iola, WI 54990 (www.toycarsmag.com) is an excellent publication with stories, pricing information and ads for collectors. A great book on this topic is *O'Brien's Collecting Toy Cars & Trucks: Identification & Price Guide* edited by Karen O'Brien. It pictures 2,800 toy vehicles made by over 300 companies and provides 12,000 value listings for them. It's a great book to have at your side when bidding on eBay items.

This 1995 S10 promotional model was purchased on eBay for $9 plus $5.80 shipping. It has a tan bucket seat interior, black wipers, dual black outside rearview mirrors, a drop-down tailgate and a nicely-detailed chassis. This is one of the prettier promos. John Gunnell photo

In addition to making "promo" models of the full-size C/K pickups, Chevy also provided miniature S10s to dealers. In this case you're looking at the 1995 4x4 Sport package version with red body finish, black wheelhouse flares, black bumpers and a chrome grille. John Gunnell photo

MANUFACTURER FILM STRIPS, TAPES, CDS & PHOTOS

Twenty years ago, in my book on collecting 1946-1972 Chevy pickups and trucks, I wrote of enthusiasts collecting dealer films and film strips. There were probably a few film strips made for 1970s Chevy trucks, since I have seen this media used to promote cars of this era. However, by the 1980s, the film strip was definitely a thing of the past, unless you count the types of film strips played in GM Mini-Theatre projectors.

The Mini Theatres were used in GM dealerships to show potential buyers the features of vehicles. Cassette-type film cartridges fit into a slot on the side of the Mini-Theatre projector. A system of mirrors then transferred the image onto a screen that looked like a primitive computer monitor. These Mini-Theatres seem to have first came into use around 1972. They were used at least through the late 1970s (possibly the early 1980s). There was probably at least one of the systems in each GM dealership, meaning that tens of thousands were produced.

At swap meets, Mini-Theatres typically sell for about $300-$400, depending upon condition, how many tapes they come with and what vehicles are on the tapes. Usually, a number of the tapes are included in the sale price. Years ago, you could find Mini-Theatres in the back rooms of GM dealerships and often purchase them very reasonably, but today they are so out-of-date that car shows, swap meets and antique stores are good places to search for them.

Another popular collectible is the "factory photo." The first of these were produced in the early years of car manufacturing and these 8 x 19 glossy "publicity stills" were still being included in Chevrolet truck press kits in the mid 1990s. In fact, the truck press kits of 1990 through 1994 are particularly nice because the include both black-and-white prints and color slides. Eventually, the nice black-and-white glossy photos were dropped and only slides were included. Then, by the mid 1990s, press kits entered the computer age. They got fancier looking, but included a pocket for a floppy disc that contained all the content other than photos, which were still in slide form. Of course, it wasn't long before the "floppy pocket" gave way to a plastic button that held a CD. The CD could hold both the written and visual content of a press kit and give members of the media the info and photos they needed to write about new Chevy trucks.

This 1993 Chevy promotional model represents a miniature version of the C1500 Silverado Bonus Cab pickup. It has Teal Green Metallic finish and features a fully-detailed chassis and bucket seat interior. Prices on these models are sure to climb in the future. John Gunnell photo

The tailgate on this plastic 1993 Silverado Bonus Cab pickup promotional model can be lowered like this, if you carefully spread the sides of the cargo box to undo the tabs. As real 1973-1998 Chevy pickups rise in value, the miniatures are sure to get more collectible. John Gunnell photo

This change in media was very apparent if you visited the press room at auto shows during this period. In the early '90s, press offices had book shelves for storing press kits and they would be filled with folios including fact sheets and photos. By the mid-'90s, if you entered the press room, the book shelves looked half empty, but in the "empty" slots you would see CDs. By the late '90s, full press kits were a rarity. A few foreign automakers and tire companies still made them up, but the GM, Ford and Chrysler press materials were almost all on CD.

ART AND ARTIFACTS

Many truckomobilia items can be broadly classified as art and artifacts related to Chevy trucks. This category is very broad and hard to define. In *Chevrolet Pickups 1946-1972*, I used the story of ex-car salesman Jay Katelle to explain how enthusiasts get into collecting art and artifacts.

Katelle had a massive collection of Chevrolet factory-and-dealer-issued items including cuff links, poker chips, tokens, sales catalogs, brochures, promo models, calendars, auto show programs, plant tour booklets, old racing programs, ball-point pens, tie tacks, ashtrays, ink blotters, key chains, pencils, cigarette lighters, playing cards, banks, rulers and advertising postcards.

Katelle started selling cars and trucks in 1964 and started collecting memorabilia in 1972. He amassed thousands of Chevrolet items and eventually turned his collection into a business. Twice every year, Katelle put together the *Automobile and Literature Collectibles Workbook* and mailed it to hobbyists in all 50 states and over a dozen foreign countries. He had automotive writer and photographer Jerry Heasley of Pampa, Texas put the book together for him and it included over 5,000 items for sale, including many Chevy truck collectibles.

Back then, Katelle sold the items only by telephone, since they were one-of-a-kind pieces and his inventory of each item was limited. Most sales were made on a person-to-person basis so no one would be disappointed by unfilled mail orders. On some days, Katelle received up to 100 phone calls. Today, it is likely he sells online, too. You can find out by contacting him by mail at Jay Katelle, 3721 Farwell, Amarillo, TX 769109.

Today, we can find such items for sale on the Internet. You start by using an Internet search engine like Yahoo. Fire up your computer, go on the Internet and enter key words. The computer will then search all "pages" put up on the Internet for your key words. You might put in search words like "1975 Chevrolet Truck key chain." If any of the key words match a page on the Internet, you'll get a "hit" that you can click on to view the match. Sometimes you'll get millions of hits, but few will be what you want. For instance, your key words might take you to a '75 Chevy key chain (from 1975) for sale or it might take you to a company in Hong Kong that makes modern key chains with pictures of old trucks on them.

If you do not get a hit or any good hits, you will want to "refine" your Internet search. Instead of typing in "1975 Chevrolet Truck key chain" you may want to type in "'75 Chevy dealer key chain" or "sales promotional key chain for '75 Chevy." Each time you re-word your search, you'll get different results. As you narrow the criteria for a search, it gets easier to find a specific item.

In addition to Websites, the computer search may take you to online classified ads (like Craig's List) or online auctions (like eBay) through which you can purchase items. Like any auction, the online variety has its positive and negative points. There are many books available on the topic of buying and selling things through online auctions. Before you jump into this game, either talk to friends who are online auction users or get one of those books and read it.

BUILDING A CHEVY TRUCK LIBRARY

If you are an enthusiast and/or collector of 1973-1998 Chevrolet trucks, you'll want to have at least a small library of books on this topic. If you're reading this, you may have started your library with *1973-1998 Chevrolet Pickup Trucks* and we thank you for that. However, you won't want to stop there.

Sales literature for your truck is a very helpful thing to have. In many years, Chevrolet put out a general "Chevy Trucks" catalog, as well as specific sales catalogs on C/K Pickups, S-10s, Suburbans, Blazers, etc. In addition, there was usually a separate guide for buyers of Commercial Trucks. Magazine advertisements and promotional brochures are also collectible. A lot of this material is available through hobby literature dealers at swap meets, via mail order and also by Internet. For 1973-1998 trucks, most sales literature should be in the $5-$15 range, although we're sure there are rare pieces that bring more.

The same dealers who sell sales literature also sell owner's manuals, service manuals, dealer service bulletins and updates, body manuals, factory assembly manuals and master parts catalogs.

In addition to factory manuals, you will probably want to have the "aftermarket" manuals such as those produced by Haynes and Chilton. These are aimed at the do-it-yourselfer. They are basically an edited version of the factory service manual, but they often include tips and advice to help mechanically-inclined owners accomplish their own at-home repairs. Sometimes they include valuable information on shortcuts in repair procedures and on how to use ordinary tools to do jobs that call for special tools in factory-type manuals.

1973-1998 CHEVY PICKUP AND BLAZER

MODELS, PRICES, WEIGHT, PRODUCTION

1: Prices/weights for V-8s, except four-cylinder or six-cylinder only trucks.
2: Engines, door options, wheelbase options and equipment additions/deletions would affect these prices.

1973

	Model No.	Body Type	Price	Weight	Production
1/2-Ton LUV — Model L/Series 82 — 102.4 in. w.b.					
	82	Mini-Pickup	2,406	2,450	18,771
El Camino — Model C/Series 13000 — 116 in. w.b. — Six					
	1AC80	Sedan-Pickup	2,976	3,725	Note 1
El Camino Custom — Model D/Series 13000 — 116 in. w.b. — V-8					
	1AD80	Custom Sedan-Pickup	3,038	3,735	Note 1

NOTE 1: *Total El Camino production was 64,987.*

	Model No.	Body Type	Price	Weight	Production
1/2-Ton Blazer 4 x 2 — Model C/Series 5 — 106.5 in. w.b.					
	CC10514	Open Utility	2,637	3,595	3,342
1/2-Ton Blazer 4 x 4 — Model K/Series 5 — 106.5 in. w.b.					
	CK10514	Open Utility	3,200	3,912	44,841
1/2-Ton Conventional — Model C/Series 10 — 117.5 in. w.b.					
	CC10703	Chassis & Cab	2,577	3,234	1,922
	CC10704	Stepside 6.5 ft.	2,763	3,664	19,408
	CC10734	Fleetside 6.5 ft.	2,763	3,560	43,987
1/2-Ton Conventional — Model C/Series 10 — 131.5 in. w.b.					
	CC10903	Chassis & Cab	2,608	3,331	877
	CC10904	Stepside 8 ft.	2,799	3,836	7,040
	CC10934	Fleetside 8 ft.	2,799	3,726	309,085
1/2-Ton Conventional 4 x 4 — Model K/Series 10 — 117.5 in. w.b.					
	CK10703	Stepside 6.5 ft.	3,510	3,989	2,112
	CK10703	Fleetside 6.5 ft.	3,510	4,108	9,605
1/2-Ton Conventional 4 x 4 — Model K/Series 10 — 129.5 in. w.b.					
	CK10906	Suburban (doors)	4,338	5,200	1,128
	CK10916	Suburban (gate)	—	—	3,770

Chevrolet Pickups 1973-1998 | 215

1973 continued

1/2-Ton Conventional 4 x 4 — Model K/Series 10 — 131.5 in. w.b.

CK10903	Stepside 8 ft.	3,546	4,085	417
CK10903	Fleetside 8 ft.	3,546	4,210	29,157

3/4-Ton Conventional — Model C/Series 20 — 131.5 in. w.b.

CC20903	Chassis & Cab	2,815	3,637	8,162
CC20903	Stepside 8 ft.	3,001	4,142	4,654
CC20903	Fleetside 8 ft.	3,001	4,032	131,624

3/4-Ton Conventional — Model C/Series 20 — 129.5 in. w.b.

CC20906	Suburban (doors)	4,009	4,817	2,424
CC20916	Suburban (gate)	4,040	4,825	7,368

NOTE 2: *Stake option included with C20 Chassis-and-Cab production.*

3/4-Ton Crew-Cab — Model C/Series 20 — 164.5 in. w.b.

CE20963	Crew-Cab Chassis	—	—	712
CE20963	Crew-Cab Pickup 8 ft.	4,001	—	7,137

NOTE 3: *Crew-Cab Model 963 was an option, average price $1,000.*

3/4-Ton Conventional 4 x 4 — Model K/Series 20 — 131.5 in. w.b.

CK20903	Chassis & Cab	3,562	4,119	880
CK20904	Stepside 8 ft.	3,747	4,514	525
CK20934	Fleetside 8 ft.	3,747	4,640	29,769

3/4-Ton Conventional 4 x 4 — Model K/Series 20 — 129.5 in. w.b.

CK20906	Suburban (doors)	4,668	5,136	780
CK20916	Suburban (gate)	—	—	1,862

1-Ton Conventional — Model C/Series 30 — 131.5 in. w.b.

CC30903	Chassis & Cab	3,075	3,811	17,422
CC30903	Stepside 8 ft.	3,087	4,321	1,939
CC30903	Fleetside 8 ft.	3,087	4,246	7,281

NOTE 3: *Stake option included with C30 Chassis-and-Cab production.*

1-Ton Conventional — Model C/Series 30 — 135.5 in. w.b.

CC31063	Crew-Cab Fleetside	2,915	3,811	479

1-Ton Conventional — Model C/Series 30 — 159.5 in. w.b.

CC31403	Crew-Cab & Chassis	2,955	3,934	12,088

1-Ton Conventional — Model C/Series 30 — 164.5 in. w.b.

CC31963	Crew-Cab & Chassis	—	—	80
CC31963	Crew-Cab Fleetside	—	—	2,925

NOTES:
1: *LUV calendar-year sales were 39,422.*
2: *Detailed Chevrolet records show the above 1973 model-year totals for U.S. production and imports from Canada. They include six-cylinder and V-8 powered trucks.*
3: *Additional C30 (1-ton) production included 1,093 motorhomes on a 127-in. wheelbase, 7,194 motorhomes on a 158.5-in. wheelbase, and 115 motorhomes on a 178-in. wheelbase.*

1974

	Model No.	Body Type	Price	Weight	Production
1/2-Ton LUV — Model L/Series 82 — 102.4 in. w.b.					
	82	Mini-Pickup	2,406	2,475	Notes
El Camino — Model C/Series 13000 — 116 in. w.b. — Six					
	1AC80	Sedan-Pickup	3,139	3,950	Notes
El Camino Classic—Model D/Series 13000 — 116 in. w.b. — V-8					
	1AD80	Classic Sedan-Pickup	3,277	3,975	Notes
1/2-Ton Blazer 4 x 4 — Model C/Series 5 — 106.5 in. w.b.					
	CC10514	Open Utility	2,936	3,606	Notes
1/2-Ton Blazer 4 x 4 — Model K/Series 5 — 106.5 in. w.b.					
	CK10514	Open Utility	3,577	3,931	Notes
1/2-Ton Conventional — Model C/Series 10 — 117.5 in. w.b.					
	CC10703	Stepside 6.5 ft.	2,971	3,563	Notes
	CC10703	Fleetside 6.5 ft.	2,971	3,664	Notes
1/2-Ton Conventional — Model C/Series 10 — 131.5 in. w.b.					
	CC10903	Chassis & Cab	3,104	3,669	Notes
	CC10904	Stepside 8 ft.	3,007	3,711	Notes
	CC10934	Fleetside 8 ft.	3,007	3,821	Notes
1/2-Ton Conventional 4 x 4 — Model K/Series 10 — 117.5 in. w.b					
	CK10703	Stepside 6.5 ft.	3,703	3,973	Notes
	CK10703	Fleetside 6.5 ft.	3,703	4,077	Notes
1/2-Ton Conventional 4 x 4 — Model K/Series 10 — 131.5 in. w.b.					
	CK10903	Stepside 8 ft.	3,739	4,175	Notes
	CK10903	Fleetside 8 ft.	3,739	4,271	Notes
3/4-Ton Conventional — Model C/Series 20 — 131.5 in. w.b.					
	CC20903	Chassis & Cab	3,104	3,669	Notes
	CC20903	Stepside 8 ft.	3,271	4,064	Notes
	CC20903	Fleetside 8 ft.	3,271	4,174	Notes
3/4-Ton Crew-Cab — Model C/Series 20 — 164.5 in. w.b.					
	CE20963	Crew-Cab Chassis	4,214	4,395	Notes
	CE20963	Crew-Cab Pickup 8 ft.	4,381	4,904	Notes
3/4-Ton Conventional 4 x 4 — Model K/Series 20 — 131.5 in. w.b.					
	CK20903	Chassis & Cab	3,974	3,981	Notes
	CK20904	Stepside 8 ft.	4,141	4,372	Notes
	CK20934	Fleetside 8 ft.	4,141	4,486	Notes
1-Ton Conventional — Model C/Series 30 — 131.5 in. w.b.					
	CC30903	Chassis & Cab	3,201	3,828	Notes
	CC30903	Stepside 8 ft.	3,368	4,271	Notes
	CC30903	Fleetside 8 ft.	3,368	4,329	Notes

1974 continued

1-Ton Conventional — Model C/Series 30 — 135.5 in. w.b.

| | CC31063 | Crew-Cab Fleetside | 4,296 | 4,459 | Notes |

1-Ton Conventional — Model C/Series 30 — 159.5 in. w.b.

| | CC31403 | Crew-Cab & Chassis | 3,251 | 3,945 | Notes |

1-Ton Conventional — Model C/Series 30 — 164.5 in. w.b.

| | CC31963 | Crew-Cab & Chassis | 4,296 | 5,469 | Notes |

NOTES:
1: LUV calendar-year sales were 30,328.
2: El Camino model-year production was 51,223.
3: Pickup and Blazer model-year production was [C10/K10] 445,699, [C20/K20] 178,829, [C30/K30] 39,964, [Blazer] 56,798,. Production includes trucks built in Canada for U.S. market.

1975

	Model No.	Body Type	Price	Weight	Production

1/2-Ton LUV — Model L/Series 82 — 102.4 in. w.b.

| | CL10503 | Mini-Pickup | 2,976 | 2,380 | Notes |

El Camino — Model C/Series 13000 — 116 in. w.b. — Six

| | 1AC80 | Sedan-Pickup | 3,828 | 3,706 | Notes |

El Camino Classic — Model D/Series 13000 — 116 in. w.b.

| | 1AD80 | Classic Sedan-Pickup | 3,966 | 3,748 | Notes |

1/2-Ton Blazer 4 x 4 — Model K/Series 5 — 106.5 in. w.b.

| | CK10514 | Open Utility | 4,569 | 4,046 | Notes |
| | CK10516 | Hardtop Utility | 4,998 | 4,313 | Notes |

1/2-Ton Conventional — Model C/Series 10 — 117.5 in. w.b.

	CC10703	Chassis & Cab	3,676	3,318	Notes
	CC10703	Stepside 6.5 ft.	3,609	3,649	Notes
	CC10703	Fleetside 6.5 ft.	3,609	3,713	Notes

1/2-Ton Conventional — Model C/Series 10 — 131.5 in. w.b.

| | CC10903 | Stepside 8 ft. | 3,652 | 3,774 | Notes |
| | CC10903 | Fleetside 8 ft. | 3,652 | 3,844 | Notes |

Add $1,089 for K10 (4 x 4) Pickups.

3/4-Ton Conventional — Model C/Series 20 — 131.5 in. w.b.

	CC20903	Chassis & Cab	3,863	3,737	Notes
	CC20903	Stepside 8 ft.	4,030	4,137	Notes
	CC20903	Fleetside 8 ft.	4,030	4,207	Notes

Add $1,009 for K20 (4 x 4) Pickups.

3/4-Ton Conventional — Model C/Series 20 — 129.5 in. w.b.

| | CC20916 | Suburban (gate) | 5,045 | 4,664 | Notes |

3/4-Ton Bonus-Cab — Model C/Series 20 — 164.5 in. w.b.

	Model No.	Body Type	Price	Weight	Production
	CE20943	Stepside 8 ft.	4,613	—	Notes
	CE20943	Fleetside 8 ft.	4,613	4,904	Notes

3/4-Ton Crew-Cab — Model C/Series 20 — 164.5 in. w.b.

	Model No.	Body Type	Price	Weight	Production
	CE20963	Chassis	4,835	4,461	Notes
	CE20963	Stepside 8 ft.	5,002	4,861	Notes
	CE20963	Fleetside 8 ft.	5,002	4,935	Notes

1-Ton Conventional — Model C/Series 30 — 131.5 in. w.b.

	Model No.	Body Type	Price	Weight	Production
	CC30903	Chassis & Cab	3,996	3,913	Notes
	CC30903	Stepside 8 ft.	4,163	4,344	Notes
	CC30903	Fleetside 8 ft.	4,163	4,379	Notes

1-Ton Conventional — Model C/Series 30 — 164.5 in. w.b.

	Model No.	Body Type	Price	Weight	Production
	CC31963	Crew-Cab & Chassis	4,988	4,517	Notes
	CC31963	Crew-Cab Stepside 8'	5,155	4,948	Notes
	CC31963	Crew-Cab Fleetside 8'.	5,155	4,987	Notes

NOTES:
1: LUV calendar-year sales were.
2: El Camino model-year production was 33,620.
3: Pickup and Blazer model-year production was [C10/K10] 318,234, [C20/K20] 144,632, [C30/K30] 44,929, [Blazer] 50,548.

1976

	Model No.	Body Type	Price	Weight	Production

1/2-Ton LUV — Model L/Series 10500 — 102.4 in. w.b.

	Model No.	Body Type	Price	Weight	Production
	CL10503	Pickup	3,285	2,460	Notes

1/2-Ton El Camino — Model C, D/Series 14000 — 116 in. w.b.

	Model No.	Body Type	Price	Weight	Production
	IAC80	Sedan-Pickup	4,333	3,791	Notes
	IAD80	Classic Sedan-Pickup	4,468	3,821	Notes

1/2-Ton Blazer 4 x 4 — Model K/Series 10500 — 106.5 in. w.b.

	Model No.	Body Type	Price	Weight	Production
	CK10516	Utility Hardtop	5,365	4,017	Notes
	CK10516	Open Utility	5,265	—	Notes

1/2-Ton Conventional — Model C/Series 10 — 117.5 in. w.b.

	Model No.	Body Type	Price	Weight	Production
	CC10703	Chassis & Cab	3,957	3,449	Notes
	CC10703	Stepside 6.5 ft.	3,863	3,790	Notes
	CC10703	Fleetside 6.5 ft.	3,863	3,848	Notes

1/2-Ton Carryall Suburban — Model C/Series 10 — 129.5 in. w.b.

	Model No.	Body Type	Price	Weight	Production
	CC10906	Suburban 9 ft. (gate)	5,087	4,335	Notes

1/2-Ton Conventional — Model CK/Series 10 — 131.5 in. w.b.

	Model No.	Body Type	Price	Weight	Production
	CC10903	Stepside 6.5 ft.	3,908	3,877	Notes
	CC10903	Fleetside 6.5 ft.	3,908	3,953	Notes

Add $1,089 for K10 (4 x 4) Pickups.

1976 continued

3/4-Ton Conventional — Model C/Series 20 — 131.5 in. w.b.

CC20903	Chassis & Cab	4,139	3,730	Notes
CC20903	Stepside	4,306	4,128	Notes
CC20903	Fleetside	4,306	4,204	Notes

Add $1,009 for K20 (4 x 4) Pickups.

1-Ton Conventional — Model C/Series 30 — 131.5 in. w.b.

CC30903	Chassis & Cab	4,279	3,887	Notes
CC30903	Stepside 8 ft.	4,446	4,316	Notes
CC30903	Fleetside 8 ft.	4,446	4,357	Notes

1-Ton Conventional — Model C/Series 30 — 164.5 in. w.b.

CC30943	Chassis & Bonus-Cab	5,210	4,420	Notes
CC30943	Bonus Cab Fleetside 8'.	5,377	4,894	Notes
CC30963	Chassis & Crew-Cab	5,320	4,497	Notes
CC30963	Crew-Cab Fleetside 8'.	5,487	5,506	Notes

NOTE 1: LUV calendar-year sales were 45,670.
NOTE 2: El Camino model-year production was 44,890.
NOTE 3: Pickup and Blazer model-year production was [C10/K10] 458,424, [C20/K20] 172,419, [C30] 45,299, [Blazer] 74,389.

1977

	Model No.	Body Type	Price	Weight	Production

1/2-Ton LUV — Model L/Series 10500 — 102.4 in. w.b.

	Model No.	Body Type	Price	Weight	Production
	CL10503	Chassis & Cab	3,084	2,380	Notes
	CL10503	Pickup	3,284	2,380	Notes

1/2-Ton El Camino — Model C, D/Series 14000 — 116 in. w.b.

	Model No.	Body Type	Price	Weight	Production
	IAC80	Sedan-Pickup	4,268	3,797	Notes
	IAD80	Classic Sedan-Pickup	4,403	3,763	Notes

Add $244 for SS package on either model.

1/2-Ton Blazer 4 x 4 — Model K/Series 10500 — 106.5 in. w.b.

	Model No.	Body Type	Price	Weight	Production
	CK10516	Utility Hardtop	5,603	4,268	Notes
	CK10516	Open Utility	5,503	—	Notes

1/2-Ton Conventional — Model C/Series 10 — 117.5 in. w.b.

	Model No.	Body Type	Price	Weight	Production
	CC10703	Chassis & Cab	4,116	3,251	Notes
	CC10703	Stepside 6.5 ft.	4,122	3,585	Notes
	CC10703	Fleetside 6.5 ft.	4,122	3,645	Notes

1/2-Ton Conventional — Model CK/Series 10 — 131.5 in. w.b.

	Model No.	Body Type	Price	Weight	Production
	CC10903	Stepside 6.5 ft.	3,908	3,877	Notes
	CC10903	Fleetside 6.5 ft.	3,908	3,953	Notes

Add $1,089 for K10 (4 x 4) Pickups.

3/4-Ton Conventional — Model C/Series 20 — 131.5 in. w.b.

	Model No.	Body Type	Price	Weight	Production
	CC20903	Chassis & Cab	4,399	3,662	Notes
	CC20903	Stepside	4,624	4,051	Notes
	CC20903	Fleetside	4,624	4,142	Notes

Add $1,009 for K20 (4 x 4) Pickups.

1-Ton Conventional — Model C/Series 30 — 131.5 in. w.b.

	Model No.	Body Type	Price	Weight	Production
	CC30903	Chassis & Cab	4,539	3,803	Notes
	CC30903	Stepside 8 ft.	4,764	4,192	Notes
	CC30903	Fleetside 8 ft.	4,764	4,283	Notes

1-Ton Conventional — Model C/Series 30 — 164.5 in. w.b.

	Model No.	Body Type	Price	Weight	Production
	CC30943	Chassis & Bonus-Cab	5,470	4,444	Notes
	CC30943	Bonus-Cab Fleetside	5,695	4,924	Notes
	CC30963	Chassis & Crew-Cab	5,580	5,475	Notes
	CC30963	Crew-Cab Fleetside	5,805	5,015	Notes

NOTE 1: LUV calendar-year sales were 67,539.
NOTE 2: El Camino model-year production was 54,321.
NOTE 3: Pickup and Blazer model-year production was [C10/K10] 525,791 and 21 percent 4 x 4, [C20/K20] 189,150 and 31 percent 4 x 4, [C30/K30] 60,779 and 8 percent 4 x 4.

1978

	Model No.	Body Type	Price	Weight	Production

1/2-Ton LUV — Model L — 102.4/117.9 in. w.b. — Four

	Model No.	Body Type	Price	Weight	Production
	CL10503	Chassis & Cab	3,721	2,095	Notes
	CL10503	Pickup	3,885	2,315	Notes

1/2-Ton El Camino — Model W — 117.1 in. w.b. — V-6

	Model No.	Body Type	Price	Weight	Production
	1AW80	Pickup	3,807	—	Notes
	1AW80	Super Sport Pickup	3,956	—	Notes

1/2-Ton El Camino — Model W — 117.1 in. w.b. — V-8

	Model No.	Body Type	Price	Weight	Production
	1AW80	Pickup	4,843	3,076	Notes
	1AW80	Super Sport Pickup	5,022	3,076	Notes

1/2-Ton Blazer — Model K10 — 106.5 in. w.b. — V-8

	Model No.	Body Type	Price	Weight	Production
	CK10516	Hardtop 4 x 4	6,397	3,928	Notes
	CK10516	Softtop 4 x 4	6,297	3,780	Notes

1/2-Ton Conventional 4 x 2 — Model C10 — 117.5 in. w.b. — V-8

	Model No.	Body Type	Price	Weight	Production
	CC10703	Chassis & Cab	4,428	3,246	Notes
	CC10703	Stepside	4,418	3,579	Notes
	CC10703	Fleetside	4,418	3,639	Notes

1/2-Ton Conventional 4 x 2 — Model C10 — 131.5 in. w.b. — V-8

	Model No.	Body Type	Price	Weight	Production
	CC10903	Stepside	4,493	3,694	Notes
	CC10903	Fleetside	4,493	3,775	Notes

1/2-Ton Diesel 4 x 2 — Model C10 Diesel — 117.5 in. w.b. — V-8

	Model No.	Body Type	Price	Weight	Production
	CC10703	Stepside	6,228	3,765	Notes
	CC10703	Fleetside	6,228	3,824	Notes

1/2-Ton Diesel 4 x 2 — Model C10 Diesel — 131.5 in. w.b. — V-8

	Model No.	Body Type	Price	Weight	Production
	CC10903	Stepside	6,303	3,841	Notes
	CC10903	Fleetside	6,303	3,962	Notes

1/2-Ton Conventional 4 x 4 — Model K10 — 117.5 in. w.b. — V-8

	Model No.	Body Type	Price	Weight	Production
	CK10703	Chassis & Cab	5,006	4,143	Notes
	CK10703	Stepside	5,006	4,477	Notes
	CK10703	Fleetside	5,006	4,537	Notes

1/2-Ton Conventional 4 x 4 — Model K10 — 131.5 in. w.b. — V-8

	Model No.	Body Type	Price	Weight	Production
	CK10903	Stepside	5,062	4,639	Notes
	CK10903	Fleetside	5,062	4,720	Notes

3/4-Ton Conventional 4 x 2 — Model C20 — 131.5 in. w.b. — V-8

	Model No.	Body Type	Price	Weight	Production
	CC20903	Chassis & Cab	4,813	3,665	Notes
	CC20903	Stepside	5,038	4,054	Notes
	CC20903	Fleetside	5,038	4,135	Notes

3/4-Ton Conventional 4 x 2 — Model C20 — 164.5 in. w.b. — V-8

	Model No.	Body Type	Price	Weight	Production
	CC20943	Chassis & Bonus-Cab	5,512	4,176	Notes
	CC20943	Bonus-Cab Fleetside	5,737	4,646	Notes
	CC20963	Chassis & Crew-Cab	5,886	4,233	Notes
	CC20963	Crew-Cab Fleetside	6,111	4,703	Notes

3/4-Ton Conventional 4 x 4 — Model K20 — 131.5 in. w.b. — V-8

	Model No.	Body Type	Price	Weight	Production
	CK20903	Chassis & Cab	5,209	4,485	Notes
	CK20903	Stepside	5,434	4,874	Notes
	CK20903	Fleetside	5,434	4,955	Notes

1-Ton Conventional 4 x 2 — Model C30 — 131.5 in. w.b. — V-8

	Model No.	Body Type	Price	Weight	Production
	CC30903	Chassis & Cab	5,055	3,792	Notes
	CC30903	Stepside	5,280	4,181	Notes
	CC30903	Fleetside	5,280	4,262	Notes

1-Ton Conventional 4 x 2 — Model C30 — 164.5 in. w.b. — V-8

	Model No.	Body Type	Price	Weight	Production
	CC30943	Chassis & Cab	5,937	4,439	Notes
	CC30943	Bonus-Cab Fleetside	6,162	4,909	Notes
	CC30943	Chassis & Crew-Cab	6,047	4,772	Notes
	CC30943	Fleetwood Crew-Cab	6,272	4,941	Notes

1-Ton Conventional 4 x 4 — Model K30 — 131.5 in. w.b. — V-8

	Model No.	Body Type	Price	Weight	Production
	CK30903	Chassis & Cab	5,589	4,956	Notes
	CK30903	Fleetside	5,814	5,426	Notes

1-Ton Conventional 4 x 4 — Model K30 — 164.5 in. w.b. — V-8

	Model No.	Body Type	Price	Weight	Production
	CK30943	Chassis & Bonus-Cab	6,250	5,370	Notes
	CK30943	Bonus-Cab Fleetside	6,745	5,840	Notes
	CK30963	Chassis & Crew-Cab	6,630	5,370	Notes
	CK30963	Fleetwood Crew-Cab	6,855	5,840	Notes

NOTE 1: LUV calendar-year sales were 71,145.
NOTE 2: El Camino model-year production was 54,286.
NOTE 3: Pickup and Blazer model-year production was [C10/K10] 540,968, [C20/K10] 176,735, [C30/K30] 68,010, [Blazer] 88,858. (Includes trucks built in Canada for U.S. market).

1979

	Model No.	Body Type	Price	Weight	Production

LUV — 1/2-Ton — 102.4 in. w.b. — Four

	Model No.	Body Type	Price	Weight	Production
	CL10503	Chassis & Cab	4,132	2,095	Notes
	CL10503	Pickup	4,276	2,345	Notes

LUV — 1/2-Ton — 117.9 in. w.b. — Four

	Model No.	Body Type	Price	Weight	Production
	CL10803	Pickup	4,486	2,405	Notes

Add $971 for 4 x 4 LUVs

El Camino — 1/2-Ton — 117.1 in. w.b. — V-8

	Model No.	Body Type	Price	Weight	Production
	1AW80	Pickup	5,377	3,242	Notes
	Z15	SS Pickup	5,579	3,242	Notes
	1AW80	Conquista	5,532	3,242	Notes

Blazer 4 x 4 — 1/2-Ton — 106.5 in. w.b. — V-8 — 4 x 4

	Model No.	Body Type	Price	Weight	Production
	CK10516	Hardtop	7,373	4,371	Notes
	CK10516	Softtop	7,273	—	Notes

C10 — 1/2-Ton — 117.5 in. w.b. — V-8

	Model No.	Body Type	Price	Weight	Production
	CC10703	Chassis & Cab	4,943	3,406	Notes
	CC10703	Stepside Pickup	5,091	3,570	Notes
	CC10703	Fleetside Pickup	5,091	3,629	Notes

1979 continued

C10 — 1/2-Ton — 131.5 in. w.b. — V-8

	Model No.	Body Type	Price	Weight	Production
	CC10903	Stepside Pickup	5,171	3,693	Notes
	CC10903	Fleetside Pickup	5,171	3,767	Notes

C10 — 1/2-Ton — 129.5 in. w.b. — V-8

	Model No.	Body Type	Price	Weight	Production
	CC10906	Suburban (gate)	6,614	4,285	Notes

Add for K10 4 x 4 models (CK prefix).

C20 — 3/4-Ton — 131.5 in. w.b. — V-8

	Model No.	Body Type	Price	Weight	Production
	CC20903	Chassis & Cab	5,481	3,693	Notes
	CC20903	Stepside Pickup	5,777	4,077	Notes
	CC20903	Fleetside Pickup	5,777	4,151	Notes

C20 — 3/4-Ton — 164.5 in. w.b. — V-8

	Model No.	Body Type	Price	Weight	Production
	CC20943	Chassis & Bonus-Cab	6,233	4,224	Notes
	CC20943	Bonus-Cab Pickup	6,516	4,682	Notes
	CC20943	Chassis & Crew-Cab	6,634	—	Notes
	CC20943	Crew-Cab Pickup	6,918	—	Notes

C20 — 3/4-Ton — 129.5 in. w.b. — V-8

	Model No.	Body Type	Price	Weight	Production
	CC20906	Suburban (gate)	7,075	—	Notes

Add for K20 4 x 4 models (CK prefix).

C30 — 1-Ton — 131.5 in. w.b. — V-8

	Model No.	Body Type	Price	Weight	Production
	CC30903	Chassis & Cab	5,941	3,899	Notes
	CC30903	Stepside Pickup	6,237	4,283	Notes
	CC30903	Fleetside Pickup	6,237	4,358	Notes

C30 — 1-Ton — 164.5 in. w.b. — V-8

	Model No.	Body Type	Price	Weight	Production
	CC30943	Chassis-Bonus-Cab	6,740	4,453	Notes
	CC30943	Chassis-Crew-Cab	7,023	4,911	Notes
	CC30943	Bonus-Cab Pickup	6,900	—	Notes
	CC30943	Crew-Cab Pickup	7,183	—	Notes

Add for K30 4 x 4 models (CK prefix).

NOTE 1: *LUV calendar-year sales were 100,192.*
NOTE 2: *El Camino model-year production was 54,008.*
NOTE 3: *Pickup and Blazer model-year production was [C10] 535,056, [C20] 148,782, [C30] 80,500, [Blazer] 90,987. (Includes trucks built in Canada for U.S. market).*

1980

	Model No.	Body Type	Price	Weight	Production

LUV — 1/2-Ton — 102.4 in. w.b. — Four

	Model No.	Body Type	Price	Weight	Production
	CL10503	Chassis & Cab	4,448	2,095	Notes
	CL10503	Pickup	4,612	2,315	Notes

LUV — 1/2-Ton — 117.9 in. w.b. — Four

	Model No.	Body Type	Price	Weight	Production
	CL10803	Long-Box Pickup	4,787	2,405	Notes

El Camino — 1/2-Ton — 117.1 in. w.b. — V-8

1AW80	Pickup	5,911	3,238	Notes
RPOZ15	Super Sport Pickup	6,128	3,238	Notes

Blazer 4 x 4 — 1/2-Ton — 106.5 in. w.b. — V-8

CK10516	Hardtop	8,233	4,429	Notes
CK10516	Softtop	8,130	—	Notes

C10 — 1/2 Ton — 117.5 in. w.b. — V-8

CC10703	Chassis & Cab	5,785	3,243	Notes
CC10703	Stepside	5,505	3,550	Notes
CC10703	Fleetside	5,505	3,609	Notes

C10 — 1/2-Ton — 129.5 in. w.b. — V-8

CC10906	Suburban	7,456	4,242	Notes

C10 — 1/2-Ton — 131.5 in. w.b. — V-8

CC10903	Stepside	5,590	3,692	Notes
CC10903	Fleetside	5,590	3,767	Notes

Add $1,120 for K10 (4 x 4) models.

C20 — 3/4-Ton — 131.5 in. w.b. — V-8

CC20903	Chassis & Cab	6,216	3,585	Notes
CC20903	Stepside	2,326	3,969	Notes
CC20903	Fleetside	6,326	4,044	Notes

C20 — 3/4-Ton — 129.5 in. w.b. — V-8

CC20906	Suburban	7,923	4,538	Notes

C20 — 3/4-Ton — 164.5 in. w.b. — V-8

CC20943	Chassis Bonus-Cab	6,964	4,330	Notes
CC20943	Fleetside Bonus-Cab	7,241	4,789	Notes
CC20943	Chassis & Crew-Cab	7,218	—	Notes
CC20943	Fleetside Crew-Cab	7,495	—	Notes

Add for K20 (4 x 4) models.

C30 — 1-Ton — 131.5 in. w.b. — V-8

CC30903	Chassis & Cab	6,399	3,848	Notes
CC30903	Stepside	6,687	4,232	Notes
CC30903	Fleetside	6,687	4,307	Notes

C30 — 1-Ton — 164.5 in. w.b. — V-8

CC30943	Chassis-Bonus-Cab	7,120	4,364	Notes
CC30943	Fleetside Bonus-Cab	7,397	—	Notes
CC30943	Chassis-Crew-Cab	7,374	—	Notes
CC30943	Fleetside Crew-Cab	7,651	—	Notes

Add for K30 (4 x 4) models.

NOTE 1: LUV calendar-year sales were 88,447.
NOTE 2: El Camino model-year production was 40,932
NOTE 3: Pickup and Blazer model-year production was [C10] 305,167, [C20] 85,553, [C30] 59,251, [Blazer] 31,776. (Includes trucks built in Canada for U.S. market).

1981

	Model No.	Body Type	Price	Weight	Production

LUV — 1/2-Ton — 104.3 in. w.b. — Four

	Model No.	Body Type	Price	Weight	Production
	CL10503	Chassis & Cab	5,913	—	Notes
	CL10503	Pickup	6,586	2,315	Notes

LUV — 1/2-Ton — 117.9 in. w.b. — Four

	Model No.	Body Type	Price	Weight	Production
	CL10803	Pickup	6,795	2,405	Notes

El Camino — 1/2-Ton — 117.1 in. w.b. — V-6

	Model No.	Body Type	Price	Weight	Production
	A1AW80	Pickup	6,988	3,181	Notes
	RPOZ15	Super Sport Pickup	7,217	3,188	Notes

Blazer 4 x 4 — 1/2-Ton — 106.5 in. w.b. — Six

	Model No.	Body Type	Price	Weight	Production
	CK10516	Hardtop	8,856	4,087	Notes
	CK10516	Softtop	8,750	—	Notes

C10 4 x 2 — 1/2-Ton — 117.5 — Six

	Model No.	Body Type	Price	Weight	Production
	CC10703	Stepside 6.5 ft.	6,012	3,328	Notes
	CC10703	Fleetside 6.5 ft.	6,012	3,391	Notes

C10 4 x 2 — 1/2-Ton — 131.5 — Six

	Model No.	Body Type	Price	Weight	Production
	CC10903	Stepside 8 ft.	6,099	3,457	Notes
	CC10903	Fleetside 8 ft.	6,099	3,518	Notes

Add $1,750 for K10 (4 x 4) Pickups.

C20 — 3/4-Ton — 131.5 w.b. — Six

	Model No.	Body Type	Price	Weight	Production
	CC20903	Chassis & Cab	6,605	3,326	Notes
	CC20903	Stepside 8 ft.	7,109	3,710	Notes
	CC20903	Fleetside 8 ft.	7,109	3,771	Notes

C20 Bonus-Cab — 3/4-Ton — 164.5 in. w.b. — Six

	Model No.	Body Type	Price	Weight	Production
	CC20943	Chassis & Cab	7,447	4,246	Notes
	CC20943	Fleetside 8-ft.	7,935	—	Notes

C20 Crew-Cab — 3/4-Ton — 164.5 in. w.b. — Six

	Model No.	Body Type	Price	Weight	Production
	CC20943	Chassis & Cab	7,737	—	Notes
	CC20943	Fleetside 8-ft.	8,225	—	Notes

Add $1,370 for K20 (4 x 4) Pickups.

C30 — 1-Ton — 131.5 in. w.b. — Six

	Model No.	Body Type	Price	Weight	Production
	CC30903	Chassis & Cab	6,720	3,893	Notes
	CC30903	Stepside 8 ft.	7,214	4,251	Notes
	CC30903	Fleetside 8 ft.	7,214	4,310	Notes

C30 Bonus-Cab — 1-Ton — 164.5 in. w.b. — Six

	Model No.	Body Type	Price	Weight	Production
	CC30943	Chassis & Cab	7,625	4.327	Notes
	CC30943	Fleetside 8-ft.	8,114	—	Notes

C30 Crew-Cab — 1-Ton — 164.5 in. w.b. — Six

	Model No.	Body Type	Price	Weight	Production
	CC30943	Chassis & Cab	7,915	—	Notes
	CC30943	Fleetside 80ft.	8,404	—	Notes

Add for K30 4 x 4 models.

NOTE 1: *U.S. Sales of LUV: 61,724.*
NOTE 2: *El Camino model-year production was 37,533*
NOTE 3: *Pickup and Blazer model-year production was [C10] 318,003, [C20] 76,288, [C30] 50,250, [Blazer] 23,635. (Includes trucks built in Canada for U.S. market).*

1982

	Model No.	Body Type	Price	Weight	Production
LUV — 1/2-Ton — 104.3 in. w.b. — Four					
	CL10503	Pickup	6,256	2,375	Notes
LUV — 1/2-Ton — 117.9 in. w.b. — Four					
	CL10803	Pickup	6,465	2,470	Notes
S-10 — 1/2-Ton — 108.3 in. w.b. — V-6					
	CS-10603	Pickup	6,600	2,476	Notes
S-10 — 1/2-Ton — 118 in. w.b. — V-6					
	CS-10803	Chassis & Cab	-	2,878	Notes
	CS-10803	Pickup	6,750	2,552	Notes
	CS-10803	Utility	-	3,276	Notes
El Camino — 1/2-Ton — 117.1 in. w.b. — V-6					
	1GW80	Sedan-Pickup	7,995	3,294	Notes
	1GW80	SS Sedan-Pickup	8,244	3,300	Notes
Blazer — 1/2-Ton — 106.5 in. w.b. — Six					
	CK10516	Hardtop 4 x 4	9,874	4,294	Notes
	CK10516	Hardtop 4 x 2	8,533	-	Notes
C10 Conventional — 1/2-Ton — 117.5 in. w.b. — Six					
	CC10703	Stepside 6.5 ft.	6,689	3,418	Notes
	CC10703	Fleetside 6.5 ft.	6,564	3,461	Notes
C10 Conventional — 1/2-Ton — 131.5 in. w.b. — Six					
	CC10903	Fleetside 8 ft.	6,714	3,613	Notes

Add $2,185 for K10 (4 x 4) Pickups.

	Model No.	Body Type	Price	Weight	Production
C20 — 3/4-Ton — 131.5 in. w.b. — Six					
	CC20903	Chassis & Cab	7,865	3,661	Notes
	CC20903	Stepside 8 ft.	7,857	3,956	Notes
	CC20903	Fleetside 8 ft.	7,732	3,999	Notes
C20 — 3/4-Ton — 164.5 in. w.b. — Six					
	CC20943	Bonus-Cab	9,123	4,748	Notes
	CC20943	Crew-Cab	9,439	4,809	Notes

Add $1,974 for K20 (4 x 4) Fleetside, add $1,849 for K20 (4 x 4) Stepside.

	Model No.	Body Type	Price	Weight	Production
C30 — 1-Ton — 131.5 in. w.b. — Six					
	CC30903	Chassis & Cab	7,990	3,973	Notes
	CC30903	Stepside 8 ft.	8,474	4,323	Notes
	CC30903	Fleetside 8 ft.	8,349	4,394	Notes

1982 continued

C30 Bonus-Cab — 1-Ton — 164.5 in. w.b. — Six

	Model No.	Body Type	Price	Weight	Production
	CC30943	Chassis & Cab	8,943	4,400	Notes
	CC30943	Fleetside 8 ft.	9,286	4,817	Notes

C30 Crew-Cab — 1-Ton — 164.5 in. w.b. — Six

	Model No.	Body Type	Price	Weight	Production
	CC30943	Chassis-& Cab	9,259	4,461	Notes
	CC30943	Fleetside 8 ft.	9,602	4,878	Notes

Add for K30 (4 x 4) Pickups.

NOTE 1: LUV calendar-year sales were 22,304.
NOTE 2: S-10 model-year production was ?
NOTE 3: El Camino model-year production was 23,104.
NOTE 4: Pickup and Blazer model-year production was: [C10/K10] 243,834 of which 17.5 percent had four-wheel drive, [C20/K20] 75,714 of which 30.5 percent had four-wheel drive, [C30/K30] 49,230 of which 16 percent had four-wheel drive, [Blazer] 24,514. (Includes all trucks with GVWs of 10,000 lb. or less built in U.S. and built in Canada for the U.S. market).

1983

	Model No.	Body Type	Price	Weight	Production

El Camino — 1/2-Ton — 117.1 in. w.b. — V-6

	Model No.	Body Type	Price	Weight	Production
	1GW80	Sedan Pickup	8,191	3,332	Notes
	1GW80	Super Sport Pickup	8,445	3,337	Notes

1/2-Ton Mini-Truck — Model S/ Series 10 — 108.3 in. w.b. — Six

	Model No.	Body Type	Price	Weight	Production
	CS-10603	Pickup	6,343	2,537	Notes

1/2-Ton Mini-Truck — Model S/Series 10 — 122.0 in. w.b. — Six

	Model No.	Body Type	Price	Weight	Production
	CS-10803	Pickup	6,496	2,618	Notes
	CS-10653	Extended Pickup	6,725	2,647	Notes

Add for S-10 four-wheel-drive models.

1/2-Ton Blazer 4 x 4 — Model S/Series 10 — 100.5 in. w.b. — V-6

	Model No.	Body Type	Price	Weight	Production
	CT10516	Hardtop (gate)	9,433	3,106	Notes

1/2-Ton Blazer 4 x 4 — Model K/Series 10 — 106.5 in. w.b. — V-8

	Model No.	Body Type	Price	Weight	Production
	CK10516	Hardtop	10,287	4,426	Notes

1/2-Ton Conventional — Model C/Series 10 — 117.5 in. w.b. — Six

	Model No.	Body Type	Price	Weight	Production
	CC10703	Stepside	6,835	3,408	Notes
	CC10703	Fleetside	6,707	3,471	Notes

1/2-Ton Conventional — Model C/Series 10 — 131.5 in. w.b. — Six

	Model No.	Body Type	Price	Weight	Production
	CC10903	Fleetside	6,860	3,633	Notes

Add for 1/2-ton K10 four-wheel-drive Pickups.

3/4-Ton Conventional — Model C/Series 20 — 131.5 in. w.b. — Six

	Model No.	Body Type	Price	Weight	Production
	CC20903	Chassis & Cab	8,032	3,614	Notes
	CC20903	Stepside	8,525	3,964	Notes
	CC20903	Fleetside	8,397	4,025	Notes

3/4-Ton Conventional — Model C/Series 20 — 164.5 in. w.b. — V-8

	Model No.	Body Type	Price	Weight	Production
	CC20943	Bonus-Cab Fleetside	9,315	4,745	Notes
	CC20943	Crew-Cab Fleetside	9,637	4,806	Notes

Add for 3/4-ton K20 four-wheel-drive Pickups.

1-Ton Conventional — Model C/Series 30 — 131.5 in. w.b. — Six.

CC30903	Chassis & Cab	8,160	3,965	Notes
CC30903	Stepside	8,654	4,319	Notes
CC30903	Fleetside	8,526	4,380	Notes

1-Ton Conventional — Model C/Series 30 — 164.5 in. w.b. — V-8.

CC30943	Chassis Bonus-Cab	9,131	4,406	Notes
CC30943	Bonus-Cab Fleetside	9,481	4,817	Notes
CC30943	Chassis Crew-Cab	9,453	4,467	Notes
CC30943	Crew-Cab Fleetside	9,803	4,878	Notes

Add for 1-ton K30 four-wheel-drive Pickups.

NOTE 1: LUV calendar-year sales were 15,530.
NOTE 2: S-10 model-year production was 179,157 of which 24.6 percent had four-wheel drive,
NOTE 3: El Camino model-year production was 22,429.
NOTE 4: Pickup and Blazer model-year production was: [C10/K10 Pickup] 219,961 of which 22.6 percent had four-wheel drive, [C20/K20 Pickup] 66,548 of which 38.4 percent had four-wheel drive, [C30/K30 Pickup] 35,625 of which 20.0 percent had four-wheel drive, [S-10 Blazer] 84,672 of which 78.8 percent had four-wheel drive and [Full-sized Blazer] 26,245. (Includes all trucks with GVWs of 10,000 lb. or less built in U.S. and built in Canada for the U.S. Market).

1984

	Model No.	Body Type	Price	Weight	Production

S-10 Pickup — 1/2-Ton — 108.3 in. w.b. — V-6

	S-10	Pickup	6,398	2,574	Notes

S-10 Pickup — 1/2-Ton — 122.9 in. w.b. — V-6

	S-10	Pickup	6,551	2,649	Notes
	S-10	Maxi-Cab Pickup	6,924	2,705	Notes

S-10 Blazer 4 x 4 — 1/2-Ton — 100.5 in. w.b. — V-6

	T10	4 x 4 Hardtop	9,685	3,146	Notes

El Camino — 1/2-Ton — 117.1 in. w.b. — V-6

	W80	Pickup	8,522	3,298	Notes
	W80	Super Sport Pickup	8,781	3,305	Notes

Full-Size Blazer 4 x 4 — 1/2-Ton — 106.5 in. w.b. — V-8

	K10	Hardtop	10,819	4,409	Notes

Series C10 — 1/2-Ton — 117.5 in. w.b. — Six

	C10	Stepside	7,101	3,434	Notes
	C10	Fleetside	6,970	3,481	Notes

Series C10 — 1/2-Ton — 131.5 in. w.b. — Six

	C10	Fleetside	7,127	3,644	Notes

Add for four-wheel-drive K10 Pickup/Suburban.

Series C20 — 3/4-Ton — 131.5 in. w.b. — Six

	C20	Chassis & Cab	8,342	3,617	Notes
	C20	Stepside	8,319	3,977	Notes
	C20	Fleetside	8,188	4,039	Notes

1984 continued

Series C20 — 3/4-Ton — 164.5 in. w.b. — Six

	Model No.	Body Type	Price	Weight	Production
	C20	Bonus-Cab	9,645	4,742	Notes
	C20	Crew-Cab	9,975	4,803	Notes

Add for four-wheel-drive K20 Pickup/Suburban.

Series C30 — 1-Ton — 131.5 in. w.b. — Six

	Model No.	Body Type	Price	Weight	Production
	C30903	Chassis & Cab	8,474	3,990	Notes
	C30903	Stepside	8,966	4,342	Notes
	C30903	Fleetside	8,834	4,404	Notes

Series C30 Bonus-Cab—1-Ton — 164.5 in. w.b. — Six

	Model No.	Body Type	Price	Weight	Production
	C30943	Chassis & Cab	9,471	4,412	Notes
	C30943	Fleetside	4,822	—	Notes

Series C30 Crew-Cab—1-Ton — 164.5 in. w.b. — Six

	Model No.	Body Type	Price	Weight	Production
	C30943	Chassis & Cab	9,802	4,473	Notes
	C30943	Fleetside	10,146	4,883	Notes

NOTE 1: S-10 model-year production was 209,377 of which 20.1 percent had four-wheel drive,
NOTE 2: El Camino model-year production was 24,244.
NOTE 3: Pickup and Blazer model-year production was: C10/K10] 275,428 of which 26.0 percent had four-wheel drive, [C20/K20] 89,811 of which 38.5 percent had four-wheel drive, [C30/K30] 45,095 of which 20.8 percent had four-wheel drive, [S-10 Blazer] 149,937 of which 72.8 percent had four-wheel drive, [K5 Blazer] 39,329 of which 100 percent had four-wheel drive. (Includes all trucks with GVWs of 10,000 lb. or less built in U.S. and built in Canada for the U.S. Market).

1985

	Model No.	Body Type	Price	Weight	Production

El Camino — 1/2-Ton — 117.1 in. w.b. — V-6

	Model No.	Body Type	Price	Weight	Production
	1GW80	Sedan Pickup	9,058	3,252	Notes
	1GW80	Super Sport Pickup	9,327	3,263	Notes

S-10 Pickup 4 x 2 — 1/2-Ton — 108.3 in. w.b. — V-6

	Model No.	Body Type	Price	Weight	Production
	CS-10603	Pickup	5,999	2,561	Notes

S-10 Pickup 4 x 2 — 1/2-Ton — 122.9 in. w.b. — V-6

	Model No.	Body Type	Price	Weight	Production
	CS-10803	Chassis Cab	6,500	2,954	Notes
	CS-10803	Pickup	6,702	2,623	Notes
	CS-10653	Maxi-Cab Pickup	7,167	3,030	Notes

S-10 Pickup 4 x 4 — 1/2-Ton — 108.3 in. w.b. — V-6

	Model No.	Body Type	Price	Weight	Production
	CT10603	Pickup	8,258	2,898	Notes

S-10 Pickup 4 x 4 — 1/2-Ton — 122.9 in. w.b. — V-6

	Model No.	Body Type	Price	Weight	Production
	CT10803	Pickup	8,412	2,623	Notes
	CT10653	Maxi-Cab Pickup	8,756	3,030	Notes

S-10 Blazer 4 x 2 — 1/2-Ton — 100.5 in. w.b. — V-6

	Model No.	Body Type	Price	Weight	Production
	CS-10516	Hardtop Utility	8,881	2,894	Notes

S-10 Blazer 4 x 4 — 1/2-Ton — 100.5 in. w.b. — V-6

CT10516	Hardtop Utility	10,134	3,151	Notes

K5 Blazer 4 x 4 — 1/2-Ton — 106.5 w.b. — V-8

K10516	Hardtop Utility	11,223	4,462	Notes

Add $2,730 and 375 lb. for diesel.

C10 — 1/2-Ton Conventional — 117.5 in. w.b. — V-6

CC10703	Stepside	7,532	3,844	Notes
CC10703	Fleetside	7,397	3,891	Notes

C10 — 1/2-Ton Conventional — 131.5 in. w.b. — V-6

CC10903	Fleetside	7,565	4,060	Notes

Add $2,322 for CK10 (4 x 4) Pickup with Vortec six engine.
Add $2,913 for 6.2-liter diesel V-8 option.

C20 — 3/4-Ton Conventional — 131.5 in. w.b. — V-6

CC20903	Stepside	8,798	4,417	Notes
CC20903	Fleetside	8,663	4,479	Notes

C20 — 3/4-Ton Heavy-Duty Conventional — 131.5 in. w.b. — V-6

CC20903	Chassis & Cab	9,198	4,057	Notes
CC20903	Stepside	9,756	4,417	Notes
CC20903	Fleetside	9,622	4,479	Notes

C20 — 3/4-Ton Conventional — 164.5 in. w.b. — V-6

CC20943	Bonus-Cab Fleetside	10,584	5,258	Notes
CC20943	Crew-Cab Fleetside	10,920	5,258	Notes

Add $1,525 for CK20 (4 x 4) Pickups with 350-cid V-8.
Add $2,276 for 6.2-liter diesel V-8 option on C20 Pickups.

C30 — 1-Ton Conventional — 131.5 in. w.b. — Six

CC30903	Chassis & Cab	9,332	4,485	Notes
CC30903	Stepside	9,849	4,838	Notes
CC30903	Fleetside	9,715	4,900	Notes

C30 Bonus-Cab — 1-Ton Conventional — 164.5 in. w.b. — V-8

CC30943	Chassis & Cab	10,349	4,912	Notes
CC30943	Fleetside	10,715	5,323	Notes

C30 Crew-Cab — 1-Ton Conventional — 164.5 in. w.b. — V-8

CC30943	Chassis & Cab	9,446	4,520	Notes
CC30943	Fleetside	11,053	5,323	Notes

Add $2,344 average for CK30 (4 x 4) models with six-cylinder engine.
Add $1,800 average for 6.2-liter diesel V-8 option on C30 models.

NOTE 1: *S-10 model-year production was 250,194.*
NOTE 2: *El Camino model-year production was 24,582.*
NOTE 3: *Pickup and Blazer model-year production was: [C/K10] 292,681, [C/K20] 91,002, [C/K30] 46,917, [S-Blazer] 231,605, [K5 Blazer] 40,011. (Includes all trucks with GVWs of 10,000 lb. or less built in U.S. and built in Canada for the U.S. Market).*

1986

	Model No.	Body Type	Price	Weight	Production
El Camino — 1/2-Ton — 117.1 in. w.b. — V-6					
	W80	Sedan Pickup	9,572	3,234	Notes
	W80	Super Sport Pickup	9,885	3,239	Notes
S-10 Pickup — 1/2-Ton — 108.3 in. w.b. — V-6					
	S14	Fleetside EL	5,990	—	Notes
	S14	Fleetside	6,999	2,574	Notes
S-10 Pickup — 1/2-Ton — 122.9 in. w.b. — V-6					
	S14	Fleetside	7,234	2,645	Notes
	S14	Maxi-Cab	7,686	2,713	Notes
S-10 Blazer 4 x 4 — 1/2-Ton — 100.5 in. w.b. — V-6					
	T18	Utility Hardtop	10,698	3,152	Notes
K10 Blazer 4 x 4 — 1/2-Ton — 106.5 in. w.b. — V-8					
	K18	Utility Hardtop	12,034	4,444	Notes
C10 Pickup — 1/2-Ton — 117.5 in. w.b. — V-6					
	C14	Stepside 6.5 ft.	7,904	3,385	Notes
	C14	Fleetside 6.5 ft.	7,764	3,432	Notes
C10 Pickup — 1/2-Ton — 131.5 in. w.b. — V-6					
	C14	Fleetside 8 ft.	7,938	3,595	Notes
Add for CK10 Pickups with 4 x 4.					
C20 Pickup — 3/4-Ton — 131.5 in. w.b. — V-6					
	C24	Chassis & Cab	9,667	3,570	Notes
	C24	Stepside	9,253	3,930	Notes
	C24	Fleetside	9,113	3,992	Notes
C20 Pickup — 3/4-Ton — 164.5 in. w.b. — I-6					
	C24	Bonus Cab Pickup	11,103	4,773	Notes
	C24	Crew Cab Pickup	11,451	4,834	Notes
Add for CK20 Pickups with 4 x 4.					
C30 Pickup — 1-Ton — 131.5 in. w.b. I-6					
	C34	Chassis & Cab	9,843	4,011	Notes
	C34	Stepside	10,381	4,426	Notes
	C34	Fleetside	10,242	4,426	Notes
C30 Pickup — 1-Ton — 164.5 in. w.b. I-6					
	C33	Chassis-Bonus-Cab	10,901	4,451	Notes
	C33	Bonus Cab Fleetside	11,282	4,862	Notes
	C33	Chassis-Crew Cab	11,253	4,512	Notes
	C33	Crew Cab Fleetside	11,633	4,923	Notes

Add for CK30 Pickups with 4 x 4.

NOTE 1: S-10 model-year production was 34,865 Maxi-Cab of which 26 percent had four-wheel drive and 138,09 regular cab of which 24 percent had four-wheel drive..

NOTE 2: El Camino model-year production was 16,229.

NOTE 3: Pickup and Blazer model-year production was: [C10/K10 cab models] 282,192 of which 31 percent had four-wheel drive, [C20/K20 regular-cab models] 75,487 of which 43 percent had four-wheel drive, [C30/K30 regular-cab models] 39,823 of which 20 percent had four-wheel drive, [C20/C30/K20/K30 Crew-Cab] 17,405 of which none had four-wheel drive, [S-10 Blazer] 132,977 of which 75 percent had four-wheel drive, [K10 Blazer] 37,310 of which 100 percent had four-wheel drive. Figures include trucks built in U.S. and Canada for the U.S. market.

1987

	Model No.	Body Type	Price	Weight	Production

S10 Fleetside Pickup — 1/2-Ton — 108.3/117.9/122.9 in. w.b. — 2.5-liter EFI L4

	Model No.	Body Type	Price	Weight	Production
	S10603	Rg. Cab Short Box EL	6,595	2,567	Notes
	S10603	Reg. Cab Short Box	7,435	2,579	Notes
	S10803	Reg. Cab Long Box	7,702	2,657	Notes
	S10653	Ext. Cab Short Box	8,167	2,721	Notes

T10 Fleetside Pickup — 1/2-Ton — 108.3/117.9/122.9 in. w.b. — 2.5-liter EFI L4

	Model No.	Body Type	Price	Weight	Production
	T10603	Reg. Cab Short Box	9,845	2,913	Notes
	T10803	Reg. Cab Long Box	10,013	2,965	Notes
	T10653	Ext. Cab Short Box	10,359	3,042	Notes

W80 El Camino Coupe-Pickup — 1/2-Ton — 117.1-in. w.b. — 4.3-liter EFI V-6

	Model No.	Body Type	Price	Weight	Production
	W80	Coupe Pickup	10,453	3,234	Notes
	W80	Conquista	10,869	3,239	Notes
	W80	SS Coupe Pickup	10,784	3,244	Notes

S10 Blazer 4 x 2 Sport Utility Wagon — 1/2-Ton — 100.5/107 in. w.b. — 2.5-liter EFI L4

	Model No.	Body Type	Price	Weight	Production
	CS10516	2-dr Tailgate	10,124	2,804	Notes

T10 Blazer 4 x 4 Sport Utility Wagon — 1/2-Ton — 100.5/107 in. w.b. — 2.5-liter EFI L4

	Model No.	Body Type	Price	Weight	Production
	CT10516	2-dr Tailgate	11,588	3,140	Notes

V10 Blazer — 1/2-Ton — 111.5 in. w.b. — 5.7-liter EFI V-8

	Model No.	Body Type	Price	Weight	Production
	V18	Utility Hardtop	13,066	4,379	Notes

R10 Pickup — 1/2-Ton Short Box — 117.5 in. w.b. — 4.3-liter EFI V-6

	Model No.	Body Type	Price	Weight	Production
	R14	Regular-Cab Stepside	8,651	3,363	Notes
	R14	Regular-Cab Fleetside	8,503	3,410	Notes

R10 Pickup — 1/2-Ton Long Box — 131.5 in. w.b. — 4.3-liter EFI V-6

	Model No.	Body Type	Price	Weight	Production
	R14	Regular-Cab Fleetside	8,687	3,565	Notes

Add $2,800 for C10 Pickups with 4 x 4

R20 Pickup — 3/4-Ton Long Box — 131.5 in. w.b. — 4.3-liter EFI V-6

	Model No.	Body Type	Price	Weight	Production
	R24	Chassis & Regular-Cab	—	4,454	Notes
	R24	Regular-Cab Stepside	10,007	3,905	Notes
	R24	Regular-Cab Fleetside	9,924	3,967	Notes
	R24	Regcab Stepside HDE	11,498	4,027	Notes
	R24	Regcab Fleetside HDE	11,351	4,089	Notes

R2500 Pickup — 3/4-Ton EEWB Long Box — 164.5 in. w.b. — 5.7-liter EFI V-8

	Model No.	Body Type	Price	Weight	Production
	R23	Bonus-Cab Fleetside	11,775	4,773	Notes
	R23	Crew-cab Fleetside	13,142	4,834	Notes

Add $2,890 for V20 Pickups with 4 x 4 5.7-liter V-8 standard in V20s

R30 HDE Pickup — 1-Ton Long Box — 131.5 in. w.b. — 5.7-liter EFI V-8

	Model No.	Body Type	Price	Weight	Production
	R34	Chassis-and-cab	—	4,026	Notes
	R34	Regular-Cab Stepside	11,712	4,364	Notes
	R34	Regular-Cab Fleetside	11,565	4,443	Notes

1987 continued

R3500 HDE Pickup — 1-Ton EEWB Long Box — 164.5 in. w.b. — 5.7-liter EFI V-8.

R33	Chassis & Bonus-Cab	—	4,450	Notes
R33	Bonus-Cab Fleetside	12,664	4,861	Notes
R33	Chassis & Crew-cab	—	4,512	Notes
R23	Crew-cab Fleetside	13,034	4,923	Notes

NOTE 1: S-10 model-year production was 34,865 Maxi-Cab and 178,842 regular cab.
NOTE 2: El Camino model-year production was 15,589.
NOTE 3: Model year production [R/V10] 183,857, [R/V20] 53,522, [R/V30] 32,384, [C/K10] 78,130, [C/K20] 16,281, [C/K30] 2,708, [S-Series Blazer] 174,797, [V10 Blazer] 32,437, Figures include trucks built in U.S. and Canada for the U.S. market. Figures include a small number of "new design" (1988 style) C/K models built from April 1987 on.

1988

	Model No.	Body Type	Price	Weight	Production

S10 Fleetside Pickup — 1/2-Ton — 108.3/117.9/122.9 in. w.b. — 2.5-liter EFI L4

	Model No.	Body Type	Price	Weight	Production
	S10603	Reg. Cab Short Box EL	6,595	2,568	Notes
	S10603	Reg. Cab Short Box	8,238	2,625	Notes
	S10803	Reg. Cab Long Box	8,412	2,703	Notes
	S10653	Ext. Cab Short Box	9,257	2,767	Notes

T10 Fleetside Pickup — 1/2-Ton — 108.3/117.9/122.9 in. w.b. — 2.5-liter EFI L4

	Model No.	Body Type	Price	Weight	Production
	T10603	Reg. Cab Short Box	10,414	2,919	Notes
	T10803	Reg. Cab Long Box	10,579	2,997	Notes
	T10653	Ext. Cab Short Box	11,197	3,061	Notes

S10 Blazer 4 x 2 Sport Utility Wagon — 1/2-Ton — 100.5/107 in. w.b. — 2.5-liter L4

	Model No.	Body Type	Price	Weight	Production
	CS10516	2-dr Tailgate	10,505	2,804	Notes

T10 Blazer 4 x 4 Sport Utility Wagon — 1/2-Ton — 100.5/107 in. w.b. — 2.8-liter EFI V-6

	Model No.	Body Type	Price	Weight	Production
	CT10516	2-dr Tailgate	12,737	3,217	Notes

K1500 Blazer — 1/2-Ton — 111.5 in. w.b. — 5.7-liter EFI V-8

	Model No.	Body Type	Price	Weight	Production
	CK10516	Utility Hardtop	14,509	4,676	Notes

NOTE 5: A $550 dealer destination charge applied to full-size Blazers

C1500 — 1/2-Ton Short Box — 117.5 in. w.b. — 4.3-liter EFI V-6

	Model No.	Body Type	Price	Weight	Production
	CC10703	Regular-cab Sportside	10,472	4,093	Notes
	CC10703	Regular-cab Fleetside	10,264	4,181	Notes

R1500 Pickup — 1/2-Ton Long Box — 131.5 in. w.b. — 4.3-liter EFI V-6

	Model No.	Body Type	Price	Weight	Production
	CC10903	Regular-cab Fleetside	10,454	4,250	Notes

R1500 Pickup — 1/2-Ton Short Box — 141.5 in. w.b. — 4.3-liter EFI V-6

	Model No.	Body Type	Price	Weight	Production
	CC10753	Extended-cab Fleetside	11,661	4,608	Notes

Add $2,077 for CK1500 Pickups with 4 x 4.

C2500 Pickup — 3/4-Ton Long Box — 131.5 in. w.b. — 4.3-liter EFI V-6

	Model No.	Body Type	Price	Weight	Production
	CC20903	Regular-cab Fleetside	11,291	4,454	Notes

C2500 Pickup — 3/4-Ton Long Box — 141.5 in. w.b. — 4.3-liter EFI V-6

	Model No.	Body Type	Price	Weight	Production
	CC20953	Extended-cab Fleetside	12,611	4,758	Notes

R2500 Pickup — 3/4-Ton EEWB Long Box — 164.5 in. w.b. — 4.8-liter EFI L6

	Model No.	Body Type	Price	Weight	Production
	RR20953	Bonus-Cab Fleetside	13,632	5,197	Notes
	RR20953	Crew-cab Fleetside	14,608	5,528	Notes

Add $1,552 for CK2500 Pickups with 4 x 4.

C3500 Pickup — 1-Ton Long Box — 131.5 in. w.b. — 5.7-liter EFI V-8

	CC30934	Chassis & Fleetside	11,451	4,032	Notes
	CC30934	Regular-cab Fleetside	11,291	4,454	Notes

C3500 Pickup — 1-Ton Long Box — 141.5 in. w.b. — 5.7-liter EFI V-8

	CC30939	Ch-&-Extended-cab	12,454	4,657	Notes
	CC30939	Extended-cab Fleetside		13,033	5,012

Notes
Add $2,020 for CK3500 Pickups with 4 x 4.

R3500 Pickup — 1-Ton EEWB Long Box — 155.5 in. w.b. — 4.8-liter EFI L6

	TR30943	Chassis & Cab	11,545	4,348	Notes
	TR30943	Bonus-Cab Fleetside	13,828	5,233	Notes
	TR30943	Crew-cab Fleetside	14,268	5,564	Notes

R3500 Pickup — 1-Ton EEWB Long Box — 164.5 in. w.b. — 4.8-liter EFI L6/5.7-liter EFI V-8.

	TR30953	Chassis & Bonus-Cab	12,700	4,859	Notes
	TR30953	Chassis & Crew-cab	13,142	5,371	Note

NOTE 1: S-10 model-year production was 42,416 Maxi-Cab and 216,301 regular cab.
NOTE 2: Model year production [C/K1500] 375,330, [C/K2500] 97,200, [C/K3500] 47,406, [S-Series Blazer] 157,264, [K Blazer] 28,446, Figures include trucks built in U.S. and Canada for the U.S. market.

1989

	Model No.	Body Type	Price	Weight	Production

S10 Fleetside Pickup — 1/2-Ton — 108.3/117.9/122.9 in. w.b. — 2.5-liter EFI L4

	S10603	Reg. Cab Short Box EL	7,927	2,624	Notes
	S10603	Reg. Cab Short Box	9,041	2,648	Notes
	S10803	Reg. Cab Long Box	9,206	2,711	Notes
	S10653	Ext. Cab Short Box	9,891	2,774	Notes

T10 Fleetside Pickup — 1/2-Ton — 108.3/117.9/122.9 in. w.b. — 2.8-liter EFI V-6

	T10603	Reg. Cab Short Box	11,731	3,103	Notes
	T10803	Reg. Cab Long Box	11,911	3,142	Notes
	T10653	Ext. Cab Short Box	12,541	3,231	Notes

NOTE 1: A $400 dealer destination charge applied to S-Series pickups

S10 Blazer 4 x 2 Sport Utility Wagon — 1/2-Ton — 100.5/107 in. w.b. — 2.8-liter EFI V-6

	CS10516	2-dr Tailgate	12,173	3,030	Notes

T10 Blazer 4 x 4 Sport Utility Wagon — 1/2-Ton — 100.5/107 in. w.b. — 2.8-liter EFI V-6

	CT10516	2-dr Tailgate	13,748	3,319	Notes

K1500 Blazer — 1/2-Ton — 111.5 in. w.b. — 5.7-liter EFI V-8

	CK10516	Utility Hardtop	15,965	4,878	Notes

C1500 Pickup — 1/2-Ton Short Box — 117.5 in. w.b. — 4.3-liter EFI V-6

	CC10703	Regular-Cab Sportside	11,163	3,751	Notes
	CC10703	Regular-Cab Fleetside	10,945	3,692	Notes

1989 continued

C1500 Pickup — 1/2-Ton Long Box — 131.5 in. w.b. — 4.3-liter EFI V-6

Model No.	Body Type	Price	Weight	Production
CC10903	Regular-Cab Fleetside	11,145	3,763	Notes
CC10903	Regular-Cab Diesel	13,931	4,105	Notes

C1500 Pickup — 1/2-Ton Short Box — 141.5 in. w.b. — 4.3-liter EFI V-6

Model No.	Body Type	Price	Weight	Production
CC10753	Extended-cab Fleetside	12,077	4,091	Notes

Add approximately $2,020 for K1500 Pickups with 4 x 4.

C2500 Pickup — 3/4-Ton Long Box — 131.5 in. w.b. — 4.3-liter EFI V-6

Model No.	Body Type	Price	Weight	Production
CC20903	Regular-Cab Fleetside	11,753	3,909	Notes
CC20903	Regular-Cab FS HD	12,987	4,780	Notes
CC20903	Reg.-Cab FS H-D diesel	14,440	4,582	Notes

C2500 Pickup — 3/4-Ton Short Box — 141.5 in. w.b. — 4.3-liter EFI V-6

Model No.	Body Type	Price	Weight	Production
CC20954	Chassis & Extended-cab	12,995	4,705	Notes
CC20953	Extended-Cab Fleetside	13,108	4,185	Notes
CC20953	Extended cab FS H-D	14,022	4,994	Notes

Add approximately $1,700 for CK2500 Pickups with 4 x 4.

C3500 Pickup — 1-Ton Long Box — 131.5 in. w.b. — 5.7-liter EFI V-8

Model No.	Body Type	Price	Weight	Production
CC30924	Regular Cab H-D	13,327	4,349	Notes
CC30903	Big Dooley	14,365	5,071	Notes

C3500 Pickup — 1-Ton Short Box — 155.5 in. w.b. — 5.7-liter V-8

Model No.	Body Type	Price	Weight	Production
CC30903	Extended-cab H-D	14,362	4,625	Notes
CC30903	Big Dooley H-D	15,400	5,330	Notes

C3500 Pickup — 1-Ton Long Box — 168.5 in. w.b. — 5.7-liter V-8

Model No.	Body Type	Price	Weight	Production
CC30933	Bonus-cab Fleetside	14,362	5,275	Notes
CC30933	Crew-cab Fleetside	14,713	5,782	Notes
CC30933	Chassis & Bonus-cab	13,928	4,859	Notes
CC30933	Crew-cab Fleetside	14,439	5,371	Notes

Add approximately $2,200 for CK3500 Pickups with 4 x 4.

NOTE 1: *S-10 model-year production was 249,758.*
NOTE 2: *Model year production [C/K1500] 369,236, [C/K2500] 106,731, [C/K3500] 24,784, [S-Series Blazer] 184,656, [K Blazer] 26,663, [RV20/30] 34,908. Figures include trucks built in U.S. and Canada for the U.S. market.*

1990

	Model No.	Body Type	Price	Weight	Production
S10 Fleetside Pickup — 1/2-Ton — 108.3/122.9 in. w.b. — 2.5-liter EFI L4					
	S10603	Reg. Cab EL X81	7,975	2,650	Notes
	S10603	Reg. Cab Short Box	9,215	2,668	Notes
	S10803	Reg. Cab Long Box	9,380	2,774	Notes
	S10653	Ext. Cab Short Box	10,165	2,732	Notes
T10 4 x 4 Fleetside Pickup — 1/2-Ton — 108.3/118/122.9 in. w.b. — 4.3-liter EFI V-6					
	T10603	Reg. Cab SWB	12,430	3,103	Notes
	T10803	Reg. Cab LWB	12,615	3,142	Notes
	T10653	Ext. Cab Short Box	13,215	3,231	Notes

S10 Blazer 4 x 2 Sport Utility Wagon — 1/2-Ton — 100.5/107 in. w.b. — 4.3-liter EFI V-6

CS10516	2-dr Tailgate	12,930	2,996	Notes

T10 Blazer 4 x 4 Sport Utility Wagon — 1/2-Ton — 100.5/107 in. w.b. — 4.3-liter EFI V-6

CT10516	2-dr Tailgate	14,595	3,279	Notes
CT10506	4-dr Tailgate	16,905	3,459	Notes
1UM05	Cargo Van	12,895	3,450	Notes
1UM06	Wagon	13,995	3,505	Notes
1UM06	Wagon CL	15,745	3,505	Notes

K1500 Blazer — 1/2-Ton — 111.5 in. w.b. — 5.7-liter EFI V-8

CK10516	Utility Hardtop	16,485	4,839	Notes

C1500 Pickup — 1/2-Ton Short Box — 117.5 in. w.b. — 4.3-liter EFI V-6

CC10703	Regular-Cab Sportside	11,625	4,167	Notes
CC10703	Regular-Cab Fleetside	11,300	4,159	Notes

C1500 Pickup — 1/2-Ton Long Box — 131.5 in. w.b. — 4.3-liter EFI V-6

CC10903	Regular-Cab Fleetside	11,580	4,293	Notes
CC10903	Regular-Cab WT	10,445	4,159	Notes

C1500 Pickup — 1/2-Ton Short Box — 141.5 in. w.b. — 4.3-liter EFI V-6

CC10753	Extended-Cab Fleetside	12,210	4,251	Notes

C1500 Pickup — 1/2-Ton Long Box — 155.5 in. w.b. — 4.3-liter EFI V-6

CC10903	Extended-Cab Fleetside	12,490	4,492	Notes

C1500 Pickup — 1/2-Ton 454SS — 117.5 in. w.b. — 7.4-liter EFI V-6

CC10703/PSS1	Regular-Cab Sportside	18,295	4,662	Notes

Add approximately $1,990 for CK1500 Pickups with 4 x 4.

C2500 Pickup — 3/4-Ton Long Box — 131.5 in. w.b. — 4.3-liter EFI V-6

CC20924	Chassis & Cab	13,038	3,836	Notes
CC20903	Regular-Cab Fleetside	12,205	4,450	Notes

C2500 Pickup — 3/4-Ton Short Box — 141.5 in. w.b. — 4.3-liter EFI V-6

CC20954	Chassis Extended-Cab	14,063	4,301	Notes
CC20953	Extended-Cab Fleetside	13,275	4,723	Notes

C2500 Pickup — 3/4-Ton Long Box — 155.5 in. w.b. — 4.3-liter EFI V-6

CC20903	Extended-Cab Fleetside	13,555	4,723	Notes

Add approximately $2,200 for CK2500 Pickups with 4 x 4.

C3500 Pickup — 1-Ton Long Box — 131.5 in. w.b. — 5.7-liter EFI V-8

CC30924	Chassis & Cab	13,393	5,006	Notes
CC30903	Regular-Cab Fleetside	13,828	5,281	Notes

C3500 Pickup — 1-Ton Long Box — 155.5 in. w.b. — 5.7-liter V-8

CC30903	Chassis Extended Cab	14,418	5,145	Notes
CC30903	Extended-Cab Fleetside	14,484	5,552	Notes

1990 continued

C3500 Pickup — 1-Ton Long Box — 168.5 in. w.b. — 5.7-liter V-8

	Model No.	Body Type	Price	Weight	Production
	CC30933	Bonus-Cab Fleetside	15,383	5,640	Notes
	CC30933	Crew-Cab Fleetside	15,913	5,538	Notes
	CC30933	Chassis & Bonus-Cab	14,938	5,125	Notes
	CC30933	Crew-Cab Fleetside	15,463	5,223	Notes

NOTE 1: *S-10 model-year production was 202,240.*
NOTE 2: *[C/K1500] 372,223, [C/K2500] 80,909, [C/K3500] 29,619, [S-Series Blazer] 175,450, [K1500 Blazer] 18,921. Figures include trucks built in U.S. and Canada for the U.S. market.*

1991

	Model No.	Body Type	Price	Weight	Production
S10 Fleetside Pickup — 1/2-Ton — 108.3/122.9 in. w.b. — 2.5-liter EFI L4					
	S10603	Reg. Cab EL X81	8,382	2,671	Notes
	S10603	Reg. Cab Short Box	9,700	2,684	Notes
	S10803	Reg. Cab Long Box	9,870	2,756	Notes
	S10653	Ext. Cab Short Box	10,970	2,793	Notes
T10 4 x 4 Fleetside Pickup — 1/2-Ton — 108.3/118/122.9 in. w.b. — 4.3-liter EFI V-6					
	T10603	Reg. Cab SWB	12,430	3,241	Notes
	T10803	Reg. Cab LWB	12,615	3,288	Notes
	T10653	Ext. Cab Short Box	13,215	3,366	Notes
	T10603	Reg. Cab SWB Baja	12,430	3,254	Notes
	T10803	Reg. Cab LWB Baja	12,615	3,301	Notes
	T10653	Ext. Cab Short Box Baja	13,215	3,379	Notes
S10 Blazer 4 x 2 Sport Utility Wagon — 1/2-Ton — 100.5/107 in. w.b. — 4.3-liter EFI V-6					
	CS10516	2-dr Tailgate	13,845	3,189	Notes
	CS10506	4-dr Tailgate	15,085	3,433	Notes
T10 Blazer 4 x 4 Sport Utility Wagon — 1/2-Ton — 100.5/107 in. w.b. — 4.3-liter EFI V-6					
	CT10516	2-dr Tailgate	15,575	3,481	Notes
	CT10506	4-dr Tailgate	17,215	3,721	Notes
K1500 Blazer — 1/2-Ton — 111.5 in. w.b. — 5.7-liter EFI V-8					
	CK10516	Utility Hardtop	17,590	4,507	Notes
C1500 Pickup — 1/2-Ton Short Box — 117.5 in. w.b. — 4.3-liter EFI V-6					
	CC10703	Regular-Cab Sportside	12,445	3,722	Notes
	CC10703	Regular-Cab Fleetside	12,115	3,692	Notes
C1500 Pickup — 1/2-Ton Long Box — 131.5 in. w.b. — 4.3-liter EFI V-6					
	CC10903	Regular-Cab Fleetside	12,415	3,838	Notes
	CC10903	Regular-Cab WT	10,625	3,838	Notes
C1500 Pickup — 1/2-Ton Short Box — 141.5 in. w.b. — 4.3-liter EFI V-6					
	CC10753	Extended-Cab Fleetside	13,065	4,051	Notes
C1500 Pickup — 1/2-Ton Long Box — 155.5 in. w.b. — 4.3-liter EFI V-6					
	CC10903	Extended-Cab Fleetside	13,365	4,153	Notes

C1500 Pickup — 1/2-Ton 454SS — 117.5 in. w.b. — 7.4-liter EFI V-6

Model No.	Body Type	Price	Weight	Production
CC10703/PSS1	Regular-Cab Sportside	19,610	4,562	Notes

Add approximately $2,290 for CK1500 Pickups with 4 x 4.

C2500 Pickup — 3/4-Ton Long Box — 131.5 in. w.b. — 4.3-liter EFI V-6

Model No.	Body Type	Price	Weight	Production
CC20924	Chassis & Cab	13,918	3,636	Notes
CC20903	Regular-Cab Fleetside	13,055	4,003	Notes

C2500 Pickup — 3/4-Ton Short Box — 141.5 in. w.b. — 4.3-liter EFI V-6

Model No.	Body Type	Price	Weight	Production
CC20954	Chassis—Extended Cab	14,988	3,901	Notes
CC20953	Extended-Cab Fleetside	14,175	4,161	Notes

C2500 Pickup — 3/4-Ton Long Box — 155.5 in. w.b. — 4.3-liter EFI V-6

Model No.	Body Type	Price	Weight	Production
CC20903	Extended-Cab Fleetside	14,455	4,268	Notes

Add approximately $1,770 for CK2500 Pickups with 4 x 4.

C3500 Pickup — 1-Ton Long Box — 131.5 in. w.b. — 5.7-liter EFI V-8

Model No.	Body Type	Price	Weight	Production
CC30924	Chassis & Cab	15,060	4,506	Notes
CC30903	Regular-Cab Fleetside	15,785	4,812	Notes

C3500 Pickup — 1-Ton Long Box — 155.5 in. w.b. — 5.7-liter V-8

Model No.	Body Type	Price	Weight	Production
CC30903	Chassis Extended Cab	16,130	4,645	Notes
CC30903	Extended-Cab Fleetside	16,855	5,124	Notes

C3500 Pickup — 1-Ton Long Box — 168.5 in. w.b. — 5.7-liter V-8

Model No.	Body Type	Price	Weight	Production
CC30933	Bonus-cab Fleetside	16,258	5,140	Notes
CC30933	Crew-Cab Fleetside	16,798	5,169	Notes
CC30933	Chassis & Bonus-cab	15,788	4,729	Notes
CC30933	Crew-Cab Fleetside	16,338	4,915	Notes
CC30934	H-D Crew-Cab Chassis	18,577	4,716	Notes

Add approximately $2,340 for CK3500 Pickups with 4 x 4.

NOTE 1: S-10 model-year production was 253,953.
NOTE 2: Model year production [C/K] 246,593, [S-Series Blazer] 81,267, [K1500 Blazer] 7,332. Figures include trucks built in U.S. and Canada for the U.S. market.

1992

	Model No.	Body Type	Price	Weight	Production

S10 Fleetside Pickup — 1/2-Ton — 108.3/117.9/122.9 in. w.b. — 2.5-liter EFI L4

Model No.	Body Type	Price	Weight	Production
S10603	Reg.-Cab EL	8,722	2,645	Notes
S10603	Reg.-Cab Short Box	9,858	2,665	Notes
S10803	Reg.-Cab Long Box	10,158	2,747	Notes
S10653	Ext.-Cab Short Box	11,358	2,826	Notes

T10 4 x 4 Fleetside Pickup — 1/2-Ton — 108.3/117.9/122.9 in. w.b. — 4.3L-liter EFI L4

Model No.	Body Type	Price	Weight	Production
T10603	Reg.-Cab EL	11,512	—	Notes
T10603	Reg.-Cab SWB	12,055	—	Notes
T10803	Reg.-Cab LS LWB	12,324	—	Notes
T10653	Ext.-Cab LS Short Box	13,402	—	Notes

1992 continued

S10 Blazer 4 x 2 Sport Utility Wagon — 1/2-Ton — 100.5/107 in. w.b. — 4.3-liter EFI V-6

CS10516	2-dr Tailgate	14,823	3,181	Notes
CS10506	4-dr Tailgate	15,783	3,369	Notes

T10 Blazer 4 x 4 Sport Utility Wagon — 1/2-Ton — 100.5/107 in. w.b. — 4.3-liter EFI V-6

CT10516	2-dr Tailgate	16,583	3,485	Notes
CT10506	4-dr Tailgate	17,953	3,712	Notes

K1500 Blazer — 1/2-Ton — 111.5 in. w.b. — 5.7-liter EFI V-8

CK10516	Utility Hardtop	19,280	4,676	Notes

C1500 Pickup — 1/2-Ton Short Box — 117.5 in. w.b. — 4.3-liter EFI V-6

CC10703	Regular-Cab Sportside	13,495	3,735	Notes
CC10703	Regular-Cab Fleetside	13,095	3,718	Notes

C1500 Pickup — 1/2-Ton Long Box — 131.5 in. w.b. — 4.3-liter EFI V-6

CC10903	Regular-Cab Fleetside	13,395	3,869	Notes
CC10903	Regular-Cab WT	10,600	3,819	Notes

C1500 Pickup — 1/2-Ton Short Box — 141.5 in. w.b. — 4.3-liter EFI V-6

CC10753	Extended-Cab Sportside	14,445	4,015	Notes
CC10753	Extended-Cab Fleetside	14,045	3,998	Notes

C1500 Pickup — 1/2-Ton Long Box — 155.5 in. w.b. — 4.3-liter EFI V-6

CC10903	Extended-Cab Fleetside	14,335	4,129	Notes

Add approximately $2,150 for CK1500 Pickups with 4 x 4.

C2500 Pickup — 3/4-Ton Long Box — 131.5 in. w.b. — 4.3-liter EFI V-6

CC20924	Chassis & Cab	15,078	3,653	Notes
CC20903	Regular-Cab Fleetside	14,035	4,023	Notes

C2500 Pickup — 3/4-Ton Short Box — 141.5 in. w.b. — 4.3-liter EFI V-6

CC20954	Chassis & Ext.-Cab	16,158	3,899	Notes
CC20953	Extended-Cab Fleetside	15,155	4,131	Notes

C2500 Pickup — 3/4-Ton Long Box — 155.5 in. w.b. — 5.7-liter EFI V-6

CC20903	Extended-Cab Fleetside	15,435	4,266	Notes

Add approximately $1,750 for CK2500 Pickups with 4 x 4.

C3500 Pickup — 1-Ton Long Box — 131.5 in. w.b. — 5.7-liter EFI V-8

CC30924	Chassis & Cab	15,138	4,269	Notes
CC30903	Regular-Cab Fleetside	15,588	4,636	Notes

C3500 Pickup — 1-Ton Long Box — 155.5 in. w.b. — 5.7-liter V-8

CC30903	Extended-Cab Fleetside	16,658	4,981	Notes

C3500 Pickup — 1-Ton Long Box — 168.5 in. w.b. — 5.7-liter V-8

CC30933	Crew-Cab Fleetside	17,047	5,279	Notes
CC30934	H-D Crew-Cab-Chassis	18,498	5,264	Notes

Add approximately $2,150 for CK3500 Pickups with 4 x 4.

NOTE 1: S-10 model-year production was 191,960.
NOTE 2: Model year production [C/K] 346,477, [S-Series Blazer] 124,965, [K1500 Blazer] 17,444. Figures include trucks built in U.S. and Canada for the U.S. market.
NOTE 3: The percentages of the above trucks with four-wheel-drive was [S10 Pickup] 13.7 percent, [C/K1500] 32.7 percent, [C/K2500] 54.5 percent, [C/K3500] 7.3 percent, [S-Blazer] 77 percent, [K-Blazer] 100 percent.

1993

Model No.	Body Type	Price	Weight	Production
S10 Fleetside Pickup — 1/2-Ton — 108.3/117.9/122.9 in. w.b. — 2.5-liter EFI L4				
S10603	Reg. Cab EL X81	8,745	2,635	Notes
S10603	Reg. Cab Short Box	10,130	2,913	Notes
S10803	Reg. Cab Long Box	10,430	3,000	Notes
S10653	Ext. Cab Short Box	11,630	3,024	Notes
T10 4 x 4 Fleetside Pickup — 1/2-Ton — 108.3/117.9/122.9 in. w.b. — 4.3-liter EFI V-6				
T10603	Reg. Cab EL X81	12,545	—	Notes
T10603	Reg. Cab SWB	13,696	—	Notes
T10803	Reg. Cab LS LWB	13,996	—	Notes
T10653	Ext. Cab LS Short Box	15,196	—	Notes
S10 Blazer 4 x 2 Sport Utility Wagon — 1/2-Ton — 100.5/107 in. w.b. — 4.3-liter EFI V-6				
CS10516	2-dr Tailgate	14,823	3,198	Notes
CS10506	4-dr Tailgate	15,783	3,365	Notes
T10 Blazer 4 x 4 Sport Utility Wagon — 1/2-Ton — 100.5/107 in. w.b. — 4.3-liter EFI V-6				
CT10516	2-dr Tailgate	16,583	3,512	Notes
CT10506	4-dr Tailgate	17,953	3,748	Notes
K1500 Blazer — 1/2-Ton — 111.5 in. w.b. — 5.7-liter Light-duty EFI V-8				
CK10516	Utility Hardtop	20,005	4,608	Notes

A $595 dealer destination charge applied to full-size Blazers effective Feb. 15, 1993.

Model No.	Body Type	Price	Weight	Production
C/K 1500 Suburban — 1/2-Ton — 131.5 in. w.b. — 5.7-liter Light-duty EFI V-8				
CC10906/ZW9	Panel Door (4 x 2)	19,170	4,657	Notes
CK10906/ZW9	Panel Door (4 x 4)	21,370	—	Notes
C1500 Pickup — 1/2-Ton Short Box — 117.5 in. w.b. — 4.3-liter EFI V-6				
CC10703	Regular-Cab Sportside	13,985	3,743	Notes
CC10703	Regular-Cab Fleetside	13,585	3,717	Notes
C1500 Pickup — 1/2-Ton Long Box — 131.5 in. w.b. — 4.3-liter EFI V-6				
CC10903	Regular-Cab Fleetside	13,885	3,860	Notes
CC10903	Regular-Cab WT	11,225	3,740	Notes
C1500 Pickup — 1/2-Ton Short Box — 141.5 in. w.b. — 4.3-liter EFI V-6				
CC10753	Extended-Cab Sportside	15,530	4,128	Notes
CC10753	Extended-Cab Fleetside	15,130	4,032	Notes
C1500 Pickup — 1/2-Ton Long Box — 155.5 in. w.b. — 4.3-liter EFI V-6				
CC10903	Extended-Cab Fleetside	15,390	4,127	Notes

Add approximately $2,250 for CK1500 Pickups with 4 x 4.

Model No.	Body Type	Price	Weight	Production
C2500 Pickup — 3/4-Ton Long Box — 131.5 in. w.b. — 4.3-liter EFI V-6				
CC20924	Chassis & Cab	15,569	4,002	Notes
CC20903	Regular-Cab Fleetside	14,425	4,021	Notes

1993 continued

C2500 Pickup — 3/4-Ton Short Box — 141.5 in. w.b. — 4.3-liter EFI V-6

	Model No.	Body Type	Price	Weight	Production
	CC20954	Chassis-Extended-Cab	17,244	—	Notes
	CC20953	Extended-Cab Fleetside	16,240	4,160	Notes

C2500 Pickup — 3/4-Ton Long Box — 155.5 in. w.b. — 4.3-liter EFI V-6

	Model No.	Body Type	Price	Weight	Production
	CC20903	Extended-Cab Fleetside	16,520	4,261	Notes

Add approximately $1,875 for CK2500 Pickups with 4 x 4.

C3500 Pickup — 1-Ton Long Box — 131.5 in. w.b. — 5.7-liter EFI V-8

	Model No.	Body Type	Price	Weight	Production
	CC30924	Chassis & Cab	15,704	4,263	Notes
	CC30903	Regular-Cab Fleetside	16,164	4,638	Notes

C3500 Pickup — 1-Ton Long Box — 155.5 in. w.b. — 5.7-liter V-8

	Model No.	Body Type	Price	Weight	Production
	CC30903	Extended-Cab Fleetside	17,824	4,874	Notes

C3500 Pickup — 1-Ton Long Box — 168.5 in. w.b. — 5.7-liter V-8

	Model No.	Body Type	Price	Weight	Production
	CC30933	Crew-Cab Fleetside	18,144	5,176	Notes
	CC30933	Crew-Cab Chassis	17,694	4,904	Notes
	CC30934	H-D Crew-Cab Chassis	18,989	5,270	Notes

Add approximately $2,240 for CK3500 Pickups with 4 x 4.

NOTE 1: S-10 model-year production was 180,342.

NOTE 2: Model year production [C/K1500] 376,592, [C/K2500] 66,847, [C/K3500] 37,904, [S-Blazer] 139,555, [K1500 Blazer] 20,205. Figures include trucks built in U.S. and Canada for the U.S. market.

NOTE 3: The percentage of above trucks with four-wheel-drive was: [S10 Pickup] 13.6 percent, [C/K1500] 33.6 percent, [C/K2500] 57.5 percent, [C/K3500] 8.1 percent, [S-Blazer] 76.5 percent, [K1500 Blazer] 100 percent.

1994

	Model No.	Body Type	Price	Weight	Production

S10 Fleetside Pickup — 1/2-Ton — 108.3/117.9/122.9 in. w.b. — 2.2-liter MFI L4

	Model No.	Body Type	Price	Weight	Production
	S10603	Reg. Cab Short Box	9,655	2,905	Notes
	S10803	Reg. Cab Long Box	9,955	3,000	Notes
	S10603	Reg. Cab LS Short Box	10,790	—	Notes
	S10803	Reg. Cab LS Long Box	11,366	—	Notes
	S10653	Ext. Cab LS Short Box	11,790	3,157	Notes

T10 4 x 4 Fleetside Pickup — 1/2-Ton — 108.3/122.9 in. w.b. — 4.3-liter EFI V-6

	Model No.	Body Type	Price	Weight	Production
	T10603	Reg. Cab SWB	14,155	—	Notes
	T10803	Reg. Cab LWB	14,455	—	Notes
	T10603	Reg. Cab LS SWB	15,290	—	Notes
	T10803	Reg. Cab LS LWB	15,866	—	Notes
	T10653	Ext. Cab LS Short Box	16,310	—	Notes

A $470 dealer destination charge applied to S-Series Pickups effective Feb. 1, 1994.

S10 Blazer 4 x 2 Sport Utility Wagon — 1/2-Ton — 100.5/107 in. w.b. — 4.3-liter EFI V-6

	Model No.	Body Type	Price	Weight	Production
	CS10516	2-dr Tailgate	15,641	3,205	Notes
	CS10506	4-dr Tailgate	16,931	3,446	Notes

T10 Blazer 4 x 4 Sport Utility Wagon — 1/2-Ton — 100.5/107 in. w.b. — 4.3-liter CPI V-6

CT10516	2-dr Tailgate	17,437	3,506	Notes
CT10506	4-dr Tailgate	19,165	3,811	Notes

K1500 Blazer 4 x 4 — 1/2-Ton — 111.5 in. w.b. — 5.7-liter EFI V-8

CK10516	Utility Hardtop	21,330	4,757	Notes

C1500 Pickup — 1/2-Ton Short Box — 117.5 in. w.b. — 4.3-liter EFI V-6

CC10703	Regular-Cab Sportside	14,690	3,748	Notes
CC10703	Regular-Cab Fleetside	14,027	3,725	Notes

C1500 Pickup — 1/2-Ton Long Box — 131.5 in. w.b. — 4.3-liter EFI V-6

CC10903	Regular-Cab Fleetside	14,307	3,865	Notes

C1500 Pickup — 1/2-Ton Short Box — 141.5 in. w.b. — 4.3-liter EFI V-6

CC10753	Extended-Cab Sportside	16,266	4,133	Notes
CC10753	Extended-Cab Fleetside	15,854	4,110	Notes

C1500 Pickup — 1/2-Ton Long Box — 155.5 in. w.b. — 4.3-liter EFI V-6

CC10903	Extended-Cab Fleetside	16,697	4,247	Notes

Add approximately $2,350 for CK1500 Pickups with 4 x 4.

C2500 Pickup — 3/4-Ton Long Box — 131.5 in. w.b. — 4.3-liter EFI V-6

CC20924	Chassis & Cab	16,233	4,007	Notes
CC20903	Regular-Cab Fleetside	15,114	4,006	Notes

C2500 Pickup — 3/4-Ton Short Box — 141.5 in. w.b. — 4.3-liter EFI V-6

CC20953	Extended-Cab Fleetside	17,642	4,270	Notes

C2500 Pickup — 3/4-Ton Long Box — 155.5 in. w.b. — 4.3-liter EFI V-6

CC10903	Extended-Cab Fleetside	18,529	4,337	Notes

Add approximately $2,025 for CK2500 Pickups with 4 x 4.

C3500 Pickup — 1-Ton Long Box — 131.5 in. w.b. — 5.7-liter EFI V-8

CC30924	Chassis & Cab	17,029	4,273	Notes
CC30903	Regular-Cab Fleetside	16,847	4,649	Notes

C3500 Pickup — 1-Ton Long Box — 155.5 in. w.b. — 5.7-liter V-8

CC30903	Extended-Cab Fleetside	20,092	5,325	Notes

C3500 Crew-Cab Pickup — 1-Ton Long Box — 168.5 in. w.b. — 5.7-liter V-8

CC30933	Fleetside	19,356	5,290	Notes
CC30933	Chassis	18,579	4,915	Notes
CC30934	H-D Cab & Chassis	20,025	5,281	Notes

Add approximately $3,300 for CK3500 Pickups with 4 x 4.

NOTE 1: *S-10 model-year production was 226,100.*
NOTE 2: *Model year production [C/K1500] 479,056, [C/K2500] 97,760, [C/K3500] 57,594, [S-Blazer] 155,511, [K1500 Blazer] 28,391. Figures include trucks built in U.S. and Canada for the U.S. market.*
NOTE 3: *The percentage of above trucks with four-wheel-drive was: [S10 Pickup] 6.2 percent, [C/K1500] 39.2 percent, [C/K2500] 58.2 percent, [C/K3500] 7.8 percent, [S-Blazer] 80.1 percent, [K1500 Blazer] 100 percent.*

1995

	Model No.	Body Type	Price	Weight	Production

S10 Fleetside Pickup — 1/2-Ton — 108.3/117.9/122.9 in. w.b. — 2.2-liter MFI L4

	Model No.	Body Type	Price	Weight	Production
	S10603	Reg.-Cab Short Box	9,823	2,905	Notes
	S10803	Reg.-Cab Long Box	10,116	3,000	Notes
	S10603	Reg.-Cab LS Short Box	11,410	—	Notes
	S10803	Reg.-Cab LS Long Box	11,705	—	Notes
	S10653	Ext.-Cab LS Short Box	12,510	3,157	Notes

T10 4 x 4 Fleetside Pickup — 1/2-Ton — 108.3/122.9 in. w.b. — 4.3-liter EFI V-6

	Model No.	Body Type	Price	Weight	Production
	T10603	Reg.-Cab SWB	14,765	—	Notes
	T10803	Reg.-Cab LWB	15,340	—	Notes
	T10603	Reg.-Cab LS SWB	15,770	—	Notes
	T10803	Reg.-Cab LS LWB	16,335	—	Notes
	T10653	Ext.-Cab LS Short Box	16,870	—	Notes

Blazer 4 x 2 Sport Utility Wagon — 1/2-Ton — 100.5/107 in. w.b. — 4.3-liter EFI V-6

	Model No.	Body Type	Price	Weight	Production
	CS10516	2-dr Tailgate	16,145	3,205	Notes
	CS10506	4-dr Tailgate	19,851	3,446	Notes

Blazer 4 x 4 Sport Utility Wagon — 1/2-Ton — 100.5/107 in. w.b. — 4.3-liter CPI V-6

	Model No.	Body Type	Price	Weight	Production
	CT10516	2-dr Tailgate	19,905	3,506	Notes
	CT10506	4-dr Tailgate	21,953	3,811	Notes

C1500 Regular-Cab Pickup — 1/2-Ton Short Box — 117.5 in. w.b. — 4.3-liter EFI V-6

	Model No.	Body Type	Price	Weight	Production
	CC10703/E62	Sportside	15,610	3,748	Notes
	CC10703/E63	Fleetside Work Truck	13,387	—	Notes
	CC10703/E63	Fleetside	14,797	3,725	Notes

C1500 Pickup — 1/2-Ton Long Box — 131.5 in. w.b. — 4.3-liter EFI V-6

	Model No.	Body Type	Price	Weight	Production
	CC10903	Regular-cab Fleetside	15,077	3,865	Notes

C1500 Extended-Cab Pickup — 1/2-Ton Short Box — 141.5 in. w.b. — 4.3-liter EFI V-6

	Model No.	Body Type	Price	Weight	Production
	CC10753	Sportside	17,269	4,133	Notes
	CC10753	Fleetside	16,757	4,110	Notes

C1500 Extended-Cab Pickup — 1/2-Ton Long Box — 155.5 in. w.b. — 4.3-liter EFI V-6

	Model No.	Body Type	Price	Weight	Production
	CC10903	Fleetside	17,700	4,247	Notes

Add approximately $2,350 for CK1500 Pickups with 4 x 4.

C2500 Pickup — 3/4-Ton Long Box — 131.5 in. w.b. — 4.3-liter EFI V-6

	Model No.	Body Type	Price	Weight	Production
	CC20924	Chassis & Cab	—	4,007	Notes
	CC20903	Regular-cab Fleetside	15,759	4,006	Notes

C2500 Extended-Cab Pickup — 3/4-Ton Short Box — 141.5 in. w.b. — 4.3-liter EFI V-6

	Model No.	Body Type	Price	Weight	Production
	CC20953	Fleetside	18,770	4,270	Notes

C2500 Extended-Cab Pickup — 3/4-Ton Long Box — 155.5 in. w.b. — 4.3-liter EFI V-6

	Model No.	Body Type	Price	Weight	Production
	CC10903	Fleetside	18,827	4,337	Notes

Add approximately $2,025 for CK2500 Pickups with 4 x 4.

C3500 Pickup — 1-Ton Long Box — 131.5 in. w.b. — 5.7-liter EFI V-8

	Model No.	Body Type	Price	Weight	Production
	CC30924	Chassis & Cab	—	4,273	Notes
	CC30903	Regular-cab Fleetside	17,458	4,649	Notes

C3500 Extended-Cab Pickup — 1-Ton Long Box — 155.5 in. w.b. — 5.7-liter V-8

	Model No.	Body Type	Price	Weight	Production
	CC30903	Fleetside	20,784	5,325	Notes

C3500 Crew-Cab Pickup — 1-Ton Long Box — 168.5 in. w.b. — 5.7-liter V-8

	Model No.	Body Type	Price	Weight	Production
	CC30933	Fleetside	20,044	5,290	Notes
	CC30933	Cab & chassis	—	4,915	Notes
	CC30934	H-D Cab & chassis	—	5,281	Notes

Add approximately $2,000 for CK2500 Pickups with 4 x 4.

NOTE 1: S-10 model-year production was 245,374.
NOTE 2: Model year production [C/K1500] 407,968, [C/K2500] 93,700, [C/K3500] 49,640, [S-Blazer] 220,833. Figures include trucks built in U.S. and Canada for the U.S. market.
NOTE 3: The percentage of above trucks with four-wheel-drive was: [S10 Pickup] 13.1 percent, [C/K1500] 30.4 percent, [C/K2500] 50.0 percent, [C/K3500] 29.8 percent, [Blazer] 80.9 percent.

1996

	Model No.	Body Type	Price	Weight	Production

S14 Compact Regular Cab Pickup – ½-Ton – 108.3/117.9/122.9 in. wb.—2.2-liter V-6

	Model No.	Body Type	Price	Weight	Production
	S14	Fleetside Short Box	11,070	2,822	Notes
	S14	Sportside Short Box	13,170	3,070	Notes
	S14	Fleetside Long Box	11,380	2,874	Notes

S17 Compact Extended Cab Pickup – ½-Ton – 108.3/117.9/122.9 in. wb.—2.2-liter V-6

	Model No.	Body Type	Price	Weight	Production
	S19	Fleetside	13,585	3,081	Notes
	S19	Sportside	14,870	3,246	Notes

Add approximately $2,700 for T10 four-wheel-drive models.
Add approximately $200 for third door.

S-Blazer Compact SUV (4 x 2) – ½-Ton – 100.5/107 in. wb.— 4.3-liter V-6

	Model No.	Body Type	Price	Weight	Production
	S18	2d Utility	19,444	3,500	Notes
	S13	4d Utility	21,150	3,654	Notes

S-Blazer Compact SUV (4 x 4) – ½-Ton – 100.5/107 in. wb.— 4.3-liter V-6

	Model No.	Body Type	Price	Weight	Production
	T18	2d Utility	19,444	3,500	Notes
	T13	4d Utility	21,150	3,654	Notes

C1500 Regular Cab Work Truck Pickup – 1/2-Ton Short Box– 117.5 in. wb.— 4.3-liter V-6

	Model No.	Body Type	Price	Weight	Production
	C14	Fleetside	14,016	3,851	Notes

C1500 Regular Cab Work Truck Pickup – 1/2-Ton Long Box– 131.5 in. wb.— 4.3-liter V-6

	Model No.	Body Type	Price	Weight	Production
	C14	Sportside	14,416	3,990	Notes

C1500 Regular Cab Pickup – 1/2-Ton Short Box– 117.5 in. wb.— 5.7-liter V-8

	Model No.	Body Type	Price	Weight	Production
	C14	Fleetside	15,426	3,851	Notes
	C14	Sportside	16,239	3,840	Notes

C1500 Regular Cab Pickup – 1/2-Ton Long Box– 131.5 in. wb.— 5.7-liter V-8

	Model No.	Body Type	Price	Weight	Production
	C14	Fleetside	15,706	3,990	Notes

C1500 Extended Cab Pickup – 1/2-Ton Short Box– 141.5 in. wb.— 5.7-liter V-8

	Model No.	Body Type	Price	Weight	Production
	C19	Fleetside	17,486	4,121	Notes
	C19	Sportside	17,998	4,121	Notes

C1500 Extended Cab Pickup – 1/2-Ton Long Box– 155.5 in. wb.— 5.7-liter V-8

	Model No.	Body Type	Price	Weight	Production
	C19	Fleetside	18,429	4,351	Notes

1996 continued

C2500 Regular Cab Pickup – 3/4-Ton – 131.5 in. wb.— 5.7-liter V-8

	Model No.	Body Type	Price	Weight	Production
	C24	Chassis & Cab	18,429	4,351	Notes

C2500 Regular Cab Pickup – 3/4-Ton Long Box – 131.5 in. wb.— 5.7-liter V-8

	C24	Fleetside	18,429	4,351	Notes

C2500 Heavy-Duty Pickup – 3/4-Ton Long Box – 131.5 in. wb.— 5.7-liter V-8

	C24	Fleetside	17,926	4,269	Notes

C2500 Extended Cab Pickup – 3/4-Ton Short Box – 141.5 in. wb.— 5.7-liter V-8

	C29	Fleetside	19,499	4,400	Notes

C2500 Extended Cab Pickup – 3/4-Ton Long Box – 155.5 in. wb.— 5.7-liter V-8

	C29	Fleetside	19,556	4,961	Notes

C3500 Regular Cab Pickup – 1-Ton – 141.5 in. wb.— 5.7-liter V-8

	C34	Chassis & Cab	17,640	4,806	Notes

C3500 Regular Cab Pickup – 1-Ton Long Box – 131.5 in. wb.— 5.7-liter V-8

	C34	Fleetside	18,087	4,798	Notes

C3500 Heavy-Duty Pickup – 1-Ton Long Box – 131.5 in. wb.— 5.7-liter V-8

	C34	Fleetside	22,278	5,095	Notes

C3500 Extended Cab Pickup – 1-Ton Long Box – 155.5 in. wb.— 5.7-liter V-8

	C39	Fleetside	21,513	5,074	Notes

C3500 Crew Cab Pickup – 1-Ton – 168.5 in. wb.— 5.7-liter V-8

	C33	Chassis & Crew Cab	20,278	5,095	Notes

C3500 Crew Cab Pickup – 1-Ton Long Box – 168.5 in. wb.— 5.7-liter V-8

	C33	Fleetside	21,221	5,475	Notes

Add approximately $250 for third door.
Add approximately $2,350 for K1500/K2500/K3500 with four-wheel drive.
NOTE 1: *S-10 model-year production was 207,631.*
NOTE 2: *Model year production [C/K1500] 338,604, [C/K2500] 56,178, [C/K3500] 44,199, [S-Blazer] 254,590. Figures include trucks built in U.S. and Canada for the U.S. market.*
NOTE 3: *The percentage of above trucks with four-wheel-drive was: [S10 Pickup] 12.7 percent, [C/K1500] 42.9 percent, [C/K2500] 42.7 percent, [C/K3500] 31.1 percent, [Blazer] 80.0 percent.*

1997

	Model No.	Body Type	Price	Weight	Production

S14 Compact Regular Cab Pickup – ½-Ton – 108.3/117.9/122.9 in. wb.—2.2-liter V-6

	Model No.	Body Type	Price	Weight	Production
	S14	Fleetside Short Box	11,553	3,062	Notes
	S14	Sportside Short Box	12,903	3,062	Notes
	S14	Fleetside Long Box	11,853	3,098	Notes

S17 Compact Extended Cab Pickup – ½-Ton – 108.3/117.9/122.9 in. wb.—2.2-liter V-6

	S19	Fleetside	14,353	3,246	Notes
	S19	Sportside	14,803	3,246	Notes

Add approximately $2,850 for T10 four-wheel-drive models.
Add approximately $250 for third door.

S-Blazer Compact SUV (4 x 2) – ½-Ton – 100.5/107 in. wb.— 4.3-liter V-6

	S18	2d Utility	20,516	3,515	Notes
	S13	4d Utility	22,041	3,686	Notes

S-Blazer Compact SUV (4 x 4) – ½-Ton – 100.5/107 in. wb.— 4.3-liter V-6

	T18	2d Utility	22,116	3,880	Notes
	T13	4d Utility	24,116	4,046	Notes

C1500 Regular Cab Work Truck Pickup – 1/2-Ton Short Box– 117.5 in. wb.— 4.3-liter V-6

	C14	Fleetside	14,532	3,869	Notes

C1500 Regular Cab Work Truck Pickup – 1/2-Ton Long Box– 131.5 in. wb.— 4.3-liter V-6

	C14	Fleetside	14,852	4,021	Notes

C1500 Regular Cab Pickup – 1/2-Ton Short Box– 117.5 in. wb.— 5.7-liter V-8

	C14	Fleetside	15,942	3,869	Notes
	C14	Sportside	16,517	3,879	Notes

C1500 Regular Cab Pickup – 1/2-Ton Long Box – 131.5 in. wb.— 5.7-liter V-8

	C14	Fleetside	15,942	4,021	Notes

C1500 Extended Cab Pickup – 1/2-Ton Short Box– 141.5 in. wb.— 5.7-liter V-8

	C19	Fleetside	18,022	4,160	Notes
	C19	Sportside	16,597	4,170	Notes

C1500 Extended Cab Pickup – 1/2-Ton Long Box– 155.5 in. wb.— 5.7-liter V-8

	C19	Fleetside	19,017	4,407	Notes

C2500 Regular Cab Pickup – 3/4-Ton – 131.5 in. wb.— 5.7-liter V-8

	C24	Chassis & Cab	17,816	4,351	Notes

C2500 Regular Cab Pickup – 3/4-Ton Long Box – 131.5 in. wb.— 5.7-liter V-8

	C24	Fleetside	17,419	4,294	Notes

C2500 Heavy-Duty Regular Cab Pickup – 3/4-Ton Long Box – 131.5 in. wb.— 5.7-liter V-8

	C24	Fleetside	18,267	4,699	Notes

C2500 Extended Cab Pickup – 3/4-Ton Short Box – 141.5 in. wb.— 5.7-liter V-8

	C29	Fleetside	20,035	4,445	Notes

C2500 Heavy-Duty Extended Cab Pickup – 3/4-Ton Long Box – 155.5 in. wb.— 5.7-liter V-8

	C29	Fleetside	19,872	5,442	Notes

C3500 Regular Cab Pickup – 1-Ton – 141.5 in. wb.— 5.7-liter V-8

	C34	Chassis & Cab	17,955	4,806	Notes

C3500 Regular Cab Pickup – 1-Ton Long Box – 131.5 in. wb.— 5.7-liter V-8

	C34	Fleetside	18,406	4,845	Notes

C3500 Heavy-Duty Pickup – 1-Ton Long Box – 131.5 in. wb.— 5.7-liter V-8

	C34	Chassis & Cab	22,391	5,095	Notes

C3500 Extended Cab Pickup – 1-Ton Long Box – 155.5 in. wb.— 5.7-liter V-8

	C39	Fleetside	21,829	5,395	Notes

C3500 Crew Cab Pickup – 1-Ton – 168.5 in. wb.— 5.7-liter V-8

	C33	Chassis & Crew Cab	20,593	5,095	Notes

C3500 Crew Cab Pickup – 1-Ton Long Box – 168.5 in. wb.— 5.7-liter V-8

	C33	Fleetside	21,536	5,504	Notes

Add approximately $300 for third door.
Add approximately $2,500 for K1500/K2500/K3500 with four-wheel drive.
NOTE 1: S-10 model-year production was 180,261.
NOTE 2: Model year production [C/K1500] 340,000, [C/K2500] 108,400, [C/K3500] 68,710, [Blazer] 211,707. Figures include trucks built in U.S. and Canada for the U.S. market.
NOTE 3: The percentage of above trucks with four-wheel-drive was: [S10 Pickup] 10.4 percent, [C/K1500] 43.7 percent, [C/K2500] 42.0 percent, [C/K3500] 31.8 percent, [Blazer] 84.0 percent.

1998

	Model No.	Body Type	Price	Weight	Production
S14 Compact Regular Cab Pickup – ½-Ton – 108.3/117.9/122.9 in. wb.—2.2-liter V-6					
	S14	Fleetside Short Box	11,998	3,003	Notes
	S14	Sportside Short Box	13,665	3,003	Notes
	S14	Fleetside Long Box	12,662	3,040	Notes
S17 Compact Extended Cab Pickup – ½-Ton – 108.3/117.9/122.9 in. wb.—2.2-liter V-6					
	S19	Fleetside	15,230	3,222	Notes
	S19	Sportside	15,705	3,222	Notes

Add approximately $2,850 for T10 four-wheel-drive models.
Add approximately $250 for third door.

	Model No.	Body Type	Price	Weight	Production
S-Blazer Compact SUV (4 x 2) – ½-Ton – 100.5/107 in. wb.— 4.3-liter V-6					
	S18	2d Utility	21,663	3,515	Notes
	S13	4d Utility	23,188	3,685	Notes
S-Blazer Compact SUV (4 x 4) – ½-Ton – 100.5/107 in. wb.— 4.3-liter V-6					
	T18	2d Utility	23,651	3,874	Notes
	T13	4d Utility	25,176	4,046	Notes
C1500 Regular Cab Work Truck Pickup – 1/2-Ton Short Box– 117.5 in. wb.— 4.3-liter V-6					
	C14	Fleetside	14,930	3,876	Notes
C1500 Regular Cab Work Truck Pickup – 1/2-Ton Long Box– 131.5 in. wb.— 4.3-liter V-6					
	C14	Fleetside	15,250	4,024	Notes
C1500 Regular Cab Pickup – 1/2-Ton Short Box– 117.5 in. wb.— 5.7-liter V-8					
	C14	Fleetside	16,355	3,876	Notes
	C14	Sportside	16,930	3,876	Notes
C1500 Regular Cab Pickup – 1/2-Ton Long Box– 131.5 in. wb.— 5.7-liter V-8					
	C14	Fleetside	16,655	4,024	Notes
C1500 Extended Cab Pickup – 1/2-Ton Short Box– 141.5 in. wb.— 5.7-liter V-8					
	C19	Fleetside	18,355	4,145	Notes
	C19	Sportside	23,099	4,145	Notes
C1500 Extended Cab Pickup – 1/2-Ton Long Box– 155.5 in. wb.— 5.7-liter V-8					
	C19	Fleetside	19,150	4,406	Notes
C2500 Regular Cab Pickup – 3/4-Ton Long Box – 131.5 in. wb.— 5.7-liter V-8					
	C24	Fleetside	17,832	4,292	Notes
C2500 Heavy-Duty Regular Cab Pickup – 3/4-Ton Long Box – 131.5 in. wb.— 5.7-liter V-8					
	C24	Fleetside	18,880	5,107	Notes
C2500 Extended Cab Pickup – 3/4-Ton Short Box – 141.5 in. wb.— 5.7-liter V-8					
	C29	Fleetside	20,448	4,432	Notes
C2500 Heavy-Duty Extended Cab Pickup – 3/4-Ton Long Box – 155.5 in. wb.— 5.7-liter V-8					
	C29	Fleetside	20,484	5,107	Notes
C3500 Regular Cab Pickup – 1-Ton Long Box – 131.5 in. wb.— 5.7-liter V-8					
	C34	Fleetside	19,019	4,681	Notes
C3500 Extended Cab Pickup – 1-Ton Long Box – 155.5 in. wb.— 5.7-liter V-8					
	C39	Fleetside	22,442	5,458	Notes
C3500 Crew Cab Pickup – 1-Ton Long Box – 168.5 in. wb.— 5.7-liter V-8					
	C33	Fleetside	22,149	5,588	Notes

Add approximately $300 for third door.
Add approximately $2,500 for K1500/K2500/K3500 with four-wheel drive.
NOTE 1: S-10 model-year production was 216,212.
NOTE 2: Model year production [C/K1500] 389,477, [C/K2500] 90,859, [C/K3500] 63,200, [Blazer] 241,972. Figures include trucks built in U.S. and Canada for the U.S. market.
NOTE 3: The percentage of above trucks with four-wheel-drive was: [S10 Pickup] 10.4 percent, [C/K1500] 54.5 percent, [C/K2500] 56.0 percent, [C/K3500] 40.6 percent, [Blazer] 76.2 percent.

INFORMATION DEPARTMENT

100 SOURCES OF RESTORATION HELP

As a collector of 1973-1998 Chevy pickups or other trucks, you'll need parts for your vehicle, special restoration tools and other sources of hobby information. You may also want to join a club.

Listed here are 100 suppliers of parts, services and literature, a number of tool companies, a few clubs open to these pickups and some of the leading hobby magazines, books and Websites.

Most listings show full contact information, including websites. Just think how improved this is from 20 years ago, when I wrote *Chevrolet Pickups 1946-1972*. Back then, you had to write a letter, get a stamp and include an SASE (self-addresses-stamped envelope) when contacting hobby vendors. Today, you can visit the vendor's Website on the Internet from your home computer. Wow!

Although 100 sources are listed here. there are dozens of others you may be dealing with later as your restoration progresses. We selected the companies and people on this list because we have had personal dealings with them and were satisfied with the results. However, there are hundreds of reputable dealers we have not dealt with yet.

It's a good idea to keep your own notebook in which you can add additional names and addresses as time goes by. A handy way to do this is to purchase a business card book, which is a loose-leaf with plastic pages designed to hold the business cards you'll be getting through the mail or at old truck shows. With one of these books, you can organize the cards into different categories and create your own restorer's guide.

Chevrolet Pickups 1973-1998 | 249

BODY PARTS

Auto Body Specialties, Inc.
PO Box 455 Rte 66
Middlefield, CT 06455
(888) 277-1960
www.autobodyspecialt.com

BOOKS

Binder Books
PO Box 230269
Tigard, OR 97281
(503) 684-2024
www.binderbooks.com

Driveline Publishing
(800) 767-5828
www.antiquepowergiftshop.com

Krause Books
700 E. State St.
Iola, WI 54990
(800) 258-0929
www.krausebooks.com

BRAKE PARTS

ABS Power Brake, Inc.
233 N. Lemon St.
Orange, CA 92866
(714) 771-6549
www.abspowerbrake.com

Apple Hydraulics
1610 Middle Road
Calverton, NY 11933
(800) 882-7753
www.applehydraulics.com

Brake & Equipment Warehouse
455 Harrison St. N.E.
Minneapolis, MN 55413
(800) 233-4053
www.brakeplace.com

Power Brake Exchange, Inc.
260 Phelan Ave.
San Jose, CA 95112
(800) 322-1775
www.powerbrakeexchange.com

White Post Restorations
One Old Car Dr.
White Post, VA 22663
(540) 837-1140
www.whitepost.com

BUMPERS

Bumper Boyz
2435 E. 54th St.
Los Angeles, CA 90058
(800) 995-1703
www.bumperboyz.com

CARPETS

ACS/Dorsett
PO Box 129
Dalton, GA 30722-0129
(706) 277-1181
www.acsdorsettcarpet.com

Auto Custom Carpets, Inc.
PO Box 1350
Anniston, AL 36201
(800) 633-2358
www.accmats.com

Quality Auto Interior
PO Box 390478
Chicago, IL 60639-0478
(773) 622-7404
www.qualityautocarpets.com

CHROME PLATING

Custom Plating Specialists
W797 Cty K
Brillion, WI 54110
(920) 756-3284
www.customplatingspecialist.com

Paul's Chrome Plating, Inc.
90 Pattison St.
Evans City, PA 16033
(800) 245-8679
www.paulschrome.com

Qual Krom
4725 Iroquois Ave.
Erie, PA 16511
(800) 673-2427
www.qualkrom.com

CLUBS

American Truck Historical Society
(816) 891-9900
www.aths.org

Antique Truck Club of America
85 South Walnut St.
Boyertown, PA 19512
(610) 367-2567
www.antiquetruckclubofamerica.com

Vintage Chevrolet Club of America
PO Box 5387
Orange, CA 92863-5387
(626) 963-2438
www.vcca.org

ENGINE PARTS

Tim S. Archer
J & C Enterprises
612 Virginia Ave.
Fairmont, WV 26554
(304) 366-4536
(email) tsarcher@aol.com

Crower Camshafts
6180 Business Center Court
San Diego, CA 92154
(619) 861-8477
www.crower.com

Egge Obsolete Engine Parts
11707 Stauson Ave.
Santa Fe Springs, CA 90670-2217
(800) 866-EGGE
www.egge.com

ENGINE REBUILDING

Promar Precision Engines
Paterson, N.J.
(800) 422-6022
www.promarengine.com

EVENTS

ATHS Rocky Mountain Annual Truck Show
Art Robinson Transport Museum
C/o Dan Ackley
3105 West Skyvue Circle
West Jordan, UT 84088
(801) 263-6547

Hawkeye Downs Swap Meet
C/o Cedar Rapids Region AACA
Box 9272
Cedar Rapids, IA 52404
(800) 367-3388

Iola Old Working Wheels Show
PO Box 1
Iola, WI 54945
(715) 445-4000
www.IolaOldCarShow.com

Rough & Tumble Thresherman's Reunion & Truck Show
Box 9
Kinzers, PA 17535
(717) 442-4249
www.roughandtumble.org

Vintage Truck & Craft Show
PO Box 838
Yellow Springs, OH 45387
(800) 767-5828
jamielee@ertelpublishing.com

FASTENERS

Bolt Locker
7509 US Hwy 53 South
Eau Claire, WI 54701
(877) 839-0556
www.boltlocker.com

GENERAL PARTS

Al Suehring Flywheel Ring Gears
Krogwald Road
Iola, WI
(715) 677-3809
al@suehring.com

Kanter Auto Products
Boonton, N.J.
(800) 526-1096
www.kanter.com

Northwestern Auto Supply
1101 S. Division Street
Grand Rapids, MI 49507
(800) 704-1078
www.northwesternautosupply.com

Mr. G's Fasteners
5613 Elliott Reeder Rd
Ft. Worth, TX 76117
(817) 831-3501
www.mrgusa.com

Parts 123.com
1833 Windsor Place
Louisville, KY 40204
(800) 203-9966
www.parts123.com

Restoration Specialties & Supply
PO Box 328
Windber, PA 15963
(814) 467-9842

Rock Auto.com
Madison, WI
(866) ROCKAUTO
www.rockauto.com

Terrill Machine, Inc.
1000 CR 454
De Leon, TX 76444
(254) 893-2610

J.C. Whitney
761 Progress Parkway
LaSalle, IL 61301-0300
(800) 529-4486
www.jcwhitney.com

GLASS

Pilkington North America, Inc.
4458 Alum Creek Dr. Ste C
Columbus, OH 43207
(800) 848-1351
www.pilkington.com

Vintage Glass USA
PO Box 336
326 S. River Road
Tolland, CT 06084
(800) 889-3826

HOOD HINGES

SMS Auto Restoration Services
1320 Route 9
Champlain, NY 12919
(800) 989-6660
www.sms-auto.com

INSURANCE

Condon & Skelly
121 E. Kings Highway Ste 203
Maple Shade, NJ 08052
(800) 257-9496
www.condonskelly.com

Grundy Worldwide
400 Horsham Road
Horsham, PA 19044
(800) 338-4005
www.grundy.com

Hagerty Classic Insurance
141 Rivers Edge Dr. Ste 200
Traverse City, MI 49684
(800) 922-4050
www.hagerty.com

J.C. Taylor
320 S. 69th Street
Upper Darby, PA 19082
(888) 268-4783
www.jctaylor.com

INTERIOR

Dash Specialists
1910 Redbud Lane
Medford, OR 97504
(541) 776-0040

OK Dash Cap
PO Box 1111
Harriman, TN 37748
(865) 898-4200
rewalls@bellsouth.net

RodDoors
(800) 509-7537
www.roddoors.com

LIFTS

Backyard Buddy
140 Dana St.
Warren, OH 44483
(800) 837-9353
www.backyardbuddy.com

Complete Hydraulics Service & Sales, Inc.
130 Commerce Park Dr.
Franklin, IN 46131
www.completehydraulic.com

Direct-Lift
(866) 347-5438
www.directlift.com

LINES

Classic Tube
80 Rotech Drive
Lancaster, NY 14086
(716) 759-1800
www.classictube.com

Inline Tube
15066 Technology Dr.
Shelby Township, MI 48315
(800) 385-9452
www.inlinetube.com

MAGAZINES

Old Cars Weekly
700 E. State St.
Iola, WI 54990
(715) 445-2214
www.oldcarsweekly.com

Vintage Truck
PO Box 838
Yellow Springs, OH 45387
(888) 760-8108
www.vintagetruckmagazine.com

PAINT

Auto Paint Specialists, Inc.
740 Industry Court
Green Bay, WI
(920) 496-0400

BASF Corp.
100 Campos Dr.
Floram Park, NJ 07932
(800) 325-3000
www.BASF.com

Jochem's Auto Parts
1806 Western Ave.
Manitowoc, WI 54220
(800) 433-0496
www.autotouchuppaint.com

POR-15
PO Box 1235
Morristown, NJ 07962-1235
(800) 725-0177
www.POR15.com

Tower Paint & Design
922 Oregon
Oshkosh, WI 54903
(800) 779-6520
www.towerpaint.com

POWDER COATING

Spence Industries, Inc.
1505 Cornell Rd.
Green Bay, WI 54313
(920) 662-0720
www.spenceindustries98@sbcglobal.net

POWER STEERING

Midwest Remanufacturing
5836 W. 66th St.
Bedford Park, IL 60638
(800) 634-5829
www.pwrsteering.com

PRICE GUIDES

Old Cars Price Guide
700 E. State St.
Iola, WI 54990
(715) 445-2214
www.oldcarsweekly.com

RADIATOR

Cool Craft Components
(602) 269-3271
www.coolcraft.com

Glen-ray Radiators
2105 North Sixth St.
Wausau, WI 54403
(800) 537-3775

RESTORATION ROTISSERIES

Accessible Systems
104 Minga Dr.
Johnson City, TN 37604
(877) 283-9755
www.accessiblesysytems.com

Auto Twirler
688 Tower Rd. Ste 112
Plainfield, IN 46168
(317) 839-6210
www.autotwirler.com

ROLLER HOOP

DSK Auto Products LLC
712 W. Cornhusker Hwy
Lincoln, NE 68521
(402) 475-9968
www.rollerhoop.com

Whirly Jig
(731) 642-0660
www.whirlyjig.com

RUBBER

Steele Rubber Products
(888) 409-4647
www.steelerubber.com

SEAT BELTS

Ssnake-Oyl
114 North Glenwood Ste 400
Tyler, TX 75702
(800) 284-7777
www.ssnake-oyl.com

SHOP MANUALS

Helm, Inc.
14310 Hamilton Ave.
Highland Park, MI 48203
(800) 782-4356
www.helminc.com

SPEEDOMETERS

Bob's Speedometer
10123 Bergin Rd.
Howell, MI 48843
(800) 592-9673
www.bobsspeedometer.com

STAINLESS STEEL RESTORATION

Vintage Vehicles Co.
N1940 20th Dr.
Wautoma. WI 54982
(920) 787-2656
www.vintagevehicles.com

SUSPENSION PARTS

Rare Parts, Inc.
(800) 315-8539
www.rareparts.com

TIRES

Coker Tire Company
1317 Chestnut St.
Chattanooga, TN 37402
(800) 251-6336
www.coker.com

Kelsey Tire, Inc.
Box 564
Camdenton, MO 65020
(800) 845-7581
www.kelseytire.com

Lucas Automotive
2850 Temple Ave.
Long Beach, CA 90806
(800) 952-4333
www.lucasclassictires.com

Universal Tire Company
Hershey, PA
(800) 233-3827
www.universaltire.com

Wallace W. Wade
530 Regal Row
Dallas, TX 75247
(800) 666-TYRE
www.wallacewade.com

TOOLS

The Eastwood Company
263 Shoemaker Road
Pottstown, PA 19464
(610) 323-2200
www.eastwood.com

TP Tools & Equipment
7075 Rt 446
Canfield, OH 44406
(800) 321-9260
www.tptools.com

TOY TRUCKS & MODELS

Mini Metals
3401 Silica Road
Sylvania, OH 43560
www.classicmetalworks.com

TRANSMISSION

Fatsco Transmission Parts
PO Box 635
337 Change Bridge Rd.
Pinebrook, NJ 07058
(800) 524-0485
www.fatsco.com

Northwest Transmission Parts
(800) 327-1955
www.nwtparts.com

TRUCK PARTS

Brother's
801 E. Parkridge Ave.
Corona, CA 92879
(800) 977-2767
www.brotherstruck.com

Bruce Horkey's Wood & Parts
46284 440th St.
Windom, MN 56101
(507) 831-5625
www.horkeyswoodandparts.com

Cheyenne Pickup Parts
Box 959
Noble, OK 73068
(405) 872-3399
www.chetennepickup.com

Classic Chevrolet Parts, Inc.
8723 South I-35
Oklahoma City, OK 73149
(800) 354-4040
www.classicchevroletparts.com

Classic Parts
(800) 741-1678
www.classicparts.com

Clester's Auto Reproductions
PO Box 1113
Salisbury, NC 28144
(800) 457-8223
www.clestersauto.com

The Filling Station
990 So. Second St.
Lebanon, OR 97355-3227
(800) 841-6622

Golden State Parts
3493 Arrowhead Drive
Carson City, NV 89706
(888) 536-6668
www.golden-state-parts.com

H & H Classic Parts for Chevys
12325 West Highway 72
Bentonville, AR
(479) 787-5575
www.hhclassics.com

LMC Truck
PO Box 14991
Lenexa, KS 66285-4991
(800) LMC-TRUCK
www.LMCTRUCK.com

Vintage Chevy Trucks
(510) 651-5874
www.vintagechevytrucks.com

Year One
PO Box 521
Braselton, GA 30517
(800) YEAR-ONE
www.yearone.com

WEATHER-STRIPPING

SoffSeal, Inc.
104 May Dr.
Harrison, OH 45030
(800) 426-0902
www.soffseal.com

WINDSHIELD WIPERS

Midwest Remanufacturing
5836 W. 66th St.
Bedford Park, IL 60638
(800) 634-5829
www.walshwiper.com

CHEVROLET TRUCKS PRICES

VEHICLE CONDITION SCALE

1. *Excellent:*	Restored to current maximum professional standards of quality in every area, or perfect original with components operating and appearing as new. A 95-plus point show car that is not driven.
2. *Fine:*	Well-restored or a combination of superior restoration and excellent original parts. Also, an extremely well-maintained original vehicle showing minimal wear.
3. *Very Good:*	Completely operable original or older restoration. Also, a good amateur restoration, all presentable and serviceable inside and out. Plus, a combination of well-done restoration and good operable components or a partially restored car with all parts necessary to complete and/or valuable NOS parts.
4. *Good:*	A driveable vehicle needing no or only minor work to be functional. Also, a deteriorated restoration or a very poor amateur restoration. All components may need restoration to be "excellent," but the car is mostly useable "as is."
5. *Restorable:*	Needs complete restoration of body, chassis and interior. May or may not be running, but isn't weathered, wrecked or stripped to the point of being useful only for parts.
6. *Parts car:*	May or may not be running, but is weathered, wrecked and/or stripped to the point of being useful primarily for parts.

Note: Prices taken from *Old Cars Price Guide* and include some models and years not covered in this book.

	6	5	4	3	2	1
1973-77 El Camino, V-8						
PU	600	1,800	3,000	6,750	10,500	15,000
Cus PU	620	1,860	3,100	6,980	10,850	15,500
NOTE: Add 25 percent for 454 engine option.						
1973-80 Vega						
Panel	360	1,080	1,800	4,050	6,300	9,000
1973-80 LUV						
PU	312	936	1,560	3,510	5,460	7,800
1973-80 Blazer K10, V-8						
Blazer 2WD	620	1,860	3,100	6,980	10,850	15,500
Blazer (4x4)	700	2,100	3,500	7,880	12,250	17,500
1973-80 C10, 1/2-Ton, V-8						
Stepside (SBx)	660	1,980	3,300	7,430	11,550	16,500
Stepside (LBx)	620	1,860	3,100	6,980	10,850	15,500
Fleetside (SBx)	620	1,860	3,100	6,980	10,850	15,500
Fleetside (LBx)	600	1,800	3,000	6,750	10,500	15,000
Suburban	620	1,860	3,100	6,980	10,850	15,500
1973-80 K10, 4x4, 1/2-Ton, V-8						
Stepside (SBx)	680	2,040	3,400	7,650	11,900	17,000
Stepside (LBx)	660	1,980	3,300	7,430	11,550	16,500
Fleetside (SBx)	640	1,920	3,200	7,200	11,200	16,000
Fleetside (LBx)	620	1,860	3,100	6,980	10,850	15,500
Suburban	640	1,920	3,200	7,200	11,200	16,000
1973-80 C20, 3/4-Ton						
Stepside (LBx)	360	1,080	1,800	4,050	6,300	9,000
Fleetside (LBx)	368	1,104	1,840	4,140	6,440	9,200
6P (LBx)	352	1,056	1,760	3,960	6,160	8,800
Suburban	460	1,380	2,300	5,180	8,050	11,500
1973-80 K20, 4x4, 3/4-Ton, V-8						
Stepside (LBx)	420	1,260	2,100	4,730	7,350	10,500
Fleetside (LBx)	420	1,260	2,100	4,730	7,350	10,500
6P (LBx)	376	1,128	1,880	4,230	6,580	9,400
Suburban	480	1,440	2,400	5,400	8,400	12,000
NOTE: Deduct 20 percent for 6-cyl.						
1978-80 El Camino, V-8						
PU	520	1,560	2,600	5,850	9,100	13,000
Cus PU	540	1,620	2,700	6,080	9,450	13,500
NOTE: Deduct 20 percent for V-6.						
1981-82 Luv, 1/2-Ton, 104.3" or 117.9" wb						
PU (SBx)	264	792	1,320	2,970	4,620	6,600
PU (LBx)	268	804	1,340	3,020	4,690	6,700
1981-82 El Camino, 1/2-Ton, V-8, 117" wb						
PU	460	1,380	2,300	5,180	8,050	11,500
SS PU	560	1,680	2,800	6,300	9,800	14,000
1981-82 Blazer K10, 1/2-Ton, V-8, 106.5" wb						
Blazer (4x4), V-8	620	1,860	3,100	6,980	10,850	15,500
1981-82 C10, 1/2-Ton, V-8, 117" or 131" wb						
Stepside PU (SBx)	452	1,356	2,260	5,090	7,910	11,300
Stepside PU (LBx)	448	1,344	2,240	5,040	7,840	11,200
Fleetside PU (SBx)	480	1,440	2,400	5,400	8,400	12,000
Fleetside PU (LBx)	580	1,740	2,900	6,530	10,150	14,500
Suburban	480	1,440	2,400	5,400	8,400	12,000
1981-82 C20, 3/4-Ton, V-8, 131" or 164" wb						
Stepside PU (LBx)	448	1,344	2,240	5,040	7,840	11,200
Fleetside PU (LBx)	452	1,356	2,260	5,090	7,910	11,300
Fleetside PU Bonus Cab (LBx)	460	1,380	2,300	5,180	8,050	11,500

	6	5	4	3	2	1
Fleetside PU Crew Cab (LBx)	456	1,368	2,280	5,130	7,980	11,400
Suburban	468	1,404	2,340	5,270	8,190	11,700

NOTE: Add 15 percent for 4x4. Deduct 20 percent for 6-cyl.

1983-87 El Camino, 1/2-Ton, 117" wb

	6	5	4	3	2	1
PU	420	1,260	2,100	4,730	7,350	10,500
SS PU	520	1,560	2,600	5,850	9,100	13,000

NOTE: Deduct 20 percent for V-6. Add 30 percent for ChooChoo model where available.

1983-87 S10, 1/2-Ton, 100.5" wb

	6	5	4	3	2	1
Blazer 2WD	320	960	1,600	3,600	5,600	8,000
Blazer (4x4)	340	1,020	1,700	3,830	5,950	8,500

1983-87 Blazer K10, 1/2-Ton, 106.5" wb

	6	5	4	3	2	1
Blazer (4x4)	480	1,440	2,400	5,400	8,400	12,000

1983-87 S10, 1/2-Ton, 108" or 122" wb

	6	5	4	3	2	1
Fleetside PU (SBx)	288	864	1,440	3,240	5,040	7,200
Fleetside PU (LBx)	292	876	1,460	3,290	5,110	7,300
Fleetside PU Ext Cab	300	900	1,500	3,380	5,250	7,500

1983-87 C10, 1/2-Ton, 117" or 131" wb

	6	5	4	3	2	1
Stepside PU (SBx)	372	1,116	1,860	4,190	6,510	9,300
Fleetside PU (SBx)	376	1,128	1,880	4,230	6,580	9,400
Fleetside PU (LBx)	364	1,092	1,820	4,100	6,370	9,100
Suburban	432	1,296	2,160	4,860	7,560	10,800

1983-87 C20, 3/4-Ton, 131" or 164" wb

	6	5	4	3	2	1
Stepside PU (LBx)	368	1,104	1,840	4,140	6,440	9,200
Fleetside PU (LBx)	372	1,116	1,860	4,190	6,510	9,300
Fleetside PU Bonus Cab (LBx)	424	1,272	2,120	4,770	7,420	10,600
Fleetside PU Crew Cab (LBx)	364	1,092	1,820	4,100	6,370	9,100
Suburban	432	1,296	2,160	4,860	7,560	10,800

NOTE: Add 15 percent for 4x4. Deduct 20 percent for 6-cyl. on full-size vehicles.

1988-91 Blazer, 106.5" wb

	6	5	4	3	2	1
V10 (4x4)	600	1,800	3,000	6,750	10,500	15,000
S10 2WD	320	960	1,600	3,600	5,600	8,000
S10 (4x4)	440	1,320	2,200	4,950	7,700	11,000

1988-91 S10 Pickup, 108.3" or 122.9" wb

	6	5	4	3	2	1
Fleetside (SBx)	280	840	1,400	3,150	4,900	7,000
Fleetside (LBx)	288	864	1,440	3,240	5,040	7,200
Fleetside Ext Cab	300	900	1,500	3,380	5,250	7,500

1988-91 C1500, 1/2-Ton, 117.5" or 131" wb

	6	5	4	3	2	1
Sportside PU (SBx)	400	1,200	2,000	4,500	7,000	10,000
SS 454 PU (SBx), 1990 & 1991 only	760	2,280	3,800	8,550	13,300	19,000
Fleetside PU (SBx)	400	1,200	2,000	4,500	7,000	10,000
Fleetside PU (LBx)	420	1,260	2,100	4,730	7,350	10,500
Fleetside PU Ext Cab (LBx)	460	1,380	2,300	5,180	8,050	11,500
Suburban	640	1,920	3,200	7,200	11,200	16,000

1988-91 C2500, 3/4-Ton, 129.5" or 164.5" wb

	6	5	4	3	2	1
Stepside PU (LBx)	560	1,680	2,800	6,300	9,800	14,000
Fleetside PU (LBx)	560	1,680	2,800	6,300	9,800	14,000
Bonus Cab PU (LBx)	460	1,380	2,300	5,180	8,050	11,500
Crew Cab PU (LBx)	472	1,416	2,360	5,310	8,260	11,800
Suburban	680	2,040	3,400	7,650	11,900	17,000

1992 K1500 Blazer, V-8

	6	5	4	3	2	1
2d SUV (4x4)	700	2,150	3,600	8,100	12,600	18,000

1992 S10 Blazer, V-6

	6	5	4	3	2	1
2d SUV	400	1,200	2,000	4,500	7,000	10,000
2d SUV (4x4)	450	1,300	2,200	4,950	7,700	11,000
4d SUV	600	1,750	2,900	6,530	10,200	14,500
4d SUV (4x4)	600	1,850	3,100	6,980	10,900	15,500

1992 Astro Van, V-6

	6	5	4	3	2	1
3d Van	250	800	1,350	3,020	4,700	6,700

1992 Lumina, V-6

	6	5	4	3	2	1
3d Van	250	800	1,300	2,930	4,550	6,500

1992 Suburban 1500, V-8

	6	5	4	3	2	1
4d Sta Wag	750	2,300	3,800	8,550	13,300	19,000
4d Sta Wag (4x4)	800	2,400	4,000	9,000	14,000	20,000

1992 Suburban 2500, V-8

	6	5	4	3	2	1
4d Sta Wag	800	2,400	4,000	9,000	14,000	20,000
4d Sta Wag (4x4)	850	2,500	4,200	9,450	14,700	21,000

1992 S10, 1/2-Ton, V-6

	6	5	4	3	2	1
2d PU (SBx)	450	1,300	2,200	4,950	7,700	11,000
2d PU (LBx)	450	1,300	2,200	4,950	7,700	11,000

NOTE: Add $1,500 for 4x4.

1992 C1500, 1/2-Ton, V-8

	6	5	4	3	2	1
2d Sportside PU (SBx)	560	1,680	2,800	6,300	9,800	14,000
2d Fleetside PU (SBx)	560	1,680	2,800	6,300	9,800	14,000
2d Fleetside PU (LBx)	560	1,680	2,800	6,300	9,800	14,000

NOTE: Add $2,000 for 4x4. Add 25 percent for 454 SS pkg.

1992 C2500, 3/4-Ton, V-8

	6	5	4	3	2	1
2d Fleetside PU (LBx)	600	1,800	3,000	6,750	10,500	15,000

1993 K1500 Blazer, V-8

	6	5	4	3	2	1
2d SUV 4x4	750	2,300	3,800	8,550	13,300	19,000

1993 S10 Blazer, V-6

	6	5	4	3	2	1
2d SUV 2WD	350	1,000	1,700	3,830	5,950	8,500
4d SUV 2WD	350	1,050	1,750	3,960	6,150	8,800
2d SUV 4x4	600	1,750	2,900	6,530	10,200	14,500
4d SUV 4x4	600	1,800	3,000	6,750	10,500	15,000

1993 Astro, V-6

	6	5	4	3	2	1
Van	250	700	1,200	2,700	4,200	6,000

1993 Lumina, V-6, FWD

	6	5	4	3	2	1
Van	250	700	1,200	2,700	4,200	6,000

1993 G Van, V-8

	6	5	4	3	2	1
Spt Van	250	800	1,300	2,930	4,550	6,500

1993 Suburban C1500/C2500, V-8

	6	5	4	3	2	1
4d Sta Wag 1500	800	2,400	4,000	9,000	14,000	20,000
4d Sta Wag 2500	800	2,400	4,000	9,000	14,000	20,000

1993 S10, V-6

	6	5	4	3	2	1
2d PU (SBx)	350	1,100	1,850	4,140	6,450	9,200
2d PU (LBx)	400	1,150	1,900	4,280	6,650	9,500

1993 C1500/C2500, V-8

	6	5	4	3	2	1
2d PU 1500 (SBx)	550	1,700	2,850	6,390	9,950	14,200
2d PU 1500 (LBx)	600	1,750	2,900	6,530	10,200	14,500
2d PU 2500 (SBx)	600	1,750	2,900	6,530	10,200	14,500
2d PU 2500 (LBx)	600	1,750	2,950	6,620	10,300	14,700

1994 K1500 Blazer, V-8

	6	5	4	3	2	1
2d SUV 4x4	700	2,150	3,600	8,100	12,600	18,000

1994 S10 Blazer, V-6

	6	5	4	3	2	1
2d SUV	350	1,100	1,800	4,050	6,300	9,000
4d SUV	350	1,100	1,850	4,140	6,450	9,200
2d SUV 4x4	500	1,450	2,400	5,400	8,400	12,000

	6	5	4	3	2	1
4d SUV 4x4	500	1,550	2,600	5,850	9,100	13,000
1994 Astro, V-6						
Cargo Van	350	1,000	1,700	3,830	5,950	8,500
Cargo Van LWB	350	1,100	1,800	4,050	6,300	9,000
CS Van	400	1,150	1,900	4,280	6,650	9,500
CS Van LWB	400	1,250	2,100	4,730	7,350	10,500
1994 Lumina, V-6						
Cargo Van	300	850	1,400	3,150	4,900	7,000
Window Van	350	1,000	1,700	3,830	5,950	8,500
1994 G10, V-8						
Van	400	1,250	2,100	4,730	7,350	10,500
1994 G20, V-8						
Van	500	1,450	2,400	5,400	8,400	12,000
Van Spt	500	1,550	2,600	5,850	9,100	13,000
1994 Suburban, V-8						
4d C1500	700	2,150	3,600	8,100	12,600	18,000
4d C2500	750	2,300	3,800	8,550	13,300	19,000
1994 S10, V-6						
2d PU 6 ft.	300	900	1,500	3,380	5,250	7,500
2d PU 7-1/2 ft.	300	900	1,500	3,420	5,300	7,600
2d PU 6 ft. Ext Cab	400	1,150	1,900	4,280	6,650	9,500

	6	5	4	3	2	1
1994 C1500, V-8						
2d PU 6-1/2 ft.	350	1,100	1,800	4,050	6,300	9,000
2d PU 8 ft.	400	1,150	1,900	4,280	6,650	9,500
2d PU 6-1/2 ft. Ext Cab	540	1,620	2,700	6,080	9,450	13,500
2d PU 8 ft. Ext Cab	550	1,700	2,800	6,300	9,800	14,000
NOTE: Deduct 10 percent for V-6.						
1994 C2500, V-8						
2d PU 8 ft.	450	1,300	2,200	4,950	7,700	11,000
2d PU 6 ft. Ext Cab	550	1,700	2,800	6,300	9,800	14,000
2d PU 8 ft. Ext Cab	600	1,800	3,000	6,750	10,500	15,000
1995 Tahoe, V-8						
LS 4d SUV	550	1,700	2,800	6,300	9,800	14,000
2d SUV, 4x4	600	1,750	2,900	6,530	10,200	14,500
LS 2d SUV, 4x4	600	1,800	3,000	6,750	10,500	15,000
LS 4d SUV, 4x4	650	1,900	3,200	7,200	11,200	16,000
1995 Blazer, V-6						
2d SUV	300	950	1,600	3,600	5,600	8,000
4d SUV	350	1,100	1,800	4,050	6,300	9,000
2d SUV, 4x4	350	1,100	1,850	4,190	6,500	9,300
4d SUV, 4x4	400	1,250	2,050	4,640	7,200	10,300
1995 Astro, V-6						
Cargo Van	350	1,000	1,700	3,830	5,950	8,500
CS Van	400	1,150	1,900	4,280	6,650	9,500

	6	5	4	3	2	1
1995 Lumina, V-6						
Cargo Van	300	850	1,400	3,150	4,900	7,000
Window Van	350	1,000	1,700	3,830	5,950	8,500
1995 G-10, V-8						
Van	400	1,250	2,100	4,730	7,350	10,500
1995 G-20, V-8						
Van	500	1,450	2,400	5,400	8,400	12,000
Van Spt	500	1,550	2,600	5,850	9,100	13,000
1995 Suburban, V-8						
4d C1500	700	2,150	3,600	8,100	12,600	18,000
4d C1500 LS	750	2,200	3,700	8,330	13,000	18,500
4d C1500 LT	750	2,300	3,800	8,550	13,300	19,000
4d C2500	750	2,300	3,800	8,550	13,300	19,000
4d C2500 LS	800	2,350	3,900	8,780	13,700	19,500
4d C2500 LT	800	2,400	4,000	9,000	14,000	20,000
1995 S-10, V-6						
2d PU, 6 ft.	300	900	1,500	3,380	5,250	7,500
2d PU, 7-1/2 ft.	300	900	1,500	3,420	5,300	7,600
2d PU, 6 ft. Ext Cab	400	1,150	1,900	4,280	6,650	9,500
NOTE: Deduct 10 percent for 4-cyl. Add $2,000 for 4x4.						
1995 C1500, V-8						
2d Fleetside WT PU, 6-1/2 ft.	350	1,100	1,800	4,050	6,300	9,000
2d Fleetside WT PU, 8 ft.	380	1,140	1,900	4,280	6,650	9,500
2d Sportside PU, 6-1/2 ft.	440	1,320	2,200	4,950	7,700	11,000
2d Fleetside PU, 6-1/2 ft.	460	1,380	2,300	5,180	8,050	11,500
2d Fleetside PU, 8 ft.	480	1,440	2,400	5,400	8,400	12,000
2d Fleetside PU, 6-1/2 ft. Ext Cab	550	1,600	2,700	6,080	9,450	13,500
2d Fleetside PU, 8 ft. Ext Cab	550	1,700	2,800	6,300	9,800	14,000
2d Sportside PU, 6-1/2 ft. Ext Cab	550	1,700	2,800	6,300	9,800	14,000
NOTE: Deduct 10 percent for V-6.						
1995 C2500, V-8						
2d Fleetside PU, 8 ft.	440	1,320	2,200	4,950	7,700	11,000
2d Fleetside PU, 6-1/2 ft. Ext Cab	550	1,700	2,800	6,300	9,800	14,000
2d Fleetside PU, 8 ft. Ext Cab	600	1,800	3,000	6,750	10,500	15,000
1996 Tahoe, V-8						
2d SUV	450	1,400	2,350	5,310	8,250	11,800
LS 2d SUV	500	1,500	2,500	5,630	8,750	12,500
LS 4d SUV	500	1,550	2,600	5,850	9,100	13,000
2d SUV, 4x4	550	1,600	2,700	6,080	9,450	13,500
LS 2d SUV, 4x4	550	1,700	2,800	6,300	9,800	14,000
LS 4d SUV, 4x4	600	1,800	3,000	6,750	10,500	15,000
NOTE: Add 10 percent for turbo diesel V-8.						
1996 Blazer, V-6						
2d SUV	300	850	1,400	3,150	4,900	7,000
4d SUV	300	950	1,600	3,600	5,600	8,000
2d SUV, 4x4	350	1,000	1,650	3,740	5,800	8,300
4d SUV, 4x4	350	1,100	1,850	4,190	6,500	9,300

	6	5	4	3	2	1
1996 Astro, V-6						
Cargo Van	300	900	1,500	3,380	5,250	7,500
Van	340	1,020	1,700	3,830	5,950	8,500
NOTE: Add 15 percent for 4x4.						
1996 Lumina, V-6						
Cargo Van	250	700	1,200	2,700	4,200	6,000
Window Van	300	900	1,500	3,380	5,250	7,500
1996 G10, V-8						
Van	400	1,150	1,900	4,280	6,650	9,500
Express Van	400	1,250	2,100	4,730	7,350	10,500
1996 G20, V-8						
Van	450	1,300	2,200	4,950	7,700	11,000
Express Van	500	1,450	2,400	5,400	8,400	12,000
1996 Suburban, V-8						
4d C1500	700	2,050	3,400	7,650	11,900	17,000
4d C1500 LS	700	2,100	3,500	7,880	12,300	17,500
4d C1500 LT	700	2,150	3,600	8,100	12,600	18,000
4d C2500	700	2,150	3,600	8,100	12,600	18,000
4d C2500 LS	750	2,200	3,700	8,330	13,000	18,500
4d C2500 LT	760	2,280	3,800	8,550	13,300	19,000
NOTE: Add 10 percent for turbo diesel V-8. Add 10 percent for 4x4.						
1996 S10, V-6						
2d PU, 6 ft.	250	800	1,300	2,930	4,550	6,500
2d PU, 7-1/2 ft.	250	800	1,300	2,970	4,600	6,600
2d PU, 6 ft. Ext Cab	340	1,020	1,700	3,830	5,950	8,500
NOTE: Deduct 10 percent for 4-cyl. Add $2,000 for 4x4.						
1996 C1500, V-8						
2d Fleetside WT PU, 6-1/2 ft.	300	950	1,600	3,600	5,600	8,000
2d Fleetside WT PU, 8 ft.	340	1,020	1,700	3,830	5,950	8,500
2d Sportside PU, 6-1/2 ft.	400	1,200	2,000	4,500	7,000	10,000
2d Fleetside PU, 6-1/2 ft.	420	1,260	2,100	4,730	7,350	10,500
2d Fleetside PU, 8 ft.	440	1,320	2,200	4,950	7,700	11,000
2d Fleetside PU, 6-1/2 ft. Ext Cab	500	1,500	2,500	5,630	8,750	12,500
2d Fleetside PU, 8 ft. Ext Cab	500	1,550	2,600	5,850	9,100	13,000
2d Sportside PU, 6-1/2 ft. Ext Cab	500	1,550	2,600	5,850	9,100	13,000
1996 C2500, V-8						
2d Fleetside PU, 8 ft.	400	1,200	2,000	4,500	7,000	10,000
2d Fleetside PU, 6-1/2 ft. Ext Cab	500	1,550	2,600	5,850	9,100	13,000
2d Fleetside PU, 8 ft. Ext Cab	560	1,680	2,800	6,300	9,800	14,000
NOTE: Add $2,000 for 4x4. Add 10 percent for turbo diesel V-8.						
1997 Tahoe, V-8						
2d SUV	472	1,416	2,360	5,310	8,260	11,800
LS 2d SUV	500	1,500	2,500	5,630	8,750	12,500
LS 4d SUV	520	1,560	2,600	5,850	9,100	13,000
2d SUV, 4x4	540	1,620	2,700	6,080	9,450	13,500
LS 2d SUV, 4x4	560	1,680	2,800	6,300	9,800	14,000
LS 4d SUV, 4x4	600	1,800	3,000	6,750	10,500	15,000
NOTE: Add 10 percent for turbo diesel V-8.						

	6	5	4	3	2	1
1997 Blazer, V-6						
2d SUV	280	840	1,400	3,150	4,900	7,000
4d SUV	320	960	1,600	3,600	5,600	8,000
2d SUV, 4x4	332	996	1,660	3,740	5,810	8,300
4d SUV, 4x4	372	1,116	1,860	4,190	6,510	9,300
1997 Astro, V-6						
Cargo Van	300	900	1,500	3,380	5,250	7,500
Van	340	1,020	1,700	3,830	5,950	8,500
NOTE: Add 15 percent for 4x4.						
1997 Venture, V-6						
2d Van	240	720	1,200	2,700	4,200	6,000
4d Van	300	900	1,500	3,380	5,250	7,500
NOTE: Add 5 percent for extended model.						
1997 G Series, V-8						
G10 Van	380	1,140	1,900	4,280	6,650	9,500
G10 Express Van	420	1,260	2,100	4,730	7,350	10,500
G20 Van	440	1,320	2,200	4,950	7,700	11,000
G20 Express Van	480	1,440	2,400	5,400	8,400	12,000
NOTE: Add 10 percent for turbo diesel V-8. Add 5 percent for 7.4L V-8.						
1997 Suburban, V-8						
4d C1500	680	2,040	3,400	7,650	11,900	17,000
4d C1500 LS	700	2,100	3,500	7,880	12,250	17,500
4d C1500 LT	720	2,160	3,600	8,100	12,600	18,000
4d C2500	720	2,160	3,600	8,100	12,600	18,000
4d C2500 LS	740	2,220	3,700	8,330	12,950	18,500
4d C2500 LT	760	2,280	3,800	8,550	13,300	19,000
4d K1500	700	2,100	3,500	7,880	12,250	17,500
4d K1500 LS	720	2,160	3,600	8,100	12,600	18,000
4d K1500 LT	760	2,280	3,800	8,550	13,300	19,000
4d K2500	740	2,220	3,700	8,330	12,950	18,500
4d K2500 LS	780	2,340	3,900	8,780	13,650	19,500
4d K2500 LT	800	2,400	4,000	9,000	14,000	20,000
NOTE: Add 10 percent for turbo diesel V-8. Add 10 percent for 4x4.						

	6	5	4	3	2	1
1997 S10, V-6						
2d PU, 6 ft.	260	780	1,300	2,930	4,550	6,500
2d PU, 7-1/2 ft.	264	792	1,320	2,970	4,620	6,600
2d PU, 6 ft. Ext Cab	340	1,020	1,700	3,830	5,950	8,500
NOTE: Deduct 10 percent for 4-cyl. Add $2,000 for 4x4.						
1997 C1500, V-8						
2d Fleetside WT PU, 6-1/2 ft.	320	960	1,600	3,600	5,600	8,000
2d Fleetside WT PU, 8 ft.	340	1,020	1,700	3,830	5,950	8,500
2d Sportside PU, 6-1/2 ft.	400	1,200	2,000	4,500	7,000	10,000
2d Fleetside PU, 6-1/2 ft.	420	1,260	2,100	4,730	7,350	10,500
2d Fleetside PU, 8 ft.	440	1,320	2,200	4,950	7,700	11,000
2d Fleetside PU, 6-1/2 ft. Ext Cab	500	1,500	2,500	5,630	8,750	12,500
2d Fleetside PU, 8 ft. Ext Cab	520	1,560	2,600	5,850	9,100	13,000
2d Sportside PU, 6-1/2 ft. Ext Cab	520	1,560	2,600	5,850	9,100	13,000
NOTE: Add $2,000 for 4x4. Add 10 percent for turbo diesel V-8.						
1997 C2500, V-8						
2d Fleetside PU, 8 ft.	400	1,200	2,000	4,500	7,000	10,000
2d Fleetside PU, 6-1/2 ft. Ext Cab	520	1,560	2,600	5,850	9,100	13,000
2d Fleetside PU, 8 ft. Ext Cab	560	1,680	2,800	6,300	9,800	14,000
NOTE: Add $2,000 for 4x4. Add 10 percent for turbo diesel V-8.						
1998 Tracker, 4-cyl.						
2d Utly Conv	210	620	1,040	2,340	3,640	5,200
4d SUV	230	680	1,140	2,570	3,990	5,700
2d Utly Conv, 4x4	250	740	1,240	2,790	4,340	6,200
4d SUV, 4x4	270	800	1,340	3,020	4,690	6,700

	6	5	4	3	2	1
1998 Tahoe, V-8						
2d SUV	470	1,420	2,360	5,310	8,260	11,800
LS 2d SUV	500	1,500	2,500	5,630	8,750	12,500
LS 4d SUV	520	1,560	2,600	5,850	9,100	13,000
2d SUV, 4x4	540	1,620	2,700	6,080	9,450	13,500
LS 2d SUV, 4x4	560	1,680	2,800	6,300	9,800	14,000
LS 4d SUV, 4x4	600	1,800	3,000	6,750	10,500	15,000

NOTE: Add 10 percent for turbo diesel V-8.

	6	5	4	3	2	1
1998 Blazer, V-6						
2d SUV	280	840	1,400	3,150	4,900	7,000
4d SUV	320	960	1,600	3,600	5,600	8,000
2d SUV, 4x4	330	1,000	1,660	3,740	5,810	8,300
4d SUV, 4x4	370	1,120	1,860	4,190	6,510	9,300
1998 Astro, V-6						
Cargo Van	300	900	1,500	3,380	5,250	7,500
Van	340	1,020	1,700	3,830	5,950	8,500

NOTE: Add 15 percent for 4x4.

	6	5	4	3	2	1
1998 Venture, V-6						
2d Van	240	720	1,200	2,700	4,200	6,000
4d Van	300	900	1,500	3,380	5,250	7,500

NOTE: Add 5 percent for extended model.

	6	5	4	3	2	1
1998 G Series, V-8						
G15 Van	380	1,140	1,900	4,280	6,650	9,500
G15 Express Van	420	1,260	2,100	4,730	7,350	10,500
G20 Van	440	1,320	2,200	4,950	7,700	11,000
G20 Express Van	480	1,440	2,400	5,400	8,400	12,000

NOTE: Add 5 percent for extended model. Add 10 percent for turbo diesel V-8. Add 5 percent for 7.4L V-8.

	6	5	4	3	2	1
1998 Suburban, V-8						
4d C1500	680	2,040	3,400	7,650	11,900	17,000
4d C1500 LS	700	2,100	3,500	7,880	12,250	17,500
4d C1500 LT	720	2,160	3,600	8,100	12,600	18,000
4d C2500	720	2,160	3,600	8,100	12,600	18,000
4d C2500 LS	740	2,220	3,700	8,330	12,950	18,500
4d C2500 LT	760	2,280	3,800	8,550	13,300	19,000
4d K1500	700	2,100	3,500	7,880	12,250	17,500
4d K1500 LS	720	2,160	3,600	8,100	12,600	18,000
4d K1500 LT	760	2,280	3,800	8,550	13,300	19,000
4d K2500	740	2,220	3,700	8,330	12,950	18,500
4d K2500 LS	780	2,340	3,900	8,780	13,650	19,500
4d K2500 LT	800	2,400	4,000	9,000	14,000	20,000

NOTE: Add 10 percent for turbo diesel V-8. Add 10 percent for 4x4.

	6	5	4	3	2	1
1998 S10, V-6						
2d PU, 6 ft.	260	780	1,300	2,930	4,550	6,500
2d PU, 7-1/2 ft.	260	790	1,320	2,970	4,620	6,600
2d PU, 6 ft. Ext Cab	340	1,020	1,700	3,830	5,950	8,500
2d PU, 7-1/2 ft. Ext Cab	340	1,030	1,720	3,870	6,020	8,600

NOTE: Deduct 10 percent for 4-cyl. Add $2,000 for 4x4.

1998 C1500, V-8						
2d Fleetside WT PU (V-6)	320	960	1,600	3,600	5,600	8,000
2d Fleetside PU	360	1,080	1,800	4,050	6,300	9,000
2d Sportside PU	400	1,200	2,000	4,500	7,000	10,000

NOTE: Add 5 percent for extended cab. Add $2,000 for 4x4. Add 10 percent for turbo diesel V-8. Add 5 percent for 7.4L V-8.

1998 C2500, V-8						
2d Fleetside PU	400	1,200	2,000	4,500	7,000	10,000
2d HD Fleetside PU	480	1,440	2,400	5,400	8,400	12,000

NOTE: Add 5 percent for extended cab. Add $2,000 for 4x4. Add 10 percent for turbo diesel V-8. Add 5 percent for 7.4L V-8.

1999 Tracker, 4-cyl.						
2d Utly Conv	210	620	1,040	2,340	3,640	5,200
4d SUV	230	680	1,140	2,570	3,990	5,700
2d Utly Conv, 4x4	250	740	1,240	2,790	4,340	6,200
4d SUV, 4x4	270	800	1,340	3,020	4,690	6,700

1999 Tahoe, V-8						
2d SUV	470	1,420	2,360	5,310	8,260	11,800
LS 2d SUV	500	1,500	2,500	5,630	8,750	12,500
LS 4d SUV	520	1,560	2,600	5,850	9,100	13,000
LT 2d SUV	540	1,620	2,700	6,080	9,450	13,500
LT 4d SUV	560	1,680	2,800	6,300	9,800	14,000
2d SUV, 4x4	540	1,620	2,700	6,080	9,450	13,500
LS 2d SUV, 4x4	560	1,680	2,800	6,300	9,800	14,000
LS 4d SUV, 4x4	600	1,800	3,000	6,750	10,500	15,000
LT 2d SUV, 4x4	600	1,800	3,000	6,750	10,500	15,000
LT 4d SUV, 4x4	620	1,860	3,100	6,980	10,850	15,500

NOTE: Add 10 percent for turbo diesel V-8.

1999 Blazer, V-6						
2d SUV	280	840	1,400	3,150	4,900	7,000
4d SUV	320	960	1,600	3,600	5,600	8,000
2d SUV, 4x4	330	1,000	1,660	3,740	5,810	8,300
4d SUV, 4x4	370	1,120	1,860	4,190	6,510	9,300

NOTE: Add 5 percent for LS, LT, Trailblazer, or ZR2 Pkgs.

1999 Astro, V-6						
Cargo Van	300	900	1,500	3,380	5,250	7,500
Van	340	1,020	1,700	3,830	5,950	8,500

NOTE: Add 15 percent for 4x4. Add 5 percent for LS or LT Pkgs.

1999 Venture, V-6						
2d Van	240	720	1,200	2,700	4,200	6,000
4d Van	300	900	1,500	3,380	5,250	7,500

NOTE: Add 5 percent for extended model. Add 5 percent for LS or LT Pkgs.

1999 G Series, V-8						
G15 Van	380	1,140	1,900	4,280	6,650	9,500
G15 Express Van	420	1,260	2,100	4,730	7,350	10,500
G25 Van	440	1,320	2,200	4,950	7,700	11,000
G25 Express Van	480	1,440	2,400	5,400	8,400	12,000

NOTE: Add 5 percent for extended model. Add 5 percent for LS Pkg. Add 10 percent for turbo diesel V-8. Add 5 percent for 7.4L V-8. Deduct 5 percent for V-6.

	6	5	4	3	2	1
1999 Suburban, V-8						
4d C1500	680	2,040	3,400	7,650	11,900	17,000
4d C1500 LS	700	2,100	3,500	7,880	12,250	17,500
4d C1500 LT	720	2,160	3,600	8,100	12,600	18,000
4d C2500	720	2,160	3,600	8,100	12,600	18,000
4d C2500 LS	740	2,220	3,700	8,330	12,950	18,500
4d C2500 LT	760	2,280	3,800	8,550	13,300	19,000
4d K1500	700	2,100	3,500	7,880	12,250	17,500
4d K1500 LS	720	2,160	3,600	8,100	12,600	18,000
4d K1500 LT	760	2,280	3,800	8,550	13,300	19,000
4d K2500	740	2,220	3,700	8,330	12,950	18,500
4d K2500 LS	780	2,340	3,900	8,780	13,650	19,500
4d K2500 LT	800	2,400	4,000	9,000	14,000	20,000

NOTE: Add 10 percent for turbo diesel V-8. Add 10 percent for 4x4. Add 5 percent for 7.4L V-8.

1999 S10, V-6						
2d Fleetside PU	260	780	1,300	2,930	4,550	6,500
2d Sportside PU	260	790	1,320	2,970	4,620	6,600
2d Fleetside Ext Cab PU	340	1,020	1,700	3,830	5,950	8,500
2d Sportside Ext Cab PU	340	1,030	1,720	3,870	6,020	8,600

NOTE: Add 5 percent for LS, Extreme, or ZR2 Pkgs. Deduct 10 percent for 4-cyl. Add $2,000 for 4x4.

1999 C1500, V-8						
2d LS Ext Cab PU	400	1,200	2,000	4,500	7,000	10,000
2d Silverado Fleetside PU	360	1,080	1,800	4,050	6,300	9,000
2d Silverado Sportside PU	400	1,200	2,000	4,500	7,000	10,000

NOTE: Add 5 percent for Silverado extended cab. Add 5 percent for LS or LT Pkgs. Add $2,000 for 4x4. Add 10 percent for turbo diesel V-8. Add 5 percent for 7.4L V-8. Deduct 5 percent for V-6.

1999 C2500, V-8						
2d Fleetside PU	400	1,200	2,000	4,500	7,000	10,000
2d HD Fleetside PU (6.0L V-8)	420	1,260	2,100	4,730	7,350	10,500
4d Fleetside Crew Cab PU	480	1,440	2,400	5,400	8,400	12,000

NOTE: Add 5 percent for extended cab. Add 5 percent for LS or LT Pkgs. Add $2,000 for 4x4. Add 10 percent for turbo diesel V-8. Add 5 percent for 7.4L V-8.

2000 Tracker, 4-cyl.						
2d Utly Conv	210	640	1,060	2,390	3,710	5,300
4d SUV	230	700	1,160	2,610	4,060	5,800
2d Utly Conv, 4x4	250	760	1,260	2,840	4,410	6,300
4d SUV, 4x4	270	820	1,360	3,060	4,760	6,800

NOTE: Add 5 percent for Hang Ten Ed.

2000 Tahoe, V-8						
Limited 4d SUV	480	1,430	2,380	5,360	8,330	11,900
Z71 4d SUV, 4x4	540	1,620	2,700	6,080	9,450	13,500

2000 New Tahoe, V-8						
4d SUV	470	1,420	2,360	5,310	8,260	11,800
LS 4d SUV	520	1,560	2,600	5,850	9,100	13,000
4d SUV, 4x4	560	1,680	2,800	6,300	9,800	14,000
LS 4d SUV, 4x4	600	1,800	3,000	6,750	10,500	15,000

NOTE: Add 5 percent for LT pkg on LS.

2000 Blazer, V-6						
LS 2d SUV	280	840	1,400	3,150	4,900	7,000
LS 4d SUV	320	960	1,600	3,600	5,600	8,000
LS 2d SUV, 4x4	330	1,000	1,660	3,740	5,810	8,300
LS 4d SUV, 4x4	370	1,120	1,860	4,190	6,510	9,300

NOTE: Add 5 percent for LT, Trailblazer, or ZR2 pkgs.

	6	5	4	3	2	1
2000 Astro, V-6						
Cargo Van	300	900	1,500	3,380	5,250	7,500
Van	340	1,020	1,700	3,830	5,950	8,500

NOTE: Add 15 percent for 4x4. Add 5 percent for LS or LT pkg.

2000 Venture, V-6						
4d Van	300	900	1,500	3,380	5,250	7,500

NOTE: Add 5 percent for extended model. Add 5 percent for LS or LT pkgs. Add 5 percent for Warner Bros. Ed.

2000 G Series, V-8						
G1500 Van	380	1,140	1,900	4,280	6,650	9,500
G1500 Express Van	420	1,260	2,100	4,730	7,350	10,500
G2500 Van	440	1,320	2,200	4,950	7,700	11,000
G2500 Express Van	480	1,440	2,400	5,400	8,400	12,000

NOTE: Add 5 percent for extended model. Add 5 percent for LS pkg. Add 10 percent for turbo diesel V-8. Add 5 percent for 7.4L V-8. Deduct 5 percent for V-6.

2000 Suburban, V-8						
4d C1500	680	2,040	3,400	7,650	11,900	17,000
4d C1500 LS	700	2,100	3,500	7,880	12,250	17,500
4d C1500 LT	720	2,160	3,600	8,100	12,600	18,000
4d C2500	720	2,160	3,600	8,100	12,600	18,000
4d C2500 LS	740	2,220	3,700	8,330	12,950	18,500
4d C2500 LT	760	2,280	3,800	8,550	13,300	19,000
4d K1500	700	2,100	3,500	7,880	12,250	17,500
4d K1500 LS	720	2,160	3,600	8,100	12,600	18,000
4d K1500 LT	760	2,280	3,800	8,550	13,300	19,000
4d K2500	740	2,220	3,700	8,330	12,950	18,500
4d K2500 LS	780	2,340	3,900	8,780	13,650	19,500
4d K2500 LT	800	2,400	4,000	9,000	14,000	20,000

NOTE: Add 10 percent for 4x4.

	6	5	4	3	2	1
2000 S10, V-6						
2d Fleetside PU	260	780	1,300	2,930	4,550	6,500
2d Sportside PU	260	790	1,320	2,970	4,620	6,600
2d Fleetside Ext Cab PU	340	1,020	1,700	3,830	5,950	8,500
2d Sportside Ext Cab PU	340	1,030	1,720	3,870	6,020	8,600

NOTE: Add 5 percent for LS, Extreme, or ZR2 pkgs. Deduct 10 percent for 4-cyl. Add $2,000 for 4x4.

2000 C1500, V-8						
2d Silverado Fleetside PU	400	1,200	2,000	4,500	7,000	10,000
2d Silverado Sportside PU	440	1,320	2,200	4,950	7,700	11,000

NOTE: Add 5 percent for Silverado extended cab. Add 5 percent for Z71, LS or LT pkgs. Add $2,000 for 4x4. Add 10 percent for turbo diesel V-8. Add 5 percent for 7.4L V-8. Deduct 5 percent for V-6.

2000 C2500, V-8						
2d Fleetside PU	420	1,260	2,100	4,730	7,350	10,500
2d HD Fleetside PU	440	1,320	2,200	4,950	7,700	11,000
4d Fleetside Crew Cab PU	500	1,500	2,500	5,630	8,750	12,500

NOTE: Add 5 percent for dual rear wheels. Add 5 percent for Z71, LS or LT pkgs. Add $2,000 for 4x4. Add 10 percent for turbo diesel V-8. Add 5 percent for 7.4L V-8.

Subscribe to  Today!

ONLY 81¢ PER ISSUE

Old Cars Weekly covers the entire field of collectible automobiles—from the classic touring cars and roadsters of the early 1900s, to the popular muscle cars of the 1960s and '70s!

Subscribe and save 73% off the cover price!

Inside each info-packed issue, you'll get:

- Technical tips and expert restoration advice
- A classified marketplace for cars, parts, and accessories
- Hot news on car shows, swap meets, and auctions
- Personal collectible stories and old car photos
- And much, much more!

Act now—subscribe today and get 1 YEAR (52 **BIG** issues) for just $41.98!

To order online, visit www.oldcarsweekly.com

To order by phone, call 877-300-0243—offer J7AHAD
(Outside the U.S. and Canada call 386-246-3431)

To order by mail, P.O. Box 420235, Palm Coast, FL 32142

In Canada: add $67 (includes GST/HST). Outside the U.S. and Canada: add $92 and remit payment in U.S. funds with order.
Please allow 4-6 weeks for first-issue delivery. Annual newsstand rate $155.48

TUNE UP YOUR SELECTION OF GARAGE GUIDES

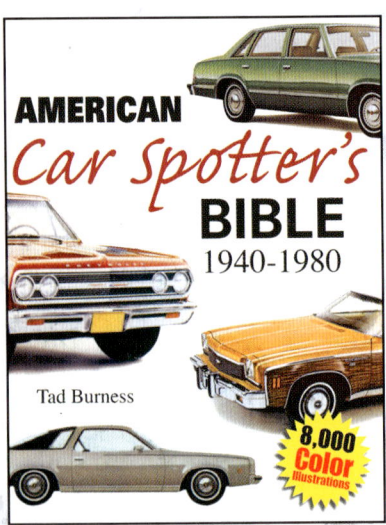

**Softcover • 8-¼ x 10-⅞ • 792 pages
8,000 color illus.
Item# SUCSG • $29.99
By Tad Burness**

Page after page of interior, exterior, and dashboard color photos and illustrations of nearly ever American-made car between 1940 and 1980 greet you when you open this book. It's like a scrapbook for car fanatics.

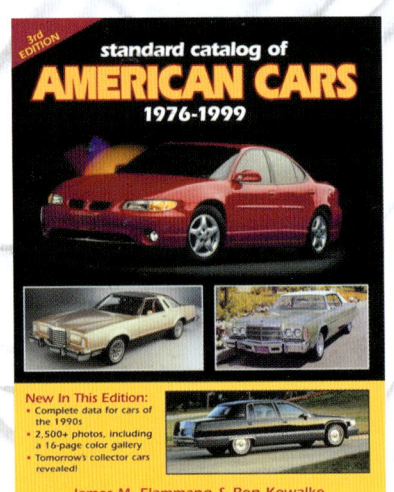

**Softcover • 8-½ x 11 • 976 pages
2,000 b&w photos • 16-page color section
Item# AD03 • $34.95
By James M. Flammang & Ron Kowalke**

Covers vehicles made from 1976 through 1999 with thousands of prices in up to 6 grades of condition. Explore complete listings of production figures, options, serial numbers, technical data, specification charts, chassis data and more.

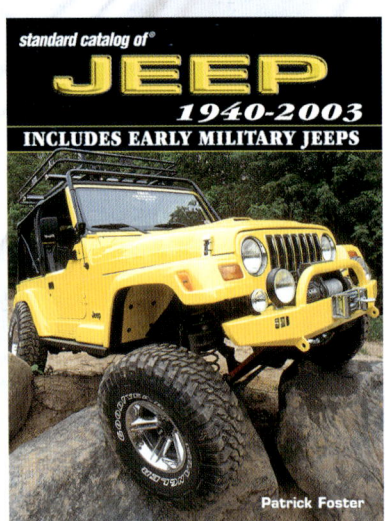

**Softcover • 8-¼ x 10-⅞ • 256 pages
300+ b&w photos • 300+ color photos
Item# JPSC1 • $24.99
By Patrick R. Foster**

This new full-color standard catalog covers every civilian Jeep model produced since the 1940s, with photographs, detailed technical specifications, developments, historical notes, and collector vehicle prices for each model through 1995.

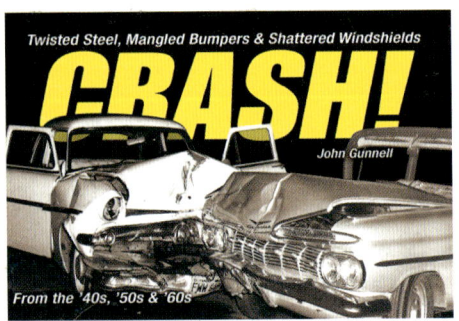

**Softcover • 8-½ x 5-½ • 192 pages
190 b&w photos
Item# Z0538 • $12.99
By John Gunnell**

Features 190 detailed photos of the most intense and humbling traffic accidents in automotive history.

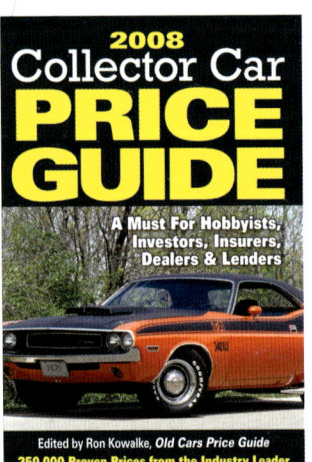

**Softcover • 6 x 9 • 784 pages
Item# Z0752 • $19.99
Edited by Ron Kowalke**

Check out collector values, in up to six grades of condition, for 250,000+ domestic cars, light trucks and various imports manufactured between 1901 and 2001.

krause publications
An imprint of F+W Publications, Inc.
P.O. Box 5009,
Iola, WI 54945-5009
www.krausebooks.com

Order directly from the publisher by calling **800-258-0929** M-F 8 am – 5 pm

Online at **www.krausebooks.com** or from booksellers nationwide and select auto parts stores.

Please reference offer **AUB7** with all direct-to-publisher orders